THE
SECOND WOR~~LD~~

19

THE
SECOND WORLD WAR
1939-45

A Strategical and Tactical History

by

Major-General
J. F. C. FULLER

"*Brute force bereft of wisdom falls to ruin by its own weight. Power with counsel tempered even the gods make greater. But might that in its soul is bent on all impiety, they hate.*"

HORACE

DA CAPO PRESS • NEW YORK

Library of Congress Cataloging in Publication Data

Fuller, J. F. C. (John Frederick Charles), 1878-1966.
  The Second World War, 1939-45: a strategical and tactical history / by J.F.C.
Fuller. — 1st Da Capo Press ed.
      p.   cm.
  Original published: 3rd impression (with revisions). New York: Duell, Sloan and
Pearce, 1954.
  Includes bibliographical references and index.
  ISBN 0-306-80506-5
  1. World War, 1939-1945 — Campaigns. I. Title. II. Title: Second World War.
D743.F85   1993   92-36812
940.54'1 — dc20   CIP

First Da Capo Press edition 1993

This Da Capo Press paperback edition of *The Second World War* is an unabridged
republication of the edition published in New York in 1954. It is
reprinted by arrangement with The Royal Society for the Prevention of Cruelty
to Animals, sole beneficiaries of the Estate of J.F.C. Fuller.

First published in 1948

Published by Da Capo Press, Inc.
A Subsidiary of Plenum Publishing Corporation
233 Spring Street, New York, N.Y. 10013

CONTENTS

MAPS and DIAGRAMS

PREFACE TO THIRD IMPRESSION

Since this book was written in 1947 there has been a vast output of war literature, which must inevitably provide reasons for modifying, in a number of respects, any book on the war written at that date. In the circumstances, I have considered carefully the propriety of allowing the publication of a third impression of this book substantially in its original form. But, in spite of the fact that I should like to recast certain sections, I have found nothing that has been written since which drastically modifies the views I expressed in 1947.

As I said in my preface to the first edition, it was at that date too early —and it still is—for a final appreciation of the tactics and strategy of either side in the many different theatres of the Second World War. What I attempted was a description in broad outline of the strategy and tactics of the war, and, as such, I believe that my book, as first written, may still serve a useful purpose. I still feel, as I did in 1947, that "however easy it is to be wise after the event . . . it is better then than never". Time has made some of our errors even plainer and others, perhaps, less serious than I thought then, but, substantially, the picture remains the same, and in an age when it is more important than ever that all who wish to play any part in creating or acting upon public opinion should know something of war, I feel that no harm can be done by letting this book remain in print, whatever its present imperfections.

If time is allowed me I may perhaps be able later to present more final conclusions based on the greater wealth of material which is now available.

J. F. C. F.

PREFACE TO THE FIRST EDITION
(abridged)

To write a full-dress history of the recent war is not my intention, because I do not believe that on the data as yet available it is a practical undertaking. Nevertheless, I do believe that if the strategy and tactics of the war are alone considered, a profitable account can be placed before the reader. Further, I believe that unless the campaigns of the war are to be anything more than of historical interest to the soldier and the layman— and to-day most laymen are soldiers actual or potential—it is now that their blunders and successes should be examined, because in the present technical age changes in the application of strategical principles and in tactical doctrines are so rapid that the happenings of yesterday are apt speedily to become relics to-morrow. Therefore, I have not attempted to examine the political, economic and psychological sides of the war, vitally important though they are. Further still, I have omitted to deal in any detail with the Battle of the Atlantic; the naval operations in the Mediterranean; partisan warfare in Russia and the German occupied countries; and the Japanese war in China. My reasons for this are that the first, and to a lesser extent the second, form so much the background of all the land campaigns in Europe that to place them in proper perspective would have taken up so much space that anything like a full examination of the military operations in the length decided upon for this book would have become cramped. As regards the third, much still remains obscure, and seems to me to be more closely related to the political than the military operations of the war. And as regards the last, to get a reasonably complete picture of it would have entailed going back to its beginning; besides, strategically and tactically, it was not a very illuminating struggle.

So far the book as a whole. Next, as to my sources of information. Roughly they fall into four groups: (1) official despatches and reports; (2) memoirs and biographies of participants; (3) war correspondents' reports and histories; and (4) the reports on the Nuremberg Trial and interviews with enemy soldiers and others. The first, though generally correct in fact, are seldom critical. They are mainly skeletons with little flesh on them; yet invaluable, because they do show in outline what operations looked like. The second, though apt to be prejudiced, are the most important of the four; but only so after a considerable number has appeared, when it becomes possible by cross-checking to get somewhere near the truth. The official Russian accounts of battles and operations—and all accounts are official—are so uninformative and so steeped in heroics that, for the most part, they would appear to have been written for people with the intelligence of a child of ten. Though no one acquainted with Russian military history doubts the stubbornness and endurance of the Russian soldier, to read time and again of redoubtable Kuban or Terek Cossacks cutting down "ten thousand Germans with the sabre" and suchlike twaddle is, to say the least of it, tedious. I may have been unfortunate, but the only book I have come across which gives a lucid description of the war in Russia is the two-volume *The Russian Campaigns of* 1941-1943 *and* 1944-1945 in the Penguin Series, by W. E. D. Allen and Paul Muratoff. On these volumes I have drawn largely for my information, which here I gratefully acknowledge. As regards the fourth source—trial reports and interviews—though they are of great interest, anyhow for the time being they should, I consider, be accepted with caution. My reasons are that: (1) Though the documents produced at Nuremberg may be accepted as authentic, this is no proof that all were in part or in whole acted upon; for as every soldier knows, plans and projects are always in a process of evolution and modification, and (2) that the veracity of defeated men is not above suspicion, because it is only human to disguise or minimize one's own errors and shift them on to the shoulders of others. That Hitler was responsible for many absurdities is true, but that he was the author of all is clearly the greatest of all absurdities; for normally in war it takes several people and many events to manufacture a first-class disaster or victory.

In commenting on such of the campaigns in which facts are sufficiently clear to lend themselves to criticism, I am fully aware how easy it is to be wise after the event. Anyhow, it is better then than never. Had historians and others been a little more critical than they were from 1919 onwards, we could not have been so mentally unprepared as we were in 1939. Further, I would like to say in extenuation of the criticism to be found in this book, that if the reader cares to look up what I wrote during the war—some of it has appeared in book form—he will find that most of it was made before, during or immediately after the events in question. Thus, I have always held that war is no more than a lethal argument, and, to be worth the fighting, it demands a sane and profitable political end. That the object of war is not slaughter and devastation, but to persuade the enemy to change his mind. That "strategic bombing" as inaugurated by Mr. Churchill, was not only morally wrong but militarily wrong and politically suicidal. That ideological wars are nonsense, not only because ideas are impervious to bullets, but, invariably, the holier the cause the more devilish the end. That bombardments of obliteration, as resorted to by so many generals, are as clumsy as they are generally unremunerative. That generalship demands audacity and imagination and not merely weight of metal and superiority of numbers. That British strategy should be based on sea power and not on land power, if only because Britain's geographical position dictates that it should be so. For the United Kingdom to attempt to play the part of a Continental power is to play the fool, a thing she has been doing ever since 1914. And lastly, taking all in all and irrespective of what your enemy does, it is more profitable to fight like a gentleman than like a cad; for a cad's war can only end in a cad's peace, and a cad's peace in yet another war, which to me seems to be silly.

One point remains which I should like to say a word on—namely, the question of numbers and casualties. As regards the former, the normal process is for all parties to minimize their own strengths and exaggerate their enemy's because this makes successes appear more brilliant and failures less culpable. Therefore, I cannot vouch for the accuracy of any strengths given in this book. As regards casualties, nearly all official figures are suspect.

Although there must be quite a number of errors in this book, as there will be in all books written on the recent war, my hope is that, as its subject is mainly strategical and tactical, there may be fewer than would be the case were it a purely heroic history, depicting for the most part events which never happened.

J. F. C. F.

THE
SECOND WORLD WAR
1939-45

CHAPTER I

BACKGROUND OF THE WAR

(1) *Immediate Causes of the War*

Saturday, 28th June, 1919, "*La journée de Versailles,*" writes Harold Nicolson in *Peacemaking* 1919, "Clemenceau is already seated under the heavy ceiling as we arrive. '*Le roi,*' runs the scroll above him, '*gouverne par lui-même.*' He looks small and yellow. A crunched *homunculus* . . . The Gardes Républicains at the doorway flash their swords into their scabbards with a loud click. '*Faites entrer les Allemands,*' says Clemenceau. They are conducted to their chairs, Clemenceau at once breaks the silence. '*Messieurs,*' he rasps, '*la séance est ouverte.*' He adds a few ill-chosen words. 'We are here to sign a Treaty of Peace.' Then St. Quentin advances towards the Germans and with the utmost dignity leads them to the little table on which the Treaty is expanded. They sign.

"Suddenly from outside comes the crash of guns thundering a salute. It announces to Paris that the second Treaty of Versailles has been signed by Dr. Müller and Dr. Bell. '*La séance est levée,*' rasped Clemenceau. Not a word more or less.

"We kept our seats while the Germans were conducted like prisoners from the dock, their eyes still fixed upon some distant point of the horizon.

"We still kept our seats to allow the Big Five to pass down the aisle. Wilson, Lloyd George, the Dominions, others. Finally, Clemenceau, with his rolling satirical gait. Painlevé, who was sitting one off me, rose to greet him. He stretched out both his hands and grasped Clemenceau's right glove. He congratulated him. '*Oui,*' says Clemenceau, '*c'est une belle journée.*' There were tears in his bleary eyes.

"Marie Murat was near me and had overheard. '*En êtes-vous sûre?*' I ask her. '*Pas du tout,*' she answers, being a woman of intelligence."[1]

Thus to the thunder of guns the First World War was buried and the Second World War conceived, and though the fundamental causes of the latter—as of the former—may be traced back through steam engines and counting houses to the instincts of tribal man, its immediate cause was the Treaty of Versailles. Not because of its severity, nor because of its lack of

[1] *Peacemaking* 1919, Harold Nicolson (1933), pp. 365-370.

17

wisdom, but because it violated the terms of the Armistice of 11th November, 1918. It is important to remember this, for it was this dishonourable action which enabled Hitler to marshal the whole of Germany behind him and to justify in the eyes of the German people each infringement of the treaty he made.

Briefly, the story is as follows: On 5th October, 1918, the German Government addressed a note to President Wilson accepting his Fourteen Points and asking for peace negotiations. Three days later the President replied, enquiring whether he was to understand that the object of the German Government in entering into discussion was to be only to agree upon the practical details of the application of the terms laid down in his Fourteen Points, Four Principles and Five Particulars? On receiving an affirmative answer, after further correspondence, on 5th November, the President transmitted to the German Government his final reply, in which he said that the Allied Governments "declare their willingness to make peace with the Government of Germany on the terms of peace laid down in the President's Address to Congress of 8th January, 1918 (the Fourteen Points), and the principles of settlement enunciated in his subsequent Addresses."

"The nature of the Contract between Germany and the Allies resulting from this exchange of documents," writes John Maynard Keynes (later Lord Keynes), "is plain and unequivocal. The terms of the peace are to be in accordance with the Addresses of the President, and the purpose of the Peace Conference is 'to discuss the details of their applications.' The circumstances of the Contract were of an unusually solemn and binding character; for one of the conditions of it was that Germany should agree to Armistice Terms which were to be such as would leave her helpless. Germany having rendered herself helpless in reliance on the Contract, the honour of the Allies was peculiarly involved in fulfilling their part and, if there were ambiguities, in not using their position to take advantage of them."[1]

They did not fulfil their part. Instead, having rendered Germany helpless, first they abandoned the procedure followed in former peace conferences—including that of Brest-Litovsk—of engaging in oral negotiations with enemy plenipotentiaries; secondly they maintained the blockade throughout the Conference; and thirdly they scrapped the terms of the Armistice, for as Harold Nicolson points out: "Of President Wilson's twenty-three conditions, only four can with any accuracy be said to have been incorporated in the Treaties of Peace."[2]

[1] *The Economic Consequences of the Peace*, John Maynard Keynes (1919), p. 55.
[2] *Peacemaking* 1919, p. 44.

As regards the first point, Signor Nitti, the Italian Prime Minister at the time of the signing of the Treaty, says in his book *Peaceless Europe*:

". . . it will remain for ever a terrible precedent in modern history that, against all pledges, all precedents and all traditions, the representatives of Germany were never even heard; nothing was left to them but to sign a treaty at a moment when famine and exhaustion and threat of revolution made it impossible not to sign it . . . In the old law of the Church it was laid down that everyone must have a hearing, even the devil: *Etiam diabulus aidutur* (Even the devil has the right to be heard). But the new democracy, which proposed to install the society of nations, did not even obey the precepts which the dark Middle Ages held sacred on behalf of the accused."[4]

As regards the second point, it should be remembered what Mr. Winston Churchill said in the House of Commons on 3rd March, 1919—namely:

"We are holding all our means of coercion in full operation, or in immediate readiness for use. We are enforcing the blockade with vigour. We have strong armies ready to advance at the shortest notice. Germany is very near starvation. The evidence I have received from the officers sent by the War Office all over Germany shows, first of all, the great privations which the German people are suffering, and, secondly, the great danger of a collapse of the entire structure of German social and national life under the pressure of hunger and malnutrition. Now is therefore the moment to settle."[5]

It is clear from this that signature at the pistol point was what was intended.

Once the Conference assembled, writes Keynes, "Then began the weaving of that web of sophistry and Jesuitical exegesis that was finally to clothe with insincerity the language and substance of the whole Treaty. The word was issued to the witches of all Paris:

> Fair is foul, and foul is fair,
> Hover through the fog and filthy air.

The subtlest sophisters and most hypocritical draftsmen were set to work,

---

[4]*Peaceless Europe*, Francesco S. Nitti (1922), p. 114. "This act of unwisdom probably discredited the treaty more than the ultimatum which preceded its signature." (*The Twenty Years' Crisis* 1919-1939, Edward Hallett Carr, 1940, p. 240.)

[5]*Hansard*, vol. 113, H.C. Deb. 5s, col. 84. In Hitler's speech to the Reichstag on 1st September, 1939, are found the following words: "A signature was forced out of us with pistols at our head and with the threat of hunger for millions of people. And then this document obtained by force was proclaimed a solemn law." (*Blue Book*, Cmd. 6106, 1939, p. 162.)

and produced many ingenious exercises which might have deceived for more than an hour a cleverer man than the President."[6]

Further, he writes:

"The future life of Europe was not their concern; its means of livelihood was not their anxiety. Their preoccupations, good and bad alike, related to frontiers and nationalities, to the balance of power, to imperial aggrandisements, to the future enfeeblement of a strong and dangerous enemy, to revenge, and to the shifting by the victors of their unbearable financial burdens on to the shoulders of the defeated.

"Two rival schemes for the future policy of the world took the field—the Fourteen Points of the President, and the Carthaginian Peace of M. Clemenceau. Yet only one of these was entitled to take the field; for the enemy had not surrendered unconditionally, but on agreed terms as to the general character of the Peace."[7]

Thus were the dragon's teeth sown, out of which was destined to sprout an even more disastrous conflict than the one this treaty of violation brought to a close.

One man at least—though a party to the proceedings—saw what the future held in store. On 25th March, 1919, Mr. Lloyd George issued a memorandum to the Peace Conference entitled, "Some Considerations for the Peace Conference before they finally draft their terms." In it he wrote:

". . . You may strip Germany of her colonies, reduce her armaments to a mere police force and her navy to that of a fifth-rate power; all the same, in the end, if she feels that she has been unjustly treated in the peace of 1919, she will find means of exacting retribution from her conquerors . . . The maintenance of peace will . . . depend upon there being no causes of exasperation constantly stirring up the spirit of patriotism, of justice or of fair play to achieve redress . . . injustice, arrogance, displayed in the hour of triumph, will never be forgotten or forgiven.

"For these reasons I am, therefore, strongly averse to transferring more Germans from German rule to the rule of some other nation than can possibly be helped. I cannot conceive any greater cause of future war than that the German people, who have certainly proved themselves one of the most vigorous and powerful nations in the world, should be surrounded by a number of small states, many of them consisting of people who have never previously set up a stable government for themselves, but each of them containing large masses of Germans clamouring for reunion with

[6] *The Economic Consequences of the Peace*, p. 47. Harold Nicolson also writes: "I have a feeling that the judgment of posterity will concentrate, not upon the errors of the Conference . . . so much as upon its appalling hypocrisy." (*Peacemaking 1919*, p. 122.)

[7] *The Economic Consequences of the Peace*, p. 51.

their native land. The proposal of the Polish Commission that we should place 2,100,000 Germans under the control of a people of a different religion and which has never proved its capacity for stable self-government throughout its history, must, in my judgment, lead sooner or later to a new war in the East of Europe . . ."[8]

This warning went unheeded. Instead, Germany was made to acknowledge her guilt for the whole war, and was debited with its entire cost. Her economic resources were ransacked and ruined, and a large slice of West Prussia was handed to Poland to create the Polish Corridor.

It is not necessary here to enter into detail, for all that need be mentioned is, that to enforce the impossible reparations demanded as well as to disrupt Germany, on 11th January, 1923, France occupied the Ruhr. This led to the financial ruin of Germany and to staggering unemployment.

What this violation of the Treaty stood for was appreciated by many people in England. Sir John Simon pronounced it to be "in fact an act of war"; Mr. Charles Roberts, M.P., that "the irrevocable steps are being taken, the ultimate result of which can only be the one of bringing about in future that great international war which, in my view, will mean the downfall of civilization . . ."; and Captain R. Berkeley, M.P., that "If ever there was a case in which an act stood on the borderland of an act of war . . . this act of the French Government in marching into the Ruhr is such an act." The *Liberal Magazine* said: "The prospect of another war in a few years' time grows more definite and certain"; and the *Liberal Year Book*, "Day by day European war is being made more and more certain . . . There is little time left for preventive measures; indeed, it may even now be too late—it may be that the wound inflicted on the German mind is already deep enough to last until the power to retaliate has been recovered."

The second French aim was the dismemberment of Germany by creating a block of independent Catholic States from Austria to the Lower Rhine. To accomplish this, while the Ruhr was occupied, an intensive propaganda was simultaneously carried out for the separation of the Rhineland and the conversion of Bavaria into an independent Catholic monarchy under the vassalage of France. By October, 1923, the separatist movement in Bavaria had so far advanced that, under French direction, the Bavarian Prime Minister decided to proclaim the independence of Bavaria on 9th November—the fifth anniversary of the establishment of the German Republic. Whereupon the man of destiny appeared—Adolf Hitler.

During the war Hitler had been a lance-corporal in the 16th Bavarian Infantry. After the Armistice he joined a minute political faction of six members who called themselves the German Labour Party, and soon after

---

[8] Quoted from *Peaceless Europe*, pp. 92-93.

becoming its head he renamed it the National Socialist German Labour Party. Strongly opposing separation and standing for "People and Father-land," on 9th November he and General Ludendorff at the head of some three thousand followers marched on the Feldherrenhalle in Munich, were stopped, fired upon and dispersed. Hitler was arrested and sentenced to five years detention in the Fortress of Landsberg. There he spent thirteen months in prison and wrote the first volume of *Mein Kampf*. Thus, as M. Follick writes, "The new Germany" was "brought into being by France herself: by French tyranny, by French violence, by French oppression."[9]

Germany had found a leader; a man awaiting only some great event to recruit his legions. This event was the economic blizzard of 1929-1931— the offspring of the financial policies of the victorious Powers. In 1928 the National Socialists (Nazis) held but twelve seats in the Reichstag, but the slump, which was then on its way, once again created conditions similar to those of 1923, and in September, 1930, they had grown to be the second largest political party in Germany. Three years later, by an astute ex-ploitation of unemployment and the general misery, Hitler became Chancellor of Germany, and once established as German Führer, he set out to repudiate clause after clause of the Treaty of Versailles, as its creators had repudiated the terms of the Armistice. On 16th March, 1935, he announced the reintroduction of conscription; on 7th March, 1936, he re-occupied the Rhineland; on 13th March, 1938, he annexed Austria; in October that same year he occupied the Sudeten-areas of Czechoslovakia; on 13th March, 1939, he occupied the whole of that country; and on 21st March he demanded that Danzig should be returned to the German Reich and that Germany should receive a route through the Corridor.

Thus did the wheel of fate turn full circle back to 25th March, twenty years before, when with true Celtic vision Mr. Lloyd George had foreseen that to place 2,000,000 Germans under the Poles "must lead sooner or later to a new war in the East of Europe."

Others also foresaw it. Mr. Follick, writing ten years after Lloyd George's prophecy, had said:

"The Polish Corridor crime was a thousand times worse than if Ger-many, having won the war, had driven a corridor across what is now the Caledonian Canal, and had given a strip to Holland, about ten miles wide, purely in order to have weakened Britain. This is more or less what France's action in giving that corridor to Poland, cloven right through one of the most fruitful parts of Germany, amounts to. In agreeing to this act

[9]*Facing Facts: A Political Survey for the Average Man*, M. Follick (1935), p. 102.

of criminality, France's allies committed one of the most violent outrages against civilization that has ever been known to history . . . In order to give Poland a seaport, another outrage was perpetrated against Germany: Danzig was taken from her and declared a Free City. Now of all that is most German in Germany, nothing is more German than Danzig . . . Sooner or later that Polish Corridor is bound to be a cause for a future war . . ." and if Poland does not return the Corridor to Germany ". . . she (Poland) must be prepared for a most disastrous war with Germany, anarchy, and, possibly, a return to the servitude from which she has but recently emerged."[10]

From this it would appear that Hitler's two requests of 21st March were not altogether unreasonable. Nevertheless, Mr. Neville Chamberlain, the British Prime Minister, rightly seeing in them a pretext of further aggression, on 31st March most unwisely gave assurance to Poland of a British guarantee of support. "In the event of any action which clearly threatened Polish independence," it was declared, "and which the Polish Government accordingly considered it vital to resist with their national forces, His Majesty's Government would feel themselves bound at once to lend the Polish Government all support in their power."[11]

In order to make sense of this guarantee, Britain turned to Russia; but Stalin, seeing profit rather than loss in another "capitalist" war, kept negotiations simmering until 23rd August, when, entering into alliance with Germany, the Polish guarantee became waste paper.

That Hitler precipitated the War of 1939-1945 there can be no possible doubt, nor can there be any doubt whatsoever who and what precipitated Hitler. It was Clemenceau, the uncontrolled and all-controlling chairman of the Peace Conference, and his masterpiece the Treaty of Versailles.

Thus it came about that, at dawn on 1st September, 1939, once again the thunder of guns was heard: this time to celebrate the burial of the Second Treaty of Versailles and the birth of the Second World War.

(2) *Aims of the Belligerents*

The war aims of the belligerents sprang directly from their respective foreign policies, because, as Clausewitz long ago pointed out: "War is nothing but a continuation of political intercourse, with a mixture of other

[10]*Ibid.*, pp. 83, 84 and 109.
[11]*Cmd.* 6106, p. 36. When in Berlin, shortly after the guarantee was given, I asked a well-known American journalist what he thought of it. His answer was: "Well, I guess your Mr. Prime Minister has made the biggest blunder in your history since you passed the Stamp Act." Further he said, and he had known Poland for thirty years: "There is no reason why you should not guarantee a powder factory so long as the rules are observed; but to guarantee one full of maniacs is a little dangerous."

means."[12] And again: ". . . the art of war in its highest point of view is policy, but no doubt, a policy which fights battles instead of writing notes."[13] What, then, were the policies of the two opposed alliances—Great Britain and France on the one hand and Germany and Russia on the other?

From the days of the Tudors to 1914, Britain's was to maintain the balance of power—that is, to keep the greater Continental nations divided through rivalry and to hold the balance between them. This balance automatically fixed who the potential enemy was. It was not the wickedest nation, but the nation whose policy more so than any other nation's threatened Britain or her Empire. And, normally, because that nation was the strongest of the Continental powers, in peace-time British statesmen favoured either the second strongest, or a group of powers which in coalition was only a little less strong than the strongest. Based on this principle, their aim in war was not to annihilate their enemy, because annihilation would permanently have upset the balance. Instead, it was to reduce his strength to a level which would enable the balance to be reinstated. Once this level was reached, peace negotiations were opened.[14]

From the days of Richelieu until to-day, French policy has been directed towards securing her eastern frontier and in keeping Germany divided. Therefore, it also was a balancing of power, not within Europe as a whole, but within and between the Germanic States, because Germany, whether Holy Roman Empire, Prussia, the Second or the Third Reich, was the sole Continental power which could rival France.[15]

When related to each other, it will be seen that these two forms of the

[12]*On War*, Carl von Clausewitz (English edition, 1908), vol. III, p. 121.

[13]*Ibid.*, vol. III, p. 126.

[14]It is instructive to note that Hitler was fully *au fait* with these various policies, as this reference and the three following show. "What England has always desired, and will continue to desire, is to prevent any one Continental power in Europe from attaining a position of world importance. Therefore England wishes to maintain a definite equilibrium of forces among the European States; for this equilibrium seems a necessary condition of England's world-hegemony." (*Mein Kampf*, English edition, 1939, p. 503.)

[15]"What France has always desired, and will continue to desire, is to prevent Germany from becoming a homogeneous Power. Therefore France wants to maintain a system of small German States, whose forces would balance one another and over which there should be no central government. Then, by acquiring possession of the left bank of the Rhine, she would have fulfilled the prerequisite conditions for the establishment and security of her hegemony in Europe" . . . "France is and will remain the implacable enemy of Germany. It does not matter what Governments have ruled or will rule in France . . . their foreign policy will always be directed towards acquiring possession of the Rhine frontier and consolidating France's position on this river by disuniting and dismembering Germany" . . . "I shall never believe that France will of herself alter her intentions towards us;

balance of power are antagonistic. Whereas the British depends on the existence of at least two equal or nearly equal great powers or groups of powers, the French depends on only one—herself. Therefore, the French aim is the opposite of the British, and, in one way or another, from the age of Louis XIV onwards the antagonism between them is to be found at the bottom of nearly every major European crisis. Hence the evil repute into which the balance of power fell.[16]

To avoid these crises, in 1919, under American persuasion, the League of Nations was agreed to by the victors, and collective security was to render balancing unnecessary. But because the United States were not a European power and could not become one even had they ratified the Peace Treaty, potentially, because France was the strongest military nation left in Europe, the balance automatically passed into her hands, whereupon French traditional policy came into play. This became apparent when, in 1923, France invaded the Ruhr, and the result was that from then onwards Britain gradually shifted back towards her traditional policy and began to favour Germany in order to balance France.[17]

Had Britain financially been in the position she held in 1913—that is, had she remained the World's Banker—this change of policy from collective security back to balance of power would have placed her in a strong position, for then she could have let Germany re-arm, always knowing that, were Germany to grow too strong, British wealth could subsidize France and increase the strength of Britain's Navy, Air Force and Army. But London was no longer the financial centre of the world; for that centre had shifted to New York, and to shift it back to London was considered essential before the balance of power could once again become operative. To assist in this, in 1925 Britain returned to the gold standard, and between then and 1931 a trade war with the United States so monopolized her limited wealth that little could be spared to finance her fighting forces. To gain time and disguise this fact, her statesmen indulged in an intensive propaganda for disarmament. They proclaimed that another war would wreck civilization, and that the sole means of preventing such a calamity

because, in the last analysis, they are only the expressions of the French instinct for self-preservation. Were I a Frenchman and were the greatness of France so dear to me as that of Germany actually is, in the final reckoning I could not and would not act otherwise than a Clemenceau . . ." (*Mein Kampf*, pp. 503-504, 505 and 548.)

[16]"The Balkanization of Europe, up to a certain degree, was desirable and indeed necessary in the light of the traditional policy of Great Britain, just as France desired the Balkanization of Germany" . . . "The final aims of French diplomacy must be in perpetual opposition to the final tendencies of British statesmanship." (*Mein Kampf*, pp. 503 and 504.)

[17]"As regards foreign politics, the action of France in occupying the Ruhr really estranged England for the first time in quite a profound way. . ." (*Mein Kampf*, p. 550.)

was collective security. Thus it came about that by the time Hitler gained power, the British people were so completely doped that had a British Government proposed rearmament, it would have been turned out of office.[18] So intense was this pacific propaganda that, when the crash came in September, 1939, the Government feared to proclaim its true war aim— namely, that as German power politics, the German way of life, the German system of finance and the German method of trading were antagonistic to Britain, and if persisted in would lead to the establishment of a German hegemony over Europe, the self-preservation of Britain as a great power depended on staying their course. Therefore, since Britain's greatness had been built and sustained by the balance of power, its future security depended upon re-establishing that balance. Consequently, the Government's war aim was not to annihilate Germany,[19] but to reduce her strength to balancing point.

Instead, when on 3rd September, 1939, war was declared, the aim was proclaimed to be a moral one. This placed the conflict on to the footing of a crusade, that is, of an ideological in contradistinction to a political war—a war to annihilate Hitler and Hitlerism, as St. George annihilated the Dragon. This is made crystal clear in the declarations of all parties in the House of Commons. Thus Mr. Chamberlain (Prime Minister) proclaimed: "I trust I may live to see the day when Hitlerism has been destroyed and a liberated Europe has been re-established." Next Mr. Greenwood (Labour): "Lastly in this titanic struggle, unparalleled I believe in the history of the world, Nazism must be finally overthrown." Then Sir A. Sinclair (Liberal): ". . . let the world know that the British people are inexorably determined, as the Prime Minister said, to end the Nazi dominion for ever and to build an order based on justice and freedom." Lastly, Mr. Churchill (Unionist): "This is not a question of fighting for Danzig or fighting for Poland. We are fighting to save a whole world from

---

[18]As late as 12th November, 1936, Mr. Baldwin, British Prime Minister, said in the House of Commons: "You will remember the election at Fulham in the autumn of 1933 . . . You will remember, perhaps, that the National Government candidate who made a most guarded reference to the question of defence was mobbed for it . . . Supposing I had gone to the country and said that Germany was rearming and that we must rearm, does anyone think that this pacific democracy would have rallied to that cry at that moment? I cannot think of anything that would have made the loss of the election from my point of view more certain." (*Hansard*, vol. 317, H. of C., Deb. 5s, col. 1144.)

[19]Writing on the 1914-1918 war, Hitler said: "With the colonial, economical and commercial destruction of Germany, England's war aims were attained. Whatever went beyond these aims was an obstacle to the furtherance of British interests. Only the enemies of England could profit by the disappearance of Germany as a Great Continental Power in Europe." (*Mein Kampf*, p. 502.)

the pestilence of Nazi tyranny and in defence of all that is most sacred to man."[20]

Thus, instead of the minds of the people being directed towards the re-establishment of the balance of power, their reason was obliterated by a spirit of hatred for the "evil thing," and to them the war became a contest between Good and Evil.[21] This emotional aim, as we shall see, not only placed the war on a total footing, but eventually led to the very end Britain had fought against for four hundred years—the establishment of a hegemony over Europe by a foreign power.

That power was fated to be Russia. Thus we come to the second alliance, which was as uneasy as the Franco-British—the alliance between Russia and Germany.

Russia is an Asiatic power more so than a European, and as Britain was the dominant European power in Asia, the destruction of the British Empire was clearly to Russia's advantage. But how to get at Britain?—that was the Russian problem. There were only two certain ways, either to link up with Germany against her, or remove Germany as a great power. In either case the British balance of power would become impossible.

From the day Stalin succeeded Lenin as Secretary-General of the Communist Party, peace was essential to the consolidation of the New Economic Policy, which slowly was to bring Russia back on to the Imperialist path the Revolution had abandoned. Therefore, according to Krivitsky, from 30th June, 1934, when by his purge Hitler firmly established his position as dictator, Stalin's set purpose was to woo him.[22] Next the purge of the Russian Army in 1937, in which 35,000 army men were sacrificed, by militarily weakening Russia, still further intensified this courtship, which,

---

[20] *The Times*, 4th September, 1939. *The Times* supported these declarations in its leading article, in which the following appeared: "The 'spiritual rejuvenation' of the Third Reich culminates in the hoariest and most illusory aspirations of pagan nationalism. No one that casts up the balance of to-day can believe for a second that the future belongs to this truculent, degraded and bankrupt faith, and it is civilization itself which is mobilizing to crush it. Hitlerism is the enemy to-day."

[21] Vattel—little read to-day—points out that as civil law is not based on emotionalism, neither must military law be, and that "The first rule of that law . . . is, *that regular war, as to its effects, is to be accounted just on both sides;* as two parties in a court are considered innocent until one is proved guilty. This," he says, "is absolutely necessary . . . if people wish to introduce any order, any regularity, into so violent an operation as that of arms, or to set any bounds to the calamities of which it is productive, and leave a door constantly open for the return of peace . . ." (See *The Law of Nations*, English edition, 1834, pp. 381-383.)

[22] See Chapter I of *I Was Stalin's Agent*, W. G. Krivitsky (1939). On 15th July, 1934, Karl Radek wrote in the *Izvestia*: "There is no reason why Fascist Germany and Soviet Russia should not get on together, inasmuch as the Soviet Union and Fascist Italy are good friends" (p. 29).

as we have seen, ended in a *marriage de convenance* on 23rd August, 1939.

What Stalin's outlook then was may be gauged from what he said in 1934—namely:

"What came of the last war? They did not destroy Germany, but in Germany they sowed such hatred for the victors and created such a rich soil for revenge that they have not been able to clean up the revolting mess they have made, even to this day, and will not perhaps be able to do so for some time. Instead, they got the smash-up of capitalism in Russia, the victory of the proletariat in Russia, and, of course—the Soviet Union. What guarantee is there that the second imperialist war will produce better results than the first?"

In 1939 this policy remained unchanged. On 24th August that year we read in the *Pravda*: "The first Imperialist war brought about a great economic *débâcle* and misery and hunger among the people. A revolution alone was able to put an end to the war and to the economic collapse . . . There is little reason to doubt that a second war . . . would result . . . in a revolution in a number of countries in Europe and Asia, and the overthrow of the governments of capitalists and landowners in those countries."

Commenting on this, Mr. Lancelot Lawton, editor of *Contemporary Russia*, wrote: "If the *Pravda* should prove to be right in its prediction, and revolutions were to occur in a number of countries, even assuming that such countries were enemies of the Allied Powers, the consequences would be catastrophic: Soviet Republics would appear on the Rhine, in the Mediterranean and in the Far East."

Clearly, then, Stalin had no intention of entering into a "capitalist" conflict if he could avoid it. On 10th March, 1939, he said:

"We must be careful not to allow our country to be involved in a conflict by instigators of war who are used to getting other people to pull the chestnuts out of the fire for them"; whereas Mekhlis, Chief Political Commissar of the Red Army, declared: "The function of the Red Army is to carry out the internationalist obligations and to increase the number of Soviet Republics." A few days later, at Kiev, he said: "Stalin, the great helmsman, will guide the mighty invincible ship of the last decisive battle to the storming of capitalism."

Stalin went into alliance with Hitler, not because he loved National Socialism, but because he feared it, and because Britain had surrendered her initiative to Poland. He knew for certain that this surrender would lead to war, a war in which the Western World might easily destroy itself. Immediately after the Polish guarantee, Dimitrov, head of the Comintern, circulated the following statement to the Communist Parties abroad: "The Soviet Government and the Comintern have . . . decided that it is best to hold aloof from the conflict, while remaining ready to intervene when the powers engaged therein are weakened by war, in the hope of securing a social revolution."

Whereas Russia's immense size was her protection, Germany's central position was her danger; and whereas England, a seabound country, could never be secure until she commanded the seas, Germany, a landlocked country, equally could never be secure until she commanded the land. This fact and not the Prussian spirit—its effect—was the cause of her militarism.

The wars of Frederick the Great, as later did the First World War, clearly proved the danger she stood in when simultaneously attacked on two fronts. Added to this, the second of these wars also showed how vulnerable she was to blockade. Therefore, in order to insure her against these two calamities, Hitler's dream was an alliance with Britain. But, such an alliance was impossible, and mainly because, immediately after he gained power, his economic policy of direct barter and subsidized exports struck a deadly blow at British and American trade.

Why, then, did he not see in a Russian alliance, which he could have cemented years earlier, an even more reliable guarantee against a war on two fronts? The answer is given in Chapter XIV of the second volume of *Mein Kampf*. In it he expounds his theory of *Lebensraum*. It is so fully detailed that it is astonishing that the question has been so often asked— "Why did Hitler invade Russia?"

He opens his argument by pointing out that "the geometrical dimensions of a State are of importance not only as the source of the nation's foodstuffs and raw materials, but also from the political and military standpoints." That from this point of view Germany never has been, and, so long as she remains confined within her then existing boundaries, never can be a world power. Compared to the world powers, she is insignificant, and what is even worse, sooner or later this lack of proportion must of necessity lead to the decline or even annihilation of the German people.

To demand the restoration of the 1914 frontiers would be totally insufficient, because they did not include all the members of the German nation. "Nor were they reasonable, in view of the geographical exigencies of military defence." They were but "temporary frontiers established in virtue of a political struggle that had not been brought to a finish; and, indeed, they were partly the chance of circumstances." The 1914 frontiers were of no significance. Conquest of foreign territories must, therefore, be undertaken.

In justification of this he writes:

"The fact that a nation has acquired an enormous territorial area is no reason why it should hold that territory perpetually. At most, the possession of such territory is proof of the strength of the conqueror and the weakness of those who submit to him. And in this strength alone lives the right of possession. If the German people are imprisoned within an impossible territorial area and for that reason are face to face with a miserable future, this is not by the command of Destiny, and the refusal to accept such a situation is by no means a violation of Destiny's laws. For just as no Higher Power has promised more territory to other nations than to the German, so it cannot be blamed for an unjust distribution of the soil. The soil on which we now live was not a gift bestowed by Heaven on our forefathers. But they had to conquer it by risking their lives. So also in the future our people will not obtain territory, and therewith the means of existence, as a favour from any other people, but will have to win it by the power of a triumphant sword."

Because colonial acquisitions will not solve the problem, and, as he writes, "all are convinced of the necessity of regulating our situation in regard to France . . . we National Socialists have purposely drawn a line through the line of conduct followed by pre-war Germany in foreign policy. We put an end to the perpetual Germanic march towards the South and West of Europe and turn our eyes towards the lands of the East."

Lastly, he divulges his plan:

"But when we speak of new territory in Europe to-day we must principally think of Russia and the border States subject to her.

"Destiny itself seems to wish to point out the way for us here. In delivering Russia over to Bolshevism, Fate robbed the Russian people of that intellectual class which had once created the Russian State and were the guarantee of its existence. For the Russian State was not organized by the constructive political talent of the Slav element in Russia, but was much more a marvellous exemplification of the capacity for State-building possessed by the Germanic element in a race of inferior worth. Thus were many powerful Empires created all over the earth. More often than once inferior races with Germanic organizers and rulers as their leaders became formidable States and continued to exist as long as the racial nucleus remained which had originally created each respective State. For centuries Russia owed the source of its livelihood as a State to the Germanic nucleus of its governing classes. But this nucleus is now almost wholly broken up and abolished. The Jew had taken its place. Just as it is impossible for the Russian to shake off the Jewish yoke by exerting of his own powers, so, too, it is impossible for the Jew to keep this formidable State in existence for any long period of time. He himself is by no means an organizing element, but rather a ferment of decomposition. This colossal Empire in the East is ripe for dissolution. And the end of the Jewish domination in Russia will also be the end of the Russian State. We are chosen by Destiny to be the witnesses of a catastrophe which will afford the strongest confirmation of the nationalist theory of race."[23]

(3) *Strategical Framework*

Vis-à-vis Continental powers, except by aircraft, Great Britain is not merely an unattackable island, but also the centre of a system of sea communications which encircle the coastline of Europe from the White Sea to the Aegean. Therefore, in the event of war, her fleet can blockade all hostile and neutral European countries, as well as support whichever power her policy of balancing favours; either directly by subsidies, munitions and armed forces, or indirectly by amphibious operations of a distracting character: by constant threat the enemy can be forced to over extend.

Time and again, as past history has shown, the strategy best fitted to these several operations is one of a defensive-offensive order. Defensive in that, so long as command of the sea is held, Britain herself is secure from attack. Offensive in that this command guarantees freedom of movement towards or against any maritime objective within the strategical field. This strategy is neither aggressive nor isolationist; instead it is purely self-interested. Related as it is to the balance of power, its aim is not to guarantee the peace of Europe, but to warn Continental nations that, in face of Britain's naval might, the making of war does not pay.

In all wars fought according to British traditional policy, this defensive-offensive strategy has proved that it does not matter how powerful a Continental nation is, or how extensive are its conquests; for so long as Britannia rules the waves the initiative remains in her hands.

The main difference between this strategy and the strategy which has been favoured on the Continent of Europe since the days of Napoleon and Clausewitz is that, whereas sea power is founded on security of base coupled with freedom to distribute forces, land power is founded on superiority of force coupled with power to concentrate it at a selected point. The rule is that, unlike land power, the strength of sea power does not spring from manpower, but instead from strategical (geographical) position.

Again and again this has been demonstrated in British history. Thus, in 1588, when England faced Spain, her population was in the neighbourhood of 4,500,000. In 1702, when confronted by France, Spain and Bavaria, it was 5,475,000. In the Seven Years' War it was 6,467,000, and in 1800 it was 8,892,000. In all these victorious wars her enemy populations vastly exceeded her own.

[23]For these quotations see *Mein Kampf*, pp. 128, 279, 523, 529, 532 and 533.

In spite of this, in 1914, Britain largely abandoned her oceanic strategy for a strategy of the continental type. Worse still, having been bled white in the war which followed, in 1919 she became a guarantor of the peace of Europe, a peace she could not guarantee, if only because she had not the manpower and wealth to do so and simultaneously maintain her position as a great trading sea power. The upshot was that, because she assumed the part of a pseudo-continental power, she was incapable of influencing events in her own interest, and in 1939 she and her ally France slid into war on no strategical basis whatever. Thus, the initiative passed to Germany.

Hitler's aim, as we have seen, was to establish his *Lebensraum*, which meant war with Russia. Having neutralized that country by alliance, should France and England fight, his strategical problem became one of subduing Poland, France and England in detail before he undertook this major operation. Behind them, as in the previous war, stood the United States; therefore, if history were not to repeat itself, at all costs that great reservoir of power had to be kept out of the war. This meant that the war must be of short duration. What type of strategy best fulfilled this demand?

The correct answer to this question is important, for without it it is difficult to understand how it came about that, with so many things in her favour, Germany was unable to bring the war to a successful conclusion before the United States entered it. Also, it explains how it came about that, though the Allied Powers utterly defeated Germany, so far as Britain is concerned, her political aim was not gained.

Not only for statesmen and soldiers, but also for history, it is tragic that Clausewitz did not live to complete his philosophy of war. Had he done so, there can be little doubt that his claim that the military aim of war is the annihilation of the enemy's fighting forces would have been modified by his belief that at times the goal should be more limited. Of his many students, Delbrück was the first to point out in his *Geschichte der Kriegskunst* that, as there were two forms of war—limited and unlimited—it follows there must be two forms of strategy. These he called the strategy of annihilation (*Niederwerfungsstrategie*) and the strategy of exhaustion (*Ermattungsstrategie*). Whereas in the first the aim is the decisive battle, in the second battle is but one of several means, such as manœuvre, economic attack, political persuasion and propaganda, whereby the political end is attained.

Following Clausewitz, who did not live long enough to elaborate the few notes he left behind him on limited warfare,[14] from the days of the elder Moltke onwards the German General Staff concentrated on the first of the above strategies as Clausewitz had expounded it, and they refused to accept Delbrück's theory that the second was as important.

[14]See *On War*, Book VIII, chaps. V, VII and VIII.

In 1914, faced with a war on two fronts and not having force enough to wage both offensively, it was essential that Germany should crush French resistance in the West in the shortest possible time, so that she might concentrate her armies against Russia. Therefore, according to Delbrück, she was justified in adopting a strategy of annihilation against France. Further, he considered that, once France was subdued, England would be incapable of continued resistance, because, as he believed, "Her past political development would make it impossible for her to raise more than a token force . . . 'Every people,' he wrote, 'is the child of its history, its past, and can no more break away from it than a man can separate himself from his youth'."[25]

This statement shows how little Delbrück, like most Germans, appreciated the potentials of sea power. For had he understood what sea power entailed, he would have seen that it was exactly the second form of strategy he was expounding which throughout England's past had led to her many successes in Continental wars. That the child of her history was not that she could not engage in a Continental war on Continental military lines, but that she was ever ready to do so on naval.

Next, when the Battle of the Marne frustrated German strategy, and a period of defensive warfare set in, it became apparent to him, because reliance upon the decisive battle was no longer possible, that Germany must seek other means of imposing her will on her enemies. Because the central position she held between her opponents enabled her to retain the initiative, he suggested that, while a firm defensive was maintained in the West, Germany should turn upon Russia and Italy in order to destroy her enemy's coalition and thereby isolate England and France. In this connection, two things were essential. The first was that "no means be adopted which might bring new allies to the Western powers," and the second that, "May God forbid that Germany enter upon the path of Napoleonic policy . . . Europe stands united in this one conviction: it will never submit to a hegemony enforced upon it by a single state." Therefore, after the Allied victory on the Marne, Delbrück urged that, in order to prove that this was not Germany's intention, she should seek a negotiated peace. "He firmly believed that the war had been caused by Russian aggression, and saw no reason why England and France should continue to fight the one power which was 'guarding Europe and Asia from the domination of *Moskowitertum*'." This conviction that Germany must negotiate was doubly reinforced when, on account of Germany's unrestricted U-boat campaign, the United States entered the war. This meant that "the battle

[25] *Makers of Modern Strategy*, edited by Edward Mead Earle (1943), p. 276. Most of what follows on Delbrück has been extracted from Mr. Gordon A. Craig's chapter II of this book, in which Delbrück's theories are examined.

was no longer an end in itself but a means. If Germany's political professions failed at first to convince the Western powers that peace was desirable, a new military offensive could be undertaken and would serve to break down that hesitation. But only such a co-ordination of the military effort with the political programme would bring the war to a successful issue."

In spite of Delbrück's pleadings, the German General Staff remained adamant, they would not recant their faith in annihilation, and the result was the abortive German offensive of March-April, 1918. Strategically, it was a faulty operation. "In the first place, the German army on the eve of the offensive was in no position to strike a knock-out blow against the enemy. Its numerical superiority was slight and, in reserves, it was vastly inferior to the enemy. Its equipment was in many respects equally inferior, and it was greatly handicapped by a faulty supply system and by insufficient stocks of fuel for its motorized units. These disadvantages were apparent before the opening of the offensive, but were disregarded by the high command."

The result was that, when Ludendorff struck he was compelled to follow the lines of least resistance instead of the line of greatest decision—the essence of the strategy of annihilation—which in this case was the separation of the English from the French armies and the rolling up of the former. This Ludendorff failed to do, for when difficulties developed in one sector, lacking a general reserve, instead of reinforcing it, he struck new blows in another, and as a result "the grand offensive degenerated into a series of separate thrusts, unco-ordinated and unproductive." "Here," writes Mr. Craig, "Delbrück returned to the major theme of all his work as historian and publicist. The relative strength of the opposing forces was such that the high command should have realized that the annihilation of the enemy was no longer possible. The aim of the 1918 offensive, therefore, should have been to make the enemy so tired that he would be willing to negotiate a peace. This in itself would have been possible only if the German Government had expressed its own willingness to make such a peace. But once this declaration had been clearly made, the German army in opening its offensive would have won a great strategical advantage. Its offensive could now be geared to the strength at its disposal. It could safely attack at the points of tactical advantage—that is, where success was easiest—since even minor victories would now have a redoubled moral effect in the enemy capitals. The high command had failed in 1918 and had lost the war because it had disregarded the most important lesson of history, the interrelationship of politics and war. 'To come back once more to that fundamental sentence of Clausewitz, no strategical idea can be considered completely without considering the political goal'."

As later on we shall see, because the Germans did not appreciate that there were two distinct and equally important forms of strategy, the strategical mistakes made by them in 1914-1918 were repeated in 1939-1945, and even more disastrously, because between the two wars a technical change occurred which went far to modify the application of both forms. This change was the shifting of fighting force from a muscular and quantitative basis on to a mechanical and qualitative one, a revolution as profound as in a former age had been the shifting of fighting force from an infantry to a cavalry basis. When the latter change occurred, the fundamental problems became one of grazing and the supply and carriage of fodder. If these were restricted or denied to the enemy, his cavalry went out of operation; whereupon his opponent—granted that he could maintain his cavalry in the field—was placed in an overwhelmingly advantageous position. Though, on account of the extent of the normal grazing areas, such occurrences were infrequent, it is notable that in the great Hunnish and Mongolian invasions their *blitzkriegs* rapidly petered out in poor grasslands.

As grass is vital for the horse, equally so is petrol vital for the machine. And because grasslands form the vital areas for the raising of great forces of cavalry,[26] so do industrial districts form the vital areas for the production of great forces of mechanized arms. Deny the former to the enemy and his source of cavalry withers; deny the latter and his supply of fighting vehicles is rapidly atrophied.

This latter change—the mechanization of armies—had a profound effect on the strategies of annihilation and exhaustion; for to deny the enemy what may be called his "vital area of operations"—that part of his country essential to the maintenance of his forces—became even more important than winning victories in the field, because it knocked the bottom out of the enemy's fighting power—his army, air force and fleet.

Therefore, in the next war, the situation of the enemy's vital areas of operations with reference to his adversary's frontier, would go far to determine which strategy should be adopted by the aggressor. Should the main vital area be sufficiently close to warrant the initial momentum of attack being maintained until it was overrun, then clearly the most profitable strategy to adopt was that of annihilation. But if instead, the vital area was distant, then, should this strategy be relied on, there was a grave risk that, in face of an enemy who was skilful in retreat, when once the momentum

[26]In this respect it is of interest to remember that in the middle of the fifth century Attila based himself on Hungary, and that in the Mongolian invasion of Europe in 1241 Hungary was the centre the Mongols made for; Kaidu after the Battle of Liegnitz moving southwards on Buda-Pest and Kadan southwards through the Carpathians and then westwards on that same city.

of the attack became exhausted, the attacker would be placed in an exceedingly disadvantageous position. Not only would he, in part at least, have outrun his supplies; but, should his opponent have kept his forces well in hand, he would be open to counter-attack before, so to speak, he could regain his wind. Therefore, should the enemy's vital area be distant, this fact alone demanded a strategy of exhaustion until sufficient ground towards that area had been gained to warrant the strategy of annihilation being put into force.

As we shall see, the failure to understand the strategical relationship between speed and space was the fundamental cause which led to German ruin.

(4) *Tactical Theories*

Taken as a whole, no body of armed men can be considered to be an army—that is, an organized fighting force—unless it reacts to the will of one man, for a multi-headed army is clearly a monster. Nor can this body be maintained as an army unless it is fed and supplied. An army is, therefore, a three-fold organization comprising a body, its combatant arms; a stomach, its administrative services; and a brain, its command. Because the destruction of any one of these parts renders the other two inoperative, it follows that there are three tactical objectives. Of these, the first, the combatant arms, which may be compared to the shell of an egg, occupies the outer or forward area, and the second and third, the command and administrative services—representing the yolk and white—occupy the inner or rear area. There are, therefore, two tactical areas of attack and defence, the forward and the rear, and the second may be compared to the vital area of operations as discussed in the preceding section.

In 1914, once trench warfare set in, fronts grew flankless. Because this made it impossible to turn or envelop a front and thereby attack the area in rear of it, the tactical problem became one of penetration. The obvious method of effecting this was to drill a hole through the enemy's front by massed artillery fire, and then pass an army through the gap. Though in idea this was sound enough, a moment's thought will show that actually it was generally impracticable, and for the following reasons: (1) The length of time taken in massing the guns gave the enemy ample warning that an attack was to be made; (2) the prolonged preliminary bombardment, by revealing to the enemy the point of attack, enabled him to deepen and adjust his defences; (3) the intensity of the bombardment so completely shattered the ground and destroyed forward communications that it became impossible to move wheeled transport over the battlefield; and (4) the substitution of a cratered area for an entrenched area in no way solved the problem of overcoming the enemy's resistance, because all that happened was that one form of earthwork was substituted for another.

At the Battle of Cambrai in November, 1917, all these difficulties were overcome by the use of tanks. They were massed rapidly and secretly; there was no preliminary bombardment and there was no shattering of the surface of the ground. Though this battle ended in failure, it nevertheless established a tactical revolution, because it clearly demonstrated that a method had been discovered whereby the forward or outer battle area could rapidly be penetrated and the rear or inner command and administrative area attacked.

As things were in 1918, this opened enormous possibilities. On the Western Front the German armies were strung out along a five hundred miles belt or zone, the forward area of which was approximately five miles deep and the rear area fifteen. In the latter were to be found their Divisional, Corps and Army Headquarters, the brains of their fighting body which occupied the former. Because penetration was now possible, and as this linear distribution not only favoured it, but hindered the Germans frustrating it, for the more they were extended the less able were they to concentrate, I put forward a project, which, by no means original in idea,[27] was novel in method. Its aim was directly to attack the enemy's command prior to attacking his fighting body, so that his fighting body, when attacked, would be paralysed through lack of command. The means was to pass powerful columns of fast-moving tanks, strongly protected by aircraft, through the forward area into the rear area and on to the German Divisional, Corps and Army Headquarters. Once they were annihilated and the forward area paralysed, in its turn it was to be attacked on normal lines.

Though these tactics of paralysation were accepted by Marshal Foch as the basis of his then projected 1919 offensive,[28] on account of the war ending in November, 1918, they were never put to the test, and remained in theoretical form until September, 1939, when, with certain modifications, the Germans tried them out in Poland and called them "*Blitzkrieg*."

Meanwhile another theory, rendered possible by mechanization, this time in the air instead of on the ground, was in the process of development. According to it, the vital area of operations was to be discovered in the will of the civil population; for were it broken by terror, the whole machinery of government and with it of military direction would collapse into anarchy.

---

[27]When cavalry was an operative arm, it frequently occurred that a successful charge on the enemy's command led to the complete dissolution of his army, as was the case at Arbela in 331 B.C., and at Otumba in 1520. At Blenheim, in 1704, it was much the same. In the days when leadership and command coincided, the mere death of a Commander-in-Chief often led to a similar catastrophe.

[28]See my *Memoirs of an Unconventional Soldier* (1936), Chapter XIII.

The most ardent exponent of this theory of attack by demoralization was the Italian General Giulio Douhet. Shortly after the conclusion of the First World War he expounded his views in his book, *The Command of the Air*.

"The armies involved in that war," he wrote, "were only the means by which the nations of each side tried to undermine the resistance of the other; so much so that, though the defeated side was the one whose armies won the most and greatest battles, when the morale of the civilian population began to weaken, these very armies either disbanded or surrendered, and an entire fleet was turned over intact to the enemy. This disintegration of nations in the last war was indirectly brought about by the actions of the armies in the field. In the future it will be accomplished directly by the actions of aerial forces. In that lies the difference between past and future wars.

"An aerial bombardment which compels the evacuation of a city of some hundreds of thousands of inhabitants will certainly have more influence on the realization of victory than a battle of the kind often fought during the last war without appreciable results. A nation which once loses the command of the air and finds itself subjected to incessant aerial attacks aimed directly at its most vital centres and without the possibility of effective retaliation, this nation, whatever its surface forces may be able to do, must arrive at the conviction that all is useless, that all hope is dead. This conviction spells defeat."[20]

Here it should be noted that Douhet's aim was not to obliterate instead of occupy the vital area of operations, in the form of those industries essential to the maintenance of the enemy's forces in the field; but something far more catastrophic—namely, to compel capitulation without the use of either army or fleet. Again and again this is made clear in his book. For instance, in one place he writes:

"At this point I want to stress one aspect of the problem—namely, that the effect of such aerial offensives upon morale may well have more influence upon the conduct of the war than their material effects. For example, take the centre of a large city and imagine what would happen among the civilian population during a single attack by a single bombing unit. For my part, I have no doubt that its impact upon the people would be terrible . . ."

Then, after describing the destruction wrought, he continues:

"What could happen to a single city in a single day could also happen to ten, twenty, fifty cities. And, since news travels fast, even without telegraph, telephone, or radio, what, I ask you, would be the effect upon civilians of other cities, not yet stricken but equally subject to bombing attacks? What civil or military authority could keep order, public services functioning, and production going under such a threat? And even if a semblance of order was maintained and some work done, would not the sight of a single enemy plane be enough to stampede the population into panic? In short, normal life would be impossible in this constant nightmare of imminent death and destruction. And if on the second day another ten, twenty, or fifty cities were bombed, who could keep all those lost, panic-stricken people from fleeing to the open countryside to escape this terror from the air?

"A complete breakdown of the social structure cannot but take place in a country subjected to this kind of merciless pounding from the air. The time would soon come when, to put an end to horror and suffering, the people themselves, driven by the instinct of self-preservation, would rise up and demand an end to the war—this before their army and navy had time to mobilize at all."[30]

These were the two outstanding tactical theories which emerged from out of the First World War, and both, it will be noted, lifted the problem of war out of the physical into the moral sphere. Whereas the aim of the attack on the enemy's command was the demoralization of the enemy's fighting forces, the aim of the attack on the enemy's civil population was to demoralize his government.

Though, in idea, these two theories ran parallel, in application they differed radically. Whereas the first demanded the integration of army and air force, the second was based on their separation, the army becoming a police force which did no more than occupy a country after it had been subdued by air attack. This form of air attack was called "strategic bombing." In the former, action was purely in the military sphere, the decisive battle still remaining the end of strategy. In the latter, action was purely in the civil sphere, the destruction of the potentials of civilized life becoming the aim of air tactics. What influence did these theories have once hostilities ended?

The first had none until the rise of Hitler in 1933. The second, because of its popular appeal was given great publicity. Already, during the war, very similar theories had been propounded by Brigadier-General William Mitchell in the United States and urged by Sir Hugh Trenchard in England. In the second of these countries, the first Independent Air Force to come into existence was created in April, 1918; the Royal Flying Corps, a co-operative air force, was converted into the Royal Air Force, a separate fighting service.

[30] *Ibid.*, pp. 51-52.

On face value this conversion appeared to fit Britain's insular position which, though it secured her against land attack, made land support of a Continental ally difficult. If the claims set out by Douhet and others of his way of thinking were true—though nothing so far had proved them to be so—then the age-old problem of how with a minimum force to intervene in a Continental war with maximum effect had been solved; air power could largely replace land power, because aerial bombardments carried out from Britain against Continental targets would obviate despatching large expeditionary forces overseas.

France was not so happily placed, for there was no English Channel between her and Germany; besides, she lacked the necessary manpower to fight another German war. To make good these deficiencies, she proceeded to turn herself into an artificial island by building the Maginot Line, which may be compared to a sea wall protecting France against the German flood. The French did not create an independent air force, and for the simple reason that they looked upon bombing aircraft as merely a means of extending the range of the guns of the Maginot Line.

From these two policies it will be seen that, if the British and French General Staffs had in mind any clear-cut idea at all, it was to start the next war at the point where the last had been broken off, the Maginot Line replacing the old trench lines of the Western Front. Therefore, the war would open as a siege operation, under cover of which ample time would be gained to produce the requisite aerial artillery to pulverize Germany and the necessary shipping to blockade her. Should this not have been the plan, then it is difficult even to imagine what it was.

Unfortunately for Britain and France, in 1933 Germany fell under the spell of a man who had a very definite policy and plan, who was realist, idealist and visionary woven into one, and who sometimes was Herr Hitler and at others Herr Gott.

" 'Who says I'm going to start a war like those fools in 1914?' cried Hitler. 'Are not all our efforts bent towards preventing this? Most people have no imagination . . . They are blind to the new, the surprising things. Even the generals are sterile. They are imprisoned in the coils of their technical knowledge. The creative genius stands always outside the circle of the experts'."[31]

As early as 1926, when he was still writing the second volume of *Mein Kampf*, he was fully aware that in the next war "motorization" would "make its appearance in an overwhelming and decisive form."[32] He believed in Clausewitz's doctrine of absolute war and in the strategy of

[31]*Hitler Speaks*, Hermann Rauschning (1939), p. 16.
[32]*Mein Kampf*, p. 537.

annihilation. He believed in war as a political instrument; therefore, as his political aim was the establishment of the German *Lebensraum,* he shaped his tactics accordingly. Their object was in the shortest possible time and with the least destruction of property to annihilate his enemy's will to fight.

He based his tactics on two theories—attack by propaganda and attack by velocity of striking power. In terms of time he reversed the Douhet theory, his aim being to strike at the enemy's civil will *before* and *not after* the outbreak of hostilities, not physically but intellectually. He said: "What is war but cunning, deception, delusion, attack and surprise? . . . There is a broadened strategy, a war with intellectual weapons . . . Why should I demoralize him (the enemy) by military means, if I can do so better and more cheaply in other ways."[33]

The following quotations from Rauschning make clear his theory:

"The place of artillery preparation for frontal attack by the infantry in trench warfare will in future be taken by revolutionary propaganda, to break down the enemy psychologically before the armies begin to function at all. The enemy people must be demoralized and ready to capitulate, driven into moral passivity, before military action can even be thought of."

"We shall have friends who will help us in all the enemy countries. We shall know how to obtain such friends. Mental confusion, contradiction of feeling, indecisiveness, panic: these are our weapons . . ."

"Within a few minutes, France, Poland, Austria, Czechoslovakia, will be robbed of their leading men. An army without a general staff. All political leaders out of the way. The confusion will be beyond belief. But I shall long have had relations with the men who will form a new government—a government to suit me."

"When the enemy is demoralized from within, when he stands on the brink of revolution, when social unrest threatens—that is the right moment. A single blow must destroy him . . . A gigantic, all-destroying blow. I do not consider consequences. I think only of this one thing."[34]

At another time he said:

"If I were going to attack an opponent, I should act quite differently from Mussolini. I shouldn't negotiate for months beforehand and make lengthy preparations, but—as I have always done throughout my life— I should suddenly, like a flash of lightning in the night, hurl myself upon the enemy."[35]

Though these three theories pointed to the next war being very different from the last, the forms and principles of attack and defence remained what they always had been, and it is of no little importance that the student

[33]*Hitler Speaks*, pp. 16-17.
[34]*Ibid.*, pp. 17-20.
[35]Quoted from *Germany's War Machine*, Albert Müller (1936), p. 30.

of war should have these forms in mind before he sets out to examine the
campaigns of 1939-1945, which were fought over every kind of terrain,
and in every kind of climate; for without them he will have no background
to his criticism.

(5) *Forms of Attack and Defence*

Though there are many subsidiary forms of attack, such as attack by
treachery (propaganda), by blockade, by feint, by distraction (drawing an
enemy away from the main strategic area), by terror and by devastation, on
the battlefield itself there are three major forms—namely, frontal attack,
flank attack and rear attack.

Of frontal attacks there are two types—attack by attrition and attack by
penetration. The technique of the first consist in contacting and fixing the
enemy, next in forcing him to draw in his reserves, and lastly in wearing
down his strength until it is no longer sufficient to resist further pressure,
when, in order to avoid annihilation, the enemy is compelled to retire and
risk being pursued. Pursuit, be it remembered, is a new attack, and, therefore, should be carried out by fresh troops.

Under modern conditions, this form of attack—the most primitive of
all—should, when possible, be avoided, because fire power in the defence
is more destructive than fire power in the attack. Therefore, even should
the defender be decisively defeated, the cost to the attacker is likely to be
disproportionately high. So long ago as the American Civil War—a muzzle-
loader conflict—this was apparent, as the following two quotations show:
"Put a man in a hole," writes Colonel Lyman, "and a good battery on a
hill behind him, and he will beat off three times his number, even if he is
not a very good soldier."[36] And Frank Wilkeson writes: "Before we left
North Anna I discovered that our infantry were tired of charging earth-
works. The ordinary enlisted men assert that one good man behind an
earthwork was equal to three good men outside of it."[37]

The classical example of the attack by penetration is the Battle of Arbela
(also called Gaugamela) fought and won by Alexander the Great on
1st October, 331 B.C. In brief his famous manœuvre was as follows:

At the head of 45,000 men Alexander advanced diagonally against the
left centre of the Persian army under Darius, which numerically was vastly
superior to his own. When closing in on it, he formed his troops into arrow-
head formation; his phalanx (heavy infantry) on his left, his light troops on
his right and his heavy cavalry, massed into a wedge, in his centre. As the

---

[36] *Meade's Headquarters*, 1863-1865, Colonel Theodore Lyman (1922), p. 224.
[37] *The Soldier in Battle, or Life in the Ranks of the Army of the Potomac*, Frank
Wilkeson (1898), p. 99.

steady advance of the phalanx struck fear into the Persian horde, Alexander, noticing a gap in its front caused by the advance of some Persian squadrons, charged that point. Breaking through, he wheeled his horsemen to the left and took the Persian right wing in reverse. Whereupon the whole of Darius's army was swept by panic.

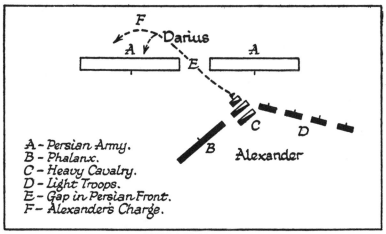

ARBELA MANŒUVRE

Of flank attacks there are also two types—the attack by single envelopment and the attack by double envelopment. Of the first there are innumerable examples, one of the most perfect being the Battle of Leuthen, fought and won by Frederick the Great on 5th December, 1757. In idea it was based on Epaminondas's famous manœuvre at the Battle of Leuctra in 371 B.C.

Advancing rapidly at the head of 36,000 men, Frederick surprised Marshal Daun and some 85,000 Austrians. Whereupon Daun hastily formed line between a bog on his right and the River Schweidenitz on his left, the village of Leuthen marking his centre. Feinting at Daun's right, under cover of a rise in the ground, Frederick marched the greater part of his army unseen across his enemy's front, and falling upon Daun's left he rolled that flank back on Leuthen. Finally, he swept the centre and all before him. Napoleon pronounced this battle to be "a masterpiece of movements, manœuvres and resolution."[38]

The classical example of the double envelopment is the Battle of Cannæ, fought and won by Hannibal on 2nd August, 216 B.C.

[38]*Correspondance de Napoléon*, vol. XXXII, p. 184.

Hannibal drew up his infantry in three divisions, his Spaniards and Gauls forming the central one and his Africans those on the flanks. On each wing of this infantry line he posted a powerful force of cavalry. Faced by the Romans under Varro, drawn up in similar order, Hannibal with his left wing cavalry charged and routed the Roman right wing cavalry. Then,

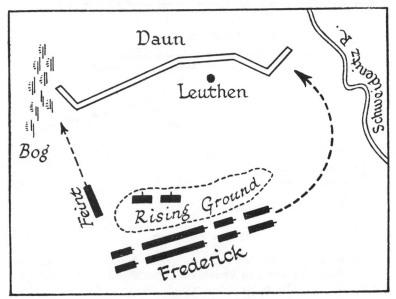

LEUTHEN MANŒUVRE

chasing the Roman left wing cavalry from the field, as the Roman infantry advanced, he formed his central division into a convex formation bulging towards his enemy. Forthwith this crescent was attacked and slowly driven back, until it became concave or hollow-shaped. Into this pocket Varro crowded his men. Suddenly, Hannibal advanced his two divisions of African infantry and wheeling them inwards closed on the Roman flanks. Thereupon the Carthaginian cavalry, returning from the pursuit, fell upon the Roman rear. Thus was Varro's army swallowed up as if by an earthquake.

Before the advent of aircraft, the rear attack proper—that is, an attack not directly consequent on an attack by penetration or envelopment—could only be carried out by a force acting independently of those engaged in the main or holding battle. An excellent example of this form of attack is the Battle of Chancellorsville. On 2nd May, 1863, General Lee ordered

Stonewall Jackson and 32,000 men to march twelve miles round Hooker's front and right flank and fall upon his rear. This Jackson successfully did and completely ruined Hooker's plan.

Of defensive tactics there are two general categories—direct and indirect defence. The latter includes defence by fire, by cover from view, defence by obstacles and reduction of target by extensions. The third of these means now includes entanglements, land-mines and a variety of tank and

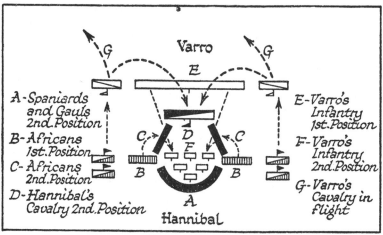

A-Spaniards and Gauls 2nd. Position
B-Africans 1st. Position
C-Africans 2nd. Position
D-Hannibal's Cavalry 2nd. Position
E-Varro's Infantry 1st. Position
F-Varro's Infantry 2nd. Position
G-Varro's Cavalry in flight

Varro

Hannibal

CANNÆ MANŒUVRE

air-landing obstacles. All these indirect means are, however, subsidiary to direct defence, of which there are three main forms—linear defence, area defence and mobile defence.

Examples of the first of these are the Great Wall of China, the Roman frontier walls, the trench lines of the First World War and the Maginot Line. Of the second—which is frequently called "defence in depth" to distinguish it from defence in length—the system adopted by the medieval castle builders and the military engineers of the seventeenth and eighteenth centuries. This system consisted in building castles or fortresses to block centres of communication and natural lines of approach, and thereby slow up an enemy's advance. These fortifications are generally distributed net-wise or chequer-wise over a deep zone.

The earliest form of mobile direct defence is the shield, later body armour, which now finds its counterpart in tank armour. But, when related to a body of men, its earliest example is the wagon laager, which was used by nomadic people—Huns, Mongols, etc.—also by the Hussites in the fifteenth century and as late as the South African War of 1899-1902 by the Boers, notably so at the Battle of Paardeburg. As we shall see, this form of defence was extensively used in the Second World War.

On first thoughts it may seem that the introduction of aircraft introduced a new form of attack and defence—namely, the vertical. But this is not so. In its day the Roman *testudo* was as important a means of defence against vertically falling projectiles as anti-aircraft fire and concrete shelters are now. And when at the Battle of Hastings, on 14th October, 1066, William the Conqueror ordered his archers to fire their arrows into the sky so that they would fall vertically on Harold's army, in an elementary way he was doing nothing more than what bombing aircraft now do, and frequently with less decisive effect.

From this brief excursion into the past, it will be seen that, though the means of attack and defence have changed out of all recognition, the forms of attack and defence remain constant. Probably the greatest change which is to be found in warfare is one which lies in the administrative more so than the tactical field—namely, the transport of supplies and troops by air. This change is radical, because it dispenses with roads and cross-country movements. Hitherto, all movements have been superficial, now spacial movement must be added to them. Therefore battles are no longer fought over areas only, let alone in lines, as for the most part they still were in 1914-1918, but in cubic spaces. Consequently, the battlefield of to-day may be compared to a box in which the armies contained in it, whether stationary or moving, are, or at least should be, constantly prepared to defend themselves on all sides—top, front, rear and flanks—or assume the offensive in one or more of these directions. War is more complex, there are more pieces to play with, but the game is still played on the same old board; for, in spite of aircraft, decision is still gained on the surface of the earth.

CHAPTER II

GERMAN INITIATIVE, ITS INITIAL SUCCESSES AND FAILURE

(1) *The Overthrow of Poland*

On 1st September, 1939, exactly twenty years after the Victorious Powers had lifted their embargo on trade with enemy countries, Germany lifted the embargo on war. While in the West the summer lightning of the guns was once again to play upon the trench lines, this time in the East there was to be lightning war: a conflict of but eighteen days in which Poland, a country three times the size of England and inhabited by over 30,000,000 courageous people, was to collapse like a house of cards.

The reasons for this were both strategical and tactical. The one because the western half of Poland formed a great salient with its snout pointing towards Berlin, flanked on the north by East Prussia and Pomerania and on the south by Silesia and Slovakia. The other because there were no natural lines of defence west of the Vistula, and because the Polish-German frontier was 850 miles in length, no army then existing could have held it defensively. Why then did the Poles decide to do so?

The main reason was that their vital areas of operations lay within the salient, and without them they could not supply their fighting forces. Of these areas there were four of major importance: (1) the Polish Silesian coalfields[1]; (2) the industrial towns of Kielce, Konskie, Opoczno, Radom and Lublin; (3) the industrial towns of Tarnow, Krosno, Drobycz and Boryslaw; and (4) the textile industries around Lodz. In the third were to be found most of the Polish armament and munition factories, aeroplanes and motor works, also coal, oil and petrol refineries. Of these areas, the first was on the German frontier and in itself formed a subsidiary salient between Upper Silesia and Slovakia. The second lay from one hundred to one hundred and fifty miles north of Slovakia; the third from twenty to sixty miles also north of Slovakia; and the fourth about eighty miles east of Silesia.

---

[1] According to the Peace Treaty, the ownership of Upper Silesia was to be decided by plebiscite; but when 707,605 votes were cast for retention by Germany and 479,359 for incorporation with Poland, it was decided to divide the territory in dispute between Germany and Poland. The north-western part of Upper Silesia

Two further strategical disadvantages faced the Poles. The first was that Germany held the naval command of the Baltic and, in spite of the Corridor, could therefore maintain close contact with East Prussia. The

THE INVASION OF POLAND, 1st-30th SEPTEMBER, 1939

second was that Poland's sole contact with her Western Allies lay by way of Rumania and the Black Sea. Strategically, Poland was a landlocked island, whose entire "coastline" was open to invasion.

went to Germany, and the south-eastern part to Poland. "It is significant that in the Polish area were to be found 53 out of the 67 coal mines, 21 out of the 37 blast furnaces, 9 out of the 14 steel-rolling mills, and 226,000 tons out of the annual output of 266,000 tons of zinc—or 70 per cent of the entire pre-war German zinc output." (*Our Own Times* 1913-1938, Stephen King-Hall, 1938, pp. 202-203.)

Tactically, the disadvantages were as great. The Polish army and air force were not only numerically inferior to Germany's, but also technically inferior. And as the area the Poles decided to defend was ideal for the rapid manœuvring of motorized forces, and more especially so in the autumn when normally the weather is fine, this alone put the Polish army at a crippling discount. Further still, in this area were living some 2,000,000 Germans, consequently little the Poles did remained unknown to their enemy.

The Polish plan was a half-measure, part offensive and part defensive. Yet in justice to its devisers it must be remembered that they expected a vigorous offensive from their allies in the West, though they had no right to rely on it for at least several months. Instinctively disliking the defensive, trusting on human valour and grossly under-estimating the potentials of armoured and aerial warfare, Marshal Smigly-Rydz, the Polish Commander-in-Chief, and his Staff decided to hold the whole salient from Grodno to Krosno and to cover all the industrial areas. His plan was to distribute six armies of thirty infantry divisions, ten reserve divisions and twenty-two cavalry brigades close to the frontier, with their reserves and a general reserve in the neighbourhood of Warsaw. Though, when mobilization was completed, he would have at his disposal some 50,000 officers and 1,700,000 men, these figures meant very little, for *vis-à-vis* the Germans the Poles were lamentably short of motorized arms. Their air force consisted of some five hundred serviceable machines, and their armoured forces of twenty-nine companies of armoured cars and nine companies of light tanks. Further, they were short of heavy, anti-aircraft and anti-tank artillery.

The German plan was to be carried out in two stages. The first was to surround and annihilate the Polish forces in the Vistula bend, and the second, by driving south from East Prussia and north from Slovakia, to cut off the whole of Poland west of Bialystok-Brest Litovsk (Brześć) and the River Bug. It, therefore, comprised two double envelopments, an inner west of Warsaw and an outer east of that city.

General von Brauchitsch was selected to carry out this plan, and he was given five armies. These were divided into two groups, the dividing line between the groups being the River Notec.

The Northern Group was under General von Bock and consisted of the Third and Fourth Armies. The former was in East Prussia and the latter in Pomerania. The main task of the Third was to thrust southwards and east of Warsaw and eventually join hands with the Fourteenth Army advancing northwards from Upper Silesia and Slovakia. That of the Fourth was, first to annihilate the enemy in Pomorze, and secondly to link up with the right of the Third Army and operate against the right flank of the Poles in Poznan.

The Southern Group, under General von Rundstedt, consisted of the Eighth, Tenth and Fourteenth Armies. The Eighth in Pomerania and Brandenburg, with its left on the River Notec and its right at Namslau (east of Breslau) was to engage the Polish forces in Poznan and co-operate with the right of the Fourth Army and the left of the Tenth. The Tenth in Lower Silesia was to thrust towards the Vistula and envelop the left of the Polish forces in Poznan. The Fourteenth, grouped in Upper Silesia, Moravia and Slovakia, was to annihilate the Polish army in the Cracow area, and with its right flank leading push northwards and join hands with the left of the Third Army.

It would appear that in all forty-five German divisions[2] were employed, which, considering the extent of the area of operations, was not a large force, but in contrast to the Polish divisions they were superbly equipped and incomparably better staffed. Though the strength of the German mechanized forces is variously given, they probably amounted to six armoured and six motorized divisions. Of their four air fleets, two were employed. No. 1 under General Kesselring and No. 4 under General Löhr; the first based on East Prussia and Pomerania and the second on Silesia and Slovakia. Their combined strength was about 2,000 machines.[3]

Though, when compared with the infantry masses, the German air and tank forces were small, and markedly so when measured against those which later on took the field, so decisive was their influence on operations that it is only necessary to examine what they accomplished in order to discover why the Polish collapse was immediate.

At 4.40 a.m. on 1st September the attack was launched in the form of an all-out German air offensive. It came as a complete surprise to the Poles; for they were thinking in the, comparatively speaking, leisurely terms of 1914: of cavalry screens, contact patrols, of the cautious feeling forward by both sides, and the gaining of time wherein to complete mobilization. In short, they were dreaming of light cavalry advanced guard actions, and were awakened by a heavy cavalry charge. Thus it came about that the Polish war brain was paralysed within forty-eight hours of the war opening.

The first object in this air assault was to gain mastery in the air. This was accomplished by destroying the Polish air force both in the air and on the

---

[2]Some sources put the infantry divisions at 37, others at 35 and 47. On 9th September Göring stated that in all there were 70 divisions in Poland. This would appear to be an exaggeration, for General Jodl stated during the Nuremberg trial that Germany entered the war with 75 divisions, and that 23 of these were left on the Western Front.

[3]A German statement gives 1,000 bombers and 1,050 fighters, which is probably correct, as on 3rd September, 1939 the total operative strength of the *Luftwaffe* (including some 300 transport aircraft) was 4,161 planes.

ground. Therefore concentrated attacks were made on aerodromes, either to compel the Polish airmen to take to the air and accept fight against superior numbers, or to see their machines destroyed where they stood. Also attacks were made on anti-aircraft defences, repair shops and broadcasting stations.

The tactics employed were as follows: Led by one or more reconnaissance machines, squadrons of nine bombers protected by fighters and flying at an altitude of some 10,000 feet made for their targets. On approaching them they came down to about 3,000 feet, and when over the target dropped their bombs in groups of three aircraft at the time. This done, the fighters dived down to within a few feet of the ground and machine-gunned any aircraft or personnel to be seen. Sometimes, before the bombing took place, a reconnaissance plane, flying low, would surround the target with a ring of white smoke.

Directly supremacy in the air was gained, as it virtually was within twenty-four hours of the campaign opening, the air object became the stopping of all enemy ground movements. During this phase of the air assault the main targets were the railways and railway junctions within the Vistula bend, care being taken not to destroy the bridges the Germans would require. Columns and convoys on the roads were also attacked, and in order to promote sabotage and treachery behind the Polish front, a number of air landings were made and parachutists dropped. "In some cases," it is stated, "detachments landed from the air attacked army headquarters or security units behind the front."[4]

The results of these attacks were that the entire chain of command throughout the Polish military hierarchy was dislocated and mobilization was thrown into inextricable confusion. The upshot was that the bulk of the Polish army never reached its concentration areas, which in several cases were overrun by the Germans within a few hours of the campaign opening.

The third object of the German air fleets was to assist and accelerate the forward movement of the troops on the ground, and more particularly the armoured and motorized divisions which formed the spearheads of all the main German attacks. It was these forces which completed the process of disorganization and demoralization induced by the air assault, by producing such confusion among the now headless bodies of fighting men that in most cases the German infantry could occupy the overrun areas with little fighting.

At the opening of the war, the German armoured divisions were somewhat cumbersome organizations, consisting as they then did of an

[4] *The Defence of Poland*, Lieut.-General M. Norwid Neugebauer (1942), p. 206.

headquarters, a divisional reconnaissance unit, a tank brigade, a motorized infantry brigade, an artillery regiment, anti-tank battalion and an engineer battalion. The tank brigade comprised two tank regiments, each regiment of two battalions and each battalion of one medium tank squadron and three light tank squadrons. In all, an armoured division possessed slightly over four hundred tanks. In order to render it more mobile, in 1942 this figure was cut by nearly a half.

German armoured tactics were based on speed more so than on fire power, for their object was to accelerate confusion. Therefore depth of penetration was generally aimed at. Consequently points of resistance, fortified areas, anti-tank positions, woods and villages were normally avoided, and the lines of least resistance leading to the enemy's rear were sought out. Exploitation after penetration was to be in depth and not laterally, which was the more prudent manœuvre laid down by the French. Though exploitation in depth was risky, because in face of an energetic enemy the exploiting units are liable to be cut off, the Germans rightly reckoned that all energy would be knocked out of their enemy by the air assault before the armoured divisions were launched. Each division was to move straight forward without considering neighbouring units, the protection of the gaps between units being entrusted to the troops in rear. When opposition was met with, if possible it was by-passed and left to the following infantry to overcome. Co-operation between the *Luftwaffe* and the armoured divisions was considered essential, and collaboration between bombers, attack air squadrons and tank squadrons was complete. Also, much reliance was placed on artillery either self-propelled or transported.

In the initial phase of the battle, should resistance be unavoidable, tank tactics were normally as follows: First, advancing in wedge formation on a narrow front of from three to four kilometres in width, a penetration of the enemy's defence system was effected. Secondly, the breach was held by storm troops following the tanks. Thirdly, fresh forces of tanks were pushed through the gap to fan laterally outwards, while others were pushed straight ahead to exploit in depth.

The Polish opposition was, however, so weak that these tactics could generally be simplified, the procedure being to push straight ahead, with the main mass of the infantry following from ten to twenty miles in rear. In this way the German Fourth Army advancing from Pomerania reached the outskirts of Warsaw "solely through the efforts of the 1st mechanized echelon, which covered 240 kilometres in eight days."[5]

---

[5]"A Neutral View of the German-Polish War," Lieut.-Colonel Dinulescu, Rumanian Army, *Journal of the Royal United Service Institution*, August, 1940, p. 403.

It is interesting to read that, in spite of German tank superiority, "The method of night attack against the headquarters and parks of armoured divisions, used on several occasions by Polish infantry, gave excellent results. The enemy was compelled to provide his tanks and armoured cars with powerful searchlights, which blinded the attacking force and, when used in accordance with a definite plan, assisted defence fire at night."[6]

To trace in any detail the operations from 1st September onwards is not our purpose, yet a few salient events must be mentioned if only to illustrate the rapidity of the campaign. On the 5th the left of the Third Army (General von Küchler) crossed the Narew near Lomza and its right joined hands with the left of the Fourth (General von Kluge), which by then had eliminated the Corridor. The Eighth (General Blaskowitz) was approaching Lodz and General Guderian's tanks had occupied Piotrkow and Kielce. The Tenth (General von Reichenau) having conquered the industrial region of Polish Silesia, was speeding towards the Vistula, and the Fourteenth (General List) had lapped round Cracow. By the 8th Guderian's tanks were outside Warsaw, the Fourteenth had reached the River San, and the whole of the Polish forces in Poznan and such as had escaped from Pormorze were squeezed into a pocket around Kutno— seventy-five miles west of Warsaw—and a week later surrendered. By the 17th practically all fighting west of the Vistula was at an end, the war having been carried to the Bug. That day, without a declaration of war, the Russians crossed the Polish eastern frontier, and the next day the Polish Government, followed by tens of thousands of fugitives, fled into Rumania. This same day William L. Shirer, an American foreign correspondent, at Zoppot, near Danzig, jotted down in his diary: "Drove all day long from Berlin through Pomerania and the Corridor to here. The roads full of motorized columns of German troops *returning* from Poland."[7] Further, he wrote: ". . . 450,000 Polish troops captured, 1,200 guns taken, and 800 airplanes either destroyed or captured; and at the end of eighteen days of fighting not a single Polish division, not even a brigade, was left intact."[8]

Warsaw held out until the 27th, when its Commander asked for an armistice, and on the 30th its garrison of 120,000 officers and men marched out and piled arms.

The German losses in this astonishing campaign were exceedingly light, and, on account of its speed, there is no reason to doubt the accuracy of the figures broadcast by Hitler—namely, 10,572 killed, 30,322 wounded and 3,400 missing. What the Polish losses were is conjectural; the Germans, however, claimed 694,000 prisoners. The booty was Poland herself. The

[6] *The Defence of Poland*, p. 213.
[7] *Berlin Diary*, William L. Shirer (1941), p. 171.
[8] *Ibid.*, p. 177.

Germans took the part of the country west of the Pissa, the Bug and the San, in all 129,400 square kilometres, and the Russians the rest—200,280.[9]

Tactically this short campaign was of outstanding importance; its very brevity acclaimed this. Not only was it the testing of the attack by paralysation; but to all of clear tactical sight it revealed that it was speed more so than fire power which in mechanized warfare is the principal means of action. Consequently, that confusion more so than destruction is the aim of the attack. It was speed which enabled the Germans to maintain their plan, and lack of speed which prevented the Poles readjusting theirs. The campaign was not decided by superiority of numbers, but by the velocity of aircraft and armoured forces operating as one integrated force. Had the Poles possessed the German air and armoured forces and had the Germans possessed the Polish, then, granted that the Poles had used them skilfully, in spite of their disadvantageous strategical position, there is no reason to doubt that they could not have reached the Oder as rapidly as the Germans reached the Vistula. But that they could have overrun Germany as speedily as they themselves were overrun is highly improbable, not only because in Germany there are more natural obstacles than in Poland, but because the main German vital centre of operations lay in the Ruhr—that is, well outside their immediate grasp. They, therefore, could not have applied the strategy of annihilation so completely as did their enemy.

The campaign also showed that, in face of mechanized attack, linear defence is outmoded. In fact, that any form of linear defence, whether consisting of permanent fortifications or hastily-dug field works, such as, again and again, halted an attacker in the First World War, is the worst possible system to rely on, because once the defensive line is penetrated by armoured forces it becomes impossible for the defender to concentrate his troops for counter-attack. He is like a man with outstretched arms facing a boxer in fighting posture; his arms must be drawn in before he can either

[9]With reference to future events, the following extracts from *A Record of the War, The First Quarter* (September-November, 1939), Sir Ronald Storrs, pp. 349-350, are of interest: "On 8th November a party of 150 officers, prisoners of war, were taken out of Lwow in lorries. Three miles beyond Jeziorna the convoy stopped and the officers were told to stand in a row facing a small stream. A detachment of G.P.U., with six machine-guns, then massacred all the 150 by shooting them in the back." . . . "The soldiers (Russian) were greatly impressed by the variety of the goods displayed in the shops of Wilno, the poorest of the large provincial towns of Poland . . . Gramophones, watches, and penknives fascinated the Red soldiers more than anything else. Within two days the entire stock of cheap watches and penknives in the shops was sold out . . . But the unhappy soldiers were not allowed to enjoy their purchases for long. As soon as these happenings reached the ears of the authorities, all the watches and penknives were taken away and strict orders were given that none of these dangerous objects were to be taken into Russia, as they might demoralize the population in the Soviet paradise."

guard or hit. Further, the campaign showed that covering detachments—forces intended to observe and delay and not to fight pitched battles—must possess the highest possible mobility, so that they can advance and retire at speed. Also, that they should be strong in anti-tank weapons.

Finally, the campaign clearly demonstrated that in the tactical conditions established by mechanized forces, in which time is fleeting because movements are rapid, command must be far more decentralized than it has been in the past, in order that the actions of subordinate commanders may be immediate. Therefore co-ordination should be sought through general idea rather than through rigid adherence to plan, velocity largely replacing method; but, nevertheless, velocity regulated by a common aim, which is clearly understood by all concerned.

(2) *The Russo-Finnish Campaign*

When Poland was being annihilated, an equally astonishing conflict was in progress in the West. Soon to be called the "Phoney War," it was better named the "*Sitzkrieg*," as may be gauged from the following quotation: "The strongest land force in the world, the French Army, had been accorded good time to take its stand in the strongest defences yet conceived by the ingenuity of man. The large and magnificently equipped and provided British Expeditionary Force had without one casualty been transported, landed and welded into this steel-hard, steel-entrenched human fortress. Thus consolidated, France and Britain had so far prevented even the menace of an attempt of any sort of *Blitz*—or other—attack on the Maginot Line."[10]

The strongest army in the world, facing no more than twenty-six divisions, sitting still and sheltering behind steel and concrete while a quixotically valiant ally was being exterminated! Yet, as a little later on we shall see—when the sawdust fell out of the effigy—there was good reason for this.

By 11th October, the British had landed 158,000 men in France, yet not until 9th December did they suffer their first casualty—Corporal T. W. Priday was shot dead when on patrol. By Christmas two more men had been killed, and by that date the total French casualties for army, navy and air force were 1,433.

Meanwhile, on 3rd September—the day Britain declared war—the Battle of the Atlantic opened with the sinking of the *Athenia* by U-boat 30 off the Donegal coast, a battle which was to strain British resources almost to breaking point and to continue until the last shot on land was fired. In the

[10] *The First Quarter*, p. 343.

air, conflict came one day later, on 4th September the Royal Air Force attacked German warships at Wilhelmshaven and Brunsbüttel, and a little after proceeded to scatter leaflets over Germany. So bloodless a war had not been seen since the Battles of Molinella and Zagonara.

On 6th October, Hitler, seconded by Mr. Molotov, Russian Commissar for Foreign Affairs, proposed peace. His proposal was rejected. Next, on 30th November, came the first of the several unexpected campaigns, Russia invaded Finland. The following day, in Berlin, Mr. Shirer wrote in his diary: "Yesterday Red air force bombers attacked Helsinki, killing seventy-five civilians, wounding several hundred. The great champion of the working class, the mighty preacher against 'Fascist aggression,' the righteous stander-up for the 'scrupulous and punctilious observation of treaties' (to quote Molotov as of a month ago) has fallen upon the most decent and workable little democracy in Europe in violation of half a dozen 'solemn' treaties."[11]

It was a war of 180,000,000 people against 3,500,000, and its duration was to be rather more than five times the length of the Polish campaign.

The Russian forces were immense, the Finnish minute. On the one side stood one hundred divisions of 1,500,000 officers and men, 9,000 tanks and 10,000 aircraft.[12] On the other, three divisions and one cavalry brigade of 33,000 officers and men, a handful of tanks, 60 battle-worthy aircraft and 250 guns, including coastal artillery. This little army was commanded by Field-Marshal Mannerheim.

The Russian plan was to bomb and demonstrate. Expecting the Finnish workers to rise and overthrow their government, in appalling weather the Soviet troops advanced in five columns, the main one, consisting of six divisions, moving against the Mannerheim Line—a zone of defensive works stretching across the Karelian Isthmus between the Gulf of Finland and Lake Ladoga. To their surprise they were met by a violent resistance which, what with the extraordinarily difficult terrain—a roadless tangle of forests, lakes, hills and ravines, feet deep in snow—soon brought them to a standstill.

Because the Russian tanks were compelled to use the forest tracks, hundreds became bogged in the snowdrifts. Many were set alight[13] by the Finns, whose ski patrols, almost invisible in their white snow-cloaks, cut circles round their enemy. Here, there and everywhere they sped through the forests, halting columns, cutting off stragglers, shooting up convoys,

[11]*Berlin Diary*, p. 202.
[12]All figures relating to Russia are more or less conjectural.
[13]*My Finnish Diary*, Sir Walter Citrine (1940), p. 118. He states that the Russian tanks were indescribably dirty and covered with oil. This explains why they took fire so easily.

field kitchens and encampments, and often so completely isolating whole brigades that the Russians had to supply them by aircraft, which they did with little success.[14] From the start, the Finns inflicted such heavy casualties on their enemy that the Russians redoubled their bombing of the civil inhabitants, expecting that it would crack their morale.

If ever there was an opportunity of testing out the Douhet theory it was now, for the Russians had absolute command of the air.[15] If Douhet were right, within a fortnight the Finns should have capitulated. Instead, their resistance became more determined. Therefore some other course of action had to be found: it was a return to the tactics of 1916-1917.

Massing twenty-seven divisions and a stupendous number of guns against the Mannerheim Line, after a prolonged artillery bombardment, on 2nd February, 1940, the Russians, under the command of Marshal Timoshenko, assaulted it. For ten days the Finns held their works; but on the 13th a penetration was made and two days later the Finns were compelled to withdraw. Not being able to resist the Russian tanks and hordes in the open, early in March they asked for an armistice. On the 10th peace negotiations followed, and two days later a treaty of peace was signed.

Insignificant though this campaign was, its lessons are illuminating. First, it showed that it is always dangerous, however weak an enemy may be, to hold him in contempt. Imagining that a show of force would be sufficient to terrify the Finns into immediate surrender, the Russians, though fully prepared to use radios, brass bands and moving pictures for purposes of propaganda, left strategy, tactics and administration unconsidered. It was faulty psychology that bogged them. As Hitler had long before written in *Mein Kampf*: ". . . man does not sacrifice himself for material interests . . . he will die for an ideal and not for a business."[16] Finland's ideal was freedom and not the business of Marx.

Secondly, to those who had open minds, it went far to explode the Douhet theory. It showed that air bombardments, like artillery bombardments, are slow and not rapid means of wearing down an enemy. Thirdly, unless weapons are fitted to ground and climate, it matters not how powerful they are, for they will be found next to useless. Fourthly, that it was the high mobility of the Finns, as it had been the high mobility of the

[14]Generally the supplies fell into Finnish hands.

[15]The Russian air force, though big, was inefficient. "Frequent 'purges' have eliminated many of the best aeronautical engineers . . . The younger men are reluctant to show any enterprise or initiative . . . The Finns are reported to have found simple multiplication tables placed with modern navigation instruments in some of the machines brought down . . . the officers are extremely conceited." "The Soviet Air Force and the War with Finland," *Journal of the United Service Institution*, May, 1940, pp. 298-299.

[16]*Mein Kampf*, p. 138.

Germans in Poland, that time and again proved superior to mere numerical strength.

Lastly, and from the point of view of future events most important of all, the gross incompetence of the Russian Command, their total lack of strategic sense and their fatuous tactics and faulty administration, must have led Hitler into believing that the Russian army of 1939-1940 was still the Russian army of 1914-1917. That if a country so small as Finland could accomplish what it did, what could not he accomplish with the might of the Reich?

(3) *The Norwegian Campaign*

While the Russians were pulverizing the Finns, the *sitzkrieg* continued unabated, and except for some desultory air raiding, the sole happenings of any interest were at sea. In mid-December the Battle of the River Plate was fought, which resulted in the sinking of the German pocket battleship, the *Graf Spee*. On 12th February a considerable fleet of transports brought the best part of two Australian and New Zealand divisions to Egypt. A week later the *Altmark*, a German armed merchantman, was boarded by British sailors in Norwegian waters and two hundred and ninety-nine prisoners of war removed from her. Though this annoyed the Norwegian Government, notwithstanding, early on 8th April, the British and French Governments informed that Government that, in order to stop German traffic along the west coast of Norway, Norwegian territorial waters had been mined during the previous night.

This being a breach of neutrality, it might easily involve Norway in the war. Were the Allied Powers ready to support her in case of German intervention? No. That night the British naval base at Scapa Flow was heavily bombed by German aircraft, and early on the morning of the 9th, when the Danes in Copenhagen were bicycling to work, they suddenly ran into a column of German soldiers marching towards the Royal Palace. At first they thought that a film was being shot.[17] A moment later the Palace guard opened fire; next the Germans returned it; and lastly, the King sent out his adjutant to stop the shooting: thus Denmark capitulated to Hitler. Such was the curtain-raiser to one of the most audacious and imaginative operations of war in history—the occupation of all the vital centres in Norway between dawn and dusk.

This astonishing operation was the first example of the Hitler strategy in practice . . . "Why should I demoralize my enemy by military means, if

[17]*Berlin Diary*, p. 250. According to evidence given in the Nuremberg trial, the invasion of Norway was being prepared as early as October, 1939.

I can do so better and more cheaply in other ways." The wisdom if not the morality of this was certainly proved, as the following brief outline of events will show.

Hitler had no intention of directly attacking the Norwegian army, small though it was,[18] because long before 9th April he had launched his direct attack against the Norwegian people. He knew that in a democratic country an army is next to useless should the people sympathize with the enemy.[19] For long his persuasive propaganda had created in Norway an extensive body of sympathizers[20] under Major Vidkun Quisling, Leader of the Norwegian Nasjonal Samling.[21] These people, who were to become known as "the Fifth Column," formed the tactical foundations of his attack, the strategical aims of which were:

(1) To restrict the power of the British Navy by establishing air and naval bases on the west coast of Norway.

(2) To open the North Sea and Atlantic to the German Fleet.

(3) To lie athwart the sea communications between Britain and Northern Russia.

(4) To secure the western Swedish iron ore sea route.

The importance of Norway to Germany was clearly explained in an article which appeared in the *Frankfurter Zeitung* of 21st April, extracts from which read as follows:

"Was it really a gigantic mistake (as the British maintain it was) to take possession of this jumping-off ground in a life and death struggle against Great Britain, instead of leaving it, plus the whole of Scandinavia with its strategic and economic advantages, to the enemy . . . Having achieved the initial success, apart from economic advantages to be derived therefrom, we shall be in a position to tie up and weaken the Franco-British air and naval forces, and to compel Britain to fight . . . The weakening of the Western Powers will be noticeable sooner or later—in the North Sea as well as in other waters, where the British and French have vital interests,

[18]It numbered only 14,500 officers and men.

[19]This is why in autocratically ruled countries their governments raise two armies, one to fight their enemies and the other to control their peoples.

[20]A profound difference between World War II and World War I was that in so many countries which the Germans overran, as well as several which they did not, the people were radically discontented with what passed for democracy. They believed that Hitler's aims were right though his methods were wrong. They believed that he stood between them and Asiatic Bolshevism, which they dreaded with a religious fear. Further, they believed that the old financial and economic systems which Hitler rejected were at the bottom of all social and international friction, unemployment and war.

[21]At one time Major Quisling had been Norwegian Military Attaché at Moscow. There he learnt to detest Communism and to fear it.

the Mediterranean in particular. The naval superiority of the Western Powers rests, not with their actual fleets, but with the margin of those fleets over other Powers. This is a very important calculation for all who look to the ending of Franco-British naval supremacy for the satisfaction of their claims to *Lebensraum*. Nowhere has the connection between the North Sea and the Mediterranean been more strongly emphasized during the last few days than in Italy."[22]

To accomplish the above strategic aims, the tactical requirements were the seizure of all the main Norwegian airfields and ports before the British could occupy them. It was here that the Fifth Columnists came in. On a given order they were to seize and hold these objectives until supported by airborne and seaborne troops. Though the first could be despatched at a few hours notice, in order to speed up the second a return was made to the ruse of the Trojan horse. A few days before the invasion was to take place, troops were embarked on ore, coal and trading vessels and sent off to their several destinations.

Simultaneously with the occupation of Denmark, which provided the Germans with airfields flanking the North Sea and Skagerrak, the Fifth Column in Norway carried out its tasks and was at once supported by airborne troops and Trojan "horsemen." Then came the seaborne troops over the Skagerrak.

Oslo, the key point of the invasion, was occupied by Fifth Columnists supported by airborne troops, while seaborne in transports, under a powerful naval escort, forced the harbour defences. In the action which took place the German 10,000-ton cruiser *Blücher* was lost as well as several other vessels, including transports. Narvik, eight hundred miles north of Oslo, was taken by Trojan horsemen protected by a naval escort. The troops landed there were Austrians trained for mountain warfare. Kristiansund, Trondheim, Bergen and Stavanger were occupied in like manner, and the most important airfield in Norway, that of Sole near Stavanger, was seized by airborne troops. By nightfall on the 9th all the above places were in German hands, whereupon General von Falkenhorst, the invasion commander, pushed columns inland from Oslo up the railways and roads leading to the above places, with the exception of Narvik, which was completely isolated.

The swiftness and suddenness of the attack temporarily paralysed the British and French Governments. Clearly the only immediate counterstroke could be by sea and air. So obvious was this that to the British public it seemed that "Hitler's adventure had delivered him into the hands of the

[22]Quoted from *A Record of the War, The Third Quarter*, Philip Graves, pp. 62-63.

British Fleet."[23] Nevertheless, and in spite of the pugnacious Mr. Churchill being at the time First Lord of the Admiralty, except for laying mines in the Skagerrak nothing was done until the 15th to impede the invaders.

That day a small British force landed north of Narvik. What for it is difficult to conceive. As Mr. Graves pertinently remarks: "If a German expedition were to surprise London and another were to establish itself at Hull, the successful landing of an American relief expedition at Inverness would not be of much assistance to the British Army struggling for life in the Midlands."[24]

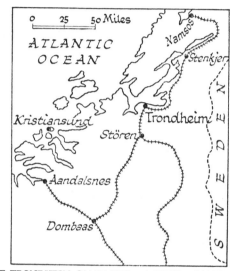

THE TRONDHEIM CAMPAIGN, 15th APRIL–3rd MAY, 1940

On the 16th followed a landing at Namsos under General Carton de Wiart, and on the 18th another at Aandalsnes under General B. C. T. Paget. These landings were planned as diversionary operations of a direct attack on Trondheim, a port of some size, possessing an airfield in its vicinity—an essential. Yet, no sooner did the diversionary forces move inland than the direct attack was abandoned because the fleet would be exposed to air attack. Had this argument been extended to include the two diversionary forces, there might have been some sense in it. But it was not, and having no air force to protect them, after an advance inland and ten days' merciless bombing, the Allied Supreme War Council decided to

[23] *Ibid.*, p. 30.
[24] *Ibid.*, p. 42.

withdraw them. This exceedingly difficult operation was successfully carried out on 2nd-3rd May, but not without heavy shipping losses.

Tactically, this short campaign showed that, unless air power is integrated with sea and land power, in themselves fleets and armies lose the greater part of their fighting values. The bombing of the Stavanger aerodrome by the R.A.F. was useless, because the Germans had all the airfields of Norway to operate from. What was required was immediate air support, and as this was not forthcoming, the expeditionary forces were doomed from the start. Further, once again this campaign showed that velocity of attack and not the size of the forces engaged is nine-tenths of the battle, not that velocity physically destroys, but because it morally upsets. There can be little doubt that the British and French Governments and their General Staffs were unhinged by the audacity and suddenness of the German attack. The steps they took to meet it definitely point to this.

The main results of the campaign were, however, not strategical, important though these were; instead they lay in the psychological and political fields. In the one, German prestige was enormously enhanced. This led to neutrals assuming that Germany was invincible. In the other, it led to a change of government in England. On 7th May a debate in the House of Commons was opened on the conduct of the war in Norway. On the 9th it was carried to a division in which the smallness of the Government's majority made it clear that the Cabinet no longer enjoyed the confidence of the House. Thereupon, on the 10th, Mr. Chamberlain resigned and Mr. Churchill succeeded him as Prime Minister.

(4) *The Collapse of Holland and Belgium*

In England the German invasion of Norway was universally acclaimed to be "a mad gamble." Even Mr. Churchill saw in it no more than another Spanish ulcer.[25] "I must declare to the House," he said on 11th April, "that I feel that we are greatly advantaged by what has occurred, provided we . . . turn to the utmost profit the strategic blunder into which our mortal enemy has been provoked."[26]

But was it a blunder? Clearly, when Hitler's *Lebensraum*—his aim—is kept in mind, and throughout the war in Europe it must be, or else his strategy becomes unintelligible, it will be seen that the conquest of Norway was the first necessary step in the conquest of the West, a conquest which

---

[25]"For myself," he said, "I consider that Hitler's action in invading Scandinavia is as great a strategic and political error as that which was committed by Napoleon in 1807 or 1808 when he invaded Spain . . ." (*Hansard*, vol. 359, H. of C., Deb. 5s, col. 359.)

[26]*Ibid.* So late as 20th April, he is reported in the *Manchester Guardian* as saying: "Allied armies . . . during the summer will purge and clean the soil of the Vikings, the soil of Norway, from the filthy pollution of Nazi tyranny."

strategically was essential before turning eastwards against Russia, so that, when her turn came, the war would be reduced to a one front operation.

To conquer the West demanded the elimination of France and England, and though France was directly attackable, England was not, not only because she was an island, but because her fleet prohibited a direct attack. To emasculate the British fleet was, therefore, the primary half of the problem, and to do so demanded: (1) The neutralization of the North Sea; (2) the establishment of air and submarine bases on the Norwegian Atlantic coast; (3) the neutralization of the English Channel; and (4) the establishment of air and submarine bases on the French Atlantic coast. Then, by operating from the Norwegian and French Atlantic coasts against English supply routes, as well as blocking all sea traffic in the North Sea and English Channel, England might be reduced to such economic straits that she would agree to a peace on terms. This, however, depended on how far America would support her.

Strategically, the third and fourth of the above requirements included the secondary half of the problem—the occupation of France—which clearly could most rapidly be solved by attacking France by way of Holland and Belgium, because this manœuvre would avoid a frontal attack on the Maginot Line, which ended at Montmédy. Also, if successful, it would overrun the main French vital area of operations in the Departments of the Nord and the Pas de Calais, without the industries and coal of which the French army could not for long hold the field. As this area was no more than one hundred and fifty to two hundreds miles from the German frontier, without being wise after the event, and bearing in mind the speed which so far had characterized all German attacks, the victory gained in Norway pointed not to the creation of a Spanish ulcer, but instead to a decisive amputation—the severance of France from England.

Therefore the German plan, suggested and elaborated by General von Manstein, was not, as has so often been asserted, a repetition of the Schlieffen plan of 1914, which was based on the Leuthen manœuvre. Instead, it was a flexible Arbela operation, the aim of which was not to outflank and then roll the enemy's left wing *inwards*, but to penetrate the enemy's front and roll that selfsame wing *outwards* and simultaneously operate against the rear of the enemy's right wing.

Opposed to this plan was one of the most suicidal ever devised. The Maginot Line ending at Montmédy,[27] from the opening of the war onwards until the Germans attacked, the British and French had been busily engaged upon linking it up with the English Channel by means of a zone of

[27]It has frequently been stated that the reason why the Maginot Line was not continued to the sea was that the Belgian Government would have considered it an unfriendly act. The main reason was that, had it been, the French had not the man-

field defences; for the French war theory was that the entrenched stalemate of the last war would repeat itself. In spite of this, in October and November, 1939, in the event of the Germans invading Holland and Belgium or Belgium alone, in accordance with what was known as Plan D, it was decided to abandon this line and move forward to the Dyle or the Escaut, not in order to attack the Germans but to take up a defensive position covered by field defences of little worth.

Subsidiary to this plan were two minor ones, those of the Dutch and the Belgians. The former's was to delay the enemy along the entire eastern frontier; hold the Valley and Raam-Peel lines (Zuider Zee at Eemnes to Grave and Grave to Weert) in strength, and if forced out of them to fall back on the Fortress of Holland and the Oost Front (Muiden-Utrecht-Corinchem). The latter's was to fight a delaying action along the Albert Canal from Antwerp to Liége, and along the Meuse from Liége to Namur, and if forced back to withdraw to the line Antwerp-Namur. There was no co-ordination between the Dutch and the Belgians, and next to none between the Belgians and the French.

The German plan was based not only on numbers, but on unity of command, directness of aim, superiority of weapons, mobility and tactics, and above all on superiority of morale.

Including the front which ran along the Maginot Line, on which the Germans had deployed Army Group C, under General von Leeb, to watch the 26 French divisions locked up in it,[28] they put into the field 150 infantry divisions to face 106 Dutch, Belgian, Polish, French[29] and

power to garrison it adequately and simultaneously maintain a field army. Had the field army they had in 1940 been highly mechanized, well led and morally healthy, there is no reason to suppose that the Maginot Line would have earned the ill name which it did. It was a shield, it wanted a sword, and not another shield to extend it to the English Channel. Instead of being a sword, the French field army was a broomstick.

[28] On this front there was complete peace. The French did not shoot because, as they said of the Germans, *"Ils ne sont pas méchants"* and "if we fire they will fire back." (*What Happened to France*, Gordon Waterfield, 1940, p. 16.) On 1st May, Mr. Shirer saw German children playing in full sight of French soldiers; Germans "punting" a football and frolicking about, and trains on both sides of the Rhine . . . "Not a shot was fired. Not a single airplane could be seen in the skies. (*Berlin Diary*, p. 254.)

[29] The French distribution was in three army groups: The first under General Billotte, 40 divisions facing Belgium; the Second under General Prétalat, 26 divisions garrisoning the Maginot Line; and the Third under General Besson, 36 divisions covering Switzerland and Italy. Also there would appear to have been 32 divisions in reserve scattered along the whole front, 8 of which were behind the Belgian front. Lord Gort had 10 divisions, the Dutch an equivalent number and the Belgians 20.

British. But, whereas they had ten armoured divisions and probably seven motorized as well, and four air fleets of 3,000 to 4,000 aircraft, their enemies had but three armoured divisions (all French) and were inferior in air power. According to General Weygand, the French could muster from 700 to 800 first line planes, the Dutch and Belgians had some 200 apiece, and the B.E.F. also about 200; for the bulk of the R.A.F. was held back in England for home defence and strategic bombing.

But it was in morale that the Germans utterly outclassed the bulk of their enemies, and as Polybius long ago wrote: "Of all the forces which are of influence in war, the spirit of the warrior is the most decisive one." The German was "fantastically good,"[30] the French, fantastically bad—"there was treachery in the French army from top to bottom."[31] The people and the army alike had been completely demoralized by the Blum Popular Front and rotted by Communist propaganda.[32] In Holland there was a strong National-Socialist movement, and in Belgium a somewhat weaker Fascist movement—the Rexists under Degrelle. Thus, a grand opportunity was offered to Hitler to put his psychological attack into operation. This he did and with surprising success.

Facing the Dutch, Belgian and Luxemburg frontiers, the Germans deployed two Army Groups and a Panzer Army Group led by General von Kleist, the northern (B) under General von Bock and the southern (A) under General von Rundstedt supported by von Kleist. Bock's aim was to overrun Holland in the shortest possible time, so that airfields might be gained to flank Belgium from the north, and Rundstedt's and Kleist's was as rapidly as possible to break through the Albert Canal defences covering Belgium, and by simultaneously advancing through the Ardennes strike the Belgian-French front between Dinant and Sedan and penetrate it.

On 7th May, rumours of an impending German attack became more persistent than at any previous date. Next, shortly after midnight on the 9th, many aircraft were heard flying over Holland. Soon after this, reports of attacks on the Dutch airfields and The Hague came in, and a little later on the news that numerous parachutists had been dropped on the airfields,

---

[30]*Berlin Diary*, p. 345. For French and German morale, see pp. 341-346.

[31]*Ibid.*, p. 342. Much information on the complete rottenness of France in 1940 will be found in *Report on France*, Thomas Kernan (1942). It is so staggering that it would not have mattered much what weapons the French Army had been armed with. It did not want to fight, and it did not intend to fight, it was like a mouse before a cat. On 2nd September, 1939, I wrote in Sir Oswald Mosley's paper, *Action*: "What will the French do? I am no prophet, yet I suggest they will sit in the Maginot Line, snip up *La Vie Parisienne*, decorate their dug-outs with very unsatisfying young ladies, and then want to go home."

[32]See *Report on France*.

THE INVASION OF HOLLAND, 10th-14th MAY, 1940

more especially on those within the Fortress of Holland, of which that of Waalhaven, the Rotterdam airport, was the most important. Other parachutists came down at Wassenaar and Valkenburg near The Hague, at Dordrecht, Moerdijk and other places, occupying bridges and linking up with groups of the Dutch Fifth Column, which rendered them invaluable assistance. Two bridges over the Maas and the bridge over the Oude Maas were seized, as well as two over the Moerdijk; most of the island of Ysselmonde and Dordrecht were occupied and The Hague was isolated. Simultaneously with these bewildering operations, a powerful German armoured column crossed the Maas at Gennap, and smashing through the left of the Raam-Peel position made directly westwards for Moerdijk. To the south, other armoured columns crossed the Maas at Lothun and Venlo and advanced on Eindhoven and Breda.

Though in many places the Dutch put up a stiff fight, and in not a few re-won airfields and other localities, the Dutch Command was so completely paralysed by the suddenness and swiftness of the attack that no co-ordinated resistance was possible. On the 11th this paralysis was increased by heavy German bombing attacks which reduced the Dutch air force to twelve machines.

On the 12th, shortly after noon, the German advanced column from Gennap made contact with the airborne troops south of Rotterdam. This meant the end, which came two days later. On the 14th the German order went out that, unless Dutch resistance ceased forthwith, Rotterdam and Utrecht would be destroyed by bombing. Apparently not waiting for an answer, which when it arrived was in the affirmative, Rotterdam was bombed by some fifty machines, and though at the time it was reported that 30,000 people were killed and 20,000 injured, this was probably a piece of German terror propaganda.

The German technique in attacking aerodromes is interesting. First came bombers which from medium levels attacked the periphery in order to drive the enemy A.A. gunners to shelter. Next came dive-bombers and machine-gunning fighters to keep the defenders in their shelters. "These were followed at once by parachute troops, dropped into the aerodrome. And so, when the defenders came up for air, they found themselves looking into the muzzles of tommy-guns."[33]

Simultaneously with the attack on Holland came the attack on Belgium. It also started with the bombing of the enemy airfields, as well as the suburbs of Brussels, Antwerp and Namur and the important railway

---

[33]*The Luftwaffe*, C. G. Grey (1944), p. 176.

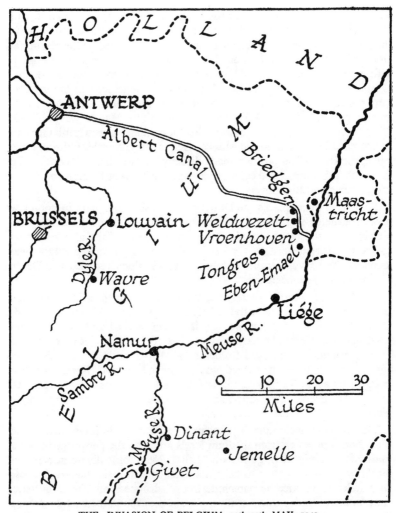

THE INVASION OF BELGIUM, 10th-13th MAY, 1940

junction of Jemelle. Parachutists were mainly used to spread alarms and seize the bridges over the Maas at Maastricht (Dutch) and those over the Albert Canal at Briedgen, Weldwezelt and Vroenhoven, as well as the fortress of Eben-Emael.

The daring of the Germans was extraordinary, as the following two accounts show:

"Troops transported by gliders were landed behind the bridges of Vroenhoven, Veldwezelt and Briedgen, whilst the German aircraft incessantly bombarded the whole of the sector. The glider troops, reinforced by parachutists, surprised the detachments guarding the bridges and captured them from the rear. The artillery of the fort of Eben-Emael, covering these bridges, had already been put out of action, by a new method of warfare. A few gliders, taking advantage of the dark, landed on the roof of the fort. Their crews succeeded, by means of explosives, in putting out of action or damaging the defensive armament of the fort."[34]

"The taking of the Maastricht bridge is a fairy tale, amazing in its daring. A plain-clothes man walked over to the sentry on the bridge on the east bank and asked him, as a friend, to allow him across the bridge for a last word with a pal on the west bank. He was allowed to pass. He walked across the bridge, and after a few minutes' conversation strolled back towards the sentry with his friend. This second man then, gangsterlike, shot the sentry and bolted back to the far bank, where he disconnected the wiring of the mines prepared for the destruction of the bridge. While this was being done, the first man possessed himself of the sentry's rifle and easily prevented any interference. The timing was a work of genius; within a few minutes, parachutists and gliders descended in a cloud on the top of the Dutch fortifications and the Belgian fortifications west of the bridge which is just in Dutch territory."[35]

On the 11th a footing on the left bank of the Albert Canal was gained. Whereupon a German armoured division rushed through the gap, and advancing beyond Tongres, by threatening to envelop the whole canal position forced its defenders, the 4th and 7th Belgian Divisions, to withdraw to the line Antwerp-Namur, where the Belgian army became merged with the French and British forces.

---

[34] *Belgium: The Official Account of What Happened*, 1939-1940, pp. 33-34.
[35] *The Diary of a Staff Officer* (1941), p. 15. The Belgian defences between south of Maastricht and south of Liége were as strong as any in the Maginot Line. Eben-Emael was so strong that the Belgians doubted it would ever be attacked. About ten gliders carrying one hundred and twenty men under Lieutenant Witzing landed upon it and completely paralysed it.

Because this curtain-raiser to the invasion of France was so largely psychological, it is not out of place here to consider a few of its effects; for they had a profound influence on the conduct of the French people and the spirit of the French troops.

Though the French people and army had watched Poland and Norway go down, and largely on account of superior German air power, it was not until their own sirens sounded that they began to learn their lessons. Strange as it may seem, air raid warning caused even more demoralization than bombings themselves. Panic thus became fertile and was accelerated by the fear of parachutists and saboteurs. "Everyone saw them being dropped, everybody was suspect, and even Allied officers and men, sometimes bearing important orders, were arrested by the French authorities."[36] This terror, coupled with the broadcasting of atrocity stories, stampeded the Belgians and sent them by hundreds of thousands over the French frontier. Roads were blocked, railway stations stormed, rumours spread, food shops and petrol depots looted, and such universal confusion produced that troop movements were delayed and in some cases rendered impossible. Under cover of this terror barrage the Germans strode out towards Brussels and through the Ardennes.

(5) *The Fall of France*

On 10th May the armies in France were distributed as follows: In the north from the Channel to the Maginot Line the First Army Group of forty divisions under General Billotte, along the Maginot Line the Second Army Group of twenty-six divisions under General Prételat, and facing the Swiss Frontier and the Maritime Alps the Third Army Group of thirty-six divisions under General Besson. In all one hundred and two divisions, of which thirty-two were scattered in reserve along the entire front. The first of these groups from left to right comprised the French Seventh Army, General Giraud; the British Expeditionary Force, General Lord Gort; the French First Army, General Blanchard; the French Ninth Army, General Corap; and the French Second Army, General Huntziger.

That day at 4.30 a.m. the British headquarters at Arras as well as Allied back areas and aerodromes were heavily bombed, and an hour later, General Georges, Commander of the French Armies of the North-East, ordered an advance to the River Dyle.[37] Thereupon, pivoting on Mézières-

---

[36]*Paratroops*, Captain F. O. Miksche (1943), pp. 38-39. This situation was in no way eased by M. Reynaud, the French Prime Minister, announcing that German parachutists were to be shot at sight.

Sedan, the above four armies wheeled to the right, and, unopposed by the *Luftwaffe*,[38] by the 12th the Allied armies took up the following positions: Belgian Army between Antwerp and Louvain; B.E.F. from Louvain to Wavre; First Army from Wavre to Namur, and Ninth from Namur to Sedan; while the French Seventh Army moved on Breda to assist the Dutch. That day Lord Gort requested the War Office to expedite the despatch of the 1st Armoured Division. Also, in his Second Despatch he states that by the 12th his fighter aircraft had been reduced to fifty machines, and that, in consequence, tactical reconnaissance had become virtually impossible.

Nothing could have suited the German plan better than the forward wheel of the Allied left wing. The hitherto closed door was now swung open, and henceforth, its ability to withstand the enemy's onrush mainly depended on the strength of its hinges. These were represented by the French Ninth Army, which consisted of two active and seven reserve or fortress divisions, whose men were elderly, under-trained and ill-armed. The active divisions were on the left, holding fifteen miles of the Meuse south of Namur; the rest of the army's front, forty miles in length, was held by three reserve and one fortress divisions, the right one of all having not a single anti-tank gun. On its right the two left divisions of the French Second Army were also composed of elderly reservists. These second-rate troops were considered adequate, because it was not believed that the Germans would attempt to advance in force through the Ardennes.[39]

Instead, it was the very locality von Rundstedt's Group was about to move through. This group consisted of the Fourth Army under General von Kluge, moving south of Aachen; the Twelfth under General von List to the south of it; and further south again General von Kleist's Group, which was advancing on the line Monthermé-Sedan. South of von Kleist

[37]General Gamelin, the Allied Commander-in-Chief, is reported to have said: "In this war the first party which comes out of its shell will be in great danger." Nevertheless, he sanctioned the forward move. (*Arms and Policy*, 1939-1944, Hoffman Nickerson, 1945, p. 101.)

[38]The anonymous author of *The Diary of a Staff Officer* writes on 13th May: "A strange, and I feel, very suspicious feature, has been the extraordinary lack of any German bombing of the B.E.F. and the French armies in their advance through Belgium . . . It looks almost as if the Germans want us where we are going" (p. 9). They certainly did.

[39]Much has been made of this. Nevertheless, the French Command were right in not making the front equally strong everywhere, and there is no gainsaying it that the Ardennes are better defensive than offensive country. Their error lay in the distribution of their reserves and in not having a sufficiency of mechanical transport to move their reserves rapidly wherever they might be needed. The misjudgment was one of speed and space rather than inadequacy of covering forces.

came the Sixteenth Army under General Busch, which was to protect von Kleist's left flank and move on the line Sedan-the Moselle River. General von Kleist's Group, which was to strike the decisive blow, consisted of two corps, the northern commanded by General Reinhardt and the southern by General Guderian. The first contained two Panzer divisions and the second three. There was also an independent Panzer division under General Rommel, which was to move direct on Houx.

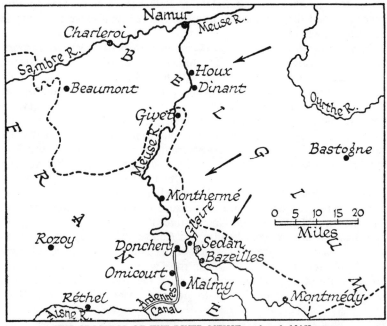

THE CROSSING OF THE RIVER MEUSE, 13th-14th MAY, 1940

On the 10th, Corap and Huntziger pushed forward their cavalry, which on the next day were violently dive-bombed by the aerial advanced guard of von Kleist's Group. Forthwith Corap asked to be reinforced, and the French Supreme Command, rightly gauging that the main blow was coming south and not north of Namur, despatched to him on the following day one armoured and three infantry divisions, to be followed on the 13th by another armoured and five infantry divisions. But the first of these reinforcements could not arrive until the 17th and the second before the 21st.

Though by the 12th von Kleist's armoured advance had outrun most of his artillery, he, nevertheless, decided to launch his 1st Panzer Division against Bouillon, which lies a few miles north of Sedan. This attack was successful, and by nightfall the whole of the east bank of the Meuse between Namur and Sedan was in German hands. From noon next day until 3 p.m. wave after wave of Stuka aircraft (dive-bombers) went to work to reduce the French pill-box defences on the west of the Meuse between the small towns of Donchery and Baszeilles which flank Sedan. By 5.30 p.m. sufficient progress was made to start bridging the Meuse at Glaire, also a 16-ton motor-tug ferry was got going by 6.30 p.m., and a second ferry was established an hour later. By 1 a.m. the 14th the bridge was finished, when column after column moved across the Meuse. Though the French were still resisting, Donchery was taken by nightfall and Sedan was found to be abandoned. The break-through was complete. About the same time General von Reinhardt succeeded in crossing the Meuse at Monthermé, and General Rommel did likewise at Houx.

Early on the 15th von Kleist turned westwards from Sedan, which necessitated crossing the Ardennes Canal. Fortunately for him, he found the bridges at Omicourt and Malmy intact. These were the only bridges which had not been blown by the French, and the story that certain bridges over the Meuse were left standing was pure fiction.[40] Meanwhile, at about midnight the 14th, to their consternation, the Allied Supreme Command learned that Sedan was in German hands and that "a salient fifteen kilometres long and some ten kilometres deep had been created."[41]

Thus, as in Poland, *Blitzkrieg*[42] swept into France. Six armoured divisions, followed by motorized divisions and supported by a mass of dive-bombers had struck at the weakest section of the French front, and had crashed through. There was no armoured force there to meet them, for the considerable number of tanks the French had was split up among the infantry to lead them into battle on 1917-1918 lines.

The next day at 8 p.m. the Germans were reported at Rozoy, twenty-seven miles west of Donchery. Further, that parachute troops and a powerful armoured column were nearing Réthel. Meanwhile the French railways were heavily bombed. That evening orders were sent to the French and British armies in Belgium to fall back on the Escaut Line. The withdrawal was begun on the night of the 16th-17th, to be completed on that of the 18th-19th.

The attack had been so sudden and so overwhelming that the French Command did not understand what was happening. They did not realize

[40]For obvious political reasons, Reynaud, in a speech on 21st May, made much heavy weather over unblown bridges, and thus pushed the blame for the disaster on to Corap's shoulders.

[41]*The Diary of a Staff Officer*, p. 10.

[42]For a detailed and clearly illustrated account of the German tank tactics of penetration see *Warfare To-day*, Odhams Press (1944), chapter IV.

that, having penetrated their enemy's front, the Germans would thrust straight ahead with their armoured and motorized troops. It would seem that they expected a pause, a build-up and then a further attack. Even Mr. Churchill referred in a B.B.C. broadcast to the "Battle of the Bulge." There was no salient, and there was no bulge. Instead, there was an ever-widening gap through which armoured forces were pouring in two directions: westwards on Amiens to sever the communications of the Allies in Belgium with their mass in France, and southwards on Rheims to cut and command the communications of the French armies in the Maginot Line.

On the 17th the breach was sixty miles wide and Brussels was occupied by the Germans. The next day Reynaud changed his Cabinet. Assuming the post of Minister of National Defence, he appointed Marshal Pétain Vice-President of the Council, and replaced General Gamelin by General Weygand. Pétain was eighty-four years old and Weygand seventy-three. On the 19th the anonymous Diarist hastily jotted down: "1500 hours. News that the *Panzers* are in Amiens. This is like some ridiculous nightmare. The B.E.F. is cut off. Our communications have gone . . . The Germans have taken every risk—criminally foolish risks—and they have got away with it . . . they have done everything that should not be done by orthodox book-trained stereotyped soldiers and they have made no mistake. The French General Staff have been paralysed by this unorthodox war of movement. The fluid conditions prevailing are not dealt with in the text books and the 1914 brains of the French generals responsible for formulating the plans of the allied armies are incapable of functioning in this new and astonishing lay-out."[43]

The arrival of the Germans in Amiens placed the Allied left wing in a critical position. As General Gort points out: "The picture was now no longer that of a line bent or temporarily broken, but of a besieged fortress. To raise such a siege, a relieving force must be sent from the south, and to meet this force a sortie on the part of the defenders was indicated."[44] This led to an action south of Arras on the 22nd, in which the 1st Army Tank Brigade[45] did well, its heavily armoured "I" tanks[46] coming as a complete surprise to the Germans.

Meanwhile, on the Somme, the Allied situation had worsened. On the 20th Abbeville had been occupied by the Germans, whereupon, without

---

[43] *The Diary of a Staff Officer*, pp. 26-7.
[44] General Gort's "Second Despatch." *Supplement to the London Gazette*, 10th October, 1941, p. 5916.
[45] This formation was distinct from the 1st Armoured Division, the three brigades of which landed in France on 16th, 22nd and 25th May.
[46] Infantry tanks were designed to co-operate closely with infantry.

pausing, the bulk of their armour swung north, overran Etaples and, on the 23rd, attacked Boulogne and Calais. This rapid advance from the south, coupled with steady pressure from the east, forced the whole of the Allied left wing into an equilateral triangle with its base between Gravelins and Terneuzen and its apex a little north of Cambrai. The northern half of its

THE INVASION OF FRANCE, 14th MAY-25th JUNE, 1940

eastern side was held by the Belgian army, which, on the 24th, was violently bombed. On the 25th it began to crumble and, on the next day, it then being apparent that there was no hope of the French armies south of the Somme attacking northwards, Lord Gort was ordered to save what he could of his army by withdrawing it to the coast. As this movement was under way, on the 28th the Belgian army under King Leopold capitulated, and what then remained of the Allied left wing was crushed into a rectangle, the base of which stretched from a few miles west of Nieuport—twenty-three miles in all.

From it and under cover of a French rearguard and Fighter Command R.A.F., operating from England, between the 26th May and 3rd June, 366,162 men were evacuated in 765 ships, mostly small craft.

How was this accomplished? It has been called a "miracle", but in war miracles are no more than exceptional operations.

The rapid German advance on the 20th May caused Rundstedt to grow nervous about his long exposed southern flank, which he expected his cornered enemy would attempt to break through. Further, he and the German Supreme Command were beginning to consider the southward move across the Somme, once the allied left wing had been rounded up. Therefore, on the 23rd, Rundstedt halted all his panzer divisions, and on the following day Hitler visited Rundstedt's headquarters and agreed that all the mobile forces could be halted on the line Lens-Béthune-Aire-St. Omer-Gravelines, while Army Group B, under Bock, pressed against the enemy: Rundstedt's troops were to provide the anvil for Bock's hammer. Further, Hitler insisted that it was necessary to conserve the armoured forces for future operations. In the circumstances, this was a wise decision as all the German armoured divisions needed overhaul—50 per cent of Kleist's tanks and 30 per cent of Hoth's were out of action—and at the time neither the German leaders nor the British Admiralty thought that a large-scale evacuation could be effected from the Channel beaches. It was this pause which enabled Lord Gort to withdraw to the coast, and when Rundstedt restarted his advance on the 27th, the B.E.F. and part of the French First Army had established themselves in the Dunkirk bridgehead, which, fortunately for them, was covered by a network of dikes and canals, which turned it into an anti-tank fortress.

Although General Halder says that Hitler prevented the complete destruction of the British Army by withdrawing the German tanks, and Rundstedt called it an "incredible blunder", Guderian, the most able of the German tank generals, was of the opposite opinion, and after reconnoitring the forward position he recommended that tanks should not be employed.

The truth about the miracle is, that the whole area was one vast tank obstacle, and that Hitler, who had a better understanding of the capabilities of tanks than most of his generals, considered that their use around Dunkirk *would be* an "incredible blunder". As long ago as the 9th October, 1939, he had laid it down that "The tank arm must be used for operations for which it is best suited. Under no circumstances must the tanks be permitted to become entangled in the endless confusion of the rows of houses in the Belgian towns". Far truer is this of the Belgian bogs.

Once the British had been driven out of France, the next German problem was to drive the French out of the war in order to isolate Great
Britain. To accomplish this, on 5th June an attack was opened against the
Weygand Line, which ran from the mouth of the Somme to the Aisne and
thence to the Maginot Line at Montmédy. Starting between Amiens and
Peronne, by the 9th the attack was extended to the Argonne, and on that
day a penetration was effected in the vicinity of Réthel. On the 10th
Châlons-sur-Marne was in German hands, and on the 17th the Swiss
frontier was reached and the entire Maginot Line boxed up.

Meanwhile, Rouen was occupied on the 10th, and on the following day
the Seine below Paris was crossed; whereupon the French Government
proclaimed the capital an open city and then retired to Tours and next to
Bordeaux, followed by many thousands of refugees. On the 14th Germans
entered Paris, and two days later M. Reynaud resigned and President
Lebrun called upon Marshal Pétain to form a government. The next
day—the 17th—Pétain asked for an armistice. It was agreed upon and
signed on the 25th. Thereupon he established his government at Vichy.

Could he have done otherwise? The only reasonable answer is "No!"—
he was no corpse-raiser, and morally France was dead long before the
campaign opened. At the time many observers, men who stood outside
the vortex of the psychological tornado which was sweeping over France,
thought otherwise. They suggested that Paris should have been held, as a
little later Mr. Churchill proclaimed he would hold London; that a *levée en
masse* should have been made, and that, failing a continuation of the war in
France, the French Government should have transferred it to North Africa.

The first was a senseless proposal, for even if psychological conditions
be set aside, what was the use of holding Paris when the northern vital area
of operations was already lost, for without it no new French armies could
be equipped. In fact, Paris was in the same position London would be in
were the whole of the Midlands in enemy hands, and not in the one which
would have faced Mr. Churchill had the Germans landed in Sussex and
Kent.

The second suggestion was fatuous, because it was the *levée en masse* of
eight to ten million Belgian and French refugees which rendered any form
of military *levée* impossible. Even had there been no refugees, what value
would hundreds of thousands of men without arms and without means of
manufacturing them have been?

The third suggestion is, however, apposite. Pétain could have retired to
Algeria and raised his standard there. For England it was extremely fortunate that he had neither the will nor the energy to do so; because had he
done so, seeing that Italy's entrance into the war on 10th June had given
the Axis the command of the Central Mediterranean, there can be no doubt

whatsoever that Hitler would have pursued him to his doom, and that before the year was out the whole of North Africa from Ceuta to Cairo would in all probability have been his. That, in spite of Pétain's surrender, Hitler did not pursue this course was, as later on we shall see, the most fatal strategical blunder he committed during the war.

This astonishing campaign, the most instructive of the entire war, shows:

(1) *War and Policy.* That when the aim of policy is constructive instead of destructive, war as the instrument of policy can be waged at high profit.

(2) *Strategy of Annihilation.* That when conditions are favourable, the advantages of the strategy of annihilation over the strategy of exhaustion are overwhelming.

(3) *Tactics of Velocity.* That the tactics demanded by the strategy of annihilation are those of velocity, in which the momentum of the initial attack is sustained until the goal is won.

(4) *Integration of Means.* That these tactics demand the integration of all arms, weapons and means, so that the maximum striking power can be concentrated at the point of impact.

(5) *Demoralization of Command.* That the ultimate aim of these tactics is psychological more so than physical—namely, the demoralization of the enemy's will in order to disorganize his body.

(6) *Preparation of Means.* That unless all the machinery of war is prepared for in advance, it is impossible to improvize it during war-time when conditions favour the strategy of annihilation.

(7) *Will to Win.* That no political, strategical, tactical, administrative or other preparations are of value, unless the people and fighting forces are possessed of a will to fight and a determination to endure.

Each of these seven items we will now discuss.

War and Policy. Setting moral considerations aside, the strength of Hitler's war policy lay in its constructiveness, whereas the weakness of his adversaries' lay in its destructiveness. His aim was economic, the establishment of a German *Lebensraum*; their's was ideological, the destruction of a political creed. In this campaign, the most successful the Germans fought, we find little bombing of cities, little destruction of enemy economic resources, and on the whole a minimum loss of life, German and enemy. Thus, Mr. Kernan informs us: "Unlike the First World War which had turned whole regions of the country into rubble, this time there had been relatively little destruction of French resources,"[47] and that the Germans

[47]*Report on France*, p. 15. Mr. Kernan was an American business man then in France.

purposely avoided damaging national monuments.[48] Mr. Waterfield also points out that the Germans "seldom bombed big industrial plant, which they could easily have done."[49] The reason was not altruistic, but purely selfish, it was, as Mr. Kernan says, to knead "all occupied France into one great industrial, commercial and agricultural plantation"[50] forming part of the German New Economic Order. "They have done," he adds, "what economists before the war said was impossible: to make military conquest immediately profitable."[51] And they did this at a ridiculously low loss in life and limb; for France was conquered at a cost of 27,074 Germans killed, 111,034 wounded and 18,384 missing—that is, considerably less than one-third of the British casualties in 1916 during the Battle of the Somme.[52]

Strategy of Annihilation. This form of strategy was greatly facilitated by the theory of solid fronts held by the French—a relic of the previous war—and also because the French would not or could not see that the tank and the aeroplane had rendered them obsolete. This solidity, which led to a vast number of French eggs becoming addled in one basket—the Maginot Line—not only deprived the French of all initiative but handed all initiative over to their enemy. Thus Hitler was enabled to attack where he liked, when he liked and with what forces he liked. What the French failed to realize was, that a defensive strategy or tactics, whether annihilative or exhaustive, must be dynamic, and because they did not realize it, they planned for a war of immobility and not of dynamic stability. The upshot was that, once their front was penetrated, their morale was also penetrated. *"Par dessus tout, on ne voulait rien risquier: cette fois encore, comme tant d'autres fois dans l'histoire, le refus d'assumer un risque raisonnable aboutit à l'extrême péril. Plus précisément, sous pretéxte de ne rien risquer, on sacrifia toutes les chances parce qu'on n'en courut aucune."[53]* This strategy

---

[48] *Ibid.*, p. 160.

[49] *What Happened to France*, p. 6. Mr. Waterfield was Reuter's War Correspondent with the French Armies.

[50] *Report on France*, p. 15.

[51] *Ibid.*, p. 67. For remarks on German finance see pp. 64, 65, 87 and 88. "Actually the strength of Hitler's propaganda in Europe lies in the fact that most Europeans in the pre-war years were convinced that European economy had come to an impasse. They knew that Europe was economically doomed unless certain fundamental changes were made" (p. 246).

[52] Though these are Hitler's figures, I see no reason to doubt their accuracy, for they are what may be expected in armoured warfare. Further, the German reports were unusually truthful. This is noted both by Mr. Kernan, "German military news was very accurate, as compared with the British and French" (p. 37); and Mr. Waterfield, "The German High Command report, which is generally accurate . . ." (p. 19). It is unlikely that, omitting prisoners, the French casualties were more than twice the German, for over half their total forces never fired a shot.

[53] *La Guerre des Cinq Continents*, The Military Critic of *La France Libre* (1943), p. 39.

à la bourgeoisie was an ideal playfield for the strategy of annihilation, and more particularly so because the French capital and main vital area of operations were within easy striking distance of Germany.

Tactics of Velocity. "The speed," writes Lord Gort, "with which the enemy exploited his penetration of the French front, his willingness to accept risks to further his aim, and his exploitation of every success to the uttermost limits emphasized, even more fully than in the campaigns of the past, the advantage which accrues to the commander who knows how best to use time to make time his servant and not his master."[54] In corroboration Mr. Shirer notes: "The Germans thrust not only with tanks and a few motorized infantry, but with *everything*." And of the German army as a whole he writes: "It is a gigantic impersonal war machine, run as coolly and efficiently, say, as our automobile industry in Detroit."[55] Therefore it was *organized* velocity which was the secret.

Not only were the various arms organized to accelerate speed, but the various services were also organized to maintain and sustain it. Thus the pioneer and engineer units were organized to repair tanks and vehicles rapidly; to clear demolitions rapidly; to maintain communications rapidly; to bridge canals and rivers rapidly; and to supply petrol and ammunition rapidly.[56]

Further, a point which was never fully appreciated by the British and later on by the Americans also, was that velocity demands the *preservation* of communications. Therefore the Germans cleared the roads leading into and through France by machine-gun fire and not by bombing; because the denial of their use to the enemy was secondary to preserving their use for themselves. "While German Stukas," writes Shirer, "put the Belgian railroad out of action, they were careful not to blow up the roads or their bridges."[57] In short, the tactics of velocity are based on time and not on high explosives.

Integration of Means. The chief instruments of velocity were the aeroplane and the tank. The Germans integrated their powers, the French and British did not; the one because the French air force had, as C. A. Grey says, "been practically disarmed" by five years of political intrigue;[58] the other because the R.A.F. was obsessed by the theory of "strategic

[54]Lord Gort's "Despatches." *Supplement to the London Gazette,* 10th October, 1941, p. 5931.
[55]*Berlin Diary,* p. 298.
[56]"Every driver knows where he can tank up when he runs short." (*Berlin Diary,* p. 298.)
[57]*Ibid.,* p. 278.
[58]*The Luftwaffe,* p. 178.

bombing." The result was that, for want of opposition, the power of the numerically superior *Luftwaffe* was vastly enhanced.

Writing on 13th May, the anonymous Diarist asserts that ". . . with five hundred more aircraft at our disposal the German advance would have been smashed," because of the "vulnerable targets offered to our aircraft in the form of close columns on the main routes of the enemy's advance."[59] Again on the 16th he says, ". . . five hundred fighters would have saved Sedan," because the German dive-bombers could have been mastered by so considerable a force.[60] On the 14th he informs us that Generals Gamelin, Georges and Gort asked the British Cabinet "to authorize the employment of the Metropolitan Bomber Force in an attempt to stop the rot within the next two hours."[61] This request was repeated on the 15th and again on the 16th, but with no result other than a bombing raid on Essen! On the critical 20th of May, instead of attempting to hold up the German advance, the R.A.F. bombed Hamm; on the 21st[62] they bombed the Ruhr, and on the 25th Aachen, Geldern, Roermond and Weert—all from one hundred and fifty to two hundred miles behind the German front!

What was the influence of this bombing on operations? Shirer, who was with the Germans, writes on the 19th: ". . . so far as I can see, the night bombings of the British have done very little damage."[63] Later that same day: ". . . these night attacks of the British have failed not only to put the Ruhr out of commission, but even to damage the German flying fields."[64] And again on 16th June: "In the Ruhr there was little evidence of the British night bombings."[65]

What the Germans realized, though the French and British did not, was that velocity of attack demands concentration of striking power at the point of impact and not at the points of initial departure, which in this campaign were from one hundred to two hundred miles behind the front. Further, that, in the time available, no damage which could have been done to the Ruhr—the main German vital area of operations—would have reduced

---

[59] *The Diary of a Staff Officer*, p. 9. He was well qualified to make this and other statements as he was on the Staff of the Commander of the British Air Force in France—Air-Marshal Sir A. S. Barrett.

[60] *Ibid.*, p. 18.

[61] *Ibid.*, p. 12.

[62] "From the 21st May onwards all arrangements for air co-operation with the B.E.F. were made by the War Office in conjunction with the Air Ministry at home." (Lord Gort's "Despatches." *Supplement to the London Gazette*, 10th October, 1941, p. 5914.)

[63] *Berlin Diary*, p. 273.

[64] *Ibid.*, p. 275.

[65] *Ibid.*, p. 318.

the speed of the German advance. Seeing in the aeroplane not only a flying siege gun, as did the R.A.F., but also a flying field-gun, which, on account of its velocity, flexibility and ability to intervene rapidly, could co-operate more closely and immediately than could normal field artillery with armoured forces, the Germans, by linking their dive-bombers up with their tanks, doubled the velocity of the latter. This also was noted by the anonymous Diarist, for he says: "It is the co-operation between the dive-bombers and the armoured divisions that is winning the war for Germany."[66]

Lord Gort also noted it; for towards the end of his *Despatches* he writes: "A commander must have at his call sufficient fighters to intercept and attack the enemy . . . The commander must, likewise, dispose of a sufficient bomber force to enable him to engage opportunity targets of vital tactical importance. Such targets were the enemy mechanized columns at Maastricht, Sedan and Boulogne . . . Successful operations on land depend more than ever before on the closest co-operation between aircraft and troops on the ground."[67]

Demoralization of Command. One example of the influence of velocity of attack on command and through command on the fighting arms is sufficient to show its superiority over attacks of a purely physical type. Writing of the operations on the Aisne, during which General Giraud was captured on the 18th, General Eon says:

"A general officer summoned by telephone to his superior was taken (prisoner) on the way.

"And while all this was going on in the rear, what was happening to the front-line troops?

"Enemy pressure was immediately intensified along the whole of the front. In each German frontal division, operations were developed aiming at strategic points, centres of communication, bridges . . .

"The primary object was not to capture our troops, but to smash our front. Skilfully planned to secure piecemeal control of the terrain, supported by tanks and by air units attached to the armies, these operations, in conjunction with those undertaken in rear, gradually paralysed all resistance.

"It was in this way that, deprived of rations, and left without leaders, the soldiers of France fell, unit by unit, into the hands of the enemy."[68]

Preparation of Means and *Will to Win.* As regards Preparation of Means—the complement of the Will to Win—it is clear that in an age in

---

[66] *The Diary of a Staff Officer*, p. 24.
[67] Lord Gort's "Despatches." *Supplement to the London Gazette*, 10th October, 1941, pp. 5932-5933.
[68] *The Battle of Flanders*, 1943, p. 21.

which speed is the dominant factor, unless a nation is as ready for war as a fire brigade is ready to extinguish a conflagration, in no circumstances can a Continental nation make good its peace-time deficiencies.

It was not that the French were altogether unprepared, they were not. It was that their preparations did not coincide with the type of war the Age of Velocity demanded. Further, though the defensive spirit which possessed them undoubtedly undermined their will to fight, the general corruption into which they fell between 1936-1939 was the most powerful factor in their defeat. It was not the men of Vichy who betrayed France, it was the men of the Popular Front.

On the other hand, Germany, though bankrupt morally, economically, politically and financially in 1932, in the seven following years, under the will of one man, became not only the most formidable military nation but also one of the most fanatical that history bears record of. Nevertheless, in 1940 she was not fully prepared to carry velocity to its final goal. This will become apparent in the next Section.

(6) *The Battle of Britain*

Before examining the next campaign—strategically the most fateful of the whole war—for a moment let us turn back to Hitler's policy, for a flaw in it now suddenly widened into a yawning chasm.

In 1923, when a prisoner in the fortress of Landsberg, and when meditating upon the causes of Germany's recent defeat, he wrote: "... glancing casually over the map of the British Empire, one is inclined easily to overlook the existence of a whole Anglo-Saxon world." Then a few paragraphs later, considering the question of alliances, he observed:

"If new territory were to be acquired in Europe it must have been mainly at Russia's cost, and once again the new German Empire should have set out on its march along the same road as was formerly trodden by the Teutonic Knights . . . For such a policy, however, there was only one possible ally in Europe. That was England . . . No sacrifice should have been considered too great if it was a necessary means of gaining England's friendship. Colonial and naval ambitions should have been abandoned and attempts should not have been made to compete against British industries."[69]

When ten years later he gained power, there can be no doubt that his one desire was to win England's friendship. Nor can there be any doubt that his failure to do so was in the main due to his economic system violently clashing with the British. Instead of making England an ally, it made her

[69] *Mein Kampf*, pp. 127-128.

his enemy, an enemy whose strength he in no way underestimated in 1923, for then he wrote:

"The British nation will therefore be considered as the most valuable ally in the world as long as it can be counted upon to show that brutality and tenacity in its government, as well as in the spirit of the broad masses, which enables it to carry through to victory any struggle that it once enters upon, no matter how long such a struggle may last or however great the sacrifice that may be necessary or whatever the means that have to be employed; and all this even though the actual military equipment at hand may be utterly inadequate when compared with that of other nations."[70]

Because, in his opinion, a friendly England would prove "the most valuable ally in the world," he should have realized that a hostile England might well prove the most dangerous enemy.[71] Therefore his war policy should have centred on the defeat of England. What had Clausewitz said?

"We may . . . establish it as a principle, that if we can conquer all our enemies by conquering one of them, the defeat of that one must be the aim of the War, because in that one we hit the common centre of gravity of the whole War."[72]

Clearly, in Hitler's case, the "one enemy" was England, as she had been the one enemy of Philip II, Louis XIV, Napoleon and William II. Yet, now in June, 1940, he found himself unable to "hit the common centre of gravity of the whole War," because the momentum of his strategy of annihilation had been halted by the English Channel, twenty odd miles of water, and how to cross them had not figured in his strategical calculations. While gazing at the map of the British Empire he had overlooked the Strait of Dover.

If its crossing was an insuperable problem, he should not have gone to war. If it were not, then he should have prepared to solve it before launching the war. He was not. Therefore, because his strategy of annihilation was now stonewalled, the sole course open to him was to re-estimate its values.

The conditions which faced him should have suggested this course. England was now left his sole enemy. She had lost not only her footing on the Continent, but also the requisite fighting manpower—that of France— to wage a Continental war. Further, she had lost the assistance of the

[70]*Ibid.*, p. 279.

[71]Though in an address given to his immediate subordinates on 23rd May, 1939, he stated that "England is . . . our enemy, and the conflict with England will be a life-and-death struggle," and "England is the driving force against Germany" (see *The Nuremberg Trial*, R. W. Cooper, p. 59), nothing so far published points to his having considered the full implications of these statements. It was not until after the fall of France that he set about preparing to deal with England.

[72]*On War*, vol. III, p. 108.

French fleet, and with Italy now in the war, she had lost the command of the Mediterranean and with it the direct sea route to Egypt. Further still, because the German air and U-boat bases now stretched from the North Cape to the Bidassoa, she must expect intensified sea and air blockade.

Single-handed, Britain could not possibly win the war, however long it might last. Henceforth, and until she could recruit another ally, her problem was a purely defensive one: to secure her homelands and to secure Egypt, and the importance of the latter did not lie in the Suez Canal, but in the fact that it was her sole remaining overseas base within striking distance of Europe. Should that base be lost, the whole of North Africa would pass into German and Italian hands. Spain could then be forced into the war; Turkey could then be pinched out; the road to Russia through Armenia and Georgia could then be opened; and, finally, Britain placed in so desperate a situation that American ardour in her support might cool to zero. Had these things happened, and they were not impossible, England must have accepted a negotiated peace, for without American economic support, and America was as vital an area of operations to her as her own Midlands, she could not with all the will in the world have continued the struggle.

Why was this course not adopted? The most probable answer is, that Hitler and his Staff were land-minded and not sea-minded.[73] They could not appreciate that the only way to force England out of the war was to strike at her indirectly and not directly—that is, by undermining her insular security in a war of attrition, and not challenge her in an assault, for which they were in no way prepared. But this meant substituting the strategy of exhaustion for the strategy of annihilation—that is, a strategy which was foreign to their whole military upbringing.

[73]Against this it must be pointed out that Göring pressed for the attack on England to be continued, and during the winter of 1940-1941 he urged Hitler to deprive Britain of access to the Mediterranean. He suggested the use of three army groups. The first to strike through Spain and capture Gibraltar; the second to invade Morocco and occupy Tunis; and the third to drive through the Balkans, seize the Dardanelles and Ankara and then advance on Suez. Hitler considered this plan, but felt that since Britain had not capitulated "she must have come to some secret agreement with Russia," and that, therefore, it was necessary to deal with Russia first. Finally, in March, 1941, convinced that the Russians were encouraging Yugoslav resistance to the Axis and that "the presence of British troops in Greece tended to confirm his suspicions of an Anglo-Russian secret agreement," he finally decided to set aside Göring's plan and deal with Russia first. After the war, on 17th September, 1946, Keitel said to Milton Shulman: "Instead of attacking Russia, we should have strangled the British Empire by closing the Mediterranean. The first step in the operation would have been the conquest of Gibraltar. That was another great opportunity we missed." (See *Defeat in the West*, pp. 55-58, also see *Ciano's Diary*, 1939-1945, English edition, 1947, p. 286.)

Hitler, therefore, did two things: On 16th July he wrote to Field-Marshal Keitel and General Jodl—the Chief of the General Staff and the Chief of his own Military Staff: "Since England, in spite of her militarily hopeless situation, shows no signs of willingness to come to terms, I have decided to prepare a landing operation against England and, if necessary, to carry it out. The aim is . . . to eliminate the English homeland as a base for the carrying on of the war against Germany. The preparations for the entire operation must be completed by mid-August."[74]

Next, three days later, he addressed the Reichstag, and after assuring its members that Germany could support the strain of a long war, he once again opened the door of peace by saying: "In this hour I feel it to be my duty before my own conscience to appeal once more to reason and common sense to Great Britain . . . I see no reason why this war must go on."[75]

From the above order and speech, three things become clear:

(1) Hitler wanted a negotiated peace with England.

(2) If England refused, he would push his direct assault.

(3) Were he forced to do so, he was by no means certain of success; therefore the possibility of a long war had to be faced.

Because Mr. Churchill and his Government paid no attention to his appeal, the die was cast, and come what might the strategy of annihilation entered its final and fateful last phase in Western Europe.

The operation visualized, rather than planned, was to land two armies of twenty-five divisions between Dover and Portsmouth, and then advance north cutting London off from the west.[76] If the time given—thirty days— in which to develop this idea into an operative plan did not appear absurd to Hitler, it certainly must have to Keitel and Jodl,[77] because in the cir-

---

According to Field-Marshal von Rundstedt, it would seem that Hitler expected the war in Russia to last no more than ten weeks (*Ibid.*, p. 65), and Count Ciano writes in his *Diary* (pp. 360 and 559): "The Germans believe that it will all be over in eight weeks." Therefore it would appear that Hitler considered that there would be ample time to deal with England once Russia had been subdued.

[74] *The Times*, 5th December, 1945, and 19th November, 1946. According to Mr. Cooper, Admiral Raeder stated at the Nuremberg trial that while "the German navy was straining every nerve in the summer of 1940 for the invasion of England, he discovered in August that Hitler was transferring troops to the Russian frontier. The Führer had deliberately deceived him by explaining these movements as a 'magnificent camouflage' to allay British suspicion. It was Raeder's navy which was providing the 'greatest deception in the history of war' for the benefit of the Russians" (*The Nuremberg Trial*, p. 250).

[75] *The Times*, 20th July, 1940.

[76] For further see *Defeat in the West*, pp. 44 and 46.

[77] Field-Marshal von Rundstedt said: "The proposed invasion of England was nonsense, because adequate ships were not available . . . I have a feeling that the Führer never really wanted to invade England." (*Ibid.*, pp. 49-50.)

cumstances of total unpreparedness it was a sheer impossibility.[78] First, there were no specially designed assault craft, therefore barges and river boats had to be collected; secondly, these craft to effect a crossing demanded an absolutely calm sea; thirdly, in order to disembark tanks, guns and vehicles from them, elaborate conversions had to be made; fourthly, the troops had no training and the staffs no experience in amphibious assaults; fifthly, the German Navy was fully aware that it was no match for the British; and lastly, the German Naval High Command appears to have held that even should the *Luftwaffe* succeed in defeating the Royal Air Force, it would be incapable of preventing the Royal Navy attacking the seaborne landing forces. In the following year, this was corroborated by the abortive German seaborne invasion of Crete.

Thus from the start the plan wobbled badly, and the sole man, it would seem, who had faith in it was Göring, who was confident that the *Luftwaffe*, of which some 2,750 machines were available, could both destroy the R.A.F. and paralyse the British fleet. This wobbling was progressive. Thus, on 16th August, the thirtieth day of preparations, the operation was put forward to 15th September. Next, on 3rd September, Z-Day was fixed for 21st September. Then, on 17th September, a further postponement was made, and on the 19th orders were issued to disperse concentrations of craft in order to avoid losses from air attack. Lastly, on 12th October, the operation was called off until the spring.

Next to the administrative and technical difficulties, which in the time were insolvable, these oscillations were due to the complete failure on the part of the *Luftwaffe* to fulfil the first half of the air programme—namely, the destruction of their opponent's Fighter Command. And it is interesting to note that the attempt made closely followed the phases laid down by Douhet.

(1) *8th August to 18th August:* Attacks on convoys and coastal objectives to draw British fighters into combat and destroy them.

(2) *19th August to 5th September:* Concentrated attacks on inland fighter aerodromes to destroy aircraft on the ground and draw fighters into action.

---

[78]It is astonishing, therefore, to find that so great a military authority as Mr. Churchill should have considered invasion imminent as early as the middle of July. On the 14th of that month in a broadcast he said: "Perhaps it will come to-night. Perhaps it will come next week. Perhaps it will never come." And again on 17th September, two days after the German maximum air attack had been smashed at an alleged loss of 185 aircraft: "The shipping available and now assembled is sufficient to carry in one voyage nearly half a million men." (*Secret Session Speeches*, 1946, p. 23.) Later on, with the command of the sea and the air in their favour, it took the British and Americans eighteen months of intense preparations before they felt ready to invade semi-friendly Algeria and Morocco.

(3) *6th September onwards:* Attacks on cities, particularly London, in order to destroy food stocks and annihilate the civil will.

These attacks were met by Air Chief Marshal Sir Hugh Dowding, C.-in-C. Fighter Command, who had at his disposal fifty-nine squadrons of fighters, and who, in spite of the odds against him—seldom less than two to one—inflicted so crushing a defeat on his enemy, that never again during the war was an all-out air battle attempted.

Besides the skilful handling of his numerically inferior forces, the following advantages were his. Fighter Command had been designed and trained for exactly this type of defensive fighting, and his enemy was foolish enough not to realize it. Because the main battle fought was between fighter craft, and because the British Spitfire was a faster climber than the German Messerschmitt, normally the former was at a marked advantage. Most important of all, Dowding had at his disposal the greatest air surprise of the war—namely, Sir Robert Watson-Watt's invention of radio-location (radar). By means of it he could tell when his adversary was on his way, his strength and the precise direction of his approach. Therefore, in spite of his numerical inferiority, he could generally concentrate a superiority of force at the decisive point.

By 12th October, on account of the stupendous losses suffered,[19] it had clearly become apparent to Hitler that the plan which was to establish peace in the west of Europe, so that he could launch his attack on Russia without fear of being attacked in rear, had failed. That though he had now conquered Poland, Norway, Denmark, Holland, Belgium and France, he had not knocked "the common centre of gravity" out of the whole war and that, consequently, the main object of his grand project remained unattained.

He had failed, not only because British fighter aircraft and British pilots were superior to German, nor because radio-location multiplied the power of the former, which it most certainly did; but above all because Douhet's theory of air supremacy was founded on a fallacy. It was that wars can be won by bombardments.

Nothing in the history of war supports this contention, because, time and again, history has shown that unless a bombardment is immediately followed up by assault or occupation, the demoralization it produces is only temporary, and, like a drug, bombardments, whatever physical damage they do, become less and less morally effective with each successive dose.

Not the least important of the many tactical lessons which may be deduced from this battle was one noted by its victor. In the *Sunday Chronicle* of 20th September, 1942, Sir Hugh Dowding wrote: "The fact

---

[19]The figures given by the British Air Ministry between 10th July and 31st October were 2,692 German aircraft destroyed; actually the number was 1,733.

is, of course, that the defence has a basic advantage which increases with the distance between the attackers and the target, and it seems not unreasonable to suppose that exclusively long-range air warfare between two remote and self-supporting opponents would result in an innocuous stalemate."

This lesson was lost on the British Air Force, which continued to hold that "strategic bombing" was the be and the end all of air power. As later on we shall see, this fallacy not only prolonged the war, but went far to render the "peace" which followed it highly unprofitable to Britain and disastrous to the world in general.

CHAPTER III

CHANGE OF THE GERMAN LINE OF OPERATIONS

(1) *The First and Second Libyan Campaigns*

Though Hitler's direct attack on England had failed, the indirect approach on her remained open, and now that Italy was his ally, strategically he was superlatively well placed to carry war over the Mediterranean and by conquering Egypt strike a devastating blow against British sea power.

Why did he not do so? The reason can only be that he did not clearly see where the centre of gravity of the war lay. That this was so, is borne out in a note—quoted by Sir Hartley Shawcross in his indictment of the Nazi Leaders at Nuremberg on 4th December, 1945—written by Admiral Raeder, in which he said: ". . . results of air raids on England (our own losses) surely caused the Führer as far back as August and September to consider whether, even prior to victory in the west, an eastern campaign would be feasible with the object of first eliminating our last serious opponents on the Continent."[1]

This note is corroborated by an order of the German Supreme Command signed by General Jodl on 6th September, 1940, stating: "Directions are given for the occupation forces in the east to be increased in the following weeks. For security reasons this should not create the impression in Russia that Germany is preparing for an eastern offensive."[2] Though Sir Hartley Shawcross points out that the attack on Russia, known as the "Barbarossa Plan," "was to be camouflaged as if it was part of the preparations for the 'Seelowe Plan' for the invasion of England," strategically this only makes sense when "Egypt" is substituted for "England"; for though a concentration in the east of Europe might point either to an attack on Egypt via the Balkans and Turkey or to an attack on Russia, it could not possibly point to a direct attack on England.

The truth would appear to be that, because Hitler did not clearly see where the centre of gravity of the war lay, he never fully realized that his true line of operations ran from Berlin to London and not from Berlin to Moscow. And though, when in May, 1940, he set out on the right line, he

---

[1] *The Times,* 5th December, 1945.   [2] *Ibid.*

was but half aware that he was travelling in the right direction. Therefore that, even during the early stages of the Battle of Britain, instead of, under cover of his *guerre de course* in the Atlantic,[3] pursuing that line via Cairo, he set about preparing to change it for what he considered a more profitable one, and thereby, following in the footsteps of Napoleon, with far less excuse, he committed one of the gravest strategical blunders in history.

Here it is as well to make clear what is meant by a line of operations. It is not the line of march which fluctuates according to tactical events, nor has it anything to do with the line of communications which links an army to its administrative base. Instead, it is the direction of the plan of war which links the plan to the centre of gravity of the war. In the present case the centre was the crippling of England as a sea power; for so long as the command of the sea was hers, the initiative was hers also: as it were, an outer initiative encircling the inner initiative of her Continental antagonist—like a bull encircled in a field by a fence. Writing on this subject, Napoleon once said: "To change one's line of operations (should the goal selected be found to be the wrong one) is an act of genius; to lose it is so great a blunder that the general who does so is a criminal."[4] Hitler did not lose it, he purposely abandoned it, and by doing so, eventually he lost the war.

While this change was in its preparatory stage, military operations swung in the very direction which Hitler should have followed—namely, to the Mediterranean, Egypt, East Africa and the Middle East—and for nine months a war was waged in that vast area between Britain and Italy, the centre of gravity of which was Egypt. And, as we shall soon see, there can be no possible doubt that, had the Italians in Libya during the autumn of 1940 been placed under German leadership, and had they been reinforced by, let us suppose, no more than one German armoured and two infantry divisions, that centre of gravity would have been eliminated, and the whole of North Africa, Middle East and East Africa would have been at the mercy of the Axis. For Britain and her Empire this would have been catastrophic, and for Hitler's projected invasion of Russia beneficial in the extreme, because it would have brought him to within measurable striking distance of Russia's most important vital area of operations—the Caucasian oilfields.

What stood between him and that goal? The British Command of the

---

[3]It must never be overlooked that throughout the war the Battle of the Atlantic was putting an enormous strain on Britain. Thus, between 3rd September, 1939, and 15th August, 1940, the British losses amounted to 1,340,404 tons, Allied 437,663, and Neutral 736,132. Later on these sinkings were considerably increased. Besides these losses hundreds of ships were damaged.

[4]*Correspondance*, vol. XVII, No. 14,343.

Middle East under General Wavell who, when Italy declared war, had at his disposal: 36,000 troops in Egypt; 9,000 in the Sudan; 5,500 in Kenya; 1,475 in British Somaliland; 27,500 in Palestine; 2,500 in Aden; and 800 in Cyprus. Of tanks he had in Egypt the 7th Armoured Division, consisting of two partly equipped brigades. His air force was minute and its machines of obsolete types.

Facing him were 215,000 Italians in Libya under Marshal Italo Balbo, and 200,000 in Italian East Africa (Eritrea, Italian Somaliland and Abyssinia) under the Duke of Aosta, both now freed by the collapse of France to turn their whole strength upon him. Further, he had to start from scratch, because up to the time of Italy's declaration of war he had been ordered to avoid taking any defence measures which might provoke the Italians. On paper, his strategical position was an all but impossible one. Of his two lines of communication, the first, by way of the Mediterranean, was three-quarters blocked by the Italians in the centre, and Malta, his sole air stepping-stone between Egypt and Gibraltar, was precariously isolated. The second, by way of the Red Sea, was threatened by the Italian fleet and air force in Eritrea and Italian Somaliland. Added to these difficulties, the adherence of Syria and French Somaliland to the Vichy Government uncovered the north of Palestine and rendered British Somaliland, which faced Aden, untenable.

With an enemy placed in so complex a situation and possessing such inadequate means, the Italian plan of war was obvious. It was, by threatening him all round, in order to keep his forces divided, to destroy them in detail. Therefore, it was in no way surprising that during the first week in July the Italians invaded the Sudan, Kenya and British Somaliland, forcing their enemy to evacuate Kassala and Gallabat in the first, doing little damage in the second, and compelling him to withdraw altogether from the third. Though the Italians started bombing Malta, they never attempted to invade it, as clearly they should have done. And having won these Chinese victories they passed away into a siesta.

The first Libyan Campaign, and in the circumstances which faced the British it is entitled to be called a campaign, was not initiated by Marshal Balbo but by General Wavell. Having established a line of defensive works from Mersa Matruh southwards—Matruh was one hundred and eighty miles west of Alexandria and linked to the latter by a single-track railway—he decided to attack his ponderous enemy, who was then occupying a position on the Egyptian frontier southwards of Bardia.

This campaign is described by Alan Morehead as follows:

The forward British forces were given a standing order and not a plan of campaign. It was, "make one man appear to be a dozen, make one tank

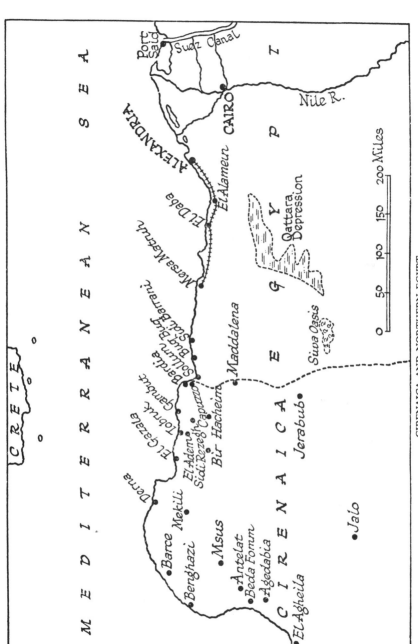

CIRENAICA AND NORTHERN EGYPT

look like a squadron, make a raid look like an advance." It was, what may be called, the strategy of exaggeration or lethal propaganda.

Continuing, Morehead writes:

"And so this little Robin Hood force, being unable to withstand any sort of determined advance by the half-dozen Italian divisions across the border, did the unpredicted, unexpected thing—it attacked. It attacked not as a combined force but in small units, swiftly, irregularly and by night. It pounced on Italian outposts, blew up the captured ammunition, and ran away. It stayed an hour, a day, or a week in a position, and then disappeared. The enemy had no clear idea of when he was going to be attacked next or where. Fort Maddalena fell, and Capuzzo. Sidi Aziz was invested. British vehicles were suddenly astride the road leading back from Bardia, shooting up convoys. Confused and anxious, the Italians rigged up searchlights and scoured the desert with them while British patrols lay grinning in the shadows. Soon, from prisoners we learned extraordinary stories were going the rounds behind the Italian lines. There were two . . . three . . . five British armoured divisions operating, they said. A large-scale British attack was imminent. Balbo drew in his horns, cut down his own patrols and called for more reinforcements from Rome."[5]

When this campaign was under way, on 28th June Balbo was killed at Tobruk in a British air raid, and on 13th August he was succeeded by Marshal Rodolfo Graziani, who during the Italo-Abyssinian War had proved himself to be a veritable snail. In the middle of September, urged on by Mussolini, he pushed his army over the Egyptian border to Sidi Barrani, seventy-five miles west of Matruh, whereupon Wavell's advanced troops fell back. There Graziani halted and began building a chain of forts south-westwards in the desert. Meanwhile, during this same month, the first reinforcements of any consequence reached Wavell. They included fifty "I" tanks, of the type which had done so well against the Germans at Arras. This time they were to prove themselves to be the decisive factor.

While Graziani was erecting monuments to his approaching defeat, on 20th October Wavell initiated the Second Libyan Campaign by instructing General Sir H. M. Wilson, commanding the British troops in Egypt, to consider the possibilities of an attack. Eight days later, Mussolini, apparently out of pique for not having been consulted about the German occupation of Rumania, declared war on Greece; whereupon Wilson's operation had to be postponed until early December, because Wavell was instructed to occupy Crete and deplete his small air force by sending three bomber and two fighter squadrons to Greece.

Graziani, who clearly should have attacked under cover of his master's

---

[5] *African Trilogy*, Alan Morehead of the *Daily Express* (1944), pp. 22-23. These tactics are similar to those I outlined for motor guerillas in my *Lectures on F.S.R.III* (1932).

Greek adventure, was believed by G.H.Q. Cairo to have 80,000 troops supported by 120 tanks and an air force three times as strong as the British distributed in or near by seven fortified camps, the names of which from north to south were Maktila, Point Ninty, Tummar East, Tummar West, Nibeiwa, Sofafi East and Sofafi South West. Some time before British patrols had discovered that between Nibeiwa and the two Sofafis there was an undefended gap of twenty miles in width, and that the camps were not built for all-round defence. Therefore, were this gap penetrated by an armoured and motorized force, it would be possible by swinging north to take the five northern Italian camps in reverse, and, what was equally important, one after the other, because no two were mutually supporting.

This, in brief, was the plan Major-General R. N. O'Connor, Commanding the Western Desert Force, decided on. His army consisted of the 7th Armoured Division (Major-General O'Moore Creagh); the 4th Indian Division; two Infantry Brigades and the 7th Bn. Royal Tank Regiment ("I" tanks). In all 31,000 men, 120 guns and 275 tanks. The air force which was to co-operate with him was under the command of Wing-Commander R. Collishaw.

The operation was planned to last for five days, and because the no-man's-land which separated the opposing armies was seventy miles in depth, several days' supplies for the whole force were first pushed forward and stored in the desert some twenty to thirty miles in advance of the British fortified lines. Next, it was decided to carry out the approach march in stages: an advance of some thirty miles on the night of 7th December; a halt in the open during daylight on the 8th, followed by another night advance after dusk, which was to culminate in an attack on the morning of the 9th.

While this extraordinarily daring movement was in progress, the Navy was to bombard Maktila, Sidi Barrani and the coastal road, and Collishaw's air force was to carry out continuous raids on the enemy airfields in order to destroy his machines on the ground.

As so frequently happens when audacity is in the saddle, everything went to plan. Nevertheless, what followed was not what had been planned, namely, a large-scale raid lasting for five days; instead, a campaign of sixty-two, which carried the Desert Army right across Cirenaica—a distance of five hundred miles—and ended with the destruction of Graziani's army. That, tactically, this was possible is astonishing; yet less so than that it was administratively possible.

This unexpected campaign—unexpected by both sides—may be divided into three phases, in each of which a different form of attack was adopted. The first was an Arbela operation; the second a series of frontal attacks; and the third a Chancellorsville battle—a rear attack.

Phase 1. Once O'Connor was through the gap, detaching the Support Group[6] of the 7th Armoured Division to pin down the garrisons of the Sofafi camps, he swung his army north, and at 7 a.m., coming up in rear of Nibeiwa—held by 3,000 Italians under General Maletti—he opened his guns upon it. Thirty-five minutes later, the 7th R.T.R., followed by infantry, struck. The Italian tanks were at once shot up,[7] and the Italian

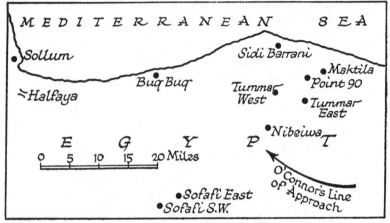

BATTLEFIELD OF SIDI BARRANI, 7th-11th DECEMBER, 1940

anti-tank gunners demoralized when they discovered that their 37 mm. pieces had no effect on the "I" tanks' heavy armour.[8] An hour later the camp[9] was in O'Connor's hands and Maletti was found killed.

Reforming his assault columns, O'Connor swept north, opened fire on Tummar West at 1.30 p.m., attacked the camp at 1.50 p.m., and carried it

[6]The tanks of the Support Group differed from the ordinary tanks in that they carried a howitzer instead of a 2-pr. gun.

[7]The Italians had two types of tanks, a light and a medium. The former I had seen in Abyssinia in 1935-1936 and had called it "a mobile coffin." In this campaign, Alexander Clifford (*Daily Mail* Correspondent) calls it "a useless death-trap."

[8]"The Italians in despair saw that their light anti-tank shells just rattled off the tanks' turrets, and even light artillery was not effective against them." (*African Trilogy*, p. 72.) Graziani wrote: "One cannot break steel armour with finger-nails alone"; also, that Mussolini had obliged him to wage the war "of the flea against the elephant." (*Ciano's Diary*, pp. 317 and 318.)

[9]The camps were as luxuriously equipped as were those of the French at Rossbach. In the latter were found pomades, perfumes, dressing-gowns, umbrellas, parrots, etc. (*Frederick the Great: His Court and Times*, Thomas Campbell, 1842-43, vol. III, p. 109) ; in the former, sheets, pomades, scents, coat-hangers, etc. (*Three Against Rommel*, Alexander Clifford, 1943, p. 42, and *African Trilogy*, p. 67). History, therefore, does sometimes repeat itself.

as he had Nibeiwa by assault. Next came Tummar East, the greater part of which was reduced by nightfall. Meanwhile, the 4th Indian Division, escorted by the 7th Armoured Division, had moved north and cut the Sidi Barrani-Buq Buq road. Thus ended the operations of the 9th.

At dawn next day an advance was made on Sidi Barrani. At 4.15 p.m. the assault was launched and the place taken by nightfall. That evening O'Connor ordered part of the 7th Armoured Division to move south and prevent the Italians withdrawing from the Sofafi camps, and part to make west in pursuit of the routed enemy. On the 11th, between Buq Buq and Sollum, 14,000 Italians were captured.

"This ended the first phase of the operation, which may be called the Battle of Sidi Barrani. It had resulted in the destruction of the greater part of five enemy divisions. Over 38,000 prisoners, 400 guns, some 50 tanks and much other war material had been captured. Our own casualties were only 133 killed, 387 wounded and 8 missing." Thus wrote General Wavell.[10]

Phase 2. The next problem was a totally different one—namely, the reduction of Bardia and Tobruk, each held by a powerful Italian detachment, and each strongly entrenched. The first, after methodical preparation— mine-clearing, anti-tank ditch filling, wire-cutting and bombardment—was carried by assault on 5th January, and the second in the same way on the 22nd; 45,000 prisoners, 462 guns and 12 tanks were taken in the one, and 30,000 prisoners, 236 guns and 87 tanks in the other.

Phase 3. On the fall of Tobruk only two strong detachments of the enemy still remained in Cirenaica: the 60th Division, less one brigade, east of Derna, and a brigade as well as 160 tanks at Mekili, fifty miles to the south of Derna. And because the Derna position was a strong one, O'Connor decided to contain it and attack the Mekili group. But during the night of 26th-27th January that group withdrew towards Barce. Thereupon Wavell saw O'Connor, and together they decided, while the 7th Armoured Division, now reduced to fifty cruiser[11] and ninety-five light tanks, was to move across the desert by way of Mekili and cut the coastal road south of Benghazi, the rest of the Desert Army was to press the enemy along that road towards Benghazi.

Early on the 30th the enemy began falling back on Barce. So soon as this was confirmed, it was decided "to move at once across the desert without

[10]General Wavell's "Despatch." *Supplement of the London Gazette* of 26th June, 1946, p. 3264.

[11]At this time there were four types of tanks in the British Army: the support tank to protect other tanks; the infantry tank, thickly armoured but slow, to co-operate with infantry; the cruiser tank, less thickly armoured but faster, to work independently; and the light tank, now becoming obsolescent. The second and third were armed with 2-pr. guns.

awaiting completion of force or of supply arrangements." Whereupon the 7th Armoured Division set out from Mekili to Msus, which was occupied by armoured cars at daybreak, 5th February. A few hours later General Creagh sent out two detachments to make straight for the coast and cut the coastal road in two places some fifty miles south of Benghazi at a point called Beda Fomm.[12]

On the evening of this same day an enemy column 5,000 strong, retreating southwards from Benghazi, suddenly came up against the 4th Armoured Brigade on the coastal road, and was so surprised and unready that it forthwith surrendered. Next, on the 6th, the main enemy column appeared including a large number of tanks. But coming into action piecemeal, it was destroyed piecemeal, eighty-four of its tanks being put out of action. Pinned down on almost twenty miles of road, blocked in front and attacked in rear; in short, so completely trapped was the Italian 60th Division that, at dawn next day, its Commander, General Berganzoli, unconditionally surrendered, and 20,000 prisoners, 120 tanks and 190 guns were added to the captures of the Desert Army.

Thus ended one of the most audacious campaigns ever fought. In all, though never more than two full British divisions were employed, between 7th December and 7th February an army of four corps, comprising nearly ten divisions, was destroyed, and 130,000 prisoners, 400 tanks and 1,240 guns captured at a cost of 500 killed, 1,373 wounded and 55 missing.

After such a victory, why did not Wavell push on? The reasons were that by now he had not only two other campaigns on his hands, but that in February the Greek Government, realizing that a German invasion of Greece was imminent, brought pressure to bear on the British Government, who in their turn instructed Wavell to send to Greece one armoured brigade and three infantry divisions under command of Sir H. M. Wilson. It was this reduction in strength and not enemy action or supply difficulties—great though they were—which brought the Second Libyan Campaign to a full stop.

Thus ended a campaign of many lessons, of which the more outstanding were: That mobility in the attack is superior to mass in the defence, because it enables the attacker to concentrate superiority of force against a single point or a series of points in rapid succession. That striking power is multiplied by novelty of tactics or means, and that it demands the closest integration of all arms. As Wavell points out, without the assistance of the Navy to keep open the sea supply lines, the campaign would not have been possible. Nor would it have been possible had Collishaw not concentrated

---

[12]The 7th Armoured Division moved from Mekili to the sea coast, a distance of 147 miles as the crow flies, in twenty-nine hours.

his numerically inferior air force in low-level attacks on the Italian aircraft on the ground. This won for him complete aerial superiority. Finally, once again the passive defence had led to ruin. To sit within a fortress is one thing, to manœuvre from or between fortresses is another. The Italians sat and they perished. This time, for many of them, the siesta was an eternal one.

(2) *The Conquest of Abyssinia*

The two campaigns, other than the Libyan, which Wavell had on hand at the time he was ordered to send an expeditionary force to Greece, were those which were to end in the conquest of Abyssinia. On 2nd December— five days before he set out to defeat Graziani—he had summoned Lieut.- General Sir William Platt, commanding the forces in the Sudan, and Lieut.-General Sir Alan A. Cunningham, commanding those in Kenya, to Cairo, and there had explained to them that he wanted the first to foster rebellion in Abyssinia and be prepared to recapture Kassala in February, and the second to maintain pressure on Moyale, and in May or June, when the rains were over, to advance on Kismayu (Chisimaio) which is situated close by the mouth of the River Juba. To Platt he allotted the 4th and 5th Indian Divisions, and to Cunningham the 1st South African Division and the 11th and 12th African Divisions. From these humble beginnings, as if by magic, was destined to sprout and grow, if not the most extensive, then certainly the most rapid pincer movement ever carried out. One base was at Khartoum, the other at Nairobi, 1,200 air miles apart.

In outline, these two remarkable campaigns, the one mainly fought through mountainous country, and the other largely over arid plainland, is as follows.

Platt's advance had been fixed for 9th February, but on account of the Italians, under General Frusci, evacuating Kassala in the middle of January, Platt set out on the 19th of that month and crossed the Eritrean border on the following day. Catching up with Frusci at Agordat, he fought and beat him there on the 31st, and then pursued him to Keren, where the Kassala-Asmara road passed through a formidable defile. At Keren the only severe fighting in the two campaigns occurred. Numerous attacks were made, and it was not until 3rd March, and at a loss of nearly 3,000 killed and wounded, that Platt was able to break through. On 1st April Asmara was occupied and three days later, after little fighting, Massawa was also. After these successes, the two remaining centres of Italian resistance were at Gondar and Amba Alagi. The latter is a conical-shaped mountain, 10,000 feet above sea level, dominating the Asmara-Addis Ababa road. In air miles it lies one hundred and eighty-five south of

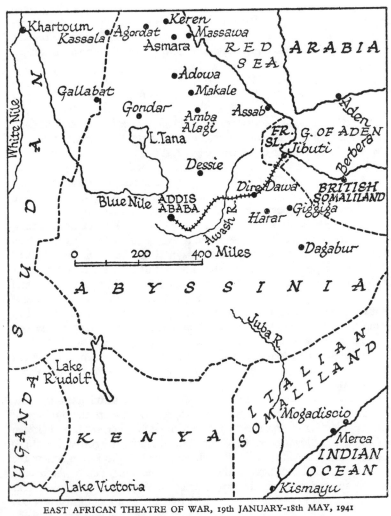

EAST AFRICAN THEATRE OF WAR, 19th JANUARY-18th MAY, 1941

Asmara, but on account of innumerable hairpin bends, by road it is nearly twice that distance. This formidable position Platt set out to attack on 4th May.

Meanwhile, nearly a thousand miles to the south of him, Cunningham started to advance on 24th January, and on 18th February he crossed the Juba river. Having obtained Wavell's permission to push on to Mogadiscio, two hundred and seventy-five miles to the north, at 6 a.m. on the 23rd he sent forward a motorized African brigade group, and, astonishing as it may seem, it entered Mogadiscio at 5 p.m. on the 25th. As astonishing, when it got there, 350,000 gallons of motor spirit and 80,000 gallons of aviation were found intact. This was a godsend, as it enabled the advance to be continued before the ports of Merca and Mogadiscio were opened.

Meanwhile Cunningham, having met with so little resistance, had asked Wavell for permission to advance on Harar by way of Giggiga, and the latter place being seven hundred and seventy-four miles by road from Mogadiscio, he also asked him to re-open the port of Berbera, which was two hundred and four miles from Giggiga, because this would eventually enable him to shorten his line of supply by five hundred and seventy miles. This Wavell agreed to do, and Berbera was occupied on 16th March by a small force based on Aden; whereupon the Italians withdrew out of British Somaliland.

Leaving Mogadiscio on 1st March, Cunningham set out for Giggiga. On the 10th, at Dagabur—five hundred and ninety miles north of Mogadiscio—his advanced troops came in contact with the enemy. Brushing them aside, Cunningham's men entered Giggiga on the 17th. Arranging to change part of his line of communications over to Berbera—it was now 1,600 miles in length from Kenya—Cunningham pushed on through the formidable Madar pass and entered Harar on the 25th. Thus, in thirty days, his advance had covered 1,054 miles at an average of thirty-five miles the day, the last sixty-five miles of which had in 1935-1936 hung up Graziani for nearly six months.

Next, turning south-west, Cunningham set out for Addis Ababa, which, abandoned by the Duke of Aosta, was occupied on 4th April. By this date Cunningham's army had captured over 50,000 prisoners, and had occupied 360,000 square miles of country at a cost of 135 men killed, 310 wounded, 52 missing and 4 captured.

On account of Wavell's commitments in Libya and Greece, it was now most urgent to open the Asmara-Addis Ababa road, in order to allow passage of troops to Egypt via Massawa. Therefore Cunningham was ordered to attack Dessie, two hundred and fifty miles north of Addis Ababa.

On the 13th he sent forward the 1st South African Brigade which, after a five days' battle in the Combolcia Pass, in which it lost ten men killed and took 8,000 Italians prisoners, occupied Dessie on the 20th. One hundred and forty air miles to the north of Dessie lay Amba Alagi, where the Duke of Aosta had entrenched the remnants of his army. There, attacked by Platt from the north and by Cunningham from the south, on 18th May he unconditionally surrendered, but nevertheless was granted the honours of war. Meanwhile, on 5th May, exactly five years after Marshal Badoglio had marched into Addis Ababa, the Emperor Haile Selassie "rode down from the hills and reclaimed his capital."

Though operations continued in outlying districts for some time—the most important of which was Gondar—to all intents and purposes the battle of Amba Alagi brought the conquest of Abyssinia to a close. Of the dual campaign Wavell writes:

"The conquest of Italian East Africa had been accomplished in four months, from the end of January to the beginning of June. In this period a force of approximately 220,000 men had been practically destroyed with the whole of its equipment, and an area of nearly a million square miles had been occupied. Some of the chief features of this remarkable campaign were the storming by British and Indian troops of the formidable mountain barriers at Keren and Amba Alagi, the boldness and skill with which the operations from East Africa were pressed over a distance of about two thousand miles from the base, and the very skilful guerilla fighting in Western Abyssinia."[13]

The most pleasing feature of these two campaigns was that both sides fought with marked chivalry. There was no bombing of the civil inhabitants, no deportations, wanton destruction, rape, murder and plundering. Even the Abyssinian guerillas on the whole behaved with moderation.

The most astonishing features were its speed on the part of the British and the lack of resistance on the part of the Italians, who seldom even put up a passive defence, relying instead in passive retirements. Only at Keren did they show any real fight. Yet, even there, the use they made of their superior air force was negligible. Though their enemy's long columns of transport were in continual movement from Kassala, not once did they bomb them. And General Cunningham informs us that one of the most "remarkable features" up to the crossing of the Juba river, "was the almost complete lack of enemy interference from the air."[14]

On the British side the opposite is to be seen. Instead of passive withdrawals there were audacious advances. In fact, the smallness of the forces employed, coupled with the enormous size of the theatre of war, which

[13]General Wavell's "Despatch." *Supplement to the London Gazette*, 9th July, 1946, p. 3530.
[14]*Ibid.*, p. 3564.

induced the Italians to protect too many places at once, were, under audacious leadership, the main factors which resulted in a mobility never before attained in war. Had the columns been larger, their supply alone would have prohibited such activity, and that the Italians were unable to concentrate in sufficient forces to compel their enemy to enlarge his columns, and, in consequence, add to his administrative difficulties, must largely be credited to the activities of the Abyssinian guerillas, who compelled vast numbers of their enemy to be scattered along his difficult lines of communication. Yet one wonders why the Marda Pass was not held and why Keren was not made impregnable to the force which attacked it.

(3) *The Conquest of Yugoslavia and Greece*

On 22nd October, 1940, when in a broadcast Mr. Churchill assured his listeners that Hitler and Mussolini were bent upon carving up France and her Empire—strategically not altogether an unsound thing to do—the first of these "bandits" was peacefully occupying Rumania, and the second was about to set out to burn his fingers in Greece. In fact, the carving up was to take place in exactly the opposite direction.

Once Rumania was swallowed, in January pressure was brought to bear on Bulgaria, which country, becoming party to the Three Power Pact,[15] was peacefully occupied by Germany on 1st March. Next, pressure was brought to bear on Yugoslavia, and it was then that the Greek Government, fearing that Hitler would come to the relief of Mussolini, by now bunkered in Albania,[16] called upon Britain to fulfil her guarantee and come to her support. From 10th March to the 20th German pressure on Yugoslavia was so increased that, on the 24th, the Yugoslav Government capitulated and joined the Three Power Pact. Three days later this surrender was reversed by a *coup d'état* carried out by General Simovitch, immediately followed by the naval battle of Matapan in which Admiral Cunningham sank seven Italian warships. On 6th April the Germans struck, simultaneously invading Yugoslavia and Greece.

At the date of the Simovitch *coup d'état*, the bulk of the Twelfth German Army, under Field-Marshal List, was stationed on the Bulgar-Turkish frontier, preparatory, as we now know, not to invade Turkey but instead Russia, once the Balkans were in the German bag. This army was ordered to invade Serbia and Macedonia, while other armies advanced from the north into Croatia and on to Belgrade. Belgrade was heavily bombed, as were the Yugoslav airfields.

[15]Signed in Berlin by Germany, Italy and Japan on 27th September, 1940.
[16]Four regiments identified in this area were the "Wolves of Tuscany," the 'Hercules of Ferrara," the "Demigods of Julia" and the "Red Devils of Piedmont."

In the brief time at their disposal, two courses were open to the Yugo-slavs: to defend their entire country, or to retire southwards into the mountains. The second was obviously the more hopeful, but as it meant abandoning the Croats and Slovenes, the first was adopted, with the inevitable result that four Yugoslav army corps were trapped. Attacked by German armoured columns as well as an Hungarian army on the Danube front, in a veritable Cannæ operation both flanks of the Yugoslav forces were rolled inwards. Their left by German and Italian armies advancing by way of Zagreb and Ljubljana; their right by a German army from Vidin. Forced back pell-mell on to Serajevo, on 17th April twenty-eight Yugoslav divisions capitulated; whereupon, General Simovitch with the King and his Ministers escaped by air to Greece.

While this campaign was being fought, Field-Marshal List fell upon Serbia and Macedonia. But before we outline what followed, it is as well to return to the middle of February, when, it will be remembered, General Wavell was instructed to despatch an expeditionary force under General Wilson to Greece.

On 22nd February conversations were held with the Greek Commander-in-Chief, General Papagos, and the various lines of defence in northern Greece were examined. There were: (1) The Metaxas Line along the eastern Rhodope Mountains, covering Macedonia; (2) the line of the Struma Valley covering Salonika; and (3) the Aliakhmon (Vistritza river) Line west of Salonika. Since the bulk of the Greek Army was facing the Italians in Albania, the first two were considered too long for the available forces to hold; therefore the third was decided on. "The main danger to it," writes Wavell, "lay in the exposure of the left flank if German forces succeeded in advancing through Southern Yugoslavia and in entering Greece by the Valley of the Cherna or Monastir Gap."[17]

A few days later, to the dismay of Generals Wavell and Wilson, General Papagos changed his mind, and, for political reasons, decided to hold the Metaxas Line, with Wilson's army on the west of the Vardar. This army consisted of the New Zealand Division, 6th and 7th Australian Divisions, the 1st Armoured Brigade and a Polish Brigade, in all 57,000 troops, 24,000 of whom were British. Its first flight began to disembark at the Piræus on 7th March.

Confronted by an enemy so mobile and pugnacious as the Germans, the Allied distribution was suicidal. On the left, west of Koritsa to the Strait of Otranto, lay the main Greek army (fourteen divisions) facing the Italians in Albania. On the right, three and a half Greek divisions held the Metaxas

---

[17]General Wavell's "Despatch." *Supplement to the London Gazette*, 2nd July, 1946, p. 3425.

THE INVASION OF GREECE, 6th-28th APRIL, 1941

Line, and three Greek divisions and the British Army were deployed on a line running from the Aegean Sea east of Mount Olympus to Veria and Edessa and thence northwards to the Yugoslav frontier; in all about one hundred miles. The weak point in this distribution was that, should the Germans succeed in penetrating through Serbia, the whole of it could be outflanked from the west. To guard against this, General Wilson established a small force, including the 3rd Royal Tank Regiment, at Amynteion (south of Florina) to watch the Monastir Gap.

Field-Marshal List decided to turn this over-extended distribution to his advantage: (1) By penetrating the Allied centre and cutting off the Greek forces in Albania; (2) by breaking through the Metaxas Line at the Rupel Pass, cutting off the Greeks in Eastern Macedonia; and (3) by simultaneously moving a column up the Strumitsa and then down the Vardar, to pinch out Salonika.

These operations, launched on 6th April, were heralded by an intense bombing attack. Tens of thousands of Yugoslav soldiers with their ox-wagons were caught in the process of taking up their defensive positions, and one hundred and fifty miles of road were jammed, bombed and blasted. Further back, Larissa and its airfields were overwhelmed, and the Piræus heavily bombed. There a burning ship ". . . ignited another vessel full of T.N.T., and in a second the harbour was savaged and battered with a volcanic explosion. Ships, wharves and buildings burned. Later, a whole cargo of Hurricanes went to the bottom."[18]

Under cover of this bombardment, List advanced four main columns, all armoured. Against the Metaxas Line he employed two, one armoured division moved down the Sturma and after some severe fighting forced the Rupel Pass. The other, consisting of one armoured and one mountain division, moved up the Strumitsa and meeting with little opposition turned down the Vardar valley. These two advances were so rapid that the leading German tanks entered Salonika on the evening of the 8th.

Meanwhile, on List's right flank, setting out from Keustendil—forty-five miles south-west of Sofia—one armoured division and a motorized division advanced on Skoplje (Uskub), which was occupied on the 7th, while another armoured division drove through Stip and reached Prilep. From there both columns moved on Monastir and entered Greece by two roads north of Florina. Thereupon, after some fighting south of Florina, the British and Greek forces holding the Vardar Front fell back to a position running from Mount Olympus along the line of the Aliakhmon river. But on account of the collapse of the Yugoslav army in Serbia and the rapid advance of the Germans through the Monastir Gap, it became obvious that

[18]*African Trilogy*, p. 146.

this position could not be held. General Wilson therefore decided to continue the withdrawal to the Pass of Thermopylæ. This withdrawal, uncovering the passes over the Pindus, placed the main Greek army, which was then retiring from Albania into Epirus, in a desperate position. On the 19th German armour crossed the Pindus range at Metsovo. This sealed the fate of the Army of Epirus. On the 21st it capitulated.

Nothing was now left to the British but to evacuate Greece as rapidly as possible, and it was decided to embark the greater part of the army in the Peloponnesus. Not only was this a more difficult operation than that of Dunkirk, because there was no fighter cover, but early on the 26th the whole programme was disrupted by a German airborne landing which seized the bridge over the Corinth Canal. These airborne troops were rapidly reinforced by the German motorized division which, after operating in Epirus, crossed the Gulf of Corinth at Patras. "This action at Corinth," writes Captain Miksche, "proved economical from the standpoint not only of time, but also of material, particularly of fuel. If Field-Marshal List had not undertaken this operation, the fighting in the Peloponnese might have continued for many more weeks."[19]

The main evacuations took place on the nights of 26th-27th and 27th-28th April, in all nearly 43,000 Imperial soldiers out of the 57,660 originally landed were got away; in the circumstances a remarkable feat and another demonstration of the value of sea power. Yet, as was the case at Dunkirk, all heavy equipment was lost. On the 27th the Germans entered Athens and hoisted the Swastika on the Acropolis.

Once again this campaign showed three things: the enormous advantage of superior air power, of superior armour, and of the superiority of the two when integrated in one striking force. Though in aircraft and armour the British were woefully outnumbered, the use they made of their small air force showed that the R.A.F. had learnt nothing from the operations in France. Instead of all machines being employed to assist the land forces, the craze for strategic bombing remained uppermost. On 7th April the railway station at Sofia was bombed—over one hundred miles behind the front! We read that the Germans "did not seem to have been materially delayed by these . . . raids on railway stations in Bulgaria"[20]: naturally, because all their movements were by road. Of the German use of aircraft we are told something very different:

"The German bombers were most dangerous to our men using roads, or holding positions on level ground, or beaches. Their attacks were very intense, for the German air force began using bases in Thessaly within a

[19] *Paratroops*, Captain F. O. Miksche (1943), p. 41.
[20] *The Seventh Quarter*, Philip Graves, p. 50.

few hours of the German forward troops having captured them. They were able to supply these forward bases by troop-carrying aircraft which brought up ground staff, fuel and munitions by air."[21]

The final point to note is, that this campaign, so far as the British were concerned, was purely a political one. It should never have been fought, for though Britain had pledged her word to support Greece, to do so with a token force in order to "save face" in the eyes of the world, was in no sense a fulfilment of her pledge, and in every sense a betrayal of General Wilson's army. Further, as we shall now see, its repercussions in Africa were disastrous.

(4) *The Third Libyan Campaign*

The destruction of Graziani's army, opening as it did the road to Tripoli, compelled Hitler to come to the assistance of his ally. Thus it came about that, when Wavell was depleting his army in order to send forces to Greece, General Erwin Rommel with German reinforcements landed in Tripolitania. Though information of this was received in Cairo, there were so few British aircraft available for long-range reconnaissance that it was not possible to ascertain what Rommel's strength was. The next difficulty was that German aircraft so persistently bombed Benghazi, now deprived of fighter aircraft and anti-aircraft artillery which had been sent to Greece, that it became too hazardous to unload ships there. This meant that supplies had to be forwarded from Tobruk—two hundred miles to the east— and eight thousand vehicles having been sent to Greece, transport was so short that unit vehicles had to be used on the line of communications. This led to the forward troops, and particularly the 2nd Armoured Division, being supplied from dumps; of these, the main petrol dump was established at Msus.

Towards the end of March the British covering forces were in position a little east of Agheila, which is one hundred and fifty miles south of Benghazi. They consisted of the 2nd Armoured Division, less one brigade in Greece, and the 9th Australian Division, with one brigade at Tobruk; also there was an Indian Motor Brigade Group at Mekili. The tanks of the 2nd Armoured Division were not only under establishment but many were in a bad condition, and several of its units were as yet untrained for desert warfare. Realizing the weakness of these troops, Wavell instructed Lieut.-General P. Neame, then commanding in Cirenaica, that, should he be attacked, he was to fight a delaying action back to Benghazi, and even to evacuate Benghazi should the situation demand it.

[21] *The Campaign in Greece and Crete*, British Ministry of Information (1942), p. 32.

On 31st March Rommel attacked. His force consisted of one German Light Armoured Division and two Italian Divisions, one armoured and the other motorized. Rommel's plan was in many ways Beda Fomm in reverse. With one section of his small army he pushed up the road towards Benghazi, and with the other he made across the desert for Mekili, his idea being to come in on the rear of his enemy retiring from Benghazi on Derna. The most novel point in it was, realizing that his enemy's main problem was petrol supply, he instructed his air force to make the destruction of the British petrol-carrying vehicles its main object.

On Rommel advancing, Neame, following his instructions, withdrew the 2nd Armoured Division. On the evening of 2nd April it arrived at a point north of Agedabia, at which it could simultaneously flank the Benghazi road and block the desert track to Mekili by way of Msus.

Next day, a report was received that a strong German armoured force was approaching Msus, whereupon the detachment guarding the dump set fire to the petrol. This over-hasty action knocked the supply bottom out of Neame's armour. Meanwhile, Benghazi having been abandoned,[22] Neame withdrew his forces to the line Wadi Derna-Mekili. Finding it impossible to hold this line, the 9th Australian Division, on the right, withdrew to Tobruk, where it arrived on the 7th. But the 2nd Armoured Division, having to regulate its movements in accordance with the petrol it could obtain, under violent air attack directed at its wireless vehicles and petrol-carrying transport, did not reach Mekili until the evening of the 6th. From there, on account of petrol shortage, its 3rd Armoured Brigade made for Derna, where it was captured. On the 7th the rest of the 2nd Armoured Division, including its headquarters, was attacked at Mekili, and that evening received orders to withdraw to el Adem, south of Tobruk. At dawn the following day an attempt to break out was made, and though the 1st Royal Horse Artillery and some Indian troops managed to escape, what remained of the 2nd Armoured Division was captured.

A further misfortune occurred on the night of the 6th-7th. Lieut.-General O'Connor and another officer had been sent forward to assist General Neame in the withdrawal. All three were taken prisoner by a German motor patrol which caught them on the Barce-Derna road.

Learning of these disasters, and having few armoured vehicles in Egypt to support the defeated army, Wavell decided to hold Tobruk, in order to prevent the thousands of tons of supplies accumulated there falling into the enemy's hands, and also to deprive the enemy of the use of the port. It

[22]At this time the reports issued by British Headquarters, Cairo, were extremely misleading. Thus, on 3rd April: "As in the autumn of 1940, the enemy is evidently seeking a propaganda success at the expense of stretching still further an already extended line of communications."

was a bold and wise decision, and because he could no longer attack, the next best thing was to strike at his enemy's mobility by denying him a forward base.   To Tobruk he despatched the 7th Australian Division and a few tanks by sea to reinforce the 9th Australian Division. These reinforcements arrived on the 7th, and on the 11th Tobruk was invested. By now Rommel's momentum being exhausted, directly he reached the Sollum escarpment he halted his weary army.

Tactically, the most interesting feature in this brief campaign of twelve days was the problem of petrol supply in mechanized operations, and the importance of keeping that supply mobile and protected against air attack. Dumping was a relic of the previous war, and though useful when conditions are static, as this campaign shows, if relied upon in a war of rapid movements, it subordinates tactics to administration, and thereby deprives leadership of liberty of action. The deduction to be made from this is: that as the most mobile means of carriage is by aircraft, every mechanized force of any size should have at its call an airborne supply column. As we shall see, and in spite of the events to be related in the next Section, this lesson was not learnt by the British in the West until near the end of the war.

But above all, what this campaign shows is: that had Rommel and his insignificant reinforcements been despatched to Graziani before instead of after the latter's defeat, the chances are that there would have been no Beda Fomm campaign and that Wavell would have been driven out of Egypt. Therefore, though Rommel was sent to the right tactical place it was at the wrong strategical time. He was four months too late; not to beat his enemy, but to change the whole course of the war. The means existed, the leader was there and his tactics were excellent; but because his master's strategy was at fault, as we shall see, hence onwards all Rommel's efforts to reach Alexandria were in vain; the strategic moment had been missed.

(5) *The Air Assault on Crete*

Simultaneously with Rommel's attack, a crisis occurred in Iraq. German propaganda had long been at work in that country, and, on 31st March, the Regent, learning of a plot to arrest him, fled to Basra and took refuge on a British warship. Whereupon the Iraqi Prime Minister, Rashid Ali Ghailani, who was in German pay, invested the British air station at Habbaniyah, sixty miles west of Baghdad. This led to a brief but annoying campaign, which fizzled out at Baghdad on 1st June. That day also ended the most extraordinary and futuristic campaign of the whole war—the German air assault on Crete.

It will be remembered that on 1st November, 1940, a small British force had occupied Crete—the key to the Aegean—but on account of the constant shortage of aircraft in the Middle East, no aircraft had been sent there. Then came the evacuation of Greece, and because many of the troops which were withdrawn were landed at Crete, when, on 30th April, Major-General Sir Bernard Freyberg was placed in command of the island to organize its defence, he found himself in command of 27,550 men. Thousands were unarmed, and equipment of all kinds was wanting.

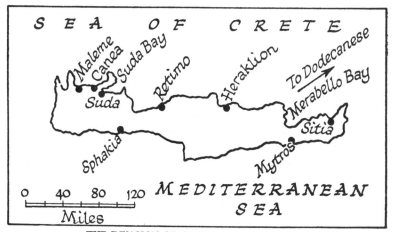

THE INVASION OF CRETE, 20th-31st MAY, 1941

On assuming command, Freyberg split his troops into four groups—at Heraklion, Retimo, Maleme and Suda Bay; the first three having aerodromes. But on account of shortage of transport, these groups were isolated and in no way mutually supporting. Further, they were constantly attacked by German aircraft, and having but few fighter planes to protect them, even had sufficient transport existed, movements could only have been made by night.

Crete was some four hundred miles from Egypt, and, therefore, outside British fighter range. German fighters were based on Dadion, Corinth, Topolia, Megara, Tanagra, Phaleron and Eleusis, and Italian on the Dodecanese, all within range of Crete. And because it was found impossible for the British aircraft on the island to maintain themselves there, on 19th May they were withdrawn.

Already, by 12th May, British Intelligence was aware that a German air attack on Crete was in preparation, and five days later Mr. Churchill announced that the island "would be held to the last man"—an ominous prediction. Nevertheless, when the attack came, as it did on the 20th, it scored a surprise, mainly on account of its strength.

The command of the operation was in the hands of Field-Marshal List, and the operation itself went under the appropriate code name of "Mercury." List, it would appear, made use of three forces: (1) The Landing Corps, consisting of the XIth Air Corps and the 3rd and 5th Mountain Divisions; (2) the Supporting Air Forces; and (3) the Transport Air Fleet of six hundred to seven hundred aircraft, mainly Junkers 52.

At 8 a.m. on the 20th a heavy bombing attack was launched, under cover of which a large number of parachutists was dropped near Maleme, south and south-west of Canea and north of Suda Bay, and fifty to one hundred gliderborne troops[23] were landed west of the Maleme aerodrome. To assist the parachutists, the ground was deliberately pitted with bomb craters so that they could find immediate ground cover. Though many of these men were killed, more attacks followed at Heraklion and Retimo. In all, it was estimated that 7,000 Germans were landed on the 20th.

During the 21st and 22nd the attack was intensified, hundreds of gliders landing on or about Maleme, although the aerodrome was under artillery fire. These men, aided by intense bomber and fighter support, which pinned the defenders to the ground during daylight, beat off every attack.

Meanwhile, on the night of 21st-22nd, and again on that of 22nd-23rd, a German seaborne invasion by caiques was attempted, but on both occasions was completely smashed by the British fleet, and in spite of lack of air cover. Nevertheless, the fleet paid a heavy price, for two cruisers and four destroyers were lost, as well as many ships receiving heavy damage.

On the 26th the Germans, who had established themselves at Retimo, were all but annihilated by a few "I" tanks; but by then the situation at Maleme and Canea had become critical. Suda Bay was now untenable and some 20,000 Germans had landed. It becoming still more critical, the next day General Freyberg decided to evacuate his army. This became urgent, because on the 28th an Italian force from the Dodecanese Islands managed to land at Sitia.

Evacuation began on the night of the 28th-29th from Sphakia. On the 30th the Germans made contact with the British rearguard and were repulsed. But on account of the heavy naval losses, it was decided that evacuation must end on the night of 31st May-1st June, which doomed many men to capture. In all, 14,580 troops were got away, 13,000 being either killed or made prisoners.

[23] The glider attack, in particular, seems to have surprised the British, because gliders could land on any ordinary ground. The ones used in this attack carried from twelve to thirty men apiece, and as many as five were towed by one aircraft at a speed of about 100 m.p.h.

Wavell gives the total German losses as "at least 12,000-15,000, of whom a very high proportion were killed."[24]

Before we comment on this remarkable battle, it will be convenient to round off Wavell's many campaigns. On 15th May he ordered an attack in the Western Desert on Sollum and Fort Capuzzo. They were taken and lost, and another attack on a larger scale was made on 15th June. What for, it is difficult to understand; anyhow, it ended in a minor disaster, for twenty-five cruiser tanks and seventy "I" tanks were lost by running on to a minefield or by enemy anti-tank gunfire. This operation showed the difficulty of combining these two types of tank, because the speed of the second, five miles the hour, was only a third that of the first.

At the same time a fresh commitment arose. Germans had been infiltrating into Syria, then under command of General Dentz, who had remained loyal to the Vichy Government. And because it was considered important to prevent Turkey being pinched out from the south, Wavell was ordered to expel them. He, thereupon, detailed the 7th Australian Division, less one brigade in Tobruk, and a formation of Free French to move into Syria from Palestine, and later supported them with the forces which had been operating in Iraq. The advance began on 8th June, was opposed by Dentz and led to some severe fighting; but on 11th July Dentz asked for an armistice, and Syria passed into Allied occupation on the 14th.

Of all the operations of the war, in audacity the air assault on Crete tops the list. Nothing like it had been attempted before, and nothing quite like it has been attempted since. It was not an air attack, it was an airborne attack; the invading army moving through the air instead of over the ground or the sea. Further, it was not decided in the air, it was decided on the ground, and without a land-moving army to assist it. And though without command of the air the assault would have failed, its most remarkable feature was air carriage: the lifting of an army into the air, and thus the dispensing with roads, railways and cross-country movements. Like the Battle of Cambrai in 1917, it was the first of its kind. And, like Cambrai, it pointed to a revolution in tactics.

That the assault on Crete succeeded was due to: (1) The amazing capacity for organization of the Germans, and (2) the equally amazing lack of imagination of the British. The first is to be attributed to hard work, and the second not only to hard luck.

As an example of the first, at the time *The Times* Australian Correspondent wrote:

[24]General Wavell's "Despatch." *Supplement to the London Gazette*, 2nd July, 1946, p. 3437.

"To augment their activity both in the air and on the land the Germans had standing reconnaissances over Crete for twenty-four hours a day . . .

"Never has wireless been used to such an extent as in Crete to control manœuvres. Contact between land forces and aircraft reconnoitring or bombing above them was continuous. The land commander could order out one of the bomber formations to assist him if he needed bomber assistance immediately. He could ask one of the standing reconnaissance aircraft above him where and what the British were doing and get a reply immediately.

"These are the incredible and complete methods of totalitarian air war organized to the nth degree . . ."[25]

As regards the second, Alexander Clifford is right in pointing out that the Battle of Crete was not lost in May, but in November and the following months.[26] In November the island had been occupied, yet no serious attempt was made between then and May to fortify it. During those six months the garrison may have been fully employed; but was it rightly employed? Otherwise, how came it that the three aerodromes were not more securely defended? It would seem that the garrison was looking out to sea and not up into the skies. Was it that the Command was so accustomed to attacks in two dimensions, that the third was overlooked?

This operation also showed the vital need for aircraft-carriers to protect a fleet at sea, which indirectly was pointed out by a writer in the *Hamburger Fremdenblatt*: "The Battle of Crete," he wrote, "as carried out by the air force, has given unquestionable proof that not even the most formidable fleet can operate within the radius of a superior enemy air force for any length of time." But unfortunately the British naval mind was still concentrated on battleships, which throughout the war played an insignificant part compared to carriers. Seldom being able to intervene in battle, these powerful and costly "two-dimensional" vessels, more often than not, became mere targets for third-dimensional attack.

As concerns the British Air Force, unlike the German, it was thinking in terms of the sky and not of the ground. Of strategic bombing, when there was nothing strategic to bomb, unless it were the Greek airfields which, seemingly, were not attacked. Thus, it appears that tactical bombing was overlooked. On this subject, Morehead writes:

"Had Freyberg been able to summon the R.A.F. . . . to bomb the Germans on Maleme, he might have won the field back, but the means of communicating with the R.A.F. Command in Cairo were archaic. An officer from Freyberg's headquarters had to find the R.A.F. group captain

[25] *The Times*, 2nd June, 1941.
[26] *Three Against Rommel*, p. 88.

and bring him back to Freyberg. The R.A.F. officer had then to return to his office to put a message to Cairo into code. Cairo had to decode it and send instructions to the Western Desert bases—by which time it was too late."[27]

This was due to the R.A.F. being separated from the Army. Coming under a separate command, it was not directly under the C.-in-C. This lack of unity of command, begotten of the erroneous theory that strategic bombing is a thing in itself and unrelated to immediate tactical requirements, was right through the war to cost the British Army and Navy dear.

(6) *The Invasion of Russia*

Though, at the time, the conquest of the Balkans and Crete, the advance of Rommel in Libya, the German intrigues in Iraq, Syria and Persia, and finally the treaty of mutual assistance signed between Germany and Turkey at Angora on 18th June, pointed to the Middle East becoming the next theatre of offensive operations, these happenings were no more than the means whereby Hitler sought to secure his rear and right flank before finally changing his line of operations.[28] That they delayed his invasion of Russia is possible, but what is more probable is that, because the German Supreme Command had decided once again to rely on the strategy of annihilation, it was essential that the initial attack should start in the most favourable Russian weather—that is, about the middle of June. According to Arvid Fredborg, a Swedish journalist then in Berlin, the original date was 12th June; but, on account of the Hungarians refusing to march against Russia, for certain minor adjustments, it was put forward to the 22nd. That it came as a political surprise to the Kremlin is unlikely;[29] but that it was a tactical surprise is all but certain. What was the German plan?

[27]*African Trilogy*, p. 156.
[28]Rudolf Hess's flight to England on 10th May also points to this.
[29]*Behind the Steel Wall*, Arvid Fredborg (1944), p. 25. The sequence of preparatory steps taken by Hitler was as follows: (1) On 18th December, 1940, a secret directive was issued to the Chiefs of Service to prepare "to crush Soviet Russia in a quick campaign before the end of the war against England." Preparations to be completed by 15th May, 1941. (2) On 3rd February, 1941, Hitler finally approved the plan, but did not fix a definite date for the attack. (3) On 1st April he decided to launch the attack during the second half of June, and on 6th June he finally fixed 22nd June as the date. (See *Defeat in the West*, pp. 60-61). Ciano, writing on 14th May, says 15th June. (*Ciano Diary*, p. 343.) "At the beginning of 1941 the clash was expected to occur in the course of the year." (*Behind the Steel Wall*, p. 32.) "Reports from travellers in Siberia showed that considerable numbers of Russian soldiers were being transported westward by rail . . ." (*The Seventh Quarter*, p. 126.) General Martel states that the Russians had been warned of the type of attack the Germans were preparing before it was launched. (*Our Armoured Forces*, p. 246.)

It was to put Russia out of the war before England had recovered sufficiently to assist her, and America came in.[30] It was not to occupy the whole of the U.S.S.R.—one-sixth of the land surface of the globe—that was manifestly impossible. Nor was it to occupy the whole of Russia in Europe—less than one-quarter of the U.S.S.R. Instead, it was to deprive Russia of her main vital areas of operation in the west, in order so drastically to reduce her economic power, that militarily she would be impotent *vis-à-vis* Germany once these vital areas were added to the Reich. This meant that the German territorial aim was to push the eastern frontier of the Reich up to the line Leningrad-Moscow-Stalingrad-Astrakhan as a minimum, or to Leningrad-the line of the Volga as a maximum. Either of these acquisitions would deprive Russia of the following vital areas:

(1) Leningrad: a highly industrialized city and the most considerable Baltic port, linked to Murmansk by rail and to Archangel by the Stalin Canal and the White Sea.

(2) Moscow: the centre of the most highly developed industries[31] in Russia; hub of the Russian railways; linked to Archangel by rail, to the Caspian and Black Sea by river and canal, and the terminus of the trans-Siberian railway.

(3) Ukraine and Donetz Basin[32]: a vast agricultural, industrial and mining area. Further, as the Ukraine and Crimea flank the Black Sea, their ports command the direct passage from Constanza in Rumania to Batum in Georgia.

(4) Kuban and Caucasia: the one a rich agricultural country, the other the main oil region in Russia, supplying ninety per cent of her oil, of which seventy per cent came from Baku alone.

To occupy the first three without the fourth was insufficient; for unless Russia was deprived of the bulk of her oil, she would continue to remain a formidable military power. Besides, above all things, Germany lacked oil.

---

[30]The original Directive (No. 21), issued by Hitler on 18th December, 1940, is no more than a general idea. Its vital sections read:

"The German Armed Forces must be prepared *to crush Soviet Russia in a quick campaign* before the end of the war against England . . ."

"The mass of the Russian Army in Western Russia is to be destroyed in daring operations by driving forward deep wedges with tanks, and the retreat of intact battle-ready troops into the wide space of Russia is to be prevented . . .

"In quick pursuit a (given) line is to be reached from where the Russian Air Force will no longer be able to attack German Reich territory. The first goal of operations is protection from Asiatic Russia from the general line Volga-Archangel. In case of necessity the last industrial area in the Urals left to Russia could be eliminated by the *Luftwaffe*." (Quoted from *The Nuremberg Trial*, R. W. Cooper, pp. 98-99.)

[31]Moscow employed over 1,000,000 industrial workers.

[32]Sixty per cent of heavy industries was concentrated here.

Therefore, Caucasia—Russia's primary vital area of operations—was Germany's strategic goal. But before it could be gained, Russian fighting power would first have to be crippled; this was Germany's tactical goal. Therefore the German problem was how to make these two goals coincide.

In examining this problem, let us start with an hypothetical solution before turning to the actual one as revealed by eventual operations; thus we shall give the latter a background to throw it into relief. In outline it is as follows:

(1) To occupy the Middle East and pinch out Turkey.

(2) To operate defensively, but not statically, on the line Riga-Pinsk.

(3) To assume the offensive between Pinsk and the middle Dniester in the direction of Kiev, Kharkov, Stalingrad.

(4) To assume the offensive between Erzerum and Tabriz in the direction Tiflis (Tiblisi) Stalingrad.

(5) Once (3) and (4) meet in the Don area, to transfer the line of communications of the latter to the Black Sea ports and move northwards on Moscow, whilst (2) assumes the offensive and moves eastwards on Moscow.

Clearly, two such vast pincer (Cannæ) operations could not possibly be carried out in a single campaign. They, therefore, could not be based on the strategy which had proved so successful in Poland and France—namely, that of annihilation. Instead, they demanded the strategy of exhaustion: several campaigns, covering two or possibly three summers. Further, they demanded that each campaign be fought in such a way that German fighting power was sufficiently economized to enable the final campaign to be based on the strategy of annihilation. Therefore, in this hypothetical solution the aim of all except the final campaign was not the annihilation of the Russian armies, but instead their immobilization by depriving them of petrol. To strike at oil and not at the enemy's mass, as Napoleon was wont to recommend, was clearly the essence of the problem, because it enabled the tactical and strategical aims to coincide.

In form, something like this hypothetical plan, but in idea very different, because it took no notice of oil, was proposed by the German General Marcks, formerly on the staff of General Schleicher, who was assassinated in the purge of 30th June, 1934. His plan was to assume the defensive from about Riga to the Upper Dniester, and to launch a single great attack from the Dniester in the direction of Rostov, from where he proposed to wheel north on Moscow, and finally fall upon the rear of the Russian armies attacking or opposing the German armies between Riga and the Upper Dniester.

Hitler would not consider this plan, apparently because he wanted to finish off Russia in a single campaign and before the Americans entered the

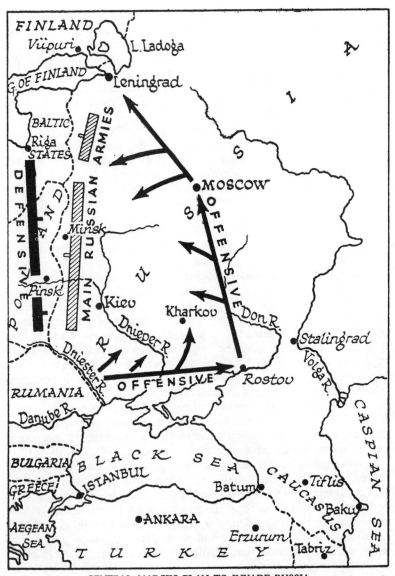

GENERAL MARCKS PLAN TO INVADE RUSSIA

field. This he imagined he could do in one mighty *blitz* operation. It is highly probable that the Russian fiasco in Finland, coupled with his detestation of Bolshevism, had hypnotized him into holding his enemy in such contempt that he expected the force of his blow to smash the Bolshevik regime as well as the Bolshevik armies. If so, then the psychologist ran away with the tactician.

The upshot was that his plan was a half-measure, or rather a mixture of measures. It was:

(1) To march on Leningrad and Moscow, and by forcing the Russians to defend those cities by opposing him, smash them in the field.

(2) To advance on Kiev, Kharkov, Rostov, Stalingrad and occupy the Caucasian oilfields.

(3) Subsidiary to these main operations, to launch an offensive north of Leningrad in conjunction with the Finns, and to launch an offensive from the Upper Pruth in conjunction with the Rumanians.

The operations against Moscow and Kiev may be compared to the fists of a boxer striking alternate blows. Moscow was to be knocked out before winter set in, and if the Russians did not then accept German terms, in the following year Caucasia would be torn from them. Thus, when compared to the hypothetical plan, the cart was placed before the horse. Instead of ending with annihilation, he began with annihilation, and, as we shall see, exhausted the German armies before an annihilating blow could be struck.

To carry out the initial attack, one hundred and twenty-one divisions,[33] of which seventeen were armoured and twelve were motorized, and three air fleets, some 3,000 aircraft in all, were organized in three Army Groups, respectively to operate in the direction of Leningrad, Smolensk and Kiev. These were:

Northern Group: Field-Marshal von Leeb's two armies under Generals Busch and Küchler, and one armoured group of four divisions commanded by General Höppner.

Central Group: Field-Marshal von Bock's three armies under Field-Marshal von Kluge and Generals Strauss and Weichs, and two armoured groups of ten divisions commanded by Generals Guderian and Hoth.

Southern Group: Field-Marshal von Rundstedt's two armies under General Stülpnagel and Field-Marshal von Reichenau, and a German-Rumanian army under General von Schobert, also one armoured group of four divisions commanded by General von Kleist.

Opposed to these army groups were from north to south the army groups

---

[33] *The Nuremberg Trial*, p. 102. This number was rapidly increased to 200 divisions.

of Marshals Voroshilov, Timoshenko and Budyonny, as of yet unknown strength.

It must not be supposed that the opposing forces were deployed on a continuous front. Instead, each front consisted of a chain of powerful groups linked together by their respective air forces, which in both cases co-operated closely with the ground forces and seldom indulged in strategical bombing on British lines.

The main strength of the Russians lay in the superiority of their reserves, their main weakness was in their command, which played into the hands of their enemy by deploying too many troops close to the frontier. Being on the defensive, their idea was to stop the Germans, when it should have been to counter-attack them once their momentum began to peter out. As attackers, the Germans had the advantage of being able to select their points of attack. Their tactics consisted in pinching out sections of the Russian front by double envelopments.

On Sunday morning, 22nd June—the day Napoleon crossed the Niemen in 1812 and abdicated in 1815—Hitler launched his mechanized armies over that same river.

Heralded by violent bombing attacks on the Russian airfields, the assault was made at dawn, and during the first week of the invasion von Leeb's and von Bock's army groups swept forward at an astonishing speed. On the 26th it was announced that two Soviet armies east of Bialystok had been surrounded; on the 30th that Riga had fallen, then Grodno, Brest-Litovsk and Minsk, and on 16th July—the twenty-fifth day of the assault—that von Bock was fighting in the outskirts of Smolensk, five hundred miles east of Warsaw and two-thirds of the way from Warsaw to Moscow.

Nevertheless, things were not going the way they had gone in Poland and France. Though outwardly the *blitz* was succeeding beyond measure, strangely enough there was little or no panic within and behind the Russian front. Already on 29th June, there appeared an article in the *Völkischer Beobachter* pointing out that "The Russian soldier surpasses our adversary in the West in his contempt for death. Endurance and fatalism make him hold out until he is blown up with his trench or falls in hand-to-hand fighting." On 6th July a somewhat similar article appeared in the *Frankfurter Zeitung*, in which it was stated that "The mental paralysis which usually follows after the lightning German break-throughs in the West did not occur to the same extent in the East. In most cases the enemy did not lose his capacity for action, but tried in his turn to envelop the arms of the German pincers." This was something new in the tactics of the war; in fact for the Germans a surprising novelty, which, later on in September, was explained as follows in the first of the above two newspapers: "At the

THE INVASION OF RUSSIA, 22nd JUNE–7th DECEMBER, 1941

German crossing of the Bug the first waves of the attack were in places able to advance quite freely: then suddenly a murderous fire was opened on the succeeding waves at the same moment that their predecessors were fired upon from the rear. One can but praise such remarkably fine discipline which enabled the defenders to hold a position which was already as good as lost."[34]

The long and the short of it was that, as Arvid Fredborg points out: "The German soldier had met an enemy who with fanatical toughness stuck to *his* political creed and who, against the German *blitz* attack, put up total resistance."[35]

Soon it became apparent that the Russians had not deployed the whole of their armies on the frontier, as the Germans expected they would do. And soon it was discovered that they themselves had profoundly misjudged the strength of the Russian reserves. Hitherto the German Intelligence had largely relied on Fifth Column assistance. In Russia, though there were to be found discontented people, there was no Fifth Column. Difficulties rapidly multiplied as they generally do in war. Some had been foreseen. For instance, that the Russian railways would have to be changed to the Continental standard gauge. Though the German engineers were prepared for this, the advance was so rapid that they could not keep pace with it. Again, though the vast open plains of Russia facilitated encircling movements, Russia was an indifferent motoring country. The roads were few and generally bad. Little stone could be obtained locally to repair them, and once the roads began to founder supply columns were delayed. Soon it was found that speed under such conditions was a boomerang turning space into a weapon, and though that weapon did not kill men, it "killed" and "wounded" the vehicles which carry the things men live on and fight with. Thus, during the first month of the invasion, the Germans found themselves faced by the strategy of exhaustion, woven on space, climate and a factor they were in no way prepared to meet—the trained partisan.

"The Russians," writes Fredborg, "had prepared for it (partisan warfare) for years, had accumulated supplies of ammunition, arms and food, installed radio stations, and trained their soldiers systematically in partisan tactics. When the regular army retreated the partisans immediately went to work . . . obviously operating on lines of high strategy. They concentrated on important centres and had their own bases in areas which they left in peace."[36]

---

[34]Quoted from *The Eighth Quarter*, p. 49.   [35]*Behind the Steel Wall*, p. 42.
[36]*Ibid.*, p. 45. It was the partisans and not the regular soldiers who rendered the war in Russia, Yugoslavia and elsewhere so brutal. The civil populations becoming involved, atrocities were committed on both sides. Had not this occurred, in Fredborg's opinion, "The general situation might certainly have developed into a European campaign against the danger from the East."

Though a series of *blitzkrieg* operations, the invasion was nevertheless methodical. In the centre it opened with a vast pincer (Cannæ) movement by von Bock's group of armies, its left advancing from Tilsit via Vilna and Molodechno, and its right from Warsaw via Brest-Litovsk, both converging on Minsk. On 10th July the Germans announced a complete victory and claimed 323,000 prisoners.[37]

From Minsk, von Bock pushed on to the Beresina—part of the semi-mythical Stalin Line. Its strength lay in its marshes and not in its works. Turning it on its right, between Lepel and Vitebsk, Bock's advanced guards reached the outskirts of Smolensk on 16th July. A gigantic tank battle for Smolensk then followed, lasting until 7th August. Though the Germans claimed 300,000 prisoners, their losses were so heavy that the Moscow time table was upset, and at Smolensk they remained on the defensive until 2nd October.

Simultaneously with the opening of the Minsk operation, von Rundstedt's left wing crossed the Carpathians and advanced eastwards, Budyonny falling back on Lutsk, Brody, Tarnopol and Chernowitz. However, not until 5th July did Rundstedt's right wing cross the Pruth. Both advances were purposely slow, and by the time Smolensk was reached the Russians were still on the west side of their 1939 frontier.

Speeding up his left wing, by the end of July fierce fighting took place about Novograd Volynsk, and by 10th August, the front had shifted east to Korosten, Zhitomir and Kazatin. To the south, between the 10th and 12th, the first great victory was won at Uman. Meanwhile, his right wing occupied Odessa, and von Kleist's tanks seized Nikolaiev. Swinging north from there, Kleist next occupied Krivoi Rog; whereupon, on 24th August, the Russians blew up the great Dnieper dam at Zaporozhe. Kiev holding out, von Rundstedt asked to be reinforced.

While von Bock was refitting at Smolensk, von Leeb was reinforced; whereupon he pushed his offensive through Estonia on to Narva and Pskov, which places he took on 20th August. Ten days later, to the north of him Field-Marshal Mannerheim, commanding the Finnish Army, occupied Viborg (Viipuri).

To the south of Smolensk von Weichs' army and Guderian's tank army advanced on Gomel, from where, on 20th August, they moved on Chernigov. This advance compelled the Russians north of Korosten, where they were covering Kiev, to fall back. At the same time, south of Kiev, von Reichenau's army reached the Dnieper at Cherkasi, and further south still, von Kleist's tanks advanced from Dnepropetrovsk to Kremenchug.

---

[37]As yet it is impossible to verify the German claims. When they were winning their claims, like those of the Russians, were frequently astronomical.

Thus, between 1st and 14th September was developed the mightiest operation of the whole campaign, the pinching out of Kiev, Guderian advancing on Nyeshin and Kleist on Lubni. On 14th September, Guderian and Kleist joined hands at Lokvitsa—one hundred and twenty miles east of Kiev.

In this vast encirclement the Germans claimed 665,000 prisoners, and whatever the correct figure may be, there can be little doubt that Budyonny's losses were catastrophic. What remained of his army withdrew eastwards, and, von Rundstedt following up, at the end of October he occupied the line Kursk-Kharkov-Stalino-Taganrog.

On the 30th of that month Field-Marshal von Manstein stormed the Isthmus of Perekop; advancing into the Crimea, he was held up before Sevastopol. On 11th November Kleist's tanks occupied Rostov; this completed the campaign in the south. Meanwhile the Russian commanders were reshuffled, Timoshenko replacing Budyonny in the Ukraine, and General Zhukov Timoshenko on the Moscow front.

Since mid-September, von Bock had been reinforced by forty-eight infantry divisions and twelve armoured, Guderian returning to him. In all he could now marshal about 1,500,000 men, and on 2nd October he set out for Moscow.

Weichs' and Guderian's armies advanced from about Gomel on Orel; Kluge's from Roslavl on Kaluga; two other armies from Smolensk on Vyazma and Rzhev with the German Ninth Army on their left flank.

This forward movement was opened on the right by the great tank battle of Trubehevsk, followed by a rapid advance on Orel. At Bryansk another considerable victory was won. Vyazma and Rzhev were taken and Medin and Tula occupied. By 15th October German armoured divisions stormed Mozhaisk—sixty-five miles west of Moscow—then their momentum petered out, and before the forces closing in on Moscow could be cranked up again, winter coming three weeks earlier than usual, the Germans were faced by an insuperable problem. Bogged in the mud of the Nara and Oka, entangled in the forests and swamps between Kalinin (Tver) and Klin (north-west of Moscow), after desperate fighting, on 5th December the last assault petered out at Klin, some thirty-five miles west of Moscow. Whereupon the very next day Marshal Zhukov vigorously counterattacked. To cover their failure, on the 8th the German Supreme Command announced that "Warfare in the East will henceforth be conditioned by the arrival of the Russian winter."

Meanwhile, von Leeb attacked Leningrad in mid-September and was repulsed. Capturing Schlüsselburg (key-citadel), thirty miles to its east, he invested the city.

Strategically the campaign had failed. The Russian armies, though severely mauled, had not been destroyed; Moscow had not been captured; the railway to Archangel had not been cut; Leningrad had not been taken; and the Caucasian oilfields were still far away. Nevertheless, the Russians had been dealt a staggering blow, and but for the unexpected early winter would probably have lost Moscow. On 6th December, 1941, the chances of victory or defeat were odds even.

Considering—in order of importance—the enormous administrative difficulties which faced the Germans; the indifference of the Russian roads; the unexpected resistance met with; the miscalculations made over the Russian reserves, and that at no time it would seem the Germans had more than twenty-five armoured divisions, the advance between 22nd June and 6th December was an astonishing feat of arms. In the main it was due to the skilful use the Germans made of the Cannæ manœuvre.

Some of the salients they forced their enemy into were enormous. The Minsk pocket was two hundred and fifty miles deep with both sides nearly as long. And when the manœuvre started, the northern flank of the Kiev pocket was one hundred and twenty miles in length, its snout sixty, and its southern flank two hundred and forty—that is, as extensive as the whole of the Western Front in France stretching from Douai to Mantes (thirty miles north-west of Paris) to Pithiviers (thirty miles south of Paris) and thence to within a few miles of Basle. Therefore, even should Russian staunchness be discounted, it is understandable why fighting in these great pockets was prolonged: they were minor theatres of war rather than battlefields.

That these boxing-up tactics were sometimes incomplete must largely be attributed to lack of cross-country transport. The bulk of the German supply vehicles ran on wheels and not on tracks; therefore the supply columns were tied to the roads, whereas the tanks they supplied were not. This limitation is in itself sufficient to account for the loss of momentum in November, when the roads began to founder. In all probability, it was not so much the resistance of the Russians—great though it was—or the effect of the weather on the *Luftwaffe*, as the bogging of the transport behind the German front which saved Moscow.

The influences of this campaign were enormous. Up to the battle of Smolensk it looked so likely to achieve its aim that, should Russia fall, in order to provide America with a pretext to intervene, not as a belligerent but as a mediator, the Atlantic Charter was brandished before the world.

The campaign gave Britain the breathing space she required, both at home and in the Middle East, wherein to set her military house in order. Egypt was relieved from the threat of war on two fronts, and General Auchinleck, who had now replaced Wavell, could henceforth concentrate his attention on one. In America, the gullibility of the people was exploited by President Roosevelt and the war party. The attack on Russia was proclaimed to be the stepping-stone to an attack on the United States. How? was not explained; nevertheless, this absurdity enabled the Administration to double its armament programme.

Further, the failure to take Moscow put new heart into the occupied countries where—particularly so in Yugoslavia under Mihailovich—the exploits of the Russian partisans became an example to follow. Thus were the brutalities of guerilla warfare fortified in Europe, and with them also the brutalities of the German Gestapo. Added to these things, when winter set in, people in Germany began to whisper of defeat. Such was the first small crack in the plaster of the German home front, and though barely visible, it was none the less a portent that foundations might be sinking.

Lastly of all its influences, those on the German Army and its Command were the most disastrous. The first never recovered the vigour it lost, and, in the eyes of the world, it was no longer the invincible army. The second was literally annihilated. First, on or about 19th December, Hitler dismissed his Commander-in-Chief, Field-Marshal von Brauchitsch, and General Halder, his Chief of Staff, who had disapproved of the entire autumn campaign, and himself assumed personal command with Generals Jodl and Zeitzler as his assistants. Secondly, Field-Marshals von Rundstedt, Ritter von Leeb, von Bock and List, as well as Generals Guderian and von Kleist, for the time being lost their commands. Such a pogrom of Generals had not been seen since the Battle of the Marne.

CHAPTER IV

JAPANESE INITIATIVE, ITS INITIAL SUCCESSES AND FAILURE

(1) *Strategical Conditions*

In the Far East, as in the West, the causes of war were mainly economic, and this particularly applies to Japan. Before her compulsory awakening by Admiral Perry in 1853, Japan was a self-sufficient land. After it, she rapidly became Westernized—that is, industrialized—and, like Germany, lacking in basic resources, she set out to seek them beyond her borders. Hence her steady march along the road of Imperialism.

Between 1875 and 1879 she acquired the Kurile, Bonin and Ryukyu Islands, and in 1891 the Volcano group. Next, in her war with China, in 1894-1895, she obtained Formosa, the Pescadores and Port Arthur, but lost the last through pressure brought to bear on her by Russia, Germany and France. In 1905, after her victorious war with Russia, she regained that strategic outpost, received from Russia the southern half of the island of Sakhalin and obtained control over Korea. In 1910, she finally annexed Korea, and in 1919, with the exception of Guam, was granted as mandated territories the Mariana, Caroline and Marshall Islands.

Overwhelmed in the great slump of 1929, even more so than most industrial countries, two years later she set out to short cut prosperity by invading Manchuria, which country she converted into a satrapy under the name of Manchukuo. This brought her into conflict with the Chinese, and on 7th July, 1937, crossing the Marco Polo bridge, near Peking, she invaded China. Like Germany, her aim was to establish a *Lebensraum*—a New Economic Order—which she called "The Great East Asia Co-Prosperity Sphere." Its purpose was to make her the sun of an economic planetary system extending from Manchukuo to Australia and from the Fiji Islands to the Bay of Bengal.

By 1941, Japan found herself so completely bogged in China that either she would have to call the war off or else cut the supply lines of her enemy. The latter demanded the closing of the Indo-China ports and the severance of the Burma Road from Lashio to Chungking.[1] This meant war with

---

[1] A third line, that from Tihua to Sian—1,200 miles in length—supplied China from the U.S.S.R. It was a highly uneconomical line as vast amounts of petrol had to be carried for the journey.

Britain, and, almost certainly, also with the United States who, throughout, had been financing China.

France, since her defeat, being unable to protect Indo-China, on 21st July, 1941, agreed to its temporary occupation by Japan. Three days later Japanese warships appeared off Camranh Bay, and, to call a halt, on the next day President Roosevelt announced the freezing of Japanese assets and credits in the U.S.A.—about £33,000,000 in value—and Britain, besides doing the same, renounced her commercial treaties of 1911, 1934 and 1937 with Japan. Soon after the Netherlands joined America and Britain.

This was a declaration of economic war, and, in consequence, it was the actual opening of the struggle. On 20th October, the new Japanese Government under General Tojo proposed a lifting of the embargo and that the United States should supply Japan with oil and cease assisting China. Obviously, these impossible proposals were put forward because Japan had already made up her mind to break the blockade by force. At the time the United States were unprepared but preparing, Britain had her hands full in Africa and the Atlantic, and Germany's rapid advance on Moscow appeared to herald Russia's speedy defeat. As we think, Ian Morrison, who knew the Japanese at first-hand, is right when he observes: "Japan went to war because she could not do anything else"[2] if she were to remain a great industrial power. The disease of the West was in her bones; she could not throw it out and live industrially. Her choice was between two evils—both gigantic. She decided to follow the one she considered the lesser—war rather than economic ruin. When eventually she struck, the Commanders-in-Chief of her Army and Navy issued a joint Order of the Day in which the following words are to be found:

"They (America and Britain) have obstructed by every means our peaceful commerce, and finally have resorted to the direct severance of economic relations, menacing gravely the existence of our Empire.

"This trend of world affairs would, if left unchecked, not only nullify our Empire's efforts of many years for the sake of the stabilization of eastern Asia, but also endanger the very existence of our nation. The situation being such as it is, our Empire for its existence and self-defence has no other recourse but to appeal to arms . . ."[3]

Having decided on war, what type of war could Japan most profitably wage?

Though well placed to overrun both British and American possessions, she was powerless to strike at the British and American homelands.

[2]*Malayan Postscript*, Ian Morrison (1942), pp. 45-46.
[3]*Ibid.*, p. 51.

Therefore, at most, Japan could only hope for a limited victory.

In the wars of 1894 and 1904 she had been faced by a similar problem. Though in the one she could not conquer China, nor in the other Russia, she had won both. Could she win this time?

In both these wars her success had been due to her ability to use her sea power in such a way that she avoided an unlimited conflict.[4] In both, because of her naval supremacy, she was able to seize limited territorial objectives, and then challenge her enemy to retake them, knowing that he was incapable of doing so, because his naval power could not challenge hers. Even if in the end the improbable occurred and Germany were defeated after defeating Russia, would not Britain be too exhausted to put much punch into yet another gigantic campaign, and by then, though it would still be impossible for Japan to knock out America, could not she establish herself in so strong a defensive position that the Americans would prefer to negotiate peace rather than continue a war which might last for many years?

To make as sure as she could of a long war, Japan would not only have to extend her conquests to include the Dutch East Indies in order to render herself economically strong enough to sustain it, but also she would have to push them deep into the Pacific, so as to deny sea and air bases to the Americans. Were she to do this, what, then, would her enemy's position be? A few figures will answer this question:

San Francisco to Honolulu is 2,400 miles, and London to Colombo is 5,600. Honolulu is 5,600 from Manila, and Colombo is 1,580 from Singapore. Singapore to Yokohama is 3,020, and Manila, via Shanghai, to Yokohama, is 2,160. Approximately 10,000 miles each way—that is, 20,000 miles of Anglo-American sea communications!

What do these figures mean logistically? Whereas a ship to make the return trip to England from east coast ports of the United States takes sixty-five days, a return trip for a ship sailing from England or the United States to Burma or China ports takes from five to six months. Further, the shipping needed for the initial landing and thirty days' maintenance of a force of 250,000 men, and several such forces would be required, is approximately 2,000,000 tons, and for every additional thirty days' maintenance this force will require 350,000 tons, or thirty to thirty-five Liberty ships and fifteen tankers. Because not many ports in the Far East can handle so much shipping, they will have to be rebuilt. This means more shipping.

Japan knew that the United States had not got anything like this

[4]See Herbert Rosinski's article "Strategy of Fear" in *Infantry Journal*, June, 1946.

shipping, and that British shipping was daily being sunk in the Atlantic and Mediterranean. She also knew that, even were her enemies able to build it, these thousands of ships would require thousands of aircraft to protect them, and that they did not yet exist. Also she knew that without advanced bases neither ships nor aircraft could operate.

As a staff exercise, therefore, the Japanese problem of limiting the war appeared not an insuperable one. Were they to deny to the British the use of Singapore, if not of Colombo as well, and were they to deny to the

JAPAN'S STRATEGIC DEFENSIVE

Americans the use of Manila, if not also of Honolulu: and simultaneously were they to push deep into the Pacific, they would establish a defence of such depth that in any former war it would have been considered impregnable, or at least one which would hold an enemy at bay for years. Thus it would appear that the Japanese High Command painted a picture of the war from sketches of previous wars. They thought backwards instead of forwards, and, in consequence, committed the common error of assuming that the history of war would repeat itself, and that the limited victories of 1895 and 1905 would be theirs again.

If this be correct, then they were guilty of a gross miscalculation. In the first of the above two wars they had attacked an enemy whose fleet was beneath contempt, and in the second an enemy whose sea power could be destroyed in detail. Now they set out to challenge not only the two greatest naval, but also the two greatest industrial powers in the world, one of whom, the United States, could not possibly be crippled even were Germany to win the war in Europe. A power whose industrial potentials were so vast that, in time, they could overcome all strategical obstacles of space and distance. A power which they should have known would choose to overcome them, and at whatever cost rather than negotiate a limited peace. Of all Japan's blunders, this was the greatest: she believed that America would be willing to barter "losing face" for a short war, when she herself was willing to risk her very existence in a long war rather than "lose face" by withdrawing from China.

Except for this psychological error, the Japanese read their strategical positions aright, and exploited to the fullest the advantages it conferred upon them. Because their aim was a limited one, they had no intention of fighting a naval war on unlimited lines—that is, to seek out their enemy's fleet and destroy it in a decisive battle. Instead, seeing that air power enabled them to convert their 2,500 insignificant islands in the Pacific into a gigantic fleet of "anchored aircraft carriers," the sea gap between any two being in no case more than five hundred miles wide, they decided to wage a war of amphibious operations. And, as we shall see, their eventual advance in the Pacific was in nearly every case covered by land-based and not carrier-borne aircraft. In short, the central tactical idea in their strategic plan was to gain air bases and not to fight pitched battles. Their strategy was, therefore, essentially one of exhaustion, and in spite of their tactics frequently being annihilative.

That they opened their offensive with a powerful carrier-borne air attack on the American fleet in Pearl Harbour, in no way contradicts this, because it may be compared to the preliminary artillery bombardment of an infantry battle. It was a subsidiary operation, the purpose of which was to open the way for the main operation. In fact, it was little more than counter-battery fire.

The essential part of the plan was to acquire Burma, Malaya, Sumatra, Java and Borneo, because these acquisitions would make Japan self-supporting as an industrial power. Further, they would compensate her for any withdrawal she might eventually have to make in China.

To gain these, it was essential during the war to occupy the Philippines, Celebes and New Guinea, in order to secure their eastern flank, and also to have something to barter with the United States for a negotiated peace, should this become necessary.

Further, in order to protect this flanking position, it was equally essential to establish east of it as strong an outpost line as possible, so as to be able to barter space for time, and draw the war out to what her enemy might be brought to consider an unprofitable length.

The outpost line may be compared to an entrenched zone: the front line running southwards from Paramushiro, the northernmost of the Kurile Islands, to Wake Island, and thence by way of the Marshall and Gilbert to the Ellice Islands, from where it swung westwards along the Solomons through New Guinea, and thence by way of Timor, Java and Sumatra to Northern Burma. Behind it the reserve line ran from the Bonin Islands (Magelhaes Archipelago) to the Mariana Islands (Ladrone), including Guam, then to Yap, Palau (Pelew) Morotai, Halmahera and Amboina to Timor, where it joined the outpost or outer line. Connecting these two lines, like a communication trench, ran the Caroline Islands from the Palau eastwards to the Marshall and Gilbert Islands. A trench which also flanked the American central Pacific line of approach running from the Hawaii Islands via Midway, Wake and Guam to Manila in Luzon.

The offensive operations were divided into two parts. The Japanese Army was given primary responsibility for the conquest of Malaya, Burma, Sumatra and Luzon, and the Navy was given primary responsibility for the raid on Pearl Harbour in the island of Oahu, and the conquest of the Southern Philippines, Borneo, Celebes, Java, New Guinea, Bismark, Solomon, Gilbert, Guam and Wake Islands. Speed was to be the dominant factor and, therefore, aircraft the dominant arm.

From the air power point of view, Japan had two overwhelming initial advantages: (1) Numerical air superiority at the start, and (2) that her air force was integrated with her navy and army, and was, therefore, not looked upon as an independent "strategic" weapon.

When, on 7th December, 1941, she struck, she had 2,625 aircraft operating with her army and fleet, earmarked for operations as follows: For Malaya, 700; for the Philippines, 475; for China, 150; for Manchuria (in reserve), 450; in Japan, 325; for the Marshall Islands, 50; for the Pearl Harbour raid, 400; and for the fleet (seaplanes), 75.[5]

Opposed to these were: U.S. Navy and Army Air Forces in the Philippines, 182 aircraft; Wake, 12; Midway, 12; Hawaii, 387; Royal Netherlands East Indies Air Forces, 200; R.A.F. in Malaya, 332; and Royal Australian Air Force in Australia, Solomons and Malaya, 165. In all 1,290[6]; but most of these planes were of obsolete types.

---

[5] *United States Bombing Survey, Summary Report (Pacific War)*, 1946, pp. 2-3.
[6] *Ibid.*, p. 3. In Malaya only 141 were fit for war.

(2) *Surprise of Pearl Harbour and the Philippines Campaign*

Few acts in history are more typical of the limitations of the military mind than the surprise attack on Pearl Harbour. On the one hand it displayed a low cunning of incredible stupidity, and on the other a lack of imagination of unbelievable profundity. We see on the one side a nation whose only hope lay in a war which would exhaust its enemy, and on the other a nation the bulk of whose people did not want war though their leader did. Therefore, should war be inevitable, then clearly the first step towards establishing a condition in which exhaustion could germinate was to force that leader to declare war against the will of the majority of his people. This might have been done had Japan sedulously avoided attacking any American possession until the United States had either committed a direct act of war or declared war upon her. Had President Roosevelt adopted the second course—the more probable of the two—then in the mind of the American people his reason for doing so could not have been other than to pull the British chestnuts out of the fire. In other words, to save the British Empire, which, however carefully the pretext was camouflaged, would not have been highly popular. Instead, by launching an undeclared war on the United States, at one blow Japan solved all Roosevelt's difficulties by galvanizing every American to his support. Her inexplicable stupidity was that, by making the Americans the laughing stock of the world, she struck more at their dignity than at their ships. Like Adam and Eve, the Americans discovered that they were naked; their eyes were most unexpectedly opened, and they suddenly realized that they had been living in a fool's paradise of their own making. That though, nearly five months before, they had declared an economic war on Japan, which, in the circumstances she was placed in, inevitably must lead to an armed conflict, they had been so lacking in imagination that like a greenhorn they had been thimble-rigged. Thirty-seven years before, Japan had played the same trick on Port Arthur, and since 1939 they had watched Hitler perform it time and again. Now they had been tricked themselves. Therefore, not because their ships had been sunk, but because they had been fooled, their dignity dictated that, however long the war might last, there could be no compromise with the trickster.

When the attack—literally out of the blue—was made on Pearl Harbour and the Hickman and Wheeler airfields on the island of Oahu at 7.50 a.m. (local time) on 7th December, the American warships were for the most part moored side by side; the troops were in barracks; many naval officers and ratings were away on leave; no protective screen of light craft had been thrown out, and the morning being cloudy the dawn air patrol had seen nothing.

The attackers came in in three waves. The first bore down on the ships, airfields and barracks; whereupon the Japanese Fifth Column on the island set to work.[7] This attack, as also the second, was little opposed, but when, at 9.15 a.m., the third wave came in, it was met by so heavy a fire from ships and shore that it was beaten back. Nevertheless, terrific damage was done. Of eight battleships, the *Arizona* was wrecked, the *Oklahoma* capsized, and three others were so badly damaged that they were resting on the bottom. In all, nineteen ships were hit; but fortunately for the Americans, at the time none of their aircraft-carriers was in harbour. Of the 202 Navy aircraft only 52 were able to take the air; 2,795 officers and men were killed, 879 wounded and 25 missing. It would appear that in all from six carriers the Japanese launched some 360 planes, of which, according to Admiral King, 60 were shot down.[8]

Simultaneously the islands of Guam and Wake were attacked. Both were but weakly garrisoned, and after severe fighting were overwhelmed. Midway Island was also attacked, but unsuccessfully.

The results of this surprisal were that, instead of the Japanese founding conditions in which strategically the war might be limited, they most successfully created a political situation which rendered it absolute. The war now assumed world-wide dimensions. Not only did these surprisals, coupled with those in the Far East, bring the United States, Britain and the Netherlands into conflict with Japan, but they also made Australia, New Zealand, South Africa, Canada, the Central American Republics and several of the South American States her enemies. Mexico broke off diplomatic relations with Germany and Italy; Italy and Germany declared war on the United States; and the sole greater power whose position remained unchanged was Russia, who maintained her neutrality towards Japan and did not even break off trade relations with her.

Before leaving this subject, it may well be asked: Seeing that Pearl Harbour itself was of far greater value to the United States than the fleet it sheltered, why did not the Japanese attempt to occupy the Hawaiian Islands or at least Oahu?

According to Mr. Rosinski, this question was examined by Admiral Yamamoto, the Japanese Commander-in-Chief, and turned down because it was considered that "For the purpose of keeping the United States from intervening during the first critical six months a crippling blow at the Pacific Fleet was enough. As the stepping-stone to an attack upon the United States themselves the Hawaiian Islands were useless to them,

[7] There were 157,000 Japanese inhabitants on the Hawaiian Islands, and according to Colonel Knox, Secretary for the U.S. Navy, "the most effective Fifth Column work of the entire war was done at Hawaii with the possible exception of Norway."

[8] *The United States News*, "Our Navy at War." Official Report by Admiral Ernest J. King, C.-in-C. U.S. Fleet, p. 7.

because such an attack was far beyond anything they could hope to propose to themselves."[9]

Accepting this as correct, then Yamamoto was no great strategist. It was not the value of the Hawaiian Islands as a Japanese base from which to attack the United States which should have struck him; instead, it was their value as an American base to attack Japan from. The whole question was in fact not an offensive but a defensive one—namely, to occupy the islands and either hold them as long as possible, or anyhow sufficiently long to permit of their naval facilities being destroyed.

Therefore, a more likely answer would appear to be that, in spite of the damage they reckoned to effect by the raid, the Japanese Naval Command realized that it would not be sufficient to warrant an occupation other than by means of a large-scale amphibious operation in which so many ships were likely to be lost that their other operations would be crippled. Relative to this, it should be remembered that the powerful coastal batteries rimming the island of Oahu had not been put out of action and that the land forces on the island, though disorganized, were still powerful. Even the tiny island of Wake, defended by 378 marines with twelve planes and six 5-inch guns, put seven Japanese warships out of action and held out for sixteen days.

Of the other Japanese operations, simultaneously launched on 7th December, the two most extensive were the invasions of the Philippines and Malaya, the first representing the left wing of the main attack.

At the time, the Philippines were garrisoned by 19,000 U.S. Army troops, 12,000 Philippine Scouts, and approximately 100,000 men of the newly-raised and partially-equipped Philippine Army. Included in these forces were 8,000 Army Air Force personnel equipped with about 200 aircraft, of which 35 were heavy bombers and 107 fighters. The whole of the garrison was under the command of General Douglas MacArthur.

As at Pearl Harbour, the Japanese surprise attack under General Homma was heralded by a systematic bombing of the airfields and key points in the island of Luzon, which resulted in the immediate destruction on the ground of about fifty per cent of the American aircraft. Next, from 10th December onwards landings were made, first on the north coast of Luzon at Aparri, then at Vigan, Legaspi and other places. Because it was impossible to meet these various attacks, MacArthur withdrew his forces to the Bataan Peninsula, between Subic and Manila Bays; the entrance to the latter was guarded by the island fortress of Corregidor. There, one of his main difficulties was the feeding of thousands of refugees who had followed the army. Though attempts were made to run the Japanese sea and air blockade, it proved so costly that it had to be abandoned, and on

---

[9] "Strategy of Fear," Herbert Rosinski, *Infantry Journal*, June, 1946, p. 27.

THE INVASION OF THE PHILIPPINES, 7th DECEMBER, 1941,-5th MAY, 1942

11th January, 1942, the garrison was reduced to half rations. Meanwhile from 1st January onwards to 10th February, fierce attacks were launched by the Japanese.

On 22nd February General MacArthur was instructed to hand the garrison over to Lieut.-General J. N. Wainwright, and then proceed by air to Australia and there assume command of the newly-created South-West Pacific Area.

In April the end came. "The Japs," writes Clark Lee, "took their time and brought in their reinforcements and brought their planes back (from Malaya), about the end of March. Meanwhile our forces, which a few weeks before had been confident of final victory, were running out of food, medicine and bullets, and out of hope, too.

"The Japs called in General Yamashita, who had blitzed Malaya and Singapore. On 1st April, with his reinforced troops, Yamashita struck. His planes hit everywhere at once. His troops smashed against our front all along the line. They landed on the cliffs on the China Sea coast and simultaneously on the level east coast of Manila Bay. They attacked everywhere in that final terrible assault.

"For eight days our forces held: the young Filipinos, the veteran Scouts, the survivors of the 31st Infantry, the aviators without airplanes.

"Then the battle of Bataan was ended."[10]

Corregidor continued to hold out until 5th May, when the Japanese, under intense air bombardment, effected a landing on the island, and the fortress fell.

An interesting point in these operations was the Japanese invasion tactics, which were uniformly employed throughout the war. The actual landing of troops was carried out in maximum force. Transports were escorted to the beaches by cruisers and destroyers, and special landing barges were used, designed to carry not only infantry, but also artillery, tanks and heavy equipment. Once ashore, the invaders concentrated on the enemy airfields, sometimes assisted by parachute troops. Fighters and dive-bombers were then flown to the airfields, and from them they protected the main landings. Each successful landing prepared the way for the next. Generally speaking, the leaps made, and particularly so in the island to island advances, were too short to permit of enemy naval interference while the invading forces were *en route*.

(3) *The Malayan Campaign and the Fall of Singapore*

Simultaneous with the invasion of the Philippines came the invasion of Malaya and the assault on Hong Kong. The latter, one of the greatest ports

[10]"Battle for Bataan," Clark Lee, *Infantry Journal*, April, 1943, pp. 22-23.

in the British Empire, was doomed from the start. Not only was there no airfield on the island, but its garrison of six infantry battalions and a volunteer force was totally inadequate to hold the Kowloon Peninsula—upon which the sole airfield was located, that of Kai Tak—because its land frontier was over fifty miles in length. Further, both Kowloon and Hong Kong were densely populated, 735,000 people inhabiting the one and 709,000 the other. On 12th December, the surrender of Hong Kong was demanded and rejected. On the night of the 18th-19th the Japanese invaded the island, and on Christmas Day its garrison capitulated.

Very different were conditions in Malaya and Singapore. The former, from the Isthmus of Kra—thirty miles across—to Cape Rumenia is seven hundred and fifty miles in length, and at the time the island of Singapore was universally held to be the strongest naval fortress in the world—£60,000,000 had been spent upon its defences. Nearly three-quarters of British Malaya was tropical jungle and considered to be all but impassable for organized military forces of any size. Communications in the peninsula were few. A single railway followed the west coast from Singapore to the Siamese frontier, with a loop line from Gemas to Kota Bharu, from where it crossed the frontier and rejoined the main line a little to the west of Singora. A good road ran down the west coast, but on the east coast communications were largely non-existent. This led to most of the fighting taking place on the former coast, though the landings were made on the latter. The population, 5,250,000 in all, was a mixture of Malayans, Chinese and Indians, 700,000 of whom inhabited Singapore, and of these seventy-five per cent was Chinese. They were so strongly disliked by the Malayans that the latter felt that "the British had sold their country out to the Chinese."[11] This, it would appear, is the true explanation why, when the Japanese landed, they found a ready-made Fifth Column to assist them.

Basing their air forces on the numerous airfields in Indo-China, on 7th December Japanese troops crossed the Indo-Chinese frontier near Siemrep, while others, convoyed in transports under naval escort, landed at Singora and Patani, both having airfields. At the same time a Japanese fleet appeared off the mouth of the Menam River, and landing troops, Bangkok was occupied on the 8th. After a token resistance, on the 21st the Siamese Government signed a treaty of alliance with Japan.

When these operations were under way, the northern airfields in British Malaya were obliterated, and, according to Ian Morrison, "For every British plane destroyed in the air over Malaya there must have been at least four destroyed on the ground."[12] Docks were also bombed, particularly those of Singapore, but communications and bridges were not attacked, presumably because the Japanese did not wish to hinder their own advance.

---

[11]*Malayan Postscript*, p. 31.   [12]*Ibid.*, pp. 93-94.

THE INVASION OF BRITISH MALAYA, 7th DECEMBER, 1941, - 30th JANUARY, 1942

This initial supremacy of their enemy in the air had the identical effect on the British troops that it had had on the French the year before. They had not time morally to accustom themselves to it, as the Germans were able to do later on in the war. The horrors of aerial warfare had been magnified during peace-time, markedly so in England, and now that air warfare had come, terror was exaggerated and in consequence morale suffered.

From Kra, Singora and Patani, by rail or by road, the Japanese pressed southwards. At the same time a detachment crossed the isthmus and seized Point Victoria. This was a grievous loss to the British, because its airfield was the stepping-stone for all aircraft flown from India and Burma to Singapore. Hence onwards, all fighter aircraft for that fortress would have to be sent to it in crates by sea.

On the 8th Singapore experienced its first air raid, and at 1.30 a.m. that day a strong Japanese force landed at Kota Bahru, and after some stiff fighting occupied its airfield.[13]

Two days later came a disaster which above all others unhinged British morale. It was the sinking by air attack of the battleships *Prince of Wales* and *Repulse*.[14] These powerful vessels had been sent out by Mr. Churchill to deter the Japanese going to war, and had arrived at Singapore on 2nd December. "With what mingled emotions," writes Morrison, "we watched the two ships as they steamed majestically to their anchorage off the Naval Base! Those strange grey shapes on the skyline, they were symbols of our new-found strength, concrete expressions of the confidence with which we faced any emergency that might arise in the Pacific. Singapore's potential naval significance was at last becoming reality."[15]

On the 9th they stood out from Singapore eastwards to intercept a falsely reported Japanese landing at Kuantan. The morning was cloudy, but when off Kuantan it began to clear, and as it did they were suddenly attacked by shore-based bombers and torpedo-carrying aircraft and sunk. Mr. O. D. Gallaher, war correspondent of the *Daily Express*, who was on board the *Repulse* at the time, describes the disaster as follows:

"The only analogy I can think of to give an impression of the *Prince of Wales* in her last moments is of a mortally wounded tiger trying to beat off the *coup de grâce*. Her outline is hardly distinguishable in the smoke and

---

[13]"If we had had 250 fighter planes in Malaya," writes Ian Morrison, "there never would have been any campaign at all, for the enemy would never have been able to set foot on Kota Bahru. Fighters and Hudsons together wrought tremendous havoc during the early hours of the Japanese landing there." (*Ibid.*, pp. 92-93.)

[14]It had been the intention of the British Admiralty to send an aircraft-carrier with them, but at the time of sailing, every carrier except one was under repair.

[15]*Malayan Postscript*, p. 16.

flame from all her guns except the fourteen-inchers. I can see one plane release a torpedo . . . It drives straight at the *Prince of Wales*. It explodes against her bows. A couple of seconds later another explodes amidships and another astern. Gazing at her turning over on the port side and her stern going under and with dots of men leaping from her, I am thrown against the bulkhead with a tremendous shock as the *Repulse* takes a torpedo on her port side astern. I am wondering where it came from when the *Repulse* shudders gigantically. Another torpedo. Now men cheering with more abandon than at a Cup Final. What the heck is this, I wonder. Then see it is another plane down. It hits the sea in flames also . . . My notebook says 'third torpedo'."[16]

The moral effect of this loss on Singapore was catastrophic.

"I still remember," writes Morrison, "the chill sense of calamity which was caused by the loss of these two ships. It was worse than calamity. It was calamity that had the premonition of further calamity . . . Blown clean away at one fell swoop was one of the main pillars on which our sense of security rested. Nor was our despondency in any way mitigated by Mr. Duff Cooper's Churchillian heroics and well-intentioned attempt to reconcile people in Singapore to the news."[17]

The strategical effect, though secondary, was also disastrous; for, when coupled with the raid on Pearl Harbour, the sinking of the two ships swung the balance of naval power in the Western Pacific, the China Seas and the Indian Ocean over to Japan. In fact, for the time being at least, the very *raison d'être* for Singapore vanished with them—it was now a naval base without a fleet.

After the Japanese success at Kota Bahru, the main fighting was rapidly transferred to Kedar on the west coast, the British falling back from the airfield at Alor Star towards the island of Penang.

On the 11th Penang had been mercilessly bombed, wave after wave diving down on the city of Georgetown to create unutterable confusion. Then came another attack on the 12th and yet another on the 13th. A *sauve qui peut* of the white population followed, which had a disastrous influence on native morale. On the 18th the Japanese occupied Penang.

From there they pressed on into Perak, and at the end of the year their troops on the east coast had reached Kuantan. The rapidity of their advance was largely due to their tactics, which were vastly superior to their enemy's. Whereas, for the greater part, the British soldiers had been trained for war in Europe or Africa and knew nothing about jungle fighting, the Japanese were adepts at it. Whereas the British soldier was loaded

[16]*Daily Express*, 12th December, 1921.
[17]*Malayan Postscript*, pp. 59-60. Mr. Duff Cooper was Resident Minister at Singapore for Far Eastern Affairs.

down with equipment—pack, gas-mask, steel helmet, etc.—and depended for supply on mechanical transport,[18] the Japanese wore a singlet, cotton shorts and rubber-soled shoes, and being rice-eaters could live off the country. Their two principal weapons were the tommy-gun and light 2-inch mortar. They made extensive use of bicycles, and their transport was the light, two-wheeled, man-hauled cart, similar to those they had used in Manchuria thirty-seven years earlier.

By 7th January the British had withdrawn to Kuala Lumpur in Selangor; at which place the Japanese surprised them by bringing into action a force of medium tanks, which caused "unspeakable confusion." Thereupon the withdrawal was hastened southwards on Tampin and Gemas, while the Japanese on the east coast pressed forward to the Endau River. By the 30th the Japanese vanguard was nearing Kulai in Johore, less than twenty miles north of Singapore. The next day at 8 a.m. the Singapore causeway was breached: the siege had begun.

Like the French behind their Maginot land-wall, the British behind their Singapore sea-wall had been living in a fool's paradise. When, on 7th December, the news of the catastrophe of Pearl Harbour was flashed through the ether, *The Times* Singapore Special Correspondent wrote:

"Singapore to-day is the core of British strength in the Far East. One is conscious of this strength as soon as one sets foot on the island . . . While the dense jungle of the northern Malay States makes it unlikely that an enemy will ever try to reach Singapore by marching down the four hundred mile peninsula, landing on the coast might well be attempted . . . In the air Malaya is far stronger, both offensively and defensively, than a year ago, thanks in large measure to American production . . . The crisis has come in this part of the world and we are not found wanting."[19]

The Maginot Line had been built to keep out the German flood from the east; the fortress of Singapore, to keep out the Japanese flood from the south. Yet, when the deluge came, in neither case did it follow the predicted path.

Thus, when on 31st January the dreamers finally awoke, they found everything in Singapore pointing in the wrong direction. The great guns

---

[18]In *The Times* of 4th February, 1941, we read: "The Indian troops which were among the reinforcements brought with them their own motor transport. They were completely mechanized, there being not a single mule or pack animal with any unit . . . The troops were soon busily engaged on training in jungle warfare tactics." But what was the use of this training with such transport? Surely there should be a relationship between the carriage and expenditure of bullets? Yet on this occasion, after reviewing these troops, the C.-in-C. remarked: "I have perfect confidence in their ability to perform the duties allotted to them." Poor devils, they had not a chance to perform them.

[19]*The Times*, 8th December, 1941.

of the fortress were gazing southwards. The Naval and R.A.F. bases were looking north. Now, they were in the front line and the enemy was facing them on the northern shore of the Strait of Johore. In fact, the fortress had become a redan, a work with an open gorge resting on a water obstacle.

It was garrisoned by some 70,000 troops under Lieut.-General A. E. Percival, G.O.C. Malaya, and of these troops some 45,000 were combatants. Food was sufficient for a long siege,[20] and the water supply was adequate, consisting of two large reservoirs in the centre of the island. The gorge was, however, in all well over thirty miles in length, and the water obstacle was narrow, varying from one thousand to two thousand yards in breadth. Outwardly the situation was not an utterly hopeless one. In fact. it looked as though the fortress might hold out for at least six months.

Inwardly it was otherwise. The Command was uninspiring; the long retreat had bred a spirit of defeatism among the troops, and labour troubles were acute.[21]

On 4th February, having by then brought up their artillery, the Japanese opened a bombardment across the Strait of Johore, and on the night of the 8th-9th, using iron barges brought with them for the purpose, on a ten mile front between Kranji Creek and Pasir Laba they landed on the island.

On the 9th two columns pressed inland, one from the first of the above named places and the other from the second. At first the situation of the defenders seemed to be well in hand, then it worsened, and on the 11th the Japanese C.-in-C., Lieut.-General Tomyuki Yamashita, dropped by aeroplane the following message on the British Command:

"I advise immediate surrender of the British forces at Singapore, from the standpoint of *bushido*, to the Japanese Army and Navy forces, which have already dominated Malaya, annihilated the British Fleet in the Far East, and acquired complete control of the China Sea, and the Pacific and Indian Oceans, as well as south-western Asia."[22]

This demand was ignored and fighting went on. Then came the final blow. The Japanese, having bridged the gap in the causeway, had passed tanks over it, and on the 14th these seized the reservoirs. Capitulation now became inevitable, and it took place at 7 p.m.—Singapore time—on the next day. Seventy thousand troops surrendered. Thus ended the most disastrous campaign fought by Great Britain since Cornwallis's capitulation at York Town in 1781.

---

[20]There was a superabundance of rice and flour and at the end of December still 125,000 pigs on the island. (*Malayan Postscript*, p. 147.)

[21]In November the Naval Base alone employed 12,000 Asiatic workmen; but in December, on account of bombing and the total lack of deep air raid shelters, this figure was frequently reduced to 800.

[22]Quoted from *Malayan Postscript*, p. 181.

Looking back on the campaign, the first thing which strikes us is that it was machine power in the form of the bomber, torpedo-carrier and fighter aircraft, which, in closest co-operation with fleet and army, enabled Japan in a little over two months to achieve so astonishing a success.

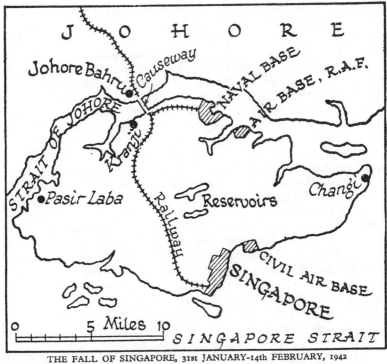

THE FALL OF SINGAPORE, 31st JANUARY-14th FEBRUARY, 1942

Unlike the great campaigns fought in the West, in which grand tactics dominated, the Japanese Malayan campaign was a triumph of minor tactics. Excepting aircraft, war machines were often an encumbrance rather than an assistance. Thus, as has been mentioned, the primitive two-wheeled carts proved far more accommodating than the British lorries, which were road-bound. Tactically, this meant that the British troops had to operate within reach of the roads, for otherwise they could not be supplied, whereas the Japanese were not so restricted. Not only could the Japanese more frequently than not by-pass their enemy, but also they could judge beforehand which would be his lines of advance and retirement. Further, whereas the Japanese soldier could live on rice alone and generally could subsist upon what he foraged, the far higher standard of living of the British soldier virtually put him out of court. From the point of view of his stomach, he simply could not compete with his antagonist.

It was this radical difference in supply which, above all things, endowed the Japanese with such remarkable mobility, coupled with the fact that in jungle warfare, so long as tactics remain primitive, the attack dominates the defence. In this fighting the deciding factor is man and not the machine. Not tanks, artillery or armoured cars, though at times they were useful; instead sharpshooters, machine-gunners and field-mortar groups—even men armed with squibs, which when detonated resembled the fire of machine-guns. Tanks were useful on the roads and aircraft invaluable in the open spaces; but in the jungle itself it was the self-reliant, lightly-equipped scout who triumphed.

(4) *The Campaigns in Burma and the Dutch East Indies*

Malaya overrun and Singapore in Japanese hands, the sole remaining strategical objectives on the mainland were Rangoon and the Burma Road: the one was within no great distance of the Kawkareik Pass—the main entrance from Siam into Lower Burma—and by road and river the other was not far short of nine hundred miles away. To defend them as well as Tenasserim—the long Burmese appendix stretching from Moulmein to Victoria Point—were two weak British divisions scattered along a one thousand six hundred miles front! The Japanese problem was, therefore, one of logistics and not of tactics—of roads and not of battles.

Though the British had been in Burma for over a hundred years, so little attention had they paid to its strategic defence that but three mule tracks—frequently impassable during the monsoon—traversed the Indo-Burmese frontier.[23] Within Burma itself, except for the Rangoon-Myitkyina-Lashio and the Rangoon-Prome railways, all trunk communications running south to north were still by river, mainly by the Irrawaddy. Therefore, to dispatch supplies to Chungking, they had to be loaded at Calcutta, sent seven hundred and fifty miles by sea to Rangoon, forwarded five hundred miles by rail to Lashio, and thence transported nine hundred miles by road.

Both the British and Japanese problems were, therefore, one of communications: on the one side to withdraw by and the other to advance by. Added to this, the British problem was vastly complicated by the fact that the Japanese held command of the air.

[23]Though the defence of the North-west Frontier monopolized the attention of the General Staff in India, in 1926, Lieut.-General Sir Andrew Skeen, then C.G.S. India, told me that, in his opinion, the North-east would one day become far more important.

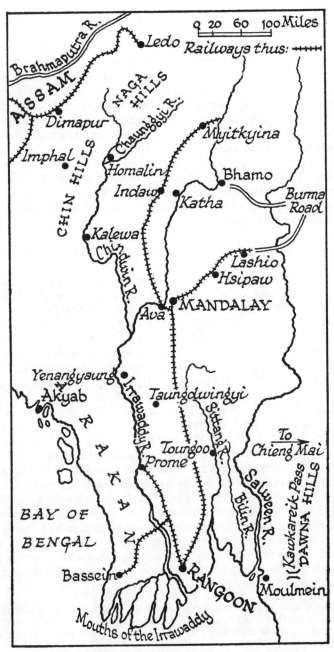

THE INVASION OF BURMA, 21st JANUARY–20th MAY, 1942

On 21st January, after some opposition, the Japanese forced the Kaw-kareik Pass through the Dawna Hills and made for Moulmein. This advance was followed by a series of withdrawals on the part of the British, in succession to the Salween, Bilin and Sittang, the only action of any severity being fought on the second of these rivers between 15th and 20th February. On 7th March it was decided to evacuate Rangoon, which meanwhile had been frequently and heavily bombed, and to carry out the withdrawal, Major-General Sir Harold Alexander took over command from Lieut.-General T. J. Hutton, who, since 28th December, had been conducting operations. He decided to retire in two columns, one up the Sittang river to link up with the Fifth and Sixth Chinese Armies,[24] which were then advancing southwards from Mandalay, under command of General Lo Cho-ying. and the other up the Irrawaddy.

Both the withdrawal and the advance were rapid. On 22nd March the Japanese were nearing Prome on the Irrawaddy and fighting the Chinese and right column at Toungoo on the Sittang. On 1st April, the left British column evacuated Prome, made north to destroy the Burma oil wells about Yenangyaung, and two days later Mandalay was laid in ruins by air attack. Next, on the 10th, a new Japanese army suddenly appeared, advancing from Chieng Mai in northern Siam. Whereupon the right column hastily made for Taungdwingyi. There the Sixth Chinese Army was surprised, routed and, apparently, never re-assembled. Pushing on at great speed towards the Burma Road, the Japanese cut it at Hsipaw on the 29th. The next day their tanks entered Lashio.

On account of this disaster, the left column, leaving the oilfields ablaze, hurried north towards Mandalay, while the right column and the Fifth Chinese Army hastened their withdrawal from Taungdwingyi to the same place. At Mandalay, it was decided that the Fifth Chinese Army should retreat on Myitkyina, so that it might keep in contact with China, while the British forces retired on Kalewa, lying on the west bank of the River Chindwin, and terminus of the motor road. Mandalay was abandoned on 1st May, and the great Ava bridge over the Irrawaddy was blown.

While the Japanese centre pushed on after the Chinese, their left pressed Alexander's army as it withdrew to the Chindwin, which, in spite of incessant bombing and machine-gunning by Japanese aircraft, it reached

[24]Each of these armies consisted of three divisions of between 2,000 and 3,000 men each. At first it was proposed to place Lieut.-General Joseph W. Stilwell, Chief of the U.S. Mission to China, in command of them; eventually, however, it was decided to leave them under General Lo Cho-ying, with Stilwell as his military adviser. Though Lo Cho-ying was under General Alexander, he communicated direct with Chiang Kai-shek, who had the last word as to the employment of the two armies. This did not help things.

on 15th May. At Kalewa all heavy equipment was destroyed, because the rest of the retreat would have to be made by a forest track. Followed by hordes of refugees the British penetrated the jungle, and by the 28th the greater part had crossed the Indian border.

Meanwhile, the Fifth Chinese Army upon reaching Indaw, finding it too hazardous to proceed further north, for by then Bhamo was in Japanese hands, Generals Lo Cho-ying and Stilwell decided to retreat into India. This they set out to do, and after abandoning all transport at Mansi, they advanced down the Chaunggyi river to Homalin. Crossing the Chindwin in small native boats and dug-out canoes, on 13th May they entered the Chin Hills as the monsoon broke, and traversing the Naga country reached Imphal on the 20th.

Thus ended a campaign as remarkable as it was disastrous. In Stilwell's words: "We took a hell of a beating."

While Burma was being overrun and the Philippines reduced, the Japanese were also busily engaged upon occupying the islands of Borneo, Tarakan, Celebes, Ceram (Serang), Bali and Timor. Practically no opposition on land was met with, and, at sea, little until 23rd January, when in a four days naval action in the Strait of Macassar several Japanese transports were sunk.

On 14th February Sumatra was invaded and Palembang occupied. Fighting continued on the island until 17th June, when the last Dutch forces surrendered. On the 27th came the Battle of the Java Sea, in which, on account of Japanese superiority in submarines and aircraft, an Allied squadron, under command of the Dutch Admiral Doorman, was all but annihilated. This victory was immediately followed by the invasion of Java, and within ten days organized Dutch resistance on the island collapsed.

Meanwhile the Japanese were carrying out a series of maritime advances, based on the Carolines, Gilbert and Marshall Islands, against the Solomon Islands, Bismarck Archipelago and New Guinea. On 23rd January a landing was effected on the island of New Britain and Rabaul was occupied. On the same day a landing was made at Kavieng in New Ireland, and by the end of the month Kieta on Bougainville in the Solomons was in Japanese hands. On 7th March the invasion of New Guinea was initiated by landings at Salamaua and Lae.

Thus, even before the struggle in the Philippines had ended, the breakdown of Allied resistance in the South Pacific was complete. Except for southern Papua, which commands the Torres Strait, the Japanese protective screen had been established. Therefore, in order to close this gap, towards the end of April the Japanese decided to seize Port Moresby, and by pushing their advance into the New Hebrides and New Caledonia cut the line of supply from Hawaii and Panama to Australia.

(5) *Battles of the Coral Sea and Midway Island*

It is a strange coincidence that, once the Japanese had beaten down all opposition, and from appearances seemed to be on the point of gaining everything they had set out to win, the tide of victory suddenly began to ebb, as in the West it had ebbed for the Germans when Europe appeared to be at their feet. And what is even stranger is, that a common factor linked these turnings of the floods of conquest. In the case of Germany it was that the fighter mastered the bomber, and by so doing maintained the might of sea power, whereas in that of Japan it was that the bomber mastered the warship, and by doing so paralysed land power. Therefore in both cases it was air power which changed the course of the war.

But before we proceed further, it is as well first to look at the problem as it faced the United States immediately after the catastrophe of Pearl Harbour.

It was not altogether unlike the one which had faced Britain after the fall of France. Because in 1940 it was vital to hold out and secure Egypt as an overseas base for eventual offensive operations, it was now as vital to hold and secure Australia for a similar reason. In the one case security demanded the establishment of the Cape route, and in the other, the establishment of the South Pacific route; for as Egypt had largely lost the use of the Mediterranean, also had Australia largely lost the use of the Indian Ocean.

The gaining of the South Pacific supply line was initiated by a series of raids, the object of which was to secure the island stepping-stones between Hawaii and Australia. On 1st February an American carrier task force raided the Marshall and Gilbert Islands; on 20th February, Rabaul in New Britain was raided; on 24th February, Wake Island; on 4th March, Marcus Island, one thousand two hundred miles south-east of Tokyo; on 10th March, Salamaua and Lae were bombed; and on 18th April General Doolittle made a carrier-borne air attack on Tokyo.

Under cover of these operations, the line of supply to Australia was consolidated. In January an air station was established on Johnston Island; the one already existing on Palmyra Island was reinforced; and at the end of the month U.S. troops occupied the Fiji Islands. In February, Christmas and Fanning Islands were occupied and Canton Island was taken over. U.S. forces were also despatched to New Caledonia and Efaté in the New Hebrides; the U.S. naval base in the Solomons was strengthened; and on 28th March work was begun on a new base on Espiritu Santo in the New Hebrides.

Meanwhile the Japanese strengthened their bases in New Guinea, New Britain and the Solomon Islands, and when on 3rd May they began to occupy Tulagi on Florida Island in the last-mentioned group, Admiral F. J. Fletcher was cruising in the Coral Sea with the carrier *Yorktown*, three cruisers and six destroyers. That day an air patrol reporting a Japanese expedition in Tulagi harbour, four planes from the *Yorktown* were sent out to bomb the shipping.[25]

On the 5th Fletcher joined up with other Allied naval forces, including the carrier *Lexington*, seven heavy cruisers, two light cruisers and nine destroyers.

On the 6th the Japanese main forces were located in the Bismarck Archipelago. This indicated an amphibious operation southwards, possibly against Port Moresby, in which case, as the enemy would have to round Milne Bay at the eastern end of New Guinea, Fletcher stationed an attack group within striking distance of the probable track of the Japanese fleet, while the remainder of his own fleet steamed northwards to discover the Japanese covering force.

On the morning of the 7th contact was made with the Japanese carrier *Shoho*. She was attacked and sunk by aircraft from the *Lexington* and *Yorktown* at the loss of five planes. Next, on the morning of the 8th, contact was made with two Japanese carriers, four heavy cruisers and several destroyers. During the counter-attack both the *Yorktown* and *Lexington* were hit, the latter so badly that she had to be abandoned.

This battle cost the Japanese one aircraft-carrier, three heavy cruisers, one light cruiser, two destroyers and several transports sunk, and more than twenty vessels damaged.

Though it was in no sense a decisive battle, for the U.S. Fleet received nearly as much as it gave, it marked the high tide of Japanese conquests in the South-west Pacific. But, in history, its chief claim to fame will always be that, of all naval engagements fought, it was the first in which surface ships did not exchange a single shot.[26]

Baulked in the Southern Pacific, the Japanese next transferred their naval operations to the Northern and Central Pacific. On 3rd June they

[25]The following account is based on the Official Report by Admiral Ernest J. King, C.-in-C. U.S. Fleet.

[26]Writing on the subject of future naval warfare in 1937, I suggested ". . . that a radical change will have to take place in our idea of the capital ship, around which present battle tactics revolve. In my opinion she will no longer be a gun-ship but a bomb-ship. In other words, our present aircraft-carriers, which are looked upon as adjuncts to battleships, will, in more efficient form, replace them as the master-ships of our fleet, and all other ships—cruisers, destroyers, submarines, and possibly also battleships—will become their auxiliaries, the moving sea fortress from which their aircraft will operate . . . Bomb-power is the key, because air-carried bombs vastly outrange gun-fired shells. As this is so, it follows that naval warfare will be very different from what it was in 1914-1918." (*Towards Armageddon*, p. 196.)

launched an air attack on Dutch Harbour, the American naval base in Unalaska Island, one of the Aleutian chain. Though its object would seem to have been a serious one, it may also have been intended as a diversion; for with it came a far more extensive operation in the Central Pacific, which led to the Battle of Midway Island.

What the object of this operation was is not clear. Merely to occupy Midway was not worth the risk, because the island was too small to be made a powerful air base. It would seem, therefore, that the Japanese aim was either to lure a weaker American force into a trap, or what appears more probable is, that it was the first step of a larger operation—the capture of the island of Oahu. Were this effected, then the U.S. line of communications with Australia would be severed at its most vital point, because Oahu was the Aden of the Pacific. Once in Japanese occupation, Australia would be isolated, as Egypt would have been, after Italy entered the war, had Aden fallen into Italian hands. Further, time would have been gained for Japan to consolidate her island defences.

Acting on the assumption that, after their defeat in the Coral Sea, the Japanese would transfer operations to the Central Pacific, the American carriers and their supporting units were ordered north. The *Yorktown* was hastily patched up, and the U.S. Central Pacific Fleet under Vice-Admiral Fletcher brought up to a strength of three carriers—the *Enterprise*, *Hornet* and *Yorktown*—seven heavy cruisers, one light cruiser, fourteen destroyers and twenty submarines. In support was a Marine Corps air group on Midway Island.

On the morning of 3rd June American naval aircraft sighted a Japanese fleet four hundred and seventy miles south-west of Midway Island on an easterly course. During the afternoon this force was bombed by a squadron of heavy bombers from Midway. Next day another fleet was observed one hundred and eighty miles to the north of Midway. Thereupon it became evident that "the largest concentration of enemy naval strength yet assembled for Pacific operations was heading eastwards with the capture of Midway as its preliminary objective."[27] At once all available Navy carrier and land-based Army and Navy aircraft were concentrated on the enemy. Three of his carriers were attacked, and one was severely damaged. As the U.S. carrier attacks were without the protection of fighters, casualties in attacking aircraft were heavy;[28] nevertheless, several hits on carriers were

[27] *Biennial Report of the Chief of Staff of the United States Army, 1st July, 1941, to 30th June, 1943* (English edition, 1943), p. 11. Most of the account of the battle is extracted from Admiral King's Official Report.

[28] Thus we read in the U.S. Navy Department's review of the operations: "Four Army torpedo-bombers, of which only two returned" . . . "six Marine Corps torpedo planes, of which only one returned" . . . "sixteen Marine Corps dive-bombers, of which only eight returned."

scored. A little later, torpedo squadrons from the *Enterprise* and *Yorktown* attacked the same three carriers, two of which were set on fire and the third sunk by a submarine.

While this action was in progress, the island of Midway was heavily attacked by Japanese aircraft, and at about the same time thirty-six aircraft from the still undamaged carrier *Hiryu* attacked the *Yorktown* and her escort. The *Yorktown* was struck in three places and abandoned. Later on she was taken in tow, but on the afternoon of the 6th was torpedoed by a Japanese submarine and sank next morning. During the attack on the *Yorktown*, planes from the *Enterprise* attacked the *Hiryu* and left her a mass of flames; later on she sank.

On the 5th the Japanese were in full retreat, and though the American air pursuit was fiercely pushed and further damage was inflicted, bad weather brought operations to an end.

The losses sustained by the Japanese were estimated to be: Four aircraft-carriers, two large cruisers, three destroyers, one transport and one auxiliary ship sunk, and three battleships, three heavy cruisers, one light cruiser, several destroyers and three transports or auxiliary ships damaged. In the air attacks the Americans lost 92 officers and 215 men.

Once again no surface ships met in combat.

This battle was decisive, probably the most decisive naval action since Tsushima, because it permanently crippled Japan's naval air power, by reducing her carrier strength to so low a level that she never was able to catch up with American construction. Japanese carriers were now reduced to five fit for action—one only large—with six under repair or building. Whereas, though the U.S. had but three large carriers left in the Pacific, no less than thirteen were on the stocks as well as fifteen escort carriers.

Hence onwards the Japanese Navy was hobbled by its weakness in carriers. So much so was this the case that, from the Battle of Midway Island on, it could only engage U.S. naval forces either at night time, or when under cover of land-based aircraft. Thus the balance of naval power in the Pacific passed to the United States. Therefore the southern line of supply to Australia was henceforth secure, and the central line ready to be won.

Looking back on the first six months of the war in the Far East, and bearing in mind that during them the Japanese conquered an area approximately half the size of the United States at the estimated ridiculously low cost of 15,000 killed and 381 aircraft destroyed,[29] the first thing which strikes the student of war is the enormous advantage preparedness, under modern conditions of warfare, confers upon an aggressor nation. The

[29] Should this figure be doubled or even trebled, it remains ridiculously small.

second is the egregious folly of underestimating a potential adversary, more especially so in a scientific age. Both the British and Americans committed this error. They looked upon the Japanese as "yellow monkeys" until they believed them to be such, and they held their noses when they passed them by, oblivious of the fact that the supremacy of the white man in Asia was not due to the colour of his skin, but to his superior weapons. Therefore that, once Asiatics were equally well armed, this supremacy would be challenged. In the end, as we shall see, it was superiority of weapon power, and, therefore, of industrial power, which was to become the final arbiter. Nevertheless, weapons themselves are but a frail reed to lean upon unless they are used with intelligence. That is, in accordance with the principles of war applied according to strategic conditions and tactical circumstances.

In the West, we have seen how the Germans, after a galaxy of victories, through lack of foresight (the higher intelligence) met with failure. They were not prepared to cross the English Channel and, as they thought, to short-cut this failure, they changed their line of operations and in the end doubled their initial error.

In the East, Japan's mistake was different. Her failure was due to selecting from the start a faulty line of operations, a line which once embarked upon it was impossible to change.

Germany, though unprepared to span the Channel, had, as we have seen, an alternative. Japan, not only unprepared, but in no circumstances could she have been prepared to span the Pacific and conquer the United States, once the Rubicon of Pearl Harbour was crossed, had no alternative.

Germany, possibly, might have erased her error, had she, instead of invading Russia, concentrated all her energies against England. Japan, *vis-à-vis* the United States, was never offered such an escape; therefore, from the start, all her brilliant victories were but Dead Sea apples.

Yet both errors had a common factor, leading to a common ruin. Whereas in the one case, error led to eventual over-extension, in the other it began with initial over-extension. In the one, the means were insufficient to accomplish the end; in the other, the means were insufficient to make certain of the beginning.

CHAPTER V
LOSS OF GERMAN INITIATIVE
(1) *The Fourth Libyan Campaign*

During the months immediately following the Third Libyan campaign[1] the main problems which faced the opposing armies, the one under Rommel and the other now commanded by General Sir Claude Auchinleck,[2] were identical. Both had to be re-equipped and reinforced before either could attack. Therefore the governing factor was communications. Whereas Auchinleck's were comparatively short by land and inordinately long by sea, Rommel's were the reverse. By road, they were approximately one thousand miles to Tripoli, his main base, and three hundred and seventy-five to Benghazi, and by sea these ports were respectively three hundred and fifty and four hundred and fifty miles from the Strait of Messina. Commanding these sea communications lay Malta; two hundred miles from Tripoli, three hundred and sixty from Benghazi and five hundred from Crete. Crete was also a German supply base and two hundred miles north of Tobruk. Clearly, then, could Rommel neutralize Malta and eliminate Tobruk, so far as communications went, the advantage would be his. Further, so long as he was compelled to invest Tobruk, he could not concentrate his army. Therefore, unless he were powerfully reinforced, he could not attack. This disadvantage is noted by General Auchinleck, who says:

"Our freedom from embarrassment in the frontier area for four and a half months is to be ascribed largely to the defenders of Tobruk. Behaving not as a hardly pressed garrison but as a spirited force ready at any moment to launch an attack, they contained an enemy force twice their strength. By keeping the enemy continually in a high state of tension, they held back four Italian divisions and three German battalions from the frontier area from April until November."[3]

Though Rommel fully realized the importance of taking Tobruk, and had attempted to carry it on 1st May,[4] it is extraordinary that the German

[1] The actual Commander-in-Chief was the Italian General Ettore Bastico, but he was no more than a figure-head.

[2] Sir Claude Auchinleck succeeded Sir Archibald Wavell on 5th July. At the same time Air Chief Marshal Sir Arthur Tedder succeeded Air Marshal Sir Arthur Longmore in command of the R.A.F. in the Middle East.

[3] General Auchinleck's "Despatches." *Supplement to the London Gazette,* 20th August, 1946, p. 4221.

[4] On this occasion, though the German tanks penetrated the outer defences, they were beaten back by anti-tank gunfire. After this failure Rommel handed the

Supreme Command failed to realize that the neutralization, or, better still, the elimination, of Malta was even more important. The only possible explanation is that, compared to the invasion of Russia, Hitler and his Staff looked upon the Libyan war as a sideshow, and of so little consequence that it did not warrant a diversion of forces which might possibly be of use in Russia. According to one writer, all "appeals for the transfer of some *Luftwaffe* from the Balkans to the Central Mediterranean were turned down by the German High Command. They persisted in sacrificing maritime needs for Continental interests. They did not even allow the Italian Navy sufficient fuel to operate."[5] The upshot was that, in August, 35 per cent of Rommel's supplies and reinforcements were sunk, and in October—63 per cent. Thus, thanks to Malta, in spite of his twelve thousand miles of sea communications, Auchinleck was able more speedily to build up his army. Not until late October, when sinkings were approaching 75 per cent, did the German Supreme Command attempt to tackle the problem. Belatedly they then diverted twenty-five U-boats from the Atlantic to the Mediterranean, which, on 13th November, scored their first success by torpedoing the British aircraft-carrier *Ark Royal*.

Meanwhile, Auchinleck, now disembarrassed from what to Wavell had been a veritable Tobruk—namely, the campaign in East Africa[6]—towards the end of August reorganized his desert forces into the Eighth Army under the command of Lieut.-General Sir Alan Cunningham.

It comprised two corps, the XIIIth under Lieut.-General A. R. Godwin-Austin, and the XXXth commanded by Lieut.-General Sir W. Norrie. In the first were the 4th Indian Division, New Zealand Division and 1st Army Tank Brigade. In the second the 7th Armoured Division (7th and 22nd Armoured Brigade and 7th Support Group), the 4th Armoured Brigade, the 1st South African Division and the 201st Guards Brigade Group. The Tobruk garrison, under the command of Lieut.-General Sir R. Scobie, comprised the 70th Division, the 32nd Army Tank Brigade and a Polish Regiment. The 2nd South African Division and the 29th Indian Infantry Brigade Group were in army reserve.

Rommel's army was roughly one-third German and two-thirds Italian. The former consisting of the Afrika Korps (15th and 21st Panzer Divisions),

---

problem of reducing the stronghold over to his air force, and up to 31st July 437 raids were made on it. Tobruk had no fighter protection.

[5]"The Mediterranean and Sea Power," Commander George Stitt, *The New English Review*, August, 1946, p. 144.

[6]The only extraneous campaign which General Auchinleck had to consider at this time was the one in Persia; but the troops he sent there were returned to him by 18th October. The objects of this campaign were to expel German agents from Persia and open a supply route to Russia.

the 90th Light Division and one Infantry Division; and the latter of the Ariete Armoured Division and six Infantry Divisions. These forces were distributed as follows: four Italian and one German divisions investing Tobruk; one Italian at Bir Hacheim; the Ariete Division at Bir el Gubi; the 15th and 21st Panzer Divisions on the coast east of Tobruk; and the 90th and one Italian division holding the frontier fortifications.

In aircraft it would appear that Rommel was numerically superior, especially in fighters.[7] The R.A.F. Component, under Air Vice Marshal A. Coningham, was nine squadrons of light bombers, twelve of fighters and six of medium bombers, with five fighter and two light bomber squadrons "kept direct under headquarters."[8] Between Bardia and Tobruk the country was broken, and some ten miles inland from the coast ran a ridge with a double escarpment, south of which the desert was flat and featureless. For tanks the escarpments were only negotiable at certain places; therefore the southern one formed a considerable obstacle to an army moving northwards across the desert.

The most pronounced tactical difference between the two armies lay in their armoured forces, not numerically but ballistically so. Rommel had 412 tanks and 194 anti-tank guns, and Cunningham 455 and 72; but Rommel's tank and anti-tank guns were of 50 mm. ($4\frac{1}{2}$-pdr.) and 75 mm. calibre, whereas Cunningham's were 2-pdrs., and the effective armour-piercing range of this gun was from eight hundred to one thousand yards less than that of the 50 mm. gun. Besides, the armour of the British "I" tank (Matilda) was not proof against the 50 mm. shell, let alone the 75 mm.

Early in November both sides were contemplating attack: Rommel, to capture Tobruk, and free his left flank and rear; Cunningham, to re-occupy Cirenaica. Cunningham's general idea was a double envelopment of his opponent's army by an attack from the south accompanied by an attack from the north by the Tobruk garrison. The XXXth Corps was to carry out the former by moving the 7th Armoured Division, 4th Armoured Brigade and the 1st South African Division from Maddalena, on the enemy's right, on to Gabr Saleh, while the XIIIth Corps held the enemy in front. Directly the enemy's armour was engaged, the XIIIth Corps was to attack, and the Tobruk garrison to fall on the enemy's left flank and rear.

Subsidiary to these operations, the 29th Infantry Brigade Group was to advance from Jarabub, capture Jalo, and from there race north-westwards and cut the Tripoli-Benghazi road. Prior to the attack, the R.A.F. orders were to harass the enemy communications, fight for air superiority, and on

---

[7] Alexander Clifford in *Three Against Rommel*, p. 161, states: "The fighter ratio was three to one in his favour."

[8] *Our Armoured Forces*, Lieut.-General Sir Giffard Martel (1945), p.124.

the morning of the attack to pound the enemy airfields. Meanwhile Naples and other Italian supply ports were to be bombed, as well as Benghazi and Triploi.

The day fixed for the attack was the 18th, but unfortunately for Cunningham on the 17th a tremendous thunderstorm burst over the two armies, and not a single one of Coningham's aircraft took off that night.[*]

BATTLEFIELD OF SIDI REZEGH, 18th NOVEMBER, 1941-17th JANUARY, 1942

Equally unfortunate, Mr. Churchill seized the opportunity to deliver himself of the following heroic passage, which roused optimism to boiling point: "The Desert Army," he said in a message to all ranks, "may add a page in history which may well rank with Blenheim and Waterloo." Fortune, however, did not altogether desert the attackers, for Rommel so little expected the attack that at the time it was launched he was actually in Rome.[10] The surprise was, therefore, complete.

The advance began before dawn, and by nightfall the 7th Armoured Brigade was ten miles north of Gabr Saleh; the 22nd Armoured Brigade in rear to the west of it, and the 4th Armoured Brigade south-east of the 7th,

[*]*Three Against Rommel*, p. 127.
[10]See "The War in the Middle East," Lieut.-General Sir Arthur F. Smith, *The Journal of the United Service Institution*, February, 1943, p. 11. Smith was Chief of Staff to Auchinleck.

while the 1st South African Division was nearing El Cuasc. No enemy was met with and no hostile aircraft was seen.

On the 19th the 7th Armoured Brigade reached the north of the Sidi Rezegh southern escarpment, whereupon the 7th Support Group occupied that locality. The 22nd Armoured Brigade attacked the Ariete Division at Bir el Gubi, apparently because it was an Italian unit, and it was considered therefore that it could easily be mopped up. This time, however, the Italians stood firm and put up a stiff fight, severely mauling their enemy. And away to the right, the 4th Armoured Brigade engaged a German tank force east of Gabr Saleh. Thus, by nightfall, the three brigades were scattered over a wide field. This lack of concentration presented Rommel with a grand opportunity to deal with his enemy in detail, and he at once seized it.

Early on the 20th he advanced a powerful force of tanks against the 4th Armoured Brigade. Whereupon General Norrie ordered the 22nd Brigade to break off its action at Bir el Gubi and hasten to the support of the 4th. Meanwhile the 4th had engaged the enemy, who withdrew and then returned to renew the conflict after the 22nd Armoured Brigade had come up. Later, the German tanks withdrew southwards, and then turned north-west and made a bee-line for Sidi Rezegh, where the 7th Armoured Brigade was being attacked by German tanks and infantry.

Soon after dawn on the 21st, the scouts of the 7th Armoured Brigade reported a force of German tanks approaching from the east. Whereupon orders were despatched to the 4th and 22nd Armoured Brigades at once to come in on its tail. But shortage of petrol delayed their start, and the German tanks caught the 7th Brigade in the middle of an engagement.

A fierce tank battle followed, during which, late in the day, the 4th and 22nd Armoured Brigades took part. To the south, the 5th South African Brigade was held up ten miles from Sidi Rezegh. The Tobruk garrison had at 6.30 a.m. started its attack, and in the east the New Zealand Division had moved round the southern flank of the enemy's fortified front, and in rear of Fort Capuzzo.

During the next two days—22nd and 23rd November—one of the most extensive tank *versus* tank battles of the war was fought around and about Sidi Rezegh. In the middle of it, General Norrie, hearing that the 5th South African Brigade was threatened by enemy tanks, sent a force of tanks to assist it. Nevertheless, the Brigade was overrun and completely disintegrated.

Meanwhile the 7th Support Group, which had been holding the Sidi Rezegh airfield, was forced back on to the southern escarpment, from where it withdrew to Gabr Saleh.

While this battle was in progress, the 70th Division from Tobruk made little way, and the 4th Indian Division of the XIIIth Corps occupied Sidi Omar.

Thus ended the first phase of the campaign. The vital escarpment of Sidi Rezegh, so easily occupied on the 19th, had been lost, and because of the initial over-extension of the 7th Armoured Division. Both sides had suffered heavy tank casualties, which were felt by the British more so than by the Germans, for the latter had an incomparably better tank recovery organization. "Their huge tracked and wheeled tank-transporters," writes Alan Morehead, "were actually going into battle with the tanks themselves. Even while the fighting was still on, the men in the transporters were prepared to dash into the battle, hook on to damaged vehicles and drag them out to a point where they could start repairs right away."[11]

Like the first phase, the second opened with a surprisal, and this time Cunningham was the victim.

On the morning of the 24th, as General Martel points out, the tactical position was such that Rommel should have pinned the British armoured forces down while they were re-organizing and attacked them in detail; for once they were smashed, "his further plans would have been made easy."[12] Though, tactically, this is incontrovertible, pinning a highly mobile force down is exceedingly difficult. Further, did the strategical situation warrant the risk of delay, let alone of failure? It was as follows: Rommel had considerable garrisons holding Bardia and Halfaya Pass—forty miles east of Sidi Rezegh; his main armoured forces were about Sidi Rezegh, and immediately in rear of them and threatening his line of retreat was the 70th Division from Tobruk. Were he to attack the 7th Armoured Division to the south and were he not immediately successful, and, meanwhile, were the New Zealand Division, then advancing westwards from Capuzzo, to link up with the 70th Division, he would almost certainly not only lose his line of retreat, but also his line of supply leading to his petrol dumps north of the escarpment between Tobruk and Bardia, and such a loss would immobolize his armour.

Ruling out the southern move—the tactically obvious one—his choice lay between an attack northwards or eastwards and a retreat westwards. The first would almost certainly lead to the 70th Division falling back on Tobruk, and the 7th Armoured Division reorganizing and once again moving northwards, while the New Zealand Division continued to advance westwards. Therefore the northwards attack, even should it succeed, was likely to place him in as bad a strategical position as the southwards one, had it been attempted and failed. To retreat westwards would not only

[11] *A Year of Battle*, Alan Morehead (1943), p. 61.
[12] *Our Armoured Forces*, p. 134.

mean abandoning the battle, but also the frontier garrisons; therefore, he decided on a gamble. It was to rush the 15th and 21st Panzer Divisions right through his enemy to Bir Sheferzen—that is, eastwards—scatter to the winds the rear services of the XXXth Corps, and thereby compel that Corps to fall back east of its starting line. Had this gamble succeeded, there can be little doubt that it would have been acclaimed a master-stroke. Therefore, as it did not, we should hesitate before dismissing it as a reckless blunder.

Crashing through, the wildest of panics followed. Morehead, who was in the middle of it, writes:

"All day for nine hours we ran. It was the contagion of bewilderment and fear and ignorance. Rumour spread at every halt, no man had orders. Everyone had some theory and no one any plan . . . I came to understand something of the meaning of panic in this long nervous drive. It was the unknown we were running away from, the unknown in ourselves and in the enemy . . . Had there been someone in authority to say, 'Stand here. Do this and that'—then half our fear would have vanished."[13]

Two pages on he sums up the situation as follows:

"It seemed indeed that Rommel had achieved a master-stroke. Cunningham had little hesitation in pointing out that the wisest course was to retire his army out of Libya to re-group. Most of his tanks appeared to be lost. He was out of touch with a great part of his army. The New Zealanders had succeeded in making contact with the Tobruk garrison at el Duda, but only for a few hours. The Germans had surged forward, broken the bridgehead, and now Tobruk was again a besieged fortress with barely forty-eight hours of twenty-five pounder ammunition left. Of the two British Corps headquarters, one, the 30th, had bolted into Tobruk and was besieged there, and the other, the 13th, was split up and out of touch . . ."[14]

From this it would appear that had Cunningham had his way, Rommel would have won a great victory. But it was not to be; for at this critical moment an outstanding example of the influence of generalship on operations is presented to us. Auchinleck flew to the desert and "opposed a final and absolute 'no' to the proposal for retreat."[15] Had he not done so, it is all but certain that Rommel would have pushed forward his tank supply columns, refilled his tanks, and a stern chase of his enemy would have followed. But entangled as he was with the 4th Indian Division, which was strenuously resisting him, directly he realized that his enemy had determined to stand, he pulled out the 15th and 21st Panzer Divisions and withdrew them to their supply bases between Tobruk and Bardia.

Having through bold generalship rectified the situation, Auchinleck

[13]*A Year of Battle,* p.65   [14]*Ibid.,* pp. 67-68.   [15]*Ibid.,* p. 68.

returned to Cairo and forthwith removed Cunningham from his command, replacing him by Major-General N. M. Ritchie.

The third phase opened on the 26th. That day the New Zealand Division drove the Germans out of Sidi Rezegh, and on the 27th linked up with the 70th Division at el Duda. But no sooner had they done so than they were heavily attacked, and once again Sidi Rezegh passed into German hands. Exhausted by several days of severe fighting, on the night of 1st-2nd December, under cover of the 1st South African Brigade, the New Zealanders were withdrawn south of the escarpment. Thus ended the third phase of the campaign; for a second time Sidi Rezegh had been lost.

On 2nd December, General Ritchie, deciding that the next blow must be struck from the south, placed the 4th Indian Division at the disposal of General Norrie and instructed him with all the tanks he could muster to secure the vital position el Adem-Sidi Rezegh.

Meanwhile Rommel, seeing that he could no longer hope to relieve his garrisons at Bardia and Halfaya Pass; that with depleted armour he now was precariously pinched in between the Tobruk garrison and the XXXth Corps—both of which flanked his line of retreat—decided to cut his losses and withdraw westwards. To secure the withdrawal he concentrated the remainder of his armoured forces at Bir el Gubi—that is, on the outer flank of the XXXth Corps. This astute move compelled that Corps to wheel westwards instead of advancing northwards. The result was that, on the 5th, the 11th Indian Brigade and the 4th Armoured Brigade, to which all available tanks had been allotted, attacked Bir el Gubi, were repulsed and counter-attacked. Reinforced by the remainder of the 4th Indian Division and the Guards Brigade, the attack was renewed and this time the position was carried. Whereupon the 15th and 21st Panzer Divisions withdrew in a north-westerly direction with the 4th Indian Division and the 4th Armoured Brigade at their heels.

On the 9th the 7th Indian Brigade and part of the XIIIth Corps linked up with the 70th Division at el Adem, and Tobruk was at length disengaged. The XIIIth Corps was then ordered to take over the pursuit from the XXXth, which, causing considerably delay, assisted Rommel in his withdrawal to el Gazala. From there, in good order, he sent the bulk of his tanks and transport via the Mekili road to Agedabia, and with the rest of his army followed the coastal road to the same place, from where on 7th January he started to withdraw to Agheila.

On 2nd January, 1942, Bardia was stormed by the 2nd South African Division, and on the 17th Halfaya surrendered. Thus ended this highly intricate campaign. In killed and wounded the Germans and Italians lost 24,500 and in prisoners 36,500, whereas the British losses were about 18,000.

(2) *The Fifth Libyan Campaign*

The Fifth Libyan Campaign followed the Fourth so rapidly that it was little more than its postscript; yet there was a basic difference between the two. This time, not only were the Germans the attackers, but during it they and the Italians held command of the Central Mediterranean. This was something new.

Already, as we have seen, late in October, 1941, the German Supreme Command suddenly became aware of what should have been obvious from the start—namely, that for Rommel to succeed, the command of the Central Mediterranean must first be won, and secondly, held By not appreciating this, they had surrendered the initiative in North Africa to their enemy, and though Rommel's next two campaigns would, as we shall see, seem to disprove this, actually they did not, because by mid-summer, 1942, the supplies which were pouring into Egypt via the Cape of Good Hope were so great that, even had the Germans held complete command of the Central Mediterranean, they would have been beaten by insufficiency of shipping. By then, for every ship they could build their enemies were building ten. Had Rommel, in November, 1941, been 50 per cent stronger than he actually was, the probabilities are that he would have taken Tobruk; that Auchinleck would never have dared to attack him; and that, after Tobruk had been eliminated, Rommel would have won Egypt.

The Fifth Libyan Campaign, small affair though it was, definitely supports this probability, because if some twelve weeks of semi, ending in complete command of the Central Mediterranean, enabled Rommel after less than a fortnight's rest, following a campaign in which he had lost a third of his army, 386 tanks out of 412 and 850 aircraft out of about 1,000, to accomplish what he did, what would not permanent command of the Central Mediterranean from the summer of 1941 onwards have enabled him to do? But nothing was done towards gaining this command until the end of October. Then, following upon the appearance of German U-boats in the Mediterranean, Malta was violently attacked from the air, and from the middle of December onwards air alerts became incessant. Between 25th and 31st December, sixty raids were made on the island, and during January—263. Simultaneously, the British fleet was harassed by U-boats, aircraft and mines. Besides the sinking of the aircraft-carrier *Ark Royal*, the battleship *Barham*, the cruisers *Neptune* and *Galatea*, the destroyer *Kandahar* and the submarines *Perseus* and *Triumph* met with the same fate. Other ships were damaged, and on the night of 18th December, the battleships *Queen Elizabeth* and *Valiant* were put out of action by "human" torpedoes in the harbour of Alexandria.

"Thus, at the end of 1941, all that the British had left to dispute command of the Eastern and Central Mediterranean were three cruisers and a handful of destroyers. As an indication of the mastery the Germans had regained, not one ton of material was lost on its way to the Afrika Korps during January, 1942, and Rommel was able to launch a counter-attack on 21st January which carried him back to el Gazala on 7th February."[16]

To this brief campaign of seventeen days we will now turn.

On arriving at Agedabia, the Eighth Army, not being able because of supply difficulties to push on against Rommel at Agheila, was faced by two choices: either to remain where it was or to retire. The first course demanded strength sufficient to resist attack. This General Ritchie did not possess. Therefore he should have retired. Nevertheless, he decided to stand. In fact, it would seem that he completely ignored his enemy and in spite of Rommel's reputation for boldness; for it would appear that his forward units did not even trouble to entrench themselves.

Between Agedabia and Agheila Ritchie had one armoured brigade scattered over a vast area; south of Benghazi there was the 7th Indian Infantry Brigade; and at Barce the rest of the 4th Indian Division. Besides these units there was little else, and the main pre-occupation was the building up of supply dumps in preparation for an advance on Tripoli.

It is highly probable that Rommel realized his adversary's situation. Anyhow, on 21st January he sent out three armoured columns which elbowed the British off the coastal road and took Agedabia at negligible loss. From there he pushed on at high speed, living largely on his enemy's dumps, and at Antelat just missed capturing the XIIIth Corps headquarters. Next, he made for Msus. From there he turned westwards on Benghazi, which he entered on the 28th, the 7th Indian Brigade escaping eastwards over the desert and the 4th Indian Division northwards to Derna. At length the retreating British rallied a little east of el Gazala, where, on 7th February, Rommel's advance was brought to a halt.

Thus, instead of the Fourth Libyan Campaign adding a page to history ranking with Blenheim and Waterloo, its postscript added one more British disaster to the many at this time tumbling in from the Far East. Most humiliating of all, as Alexander Clifford points out, was the fact that the British "let exactly the same catastrophe happen two years running."[17] Tactically, one of the most remarkable things about this brief campaign was that, in spite of British command of the air, Rommel advanced over three hundred and fifty miles in seventeen days "without any air support at all."[18]

[16]"The Mediterranean and Sea Power," Commander George Stitt, *The New English Review*, August, 1946, p. 144.

[17]*Three Against Rommel*, p. 226.

[18]"The Air Campaign in Libya and Tripolitania," Air Marshal Sir P. R. M. Drummond, *Journal of the Royal United Service Institution*, November, 1943, p. 260.

Taken together, these two campaigns are highly instructive, and of the many lessons which can be learnt from them, the first is the importance of generalship.

"The true general is not a mere prompter in the wings of the stage of war, but a participant in its mighty drama."[19] Therefore it is not sufficient for a general to elaborate plans and issue orders; for he must see that his plans are followed, or modified according to his ideas, and that his orders are carried out. Above all, as Napoleon once said: *"Un général ne doit jamais se faire de tableaux, c'est le pire de tout. Parce qu'un partisan a enlevé un poste, il ne faut pas croire que toute l'armée y est."*[20]

Rommel, though surprised on 19th November, did not lose his balance. "In war," wrote Napoleon, "one sees one's own difficulties and does not take the enemy's into consideration; one must have confidence in oneself."[21] Rommel had; yet Cunningham, it would seem, was so beset by difficulties that, when Rommel fell upon his rear services about Bir Sheferzen, he failed to take into consideration his enemy's desperate situation. Should this be correct, then Cunningham did what no general should ever do—*"faire de tableaux"*—paint a picture out of his own disasters without reference to the situation of his enemy. Auchinleck, not so involved in the turmoil, was better placed to see his enemy's difficulties as well as Cunningham's. Seeing that they balanced, his bold and cool-headed decision saved the situation, as Rommel's cool-headed decision had spared his army an initial retreat. The moral to be drawn from this is, that however technical war becomes, warfare remains an art, and in consequence the artist remains indispensable. Even should technical superiority be so overwhelming that by bludgeoning alone an enemy can be rendered insensible, unless warfare is to become pure ironmongering, the artist is still necessary.

Of the more purely tactical lessons, two in particular are outstanding. The one concerns the aim and the other the integration of forces.

In armoured warfare the tactical aim is the destruction of the enemy's armour. Seldom can armoured forces be fixed, because not only does their mobility enable them to refuse battle, but also to disengage after engagement. Therefore, in order to bring the enemy armour to battle, it is necessary to attack an objective which is of such importance that the enemy must protect it. In the Fourth Libyan Campaign, and mainly because of Tobruk, such an objective was the stretch of the escarpment between el Adem and Sidi Rezegh. Therefore, from the start, not only should that position have been laid down as *the* objective of the XXXth Corps, but

---

[19]*Generalship, its Diseases and their Cure*, J. F. C. Fuller (1933), p. 25.
[20]*Sainte-Hélène, Journal inédit*, Général Gourgaud (1899), vol. II, p. 460.
[21]*Correspondance*, No. 15,144, vol. XVIII, p. 525.

that Corps should have concentrated every available tank against it, flanking protection, etc., being relegated to the air force.

Nor is it sufficient solely to mass tanks, for though tanks can seize a position, they are wasted should they be called upon to hold it. Therefore, it is also necessary to mass artillery and infantry, the one representing mobile and the other static anti-tank fire power. The objective should, therefore, be seized by tanks protected by aircraft and artillery, and held by infantry and artillery protected by aircraft. Meanwhile, the tanks should be withdrawn to refit and refuel, after which they should take up a position from which they can counter-attack the enemy's armour should it attempt, as is probable, to recover the objective. The conclusion is, that tanks, artillery, infantry and aircraft should form one force and not four.

The British air force had still to learn this lesson, for integration between the R.A.F. and the Eighth Army would seem to have been less complete than in Wavell's campaigns.

Few military writers notice this, apparently because the separation of the air force from the army at the end of the first World War had made of the R.A.F. a specialist fighting force with strategic bombing as its controlling idea. It was, therefore, left to a civilian, Alexander Clifford, to note this defect.

Though, he writes, the R.A.F. had for the first time air superiority over the battlefield, it "did not really know what to do with it." He continues:

"The theory was still maintained that the job of the air force was to engage and destroy the opposing air force. But almost imperceptibly the air force was getting mixed up in the battles on the ground, and that gave rise to new problems. The question of army-air force co-operation came irresistibly and rather cantankerously to the fore. The matter had been given a certain amount of theoretical attention beforehand, and experts had been flown out from London to offer advice. But the whole technique was in its infancy. The very term 'army co-operation' contained in itself an implication that the R.A.F. was normally non-co-operative . . . More than once—as was unavoidable on so chaotic and changeable a front—British troops were bombed by the R.A.F. There grew up in the army a feeling that co-operation ought to be much more exact and intimate and speedy, and that the air force ought to be forced into it, even to the point of incorporation. And, on the other hand, the air force began to resist this trend, not so much with the perfectly sound arguments at its disposal, as with a blank refusal to permit the subject to be discussed at all."[22]

Two other items should be noted, for they also were of outstanding importance. The first is, that the idea of fixing an armoured force, as

[22] *Three Against Rommel,* pp. 162-163.

infantry can by fire power be pinned to their defences, because in the open they will be slaughtered, is seldom realizable, since tanks carry their field-works (armour) along with them. The more profitable method of fixing an armoured forces is to destroy, or cut it off from, or manœuvre it away from, its petrol supply. It is by starving tanks of petrol and not by attempting to pin them down that they are more readily fixed, and, except as static pill-boxes, rendered useless.

The other item is, that one never can be too strong in tank reserves, and that, as seldom one can be too strong at the point of attack, to equate these two requirements, tank recovery is essential. The side which can repair its tanks the more rapidly adds the more rapidly to its reserves. Also, be it noted, the side which loses the battlefield, loses with it its damaged armour, and the side which wins the battlefield adds a proportion of the enemy's armour to its own. Tanks are seldom totally destroyed, and though some may be heavily damaged, others can frequently be repaired in a few hours.

Late in the war this lesson was learnt by the British, and on 1st October, 1942, a new Corps was added to the Army, the Corps of Royal Electrical and Mechanical Engineers (R.E.M.E.), three of whose duties were tank maintenance, recovery and repair. Its importance may be judged from the fact that, by the end of the war, in numbers its personnel exceeded the strength of the pre-war British Regular Army.

(3) *The Sixth Libyan Campaign*

Belatedly, as we have seen, the Germans began to realize their funda-mental mistake in not recognizing that British sea power was at the bottom of their strategic problem, and that the road to Egypt—the overseas base of British sea power in the European theatre of war—ran through Malta. Were Malta occupied, Rommel could be more rapidly supplied than his adversary, and because in North Africa success and failure were mainly a problem of communications, Malta, long before this, should have been eliminated as Crete already had been. Instead, the German Supreme Com-mand decided to neutralize it by air attack, which in February was vastly assisted by the re-conquest of the Cirenaica airfields.

Thus it came about, once Rommel was brought to a halt, that the air attack on Malta was intensified. In April it reached a climax. During that month 5,715 sorties were made on the island, which having no under-ground hangars was in the main dependent for its defence upon anti-aircraft artillery. Nevertheless, under the command of Lieut.-General Sir William

Dobbie, the morale of its garrison and civil population was unshaken.[22] In conjunction with this attack, from Crete the Germans also struck at the British fleet, and on 11th May sunk three destroyers.

From Gazala the British defences ran forty miles southwards to Bir Hacheim, and this region being devoid of tactical features, General Ritchie dropped the idea of a continuous front, and behind an unmanned minefield he entrenched his troops in a series of fortified posts known as "boxes." Each was a mile or two square, prepared for all-round defence and amply provided to withstand a siege. They may be compared to medieval castles, for their object was to form refuges which could resist attack until relieved. Therefore, their tactical value largely depended on the maintenance of mobile forces which could come to their relief. Should the enemy penetrate the gaps between them, their garrisons held firm, and, when opportunity presented itself, sallied forth and worried his communications. Therefore, it was risky for the enemy to leave them intact in rear of him. Consequently, should his attack be more than a raid, he was forced to lay siege to them, when at once his adversary's mobile forces would come into play.

Of these "boxes," the four main ones were—the Gazala Box garrisoned by the 1st South African Division; to the south of it the 50th Divisional Box; in the centre, and at the junction of the Bir Hacheim-Acroma track with the Capuzzo road, the Guards Brigade Box, called "Knightsbridge"; and in the extreme south the Bir Hacheim Box manned by a Free French Brigade. Between these and in rear there were other "boxes" and the entrenched camp of Tobruk.

The two corps of the Eighth Army were still the XIIIth and the XXXth. In the first were the 1st and 2nd South African Divisions and the 50th

---

[22]This was another example of the complete failure of the Douhet theory. On 8th April Malta had its 2,000th alert. According to the protocols of Hitler's conferences with his naval commanders, published by the British Admiralty: "In the war council with Mussolini at the end of April, 1942, it was agreed to attack first in Libya at the end of May or the beginning of June, then to conquer Malta in mid-June, and only after that to mount the final offensive on Cairo and Suez. The Malta operation, the supreme importance of which was always insisted on by the German Navy, was planned on a grand scale, and was to be carried out mainly by German, not Italian, forces. . . . At the beginning of July, however, Hitler, overimpressed with Rommel's successes in Libya, suddenly postponed the Malta operation, without reference to either the Italians or his own naval staff, till after 'the conquest of Egypt' was completed, and switched supplies earmarked for the Malta offensive to Rommel instead" (*The Observer*, London, 8th June, 1947). In *Ciano's Diary* the projected attack on Malta is first mentioned on 22nd April (p. 459). On 12th May (p. 468) he stated that it was to take place "in July or August at the latest," and on 21st June (p. 483) writes: "Mussolini wrote to Hitler, saying that if we had not forty thousand tons of oil at our disposal, we should have to postpone it (the invasion of Malta) indefinitely."

Infantry Division, and in the second, the 1st Armoured Division (2nd and 22nd Armoured Brigades), the 7th Armoured Division (4th Armoured Brigade), the 201st Guards Brigade Group, a brigade of Free French, the 3rd Indian Motorized Brigade and the 29th Indian Brigade. The XIIIth Corps was commanded by Lieut.-General W. H. E. Gott and the XXXth by Lieut.-General Sir W. Norrie.

Rommel's army was composed of six Italian Infantry Divisions, the Italian XXth Mobile Corps (the Ariete Armoured Division and the Trieste Motorized Division), the Afrika Korps (15th and 21st Panzer Divisions) and the German 90th Light Division.

It was estimated that Rommel had 550 tanks and some 90 self-propelled guns. Ritchie's tank strength was 631, of which some 100 were "I" tanks and 160 Grants—an American tank armed with a 75 mm. gun. Since the last campaign Ritchie had also received a number of 6-pdr. anti-tank guns and a considerable number of tank transporters for tank recovery; therefore his army was now far better equipped.

Another improvement was the tightening up of co-operation between the R.A.F. and the Eighth Army. In future, independent air conflicts were to be avoided, and instead more direct support given to the ground forces.[24]

In early May Ritchie was preparing to assume the offensive on 7th June. But expecting that Rommel would be ready before he himself was, in the event of being attacked, he decided that the XIIIth Corps should hold the main "boxes," and that the duty of the XXXth should be to destroy the enemy's armour and protect the left flank of the XIIIth Corps. Clearly these two duties were incompatible, because protection and the offensive do not mix.

Rommel's general idea of attack was: while holding his front with his Italian infantry, to move the whole of his armour round his enemy's left flank, engage and destroy the British armoured forces and seize the position el Adem-Sidi Rezegh by the night of the first day of the offensive. On the second day, wheel westward and attack in rear his enemy on the Gazala line, and on the third day turn right about and storm Tobruk. This was lightning war with a vengeance.

His plan was as follows:

On the evening of 26th-27th May the Afrika Korps, XXth Mobile Corps and the 90th Light Division were to assemble south of Bir Hacheim, and

---

[24] "They (Tedder and Coningham) decided to throw overboard the old negative theory that the function of an air force was to neutralize the opposing air force. And in its place they put the positive proposition that a very large part of an air force's function was to take part in the battle in co-operation with the troops on the ground. They no longer thought of co-operation as the dovetailing of two jobs, but as collaboration in one job." (*Three Against Rommel*, p. 237.)

on the following morning, while the Trieste Division stormed Bir Hacheim, the Afrika Korps, Ariete Division and 90th Light Division were to advance on el Adem and *en route* destroy the enemy armour. Meanwhile, a feint attack was to be made on Gazala accompanied by a seaborne landing to the east of it, and a gap cut through the enemy's minefield where it crossed the Capuzzo road, in order to shorten supply communications should Bir Hacheim not immediately succumb.

On the afternoon of 26th May Rommel set out from Rotonda Segnali on his Leuthen manœuvre, and though his enemy knew that an attack was impending, the sole British reconnaissance aircraft sent out that day was

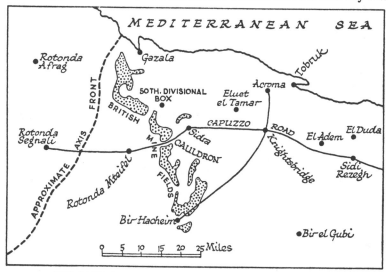

THE BATTLEFIELD OF TOBRUK, 27th MAY-30th JUNE, 1942

shot down, and it was not until early on the following morning that Ritchie became aware that a force of some 200 tanks was south of Bir Hacheim.

From his position of assembly Rommel advanced northwards in three columns, the Ariete Armoured Division on the left, the 21st Panzer Division in the centre, and the 15th Panzer Division on the right. At 7.30 a.m. he overran the 3rd Indian Motorized Brigade; next he engaged and drove back the 4th Armoured Brigade. Pushing on at high speed, he surprised the headquarters of the 7th Armoured Division and captured its G.O.C.—General Messervy—who later on escaped. Lastly, he engaged the 1st Armoured Division round Knightsbridge. Meanwhile all boxes were closed and many were attacked. By the evening of the 27th, in spite of continuous R.A.F. intervention, Rommel's advanced screen had reached

Acroma, el Duda and Sidi Rezegh, and one small column, travelling along the eastern flank of the minefield, actually reached the coastal road. Most of these columns were driven back and the landing east of Gazala was frustrated. For the British, what was more important was that, though heavily attacked, Bir Hacheim stood firm.

From the morning of the 28th until nightfall the 31st, vicious and confused fighting occurred between the contending armoured forces, the battle swaying backwards and forwards over a wide area, but most fiercely west of the Knightsbridge Box, a region which became known as the "Cauldron."

Meanwhile the German engineers cleared a lane through the minefield on the Capuzzo road, and then set to work upon clearing another lane about ten miles to the south of the first one. By the time these lanes were open, both sides were completely exhausted, and on the night of the 31st Rommel fell back on the lanes, between which stood the British 150th Brigade Box. Ritchie's opinion was that Rommel had had enough and was withdrawing. This, however, was far from being the case; for he was merely falling back, as the knights of the Middle Ages were wont to do on their wagon laagers, to rest and refit. Flanked by his enemy's minefields, to the east of the lanes and in the Cauldron area he threw out a screen of anti-tank guns, and under their cover, on 1st June, he attacked the 150th Brigade Box, and in spite of Coningham directing the whole of his air force to its support, carried it by storm and captured over 3,000 prisoners.

Ritchie and his Generals now considered a variety of plans, but on account of exhaustion and the general confusion, one after the other was discarded, and, apparently, in order to do something pending a decision, on 2nd June an attempt was made to worry Rommel's rear. That day a column of Free French occupied Segnali—Rommel's starting point—while the 7th Motorized Brigade operated against the German line of communications near Rotonda Mteifel.

Finally, Ritchie decided to launch an attack on the Cauldron. His plan was for the 10th Indian Brigade to advance on Rommel's "box" from the south on the night of the 4th, and at dawn on the 5th to follow this attack up by another made by the 22nd Armoured Brigade further north, while the 32nd Army Tank Brigade attacked towards Sidra.

This plan was put into effect and with unfortunate results; for though the 10th Indian Brigade carried its objective, the 22nd Armoured Brigade was met by such intense anti-tank fire that it was unable to make headway, while the 32nd Army Tank Brigade ran on to a minefield. Thereupon Rommel, far from intending to withdraw, issued forth from his "laager" and overran the 10th Indian Brigade.

Commenting on this battle, General Martel writes:

"It is now clear that an optimistic view had been taken of the situation. The method of attack employed by the army would have been suitable for an enemy who was withdrawing from the position, but was unsuitable under the circumstances that existed . . . This day—the 5th June—was probably the turning-point in the battle."[25]

At once Rommel seized the initiative and, in order to clear his right flank and win the desert south of Tobruk, he concentrated every available man, gun and aircraft on Bir Hacheim. Though General Ritchie strongly supported the French garrison under General Koenig by turning the R.A.F. on to the attackers, by the 10th, lack of water and ammunition, rendered the post untenable. That night, instead of surrendering, Koenig skilfully withdrew under cover of darkness, and carried three-quarters of his men northwards to safety.

Directly Bir Hacheim was his, Rommel turned northwards to resume his original plan. On the 12th he pressed his attack in the Knightsbridge and el Adem areas. There he was met by the British 2nd and 4th Armoured Brigades; but they could make no progress against his powerful anti-tank defence. That evening the remaining British tanks—170 in all—were placed at the disposal of the XIIIth Corps, and on the morning of the 13th[26] they moved to the assistance of the Knightsbridge Box; but failing to drive the enemy back, General Ritchie decided to withdraw its garrison in order to prevent it becoming isolated. The withdrawal took place on the morning of the 14th, and because it uncovered the coastal road, the 1st South African and the 50th Divisions on the Gazala front were exposed to an attack in rear. Therefore, Ritchie next ordered the withdrawal of the Eighth Army to the Egyptian frontier; but at the same time he decided to leave a garrison in Tobruk. This was contrary to the plan drawn up prior to the battle, according to which, in the event of a retreat becoming necessary, Tobruk was not to be held, because the Navy no longer had command of the Mediterranean.

The withdrawal was carried out under cover of the R.A.F. and flanked by the 1st Armoured Division, which held back the German armour west and east of Acroma. In spite of immense traffic jams, the 1st African Division cleared Tobruk on the 15th. The withdrawal of the 50th Division was, however, a far more difficult operation, because the enemy now blocked its line of retreat. Fortunately, its commander, General Gott, was

---

[25]*Our Armoured Forces*, p. 174.

[26]On 2nd July Mr. Churchill stated in the House of Commons, that on this day 230 British tanks had been destroyed in an ambush. This was quite untrue. Not only were there no more than 170 tanks still operative, but there was no sandstorm on the 13th, and therefore how a force could get ambushed in a vast flat space of desert is difficult to see.

prepared in advance for such a situation, and instead of attempting to cut his way out eastwards, he moved westwards, broke through the Italian defences and then wheeled south to Bir Hacheim, from where he moved due east, and after a march of two hundred miles brought his division back to Egypt.

Meanwhile the XXXth Corps, to which both its armoured divisions had reverted, kept the eastern exits of Tobruk open until the 17th, when an enemy armoured attack from the Sidi Rezegh area compelled it to retire over the frontier. Thus, once again, Tobruk was invested.

During the 18th Rommel vigorously pursued his retreating enemy, and in the vicinity of Gambut ambushed the 20th Indian Brigade. Then, suddenly, he wheeled round and advanced on Tobruk.

The fortress, commanded by Major-General H. B. Klopper, was garrisoned by the 2nd South African Division, less one brigade, the 32nd Army Tank Brigade—some 50 "I" tanks—and a large number of battle-worn men who had filtered in or had been left behind during the retreat. Though it was well stocked, its perimeter defences, some twenty-five miles in length, were in a bad state. Within them was much confusion, and what was nearly as bad, from without them it was impossible to provide fighter cover.

Knowing that the weakest section of its defences was in the el Duda area, Rommel at once pushed forward Italian infantry to engage it, and under their cover he rapidly assembled what remained of the Afrika Korps, the XXth Mobile Corps and the 90th Light Division. Behind them he threw out a screen of anti-tank guns supported by one tank battalion. In fact, he formed his army up into a mobile "box." Meanwhile, he assembled all his Stuka aircraft on the Gazala and el Adem airfields.

On the 20th he was ready to strike, and at dawn that day the fortress was heavily bombed in order to drive its garrison to cover and impede movement within it. Next, wave after wave of Stukas came into action and bombed the minefields. They were immediately followed by sappers, who cleared all mines which had not been exploded. Thus a lane was formed for his tanks, which, under cover of an artillery box barrage and followed by infantry, burst through the outer ring of defences. By midday, and after destroying the British tanks which had counter-attacked, Rommel was well within the fortress.

Meanwhile, Klopper had lost all control: ". . . at the very earliest moment of the attack he was bombed out (of his headquarters) and forced to go to another place. Then again the Stukas got on to him. Through these critical hours, he was hounded from one place to another, and inevitably his communications broke down . . . As in the Crete action, the senior generals had simply to sit down and wait for news, and were unable to act upon it when they got it."[27]

Because the Command was paralysed, the body of the garrison became inarticulate. Groups of men gallantly fought on, a few escaped, others gave in. There was no general surrender, instead—a general collapse. By dawn the 21st Tobruk was Rommel's. Immense booty fell into his hands, also some 30,000 prisoners.

Barely pausing to regain breath, Rommel was on the move again. On the 23rd he crossed into Egypt between Maddalena and Sidi Omar. Whereupon General Ritchie ordered a withdrawal to Mersa Matruh under cover of the R.A.F. That line was occupied on the 27th. From there further orders were issued to fall back on el Alamein, where the front between the Mediterranean and the Qattara Depression narrows to thirty-six miles. El Alamein was occupied on the 30th, and the Eighth Army was reinforced by a division from Syria.

For three days the British situation was critical, so critical that General Auchinleck was preparing to withdraw to the Alexandria defences and the Delta. But fortunately for him Rommel's army was utterly exhausted—its momentum had petered out. He had but 50 German and 75 Italian tanks fit for action, and was faced by far stronger tank forces. Though for a time both sides attempted to keep the battle fluid, by the end of July the position stabilized.

Since 27th May the initiative had been Rommel's, but now, when within sixty-five miles of his goal—Alexandria—at first gradually and then rapidly it passed to his adversary. Not only did the lengthening of his line of communications add to the difficulty of his supply, but the Axis command of the Central Mediterranean was waning. In May Spitfires had been flown to Malta from the American aircraft-carrier *Wasp* and had wrought havoc among the German dive-bombers. And between 14th-16th June, a double convoy—one fleet sailing from Gibraltar and the other from Alexandria—succeeded in re-supplying Malta; for though the eastern convoy was forced to turn back, part of the western reached the island on the 16th. Costly though this operation was, for in it the British Navy lost one cruiser, six destroyers and two escort vessels, besides twelve merchantmen sunk, it marked the turning of the tide. In North Africa, on account of an incredible lack of vision, the Germans had missed the flow, now they were to be carried to ruin on the ebb.

Of the many campaigns fought in North Africa, this one presents us with the clearest example of the fluidity of armoured battles in flat and unobstructed country, and, in consequence, their close resemblance to the

[27]*A Year of Battle*, Alan Morehead, p. 206.

fieldland battles of armoured knights in the Middle Ages. Fronts appear and disappear, localities and areas replace lines, communications are cut and abandoned and retirements are carried out in extraordinary directions. In every engagement armour dominates the field, infantry being relegated to the position of garrison troops, or the occupiers of the battlefield. The medieval castle and wagon laager reappear in the form of the "box," which so long as it can be relieved forms an obstacle, and directly it cannot be becomes a death-trap. And as "box" and armoured force attain their highest value when combined, so do tank and anti-tank gun, in the combination of which the Germans excelled the British.

In rapidity of decisions and velocity of movement the Germans completely outclassed their enemy, and mainly because Rommel, instead of delegating his command to his subordinates, normally took personal command of his armoured forces. On his enemy's side, lack of concentration of command once again led to a lack in the concentration of armour. Not only were the British armoured forces scattered over a wide area when the battle was launched, but during it they were switched in part or in whole from one corps to another, and thereby lost that personal direction which is essential to unity of action. In June, to a captured British tank brigadier Rommel is reported to have said: "What difference does it make, if you have two tanks to my one, when you spread them out and let me smash them in detail. You presented me with three brigades in succession."[28]

On Rommel's generalship, Alexander Clifford writes:

"Rommel could swing his forces round the desert at a moment's notice because he was usually commanding them directly himself. He had realized that, just as an admiral goes to sea with his fleet and directs the battle from the midst of it, so in these desert tank battles the commander must be on the spot himself. All relevant information came straight to him without any intermediary. His decision could be taken in a matter of seconds, and his orders given in a matter of minutes. He could alter the whole course of the battle before the British information had even started on its way back to headquarters."[29]

It was not that the British generals were less able than the German. It was that their education was out of date. It was built on the trench warfare of 1914-1918 and not for the armoured warfare they were called upon to direct.

(4) *The Russian* 1941-1942 *Winter Counter-Offensive*

For Germany, the failure to take Moscow was as great a strategic defeat as the Battle of Britain. And, as we shall see, it was to be followed by an identical mistake; yet another change in the line of operations.

On 7th December Berlin was paralysed. Two reports were simultaneously received. The one, that the United States were a belligerent, and the other that the day before, on the Moscow front, the temperature had dropped to 40 degrees below zero centigrade. Next, as already related, on the 8th came the announcement that henceforth the war in Russia was to be conditioned by winter. What this exactly meant was not known, but it was sufficiently explicit to awaken the memories of 1812. Arvid Fredborg, who was in Berlin at the time, relates:

"Unrest grew among the people. The pessimists remembered Napoleon's war with Russia, and all the literature about La Grande Armée suddenly had a marked revival. The fortune-tellers busied themselves with Napoleon's fate and there was a boom in astrology . . . Even the most devoted Nazi did not want a war with America. All Germans had a high respect for her strength. Nobody could help remembering how America's intervention had decided the first world war. The 1917 perspective was uncomfortable."[30]

Conversely, in the occupied countries, gloom gave way to joy. The colossus had been halted, and though its head might be of iron, its feet had been found to be of clay. In the Balkans partisan warfare was given a blood transfusion, and an ever-increasing drain on German and Italian troops set in, in order to maintain authority in the occupied countries.

At the front there was consternation; for, as the cold grew in intensity, it was brought home to every German soldier that no preparations had been made for a winter campaign; that they were neither clothed, equipped nor trained for winter warfare. The Generals counselled retreat; but Hitler, the visionary, saw that, were one undertaken, it could but end as had Napoleon's. Though it was his obstinacy which had brought the campaign to the brink of disaster, now it was his obstinacy which was to save it plunging into the abyss. By refusing to draw out of Russia, or even to the west of Smolensk, he undoubtedly saved his army from an even greater catastrophe than that of 1812.

What was Hitler's problem? The choice was not between retreating, as Napoleon's had done, and standing still. Anyhow the latter was now out of the question, and the former would place so tremendous a strain on his communications, which were literally frozen up,[31] that it might easily end in a rout. There was, in fact, no choice. There were but two things to do: the first was to get the bulk of the troops under shelter before they were

---

[30]*Behind the Steel Wall*, pp. 60-61.

[31]Thousands of the German lorries and hundreds of their locomotives were frozen up. The damage done took weeks to repair.

frozen to death, and the second was to hold on to communications so that the armies could be re-equipped and supplied.

The communications the more vitally affected in the Moscow sector of the front were the railways, Moscow-Rzhev-Velikiye Luki, Moscow-Vyazma-Smolensk, Moscow-Kaluga-Bryansk, and Moscow-Tula-Orel, all of which were linked together by the lateral line Velikiye Luki-Vitebsk-Smolensk-Bryansk-Orel. Further, from Orel a railway ran south to Taganrog on the Sea of Azov. On all these railways there were one or more advanced depots from which the front had been fed. The more important were: Staraya Russa, Rzhev, Vyazma, Kaluga, Bryansk, Orel, Kursk and Kharkov. Between them there were minor depots. They were all fully stocked and afforded shelter. It was essential to hold them and get the troops back to them.

Therefore, what Hitler decided upon was to turn these advanced depots into entrenched camps, really fortified regions, and to fall back on them. By doing so he would gain shelter for his troops, who could live on their dumps while the lines of supply were put into working order. Meanwhile new advanced depots could be established in rear of them. Consequently, Hitler's plan was not a retreat, as had been Napoleon's, instead it was a rear manœuvre, though a compulsory one.

Each of these main fortified regions covered many square miles, and in some cases they could shelter entire armies. Like the Libyan "boxes" they were provided with all-round defences, and were intended, should they be cut off, to hold out until relieved. The Germans, adopting the name given to the squares of medieval Swiss pikemen formed to resist cavalry, called these fortified localities *Igels*—"hedgehogs"—because their defences bristled in all directions. And between the main ones they established lesser ones at small towns and large villages, linking the whole together by aircraft and at times supplying them by aircraft also.

Generally speaking, the Russian advance was not so much a counter-offensive or a pursuit as a steady forward percolation lapping round the points of German resistance and flowing in between them. Movement having to be made across country more so than by road, the Russians relied extensively on Cossack divisions reinforced by sledge-mounted artillery, sledge-borne infantry and ski-troops; the landing-wheels of fighter aircraft being replaced by skis. As these divisions did not possess weight of fire power, their main use was to pour through the gaps, sweep round the greater "hedgehogs" and swamp the lesser ones. Fighting became brutal in the extreme, because the guerilla bands not only co-operated with the Cossacks, but also operated independently far behind the German front. Ferocity begot ferocity, and as a writer in the *Neue Züricher Zeitung* described: "It is now a war of destruction such as modern Europe has never known. This is the characteristic of a merciless struggle in which neither side gives nor receives quarter. As often as not a battle ends in a mad butchery."[32]

The German withdrawal embraced the entire front, and was deepest in the central or Moscow sector between Kalinin and Tula. On 16th December the former town was cleared of the Germans, and, shortly after, an extensive pincer operation was developed against Rzhev, Gzhatsk and Vyazma, the Russians moving south-westwards from Kalinin and north-westwards from Tula. Heavy fighting soon developed around Kaluga, which was captured by the Russians on the 26th, lost immediately after and recaptured by them on the 30th. This was the most important single Russian success of the whole winter campaign, because Kaluga was one of the main "hedgehogs."

From Kaluga the Russians advanced north-west on Yukhnov, a "hedgehog" due east of Smolensk and south-east of Vyazma, pushing a deep salient into the German position. Simultaneously in the north they lapped round the west of Rzhev towards Vitebsk and reached Velikiye Luki to the north of it. These two advances round Vyazma brought the Russians to within fifty miles of Smolensk. Meanwhile, on 20th-22nd January, Mozhaisk, which lay sixty-five miles west of Moscow and forty east of Gzhatsk, was occupied by the Russians.

On the northern or Leningrad front, Tikhvin was abandoned by the Germans on 9th December, the Russians pressing on and crossing the Volkhov river; whereupon the Germans linked up Schlüsselburg and Novgorod—north of Lake Ilmen—and position warfare set in. In the extreme south the Russians opened a counter-offensive in the Crimea, and north of the Sea of Azov the "hedgehogs" of Taganrog, Stalino and Artemovsk were by-passed in order to concentrate all available forces against the "super-hedgehog" of Kharkov. It, however, stood firm, though Losovaya to the south of it was taken and the advance pushed to within thirty miles of Poltava.

Once mid-winter set in, and on account of the increasing depth of the snow, the Germans expected a respite. But the Russians percolated on, though no decisive gains were won, except on the Leningrad front. There, in January, the Russians constructed a motor road over the ice of Lake Ladoga, regaining contact with Leningrad, and, on 22nd February, they cut off a considerable part of the Sixteenth Germany Army in the Staraya Russa area south of Lake Ilmen and gradually annihilated it.

On the central front, in February and March, the Russian gains were consolidated and the small "hedgehogs" of Sukhinichi and Yuknov were

---

[32]Quoted in *The Tenth Quarter*, p. 63.

captured, the second on 3rd March. In April the thaw set in, and operations were brought to a standstill except in the Crimea, where the Germans made some progress against Kerch, which had been occupied by the Russians earlier in the winter, as also was Theodosia.

The main results of this campaign were: First, its moral effect on Russia, Germany and the world in general. In November, Hitler had proclaimed that the Russian armies had been destroyed. The campaign showed that this was far from being the case. That under winter conditions the Russian soldier was more than an equal of the German, and in spite of the fact that, as Fredborg says, "the German soldiers achieved the impossible against the pressing Russian hordes."[33] Secondly, by compelling the Germans to turn their advanced bases into "hedgehogs," and in consequence to form new advanced bases in rear of them along the line of the Dnieper and Dvina, the next German campaign was set back by many miles. Thirdly, the one thing the German Generals dreaded most had happened, a war of attrition had set in. Not only were the strengths of the German armies reduced by defensive fighting and frost, but the forward troops were prevented from reorganizing and training for the coming resumption of the offensive. In the "hedgehogs" of these winter months the cutting edge of the Grand Army of 1941 was blunted, and no reinforcing with the base metal of Italian, Rumanian and other satellite levies could give it back its temper.

(5) *The German* 1942 *Summer Campaign in Russia*

To grasp the full import of the German second summer campaign in Russia, it is necessary to bear in mind the aim of their first summer campaign. It was, as we have seen, not to conquer all Russia, but instead, by advancing on the main vital areas of operations, to compel the Russian armies to protect them and to destroy those armies as and when met. Tactical annihilation was the strategic aim.

We have also seen that this strategy failed, because speed was low, space too vast and force (opposition) too great.

Having failed in the more favourable circumstances of 1941, was the same strategy likely to succeed in the less favourable of 1942? Hitler's answer was "No!"—it would be folly to repeat it. Therefore, the alternative was to substitute a strategy of exhaustion for that of annihilation. To do so by tactical attrition was out of the question; for, even had it been possible, it would have taken too long. To do so morally—that is, by fomenting a counter-Bolshevik revolution—was also out of the question; therefore the

[33]*Behind the Steel Wall*, p. 68.

sole way open was to strike at Russia's economic power—the material basis of her fighting strength. This, it was decided, could be done by depriving Russia of the Donetz industrial area, her Kuban cornfields and her Caucasian oil wells. In brief, deprive Russia of her vital area of operations in the quadrilateral Kharkov-Stalingrad-Baku-Batum, and the Russian fighting forces would in time become inoperative.

It would appear, therefore, that Hitler's plan for 1942 was as follows[34]: To cut off and occupy the quadrilateral Voronezh-Saratov-Stalingrad-Rostov by two parallel attacks, the northern along the line Kursk-Saratov and the southern along the line Taganrog-Stalingrad, and, under cover of this blockage, thrust through Caucasia to Baku.[35]

According to two historians, this plan "was confirmed by a document which fell into the hands of the Russians and which was mentioned by Premier Stalin in his speech on the twenty-fifth anniversary of the Soviet Revolution."[36] In it is given a time table for the occupation of the following towns: Borisoglebsk, east of Voronezh, by 10th July; Stalingrad by 15th July; Saratov by 10th August; Syzran by 15th August; and Arzamas, south of Gorki, by 10th September.

Though the rapidity of these occupations is startling, what is more so is that, even to a strategic tiro, it should have been apparent that success did not so much depend on the occupation of important points as on the prevention of Russian retaliation. The plan would seem to have ignored the

[34]This plan tallies with Hitler's pronouncements and the German radio commentaries of this period. The main German objective was no longer to be Moscow or the destruction of the Russian armies, instead to "control the Volga"—that is, cut all traffic from the south to the north. *Das Schwarze Korps* of 9th July pointed out that, because the Russian had the "advantage of the infinity of space . . . only by stubborn efforts can he be broken down and his material destroyed, his production centres seized, his sources of raw materials cut off, and the arteries of his economic life strangled." (*Behind the Steel Wall*, p. 120.)

[35]As early as April, this plan, in part at least, became known in Istanbul. On the 15th *The Times* Istanbul Correspondent wrote: "Turkish experts agree there are two possible German plans—the 'Caucasus plan' and the 'Volga plan'." The first "will enable the Germans to cut off the Caucasus from the rest of Russia, will deprive the Russians of their main source of oil supply . . . The Volga plan is supposed to aim . . . at the destruction of the Russian armies by first isolating them from one another, and then beating them separately. According to that plan, the main attack will be launched from Orel and Kursk north-eastwards towards Gorki (Nijni-Novgorod) on the Volga, in order to separate the Russian armies in the centre from Marshal Timoshenko's forces in the south, and to menace the rear of the Russian armies defending Moscow." (*The Times*, 16th April, 1942.) According to Ciano, Ribbentrop told him that the oil wells were the politico-military objective. "When Russia's sources of oil are exhausted, she will be brought to her knees." (*Ciano's Diary*, p. 462.)

[36]*The Russian Campaigns of* 1941-1943, W. E. D. Allen and Paul Muratoff (1944), p. 72.

existence of the Russian armies to the north of the line Voronezh-Saratov. And because it had been decided that, on account of space and force, they could not be tactically annihilated, nor, on account of the morale of the Russian people, morally annihilated, the only way to defeat the Russian armies was strategically to paralyse them, not by depriving them of future resources, such as oil, coal and wheat, but of immediate means of movement. Therefore, first of all, it was essential to occupy or invest Moscow, because, as Paris is the hub of all French railways, Moscow is the hub of all Russian. In 1914, the failure to occupy Paris had led to the German disaster on the Marne, and, as we shall see, the failure to occupy Moscow in 1942 led to the German disaster on the Volga. With Moscow in German hands, coupled with persistent strategic air attacks on Vologda, Bui, Gorki, Arzamas and Penza, all between two hundred and fifty and three hundred and fifty miles from Moscow and, therefore, within easy bombing range, not only would supplies from Archangel and reinforcements from Asiatic Russia have been blocked, but all rail movements within central Russia would have become chaotic if not altogether halted.

The armies[37] detailed to carry out this plan were placed under the command of Field-Marshal von Bock. Though their morale and training were lower than in 1941, their fire power had been increased; the clumsy armoured divisions of 400 tanks were reduced to 250 of improved patterns, and the *Luftwaffe* had been organized into assault groups which co-operated even more closely than hitherto with the ground troops. Also, a new tank tactics, ascribed to Field-Marshal Rommel, was introduced. It was called the Mot-Pulk (moving box formation), really a modernized edition of the Hussite Wagenburg. It is described by Colonel de Watteville as follows:

"This mass of manœuvre was so distributed that the tanks and anti-tank artillery represented an exterior frame which was filled by a 'soft-skinned' centre of lorry-borne infantry, anti-tank artillery, mobile repair shops and all the modern paraphernalia necessary to an army in battle . . . It was first and foremost a fighting organism of immense fire power and immense mobility covered by a powerful armoured skin . . ."[38]

Though the main German offensive was not launched until 28th June, it was preceded by important preliminary fighting. On 8th May Field-Marshal von Manstein, commanding the German Twelfth Army in the Crimea, opened an attack on Kerch, and carried that town by storm on the 13th. When this attack was in its last stage, Timoshenko, in order to

---

[37]The total forces in Russia would appear to have been 225 German divisions and 43 Satellite. The Russians had 300 divisions or more. The Germans had about 50 armoured and motorized divisions.

[38]*The Twelfth Quarter*, p. 47. For diagram of, see *Warfare To-day*, Odhams Press (1944), pp. 112-113.

THE GERMAN SUMMER CAMPAIGN IN RUSSIA, 8th MAY–15th OCTOBER, 1942

delay the German offensive, on the 12th launched a violent attack south of
Kharkov. Rapidly advancing from Losovaya towards Kharkov and
Poltava, on the 16th he captured Krasnograd and broke through the outer
defences of the Kharkov "super-hedgehog," and two days later was
fighting in the suburbs of Kharkov. On the 19th he was violently counter-
attacked, and a week later so hard pressed in the Barvenkovo-Izyum area,
that he was compelled to fall back from Krasnograd. During the withdrawal a considerable body of his troops was encircled and captured. On
1st June, the Germans proclaimed a complete victory; nevertheless, it had
given them a nasty shock.

Four days later, von Manstein opened his bombardment of Sevastopol,
prior to assaulting the fortress. It had an outer circumference of twenty
miles and an inner of eight. It was held by 75,000 troops under command
of General Petrov. After a tremendous defence, during which 50,000 tons
of shells and 25,000 of bombs were rained upon it, it was stormed on
1st July. Thus the whole of the Crimea passed into German hands.

By the middle of June the massing of German troops on the winter front
west of the Oskol river left no doubt in the Russian mind that a powerful
offensive was imminent. There von Bock had marshalled the following
forces: In the Kursk area, the Second Army, the Second Panzer Army and
an Hungarian Army under General Weichs; in the Byelgorod area, the
Sixth Army and Fourth Panzer Army under General von Hoth; and in
the Kharkov area, the Seventeenth Army and the First Panzer Army
under Field-Marshal von Kleist, with an Italian Army in reserve west of
Kharkov. South of these groups of Armies was General Schwoedler's
group, which was to be absorbed by Field-Marshal von Manstein's Twelfth
Army and a Rumanian Army, soon to move north from the Crimea.[39]

Appreciating that the German attack would come on the front Voronezh-
Rostov and be directed on the line Saratov-Stalingrad, the Russians massed
powerful forces north of Voronezh, and strongly fortified Voronezh and
Rostov as well as the line of the Donetz river.

On 22nd June a sudden German attack was made from Izyum, and
three days later the Russians were driven out of Kupyansk. Next, on the
28th, the long expected blow was struck east of Kursk, and on 1st July the
Russian front between Shigri and Tim was smashed. This blow was
immediately followed on the 2nd by a powerful attack between Byelgorod
and Kharkov. Again the Russian front was broken, and on the 5th, in the
north, the Germans reached the western outskirts of Voronezh, and in
the south the line Svatovo-Lisichensk.

[39]In all, about 40 German infantry divisions, 16 to 18 Panzer and 15 to 20
Hungarian, Italian and Rumanian divisions. (*The Russian Campaigns of 1941-1943*,
p. 80.)

The battle for Voronezh now began and, as we shall see, for the Germans it was one of the most fateful of the whole war.

On the 6th and 7th Weichs' tanks and motorized infantry forced a crossing over the Don and penetrated into Voronezh, which lies in an angle formed by the Don and a small tributary, and, in consequence, is moated on three sides. Following this assault came the German infantry, who were attacked in flank between the two rivers. "The Russian Army concentrated . . . to the north of Voronezh had arrived in time to save the situation; it perhaps even saved, for the Russians, the course of the whole campaign."[40]

There is little doubt that it did; for during the ten days of desperate fighting which followed, south of Voronezh the advance was so rapid that, when contrasted with the Russian resistance at Voronezh, the two together had, as we shall see, a strange psychological effect on the mind of Hitler.

By 12th July, von Hoth had taken Rossosh and Kantemirovka stations on the Voronezh-Rostov railway, and the next day Millerovo was captured by von Kleist's First Tank Army. Voroshilovgrad was outflanked and entered on the 20th, while von Manstein's armies moved on Rostov, which was evacuated by the Russians on the 27th.

"The whole Russian front was tottering . . . and the German Army crossed the Don on a broad front. The tone of the Russian communiques became grave, and the Russian radio revealed increasing anxiety . . . Strong demands for a second front were raised in Russia."[41]

These rapid advances towards Stalingrad, when coupled with the unexpected Russian resistance at Voronezh, would appear to have so powerfully influenced Hitler that he decided to mask Voronezh with Weichs' group of armies and direct von Hoth's group due east to co-operate with von Manstein against Stalingrad, and only when Stalingrad had been taken to resume the advance on Saratov.

Strategically, this was a blunder of such magnitude that it verges on madness. Because no attempt had been made to neutralize the Moscow railway hub, it followed that the Russian armies north of Voronezh had complete freedom of movement. Therefore that, because the occupation of Caucasia was the most important part of the German plan, the sole possibility of securing it was to establish a deep defensive block to the north of that region—namely, as in the original plan, the occupation of the quadrilateral Rostov-Stalingrad-Saratov-Voronezh. This was essential in order to obtain depth of defence and to gain room to manœuvre in. By reducing the quadrilateral to the triangle Voronezh-Stalingrad-Rostov, a salient was substituted for it, the northern flank of which—Voronezh-Stalingrad—was open to attack should the Russians move southwards from the line

[40]*Ibid.*, p. 81.   [41]*Behind the Steel Wall*, p. 120.

Voronezh-Saratov. The tactical line of operation was thus changed and the door unbolted to eventual disaster.

In accordance with this change of plan, Weichs' armies entrenched themselves before Voronezh, and a number of Hungarian, Italian and Rumanian divisions were brought forward to protect von Hoth's strategic flank which ran along the western bank of the Don. Meanwhile, von Manstein's group, advancing from Rostov, crossed the Lower Don at Tsimlyanskaya, while von Kleist's swept southwards towards the northern Caucasian steppes.

During the last week in July and the first in August, von Hoth rapidly advanced down the Don, and a fierce struggle began for the bridgeheads of Kletskaya and Kalash, where the Don bends southwards and west of Stalingrad. On 15th August a crossing at Kalash was won; but it was not until the 25th that the river at Kletskaya was crossed. Meanwhile, the German forces advancing south of the Don had been brought to a halt at Kotelnikovo, and it was not until von Hoth was over the river that they were able to move forward. On 9th September the Stalingrad-Borisoglebsk railway was cut. That day Stalingrad was heavily bombed, and to the Germans its fall appeared imminent.

While these operations were developing, von Kleist's group, having crossed the Lower Don, fanned out over the northern Caucasian plains at high speed. On 4th August Voroshilovsk was taken; on the 8th the Russians wrecked and abandoned the Maikop oilfields; on the 20th Krasnodar fell, and on the 25th Mozdok on the middle Terek and one hundred miles from the Caspian Sea was reached, the Russians withdrawing to Grozny. Lastly, on 10th September the naval Black Sea base of Novorossisk was captured, after which, on account of the difficulties of the terrain, Russian resistance, length of communications and shortage of petrol,[42] to all intents and purposes the Caucasian campaign came to an end. Everything was to be concentrated on the capture of Stalingrad.

Stalingrad, formerly Tzaritsin,[43] was a long straggling industrial city of some 500,000 inhabitants, situated on the right bank of the Volga a few miles north of its elbow. *Vis-à-vis* a German attack, its strength was due to the Volga being from two to two and a half miles wide, and, therefore,

---

[42]Fredborg writes: "I was also told that one of the reasons for the lull in the Caucasus . . . was shortage of motor fuel. The oil transports had to be diverted to Stalingrad." (*Behind the Steel Wall*, p. 125.) This is corroborated by Field-Marshal von Kleist, who in an interview given to Captain B. H. Liddell Hart said: "We ran out of petrol and came to a halt; our supplies from behind failed to keep up. But that was not the main cause of the failure. We could still have reached our goal if my forces had not been drawn away bit by bit to help the attack on Stalingrad. Hitler missed his main objective in trying to secure that lesser one—and in the end didn't even gain that." (*Sunday Dispatch*, 15th September, 1946.)

difficult to bridge, and until it was bridged the city could not be completely invested.

For the Germans, the problem was, therefore, to establish themselves on the left bank of the Volga. Once there, a comparatively small army could stop all traffic over it, and thereby starve the garrison of Stalingrad out.

In all opposed river crossings the determining factor is not width of river—though this is important—instead it is the length of river frontage held by the attacker. Should the frontage be extensive, by feinting here and there the would-be crosser can so distract his opponent that, sooner or later, he will be able to throw a bridge over the river at some unprotected or lightly held point, and establish a bridgehead on its far side. And because a wide river, such as the Volga, will take longer to bridge than a narrow one, the wider a river is the longer must be the operative stretch to feint on. Therefore the initial German problem was to establish this operative front. But instead of doing so, direct attack was resorted to—that is, an attempt was made to carry the city by batter and storm.[44]

The assault proper opened on 15th September. Thence onwards for exactly a month attack after attack was launched, to be met by so staunch a resistance by the garrison under General Chuykov that none gained more than a local or temporary advantage. The monumental folly of this should have become apparent immediately after it was found that the city could not be rushed; for though a city is not a fortress, so long as its garrison remains staunch and its supply line open, by pounding it into rubble is the most effective way of converting it into a more formidable obstacle than any fortress which has ever been built.

The losses suffered in these senseless assaults became so heavy that, after 15th October, General von Hoth was ordered to desist and systematically obliterate the city by artillery bombardment and bombing. But, what for? The only possible answer is, to sustain Hitler's prestige; for the city was already a rubble heap. Its industries had been destroyed, and the Volga had been blocked for up and down traffic.[45] This meant that the umbilical oil cord between Baku and Moscow had ceased to function. Therefore, all that was now necessary was to keep the river blockaded; the city itself was tactically of no value.

[43] It is interesting to remember that on 1st July, 1919, Tzaritsin was captured by Major E. M. Bruce and six English mechanics in a Mark V tank.

[44] According to von Kleist: "The 4th Panzer Army could have swept into it (Stalingrad) without a fight, but was diverted south to help me over the Don—quite needlessly. When it turned north a fortnight later, the Russians were able to check it." (*Sunday Dispatch*, 15th September, 1946.)

[45] On 11th September the Germans had reached the Volga South of Stalingrad, Later they occupied a five mile length of the western bank at Dubovka, thirty miles north of Stalingrad.

Thus was German initiative in Russia exhausted and at the very moment when, as we have seen, it was becoming more and more attenuated in North Africa. And though many factors go to sustain and maintain the initiative, the fundamental one is freedom of movement; therefore, conversely, restriction of enemy movement. In both North Africa and at Stalingrad—in fact in the whole of Russia—one common denominator is to be discovered. It is, over-extension of German communications coupled with the difficulty of protecting them.

From Egypt, Rommel's ran westwards for one thousand two hundred miles to Tripoli; and thence, as the crow flies, one thousand three hundred miles to the industrial centres in Germany—his source of supply. From Stalingrad, Hoth's ran westwards through Russia for one thousand miles, and thence six hundred miles to central Germany. In the one case, so long as the British held fast to Malta, they could operate against Rommel's communications; and in the other case, so long as the Russians held fast to Moscow, they maintained freedom of movement to manoeuvre against Hoth's, while their guerilla bands compelled the Germans to protect every mile of their communications, and, in consequence, deprive their field armies of hundreds of thousands of combatants.

Nevertheless, in the autumn of 1942 the economic position of Russia was a desperate one, and had it not been for the steady stream of Anglo-American supplies then pouring into Archangel, it is doubtful whether the Russians would have been able to turn to their advantage the fantastic situation in which Hitler had placed his armies.

Since June, 1941, German occupation had reduced the population under the Soviet Government from 184,000,000 to 126,000,000—that is, by over 30 per cent. Further, Russia's economic losses had been gigantic—namely, in foodstuffs, 38 per cent; in coal and electrical power, 50 per cent; in iron and steel, 60 per cent; in manganese and aluminium, 50 per cent; and in chemical industries, 33 per cent.

Therefore, the idea behind Hitler's strategic plan had been right—namely, to strike at his enemy's economic strength, the foundations of his military power. It was in its realization that blunder after blunder had been made, and the greatest was that, because the vastness of Russia prohibited him bringing his enemy to decisive battle, he failed to see that it was imperative to immobilize him before setting out to overrun his vital areas of operation. This could have been done had he occupied Moscow—the hub of Russian movements. Instead, like Charles XII, more so than Napoleon, he lost the initiative.

After his great victory at Poltava in 1709, Peter the Great entered Kiev, and there in the Church of St. Sophia he held a thanksgiving service.

Addressing the Tsar and his soldiers, a Russian monk, by name Féofan Prokopovich, said:

"When our neighbours hear what has happened, they will say, it was not into a foreign country that the Swedish army and the Swedish power ventured, but rather into some mighty sea! They have fallen in and disappeared, even as lead is swallowed in water!"[46]

This was the secret of Russia's might which Hitler in his strategy missed. Its answer could only be to deprive the Russian armies of their mobility; for then space would be transformed for them from an ally into a deadly enemy.

[46]*Peter the Great*, K. Waliszewski (1898), p. 326.

CHAPTER VI

LOSS OF JAPANESE INITIATIVE

(1) *The Allied Strategical Problems*

After the Battle of Midway Island, the problem which faced the Allies was how to sap forward through the outer and inner defences of the Japanese ocean fortress and ultimately storm its citadel—the home islands of Japan.

This problem was solved, as in the past sieges so frequently have been, by taking advantage of the contour of the fortress, which was that of a huge salient. Its base extended from Burma to Paramushiro in the Kuriles; its apex resting in the Ellice Islands pointing south-eastwards towards Fiji and Samoa.

Strategically, the salient commanded both the Western Pacific and the Indian Ocean; but fortunately for the United States and the British Empire Japan had not strength enough to occupy and hold the strategic centres in the latter and simultaneously fight a life or death struggle in the former. And it is as well to note that, had she been able to do so, the course of the entire war would have been changed; for she could then have strangled her enemies' sea routes to the Middle East and India. This would have led to three all but certain results: the occupation of Egypt by Rommel, because Auchinleck could not have been reinforced; the collapse of Timoshenko in Caucasia, because he could not have been supplied through Persia; and the collapse of Chiang Kai-shek in Central China, because he could not have been supplied from India, and though the air supply service established provided him with little enough, the mere fact that it was continuous and increasing gave him considerable moral support.

All this should be borne in mind. It was the Indian Ocean, as much so as Russia, which separated Japan from her Western allies, and throughout the war because she had her hands full in the Pacific its security was guaranteed to her enemies. This is at once made clear, by imagining that the United States had remained neutral, when there can be no shadow of doubt that, irrespective of what happened in Europe, Britain would have been impotent in the Indian Ocean, and in consequence would have lost the eastern half of her Empire; for even had Russia defeated Germany, it is fantastic to suppose that the Russians would have turned upon Japan in order to restore it to Britain.

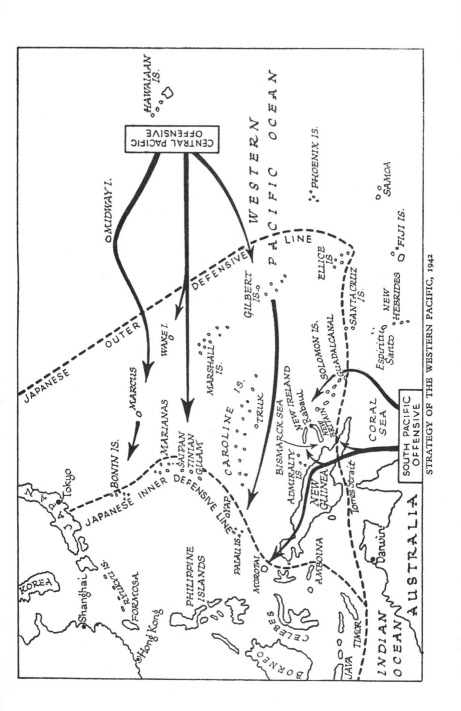

STRATEGY OF THE WESTERN PACIFIC, 1942

It was because Japan could not simultaneously hold the two flanks of the salient in sufficient force that she lost the war, and from the start it must have been clear to her that her danger lay in the likelihood of both being simultaneously attacked. Her enemies saw this with equal clarity, in fact, that their grand tactical problem was a stupendous Cannæ operation at sea. Also they saw that, strategically, they were well placed to carry it out directly they had accumulated sufficient means, because they could approach the salient from four separate bases: from India and Alaska to strike at its haunches, and from the Hawaiian Islands and Australia to strike at its flanks.

Of these two double enveloping operations, the second was the more important, because the haunches of the salient were exceedingly strong: the southern was protected by an enormous block of mountains and the northern by the Arctic weather.

Though the salient enabled Japan to operate on interior lines, a decided advantage so long as her enemies were weak, directly they became strong enough to threaten it from several directions, her shipping and air power were insufficient to permit her concentrating her forces against more than one point at the time, and simultaneously hold the rest of the enormous circumference. In fact, from the Battle of Midway onwards, the limited nature of her strategy worked in her enemies' favour, for it enabled them to gain the time needed wherein to build up their strength, and eventually by forcing her to over-extend her own, to wrest the initiative from her.

Therefore, in the long run, time was against her, and not as her strategy had first led her to suppose, on her side. Nevertheless, until her enemies were ready to strike in force, their problem remained a preparatory and defensive one.

To the Americans and British is was clear that their lines of advance from Burma and Alaska against the haunches of the salient were in importance secondary to those from Hawaii and Australia against its flanks. Further, that because the victory of Midway Island had definitely secured the former base, their immediate problem was to secure Australia. To do so demanded that the Japanese be prevented extending their occupation of New Guinea and pushing the apex of the salient south-east to include the New Hebrides, New Caledonia, Fiji and Samoa; for were they to do this, they would be powerfully placed to operate against the South Pacific line of communications from the United States to Australia, and, thereby, seriously impede the concentration of forces and supplies in the latter.

The strategic centre of this sub-theatre of the war was Rabaul in the island of New Britain, which, as we have seen, was occupied by the Japanese on 23rd January, 1942. Its importance lay in that it was centrally placed between the Bismarck Sea, which flanked the northern coast of New

Guinea, and the Coral Sea, which flanked the north-eastern coast of Australia as well as the Torres Strait. Therefore, once Rabaul was neutralized or in Allied possession, no further extension of the apex of the salient south-eastwards was to be feared.

Further still, Rabaul lay on the left flank of the line of approach from the Hawaiian Islands through the northern flank of the salient. It was a three-fold line. Its axis ran by way of Wake to Guam and Saipan Islands; its right flank ran via Midway and Marcus Islands to the Bonin Archipelago; and its left flank via the Gilbert Islands and Truk to the Palau Islands and Yap. Therefore, as Rabaul lay eight hundred miles south of Truk—the main Japanese base in the Caroline Islands—that is, within aircraft range of that island, once Rabaul and Truk were neutralized, an air-free link would be established between an advance from Australia by way of New Guinea on to the island of Morotai and an advance from Hawaii on to the Palau Islands, Yap and Guam. And, be it noted, all these terminal islands were vitally important strategic points, because they lay on the circumference of Japan's inner line of defence.

In brief, the Allied solution of the problem was as follows:

First, to neutralize Rabaul and thereby breach the southern flank of the salient as well as prevent the extension of its apex south-eastwards. Next, to breach the northern flank between Wake Island and the Gilberts. Then, once these two operations were successfully accomplished, to assault the inner line between Morotai and Guam and storm the Philippines; thereby cutting Japan off from her recently gained southern Empire. Lastly, from the Philippines to advance on the citadel.

(2) *The Guadalcanal and Papua Campaigns*

As is so often the case in war, the solution of the Allied strategical problem was shaped by events as much so as by calculations, and after the Battle of Midway Island, the next major event arose out of the Japanese decision to extend the apex of the salient by renewing their operations against Port Moresby and by establishing a powerful air base to the east of it in the southern Solomon Islands. To fulfil this second decision, in July they set about building an airfield on the northern coast of Guadalcanal, an island immediately south of the island of Florida. From it their intention was, by means of land-based aircraft, to imperil the American hold on the New Hebrides and New Caledonia, which lie to the north-west and west of the Fiji Islands and south-west of the Ellice group, as well as to protect the sea flank of their advance in Papua. In order to frustrate this extension southwards, on 7th August an American expedition, based on New

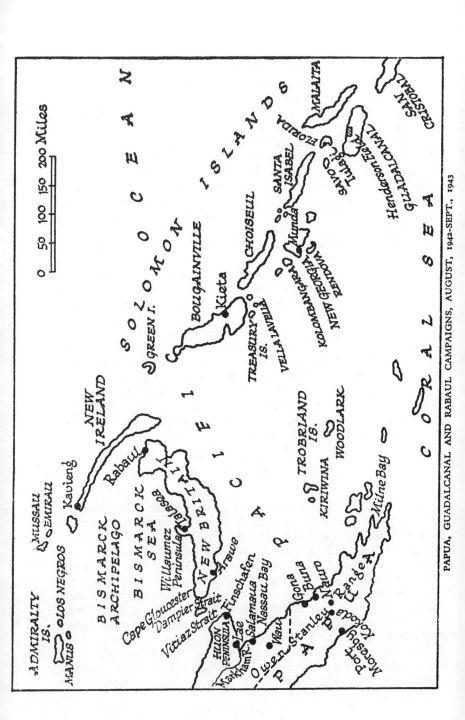

PAPUA, GUADALCANAL AND RABAUL CAMPAIGNS, AUGUST, 1942-SEPT., 1943

Zealand and protected by three aircraft-carriers, landed on the islands of Florida and Guadalcanal, and meeting with little opposition, occupied the partly finished Guadalcanal air base and named it Henderson Field. This action led to a series of naval and land battles of unprecedented violence which lasted for exactly six months.

The first of the naval engagements was the Battle of Savo Island, brought about by the Japanese attempting to frustrate the landing. It opened in the early hours of 9th August, and though the American fleet was worsted, losing four cruisers—the *Canberra* (Australian), *Quincy*, *Vincennes* and *Astoria*—in the evening the Japanese withdrew and the landing continued.

Concentrating their forces in the Rabaul area, the Japanese made ready, at all costs, to destroy the invaders. Bombing attacks and naval battles next followed in rapid succession. On 23rd-25th August the naval battle of the Eastern Solomons was fought, in which a large and strongly protected convoy of Japanese reinforcements was repulsed. In this engagement the American naval forces were built round the aircraft-carriers *Saratoga* and *Enterprise*. Next, on the night of 11th-12th October, the naval battle of Cape Esperance took place, and on the 16th large Japanese reinforcements were landed on Guadalcanal, and the American hold on the island was seriously challenged. Most of the fighting was in dense jungle and was very confused, as the following incident shows: "I remember the leading skirmish line of a platoon advancing on Tassafaronga," writes an American participant. "The regimental commander came up and went through the line to a short distance, then came back and said, 'How much farther to the front line?' I said, 'Colonel, you have just come *back* to the front line, the Japs are right over there'."[1]

Ten days later followed the naval battle of Santa Cruz Islands, in which the U.S. carrier *Hornet* was lost and the carrier *Enterprise* severely damaged. This day the Japanese made an all-out attack on Henderson Field, and were with difficulty repulsed. Next, on the nights of 13th-14th November, followed the naval battle of Guadalcanal, one of the most furious sea battles ever fought.[2] In it battleships participated, and two Japanese battleships were sunk. Of this period Lieutenant Brodie, an American naval officer, writes:

"Our possession of Henderson Field on Guadalcanal gave us not only a base for direct air attack, but also a valuable advance position of reconnaissance for our surface forces. Our planes could scout far to the north of

[1]"Lessons of Guadalcanal," Captain Gerald H. Shea, *Infantry Journal*, July, 1943.
[2]"Our Navy at War," Official Report by Admiral Ernest J. King, *The United States News*, p. 36.

the island, over waters which Japanese naval forces and transports had to cross in approaching Guadalcanal, while the Japanese were largely denied similar reconnaissance in the direction of our own approach. Thus we were able to bring our available ships to the scene when needed, and upon arriving there they were likely to enjoy all the advantages of surprise. By such devices our surface forces were able to exercise a continuity of pressure out of all proportion to the total time they spent in the disputed waters . . ."[3]

In spite of these advantages, in the next naval battle, that of Tassa-faronga, fought on 30th November, the Americans came near to disaster. "Only one of the five American cruisers engaged," writes Lieutenant Brodie, ". . . escaped damage. Fortunately, however, the Japanese vessels involved, destroyers and possibly light cruisers, failed to get home to report the havoc they had caused. The battle will probably become the classic example of how wise it may be to keep one's mouth shut about damage received, for the enemy in effect gave up a campaign as a result of a battle we thought we had lost."[4]

Though this may be true, a more important reason was that by early December the situation in Papua had become so critical that the forces assembling in the Rabaul area to reinforce the garrison of Guadalcanal on 1st February had to be diverted to Papua. Thus it came about that on the night of 7th-8th February, after having lost some 10,000 in killed and an equivalent number through disease and starvation, the remnants of the Guadalcanal garrison were withdrawn. Thus one half of the Japanese plan to push out the salient came to naught. What of the other?

The Papua half of the plan was based on three separate operations. First, a direct advance from Gona on to Port Moresby was to be made by the jungle trail which passes through the Australian Government post of Kokoda and over the Owen Stanley Range. Its object was to draw the Australian forces at Port Moresby northwards into the mountains and jungle. Secondly, while this movement was under way, a seaborne force was to occupy Milne Bay and seize the airfield in its vicinity. This done, an air base was to be established there from which, in conjunction with the one then being built on Guadalcanal, air command of the northern entrance to the Coral Sea was to be gained. Lastly, under cover of this command, a seaborne force was to move from Rabaul to Port Moresby with the dual aim of attacking in rear the Australians entangled with the

[3]"The Naval Strategy of the Pacific War," Lieut. Bernard Brodie, USNR, *Infantry Journal*, August, 1945, p. 37.
[4]*Ibid.*, p. 37.

Gona column in the mountains, and cutting the Australian line of communications between Port Moresby and Darwin.[5]

On 21st-22nd July the first part of this plan was set in motion by a Japanese landing at Gona, a village on the northern coast of Papua roughly half-way between Lae and Milne Bay. At the time there were a few Australian patrols on the coast, based on a militia battalion at Kokoda. After a spirited fight this battalion was forced back towards Port Moresby, and early in August the Japanese occupied Kokoda. From there they pushed slowly on southwards through the jungle.

On 26th August the second part of the Japanese plan was put into force. That day about 2,000 troops were landed to the north of Milne Bay, and forthwith set out to seize the airfield. They had expected little opposition, hence the smallness of their numbers. But unfortunately for them, they were met by so stubborn a resistance and such powerful air assault that, after losing the bulk of their supplies and 700 in killed, on the 29th they re-embarked and abandoned the project. That no further attempt was made to establish an air base at this vitally important point can only be explained by the fact that the operations at Guadalcanal were absorbing so many reinforcements that insufficient remained over to warrant its repetition.

Thus it came about that the whole onus of the campaign was lifted on to the shoulders of the overland column, which lacking local command of the air was unable to protect its bases as well as the jungle track leading back to Kokoda. The upshot was that the Japanese advance grew slower and slower. Scores of men died daily from starvation, and so depleted did the column become that, when on 15th September it collided with its enemy between the villages of Elfogi and Ioribaiwa, some thirty miles north of Port Moresby, it was so weak that the Japanese Command ordered it to withdraw to Nauro, ten miles to the north of the Owen Stanley main ridge. Pressing on, the Australians re-entered Kokoda on 3rd November.

The most interesting item in this advance was that the Australians relied almost entirely on air supply. Of it, Mr. Courtenay, a war correspondent present at the time, writes:

"There was nowhere to land in those mountain areas, but here and there on the sides of the razor-backs, by a sort of fortuitous geographical trick, there were open patches of jungle grass about the size of a village green. The Army Service Corps organized these little places into supply-dropping grounds, and the Australian pilots, flying the unarmed transport aircraft

[5]When the war opened, from Alice Springs in the centre of Australia to Birdun, two hundred and fifty miles south of Darwin, there was a roadless and railless gap of nearly seven hundred miles. The Australian and American engineers were given ninety days to build a road spanning this gap. This they did in eighty-eight days.

under the canopy of the fighters keeping command of the air, were able to wind their way through tortuous valleys and drop supplies to us as we marched along these mountain trails. There were no parachutes for most of the supplies, and about 80 per cent of them fell into the jungle and were never recovered; but the other 20 per cent fell in the target area and that succoured the men on the march."[6]

At Nauro the Japanese hoped to hold their enemy until they themselves were reinforced, but to their astonishment and surprise, while they were attempting to do so, they were suddenly threatened in rear by an airborne American force. Of this brilliant manœuvre General H. H. Arnold, Commanding General, U.S. Army Air Force, writes:

"All Japanese efforts to reinforce the Buna-Gona region were frustrated by our long-range heavy bombers. Our Troop Carrier Command flew a complete striking-force—troops, equipment and food—into the area. In one air movement, 3,600 troops were brought from Australia to Port Moresby, and 15,000 from Moresby over the high Owen Stanley Mountains to the air strips near Buna. These troops were not only transported but were supplied by air at a rate of more than two million pounds a week. Construction equipment and steel mats and asphalt moved by the same route. A four-gun battery of 105 mm. howitzers was ferried over by a B-17. Sick and wounded were evacuated on the way back. The entire operation proved to be of far-reaching tactical consequences."[7]

The aim of this rear attack was to harry the Japanese lines of communication and, if possible, occupy their coastal bases. And to protect them, the Japanese were forced to do what General Hooker did at Chancellorsville—namely, altogether abandon their offensive plan, and with speed withdraw to the coast and fortify Gona, Sanananda and Buna. Whereupon the Australian overland column linked up with the airborne troops and lay siege to these bases. Gona fell on 9th December, Buna on 3rd January, 1943, and Sanananda on 19th January; the Japanese fighting to the death.

Thoroughly alarmed by these disasters, the Japanese Command poured the reinforcements which at the time were earmarked for Guadalcanal into Finschhafen, Lae and Salamaua, and then set out from Mubo, a village some fifteen miles south of Salamaua, to attack Wau, the main Allied air

---

[6]"The War in the Pacific," William Courtenay, *Journal of the Royal United Service Institution*, February, 1945, p. 16.

[7]*Report of the Commanding General of the Army Air Force to the Secretary of War*, 4th January, 1944, pp. 36-37. "The most noteworthy feature of this project was the fact that only hastily prepared landing strips of the most primitive character could be made available. An unusual amount of skill and daring made possible its achievement." (*Biennial Report of the Chief of Staff of the United States Army, 1st July, 1941, to 30th June, 1943, to the Secretary of War*, p. 32.)

base in the goldfield area of North-east New Guinea. In June, 1942, an Australian Commando had been landed there, but through sickness was now reduced to some 300 men. Against this minute force the Japanese advanced a column 3,300 strong, and would certainly have overwhelmed it had not General MacArthur[8] rushed to its support 600 Australians by air transport. Discovering a mountain track unknown to the Australians, this time it was the Japanese who surprised their enemy by attacking him in rear, and, on 29th January, having advanced to within four hundred yards of Wau, they were on the point of carrying the post by assault when 1,200 reinforcements, again air transported, came to its relief. The next day a number of 25-pdrs. were also landed, and coming into action within half an hour of their arrival, the Japanese were beaten back and compelled to withdraw.

Lastly, on 3rd-4th March, was fought the Battle of the Bismarck Sea, in which a Japanese convoy, sailing from Rabaul to bring supplies and reinforcements to Lae, was literally annihilated by Allied air attack. "In this Battle of the Bismarck Sea," writes General G. C. Marshall, Chief of Staff of the United States Army, "Allied losses were one bomber and three pursuit planes, with a casualty list of thirteen men, compared to a known Japanese loss of 61 planes and 22 ships, and an estimated loss of an entire division of 15,000 men."[9]

Thus the second half of the Japanese campaign to extend the salient ended as disastrously as had the first, and though, on the part of the Allies, both halves were strategically defensive operations, the winning of Guadalcanal and Papua clearly showed that the strategic initiative was slipping out of the hands of the Japanese into their own. This loss of initiative was to be vastly accelerated in the next two campaigns.

(3) *The Rabaul Campaign and the Conquest of New Guinea*

The Battle of the Bismarck Sea was followed by several months of cleaning up Japanese detachments and reinforcing the Allied forces both in northern Papua and the southern Solomons. In the former they were built up to four American and six Australian divisions. In consequence of this, it was not until the middle of June that in both these sub-areas of the Pacific theatre of war the Allies were ready for the next campaign—the neutralization of Rabaul as the Japanese main base.

On the 22nd and 23rd of that month, General MacArthur occupied Woodlark and Kiriwina Islands in the Trobrian group, which lies to the east of the tail of New Guinea. Their value lay in that, once airfields had

---

[8]General MacArthur had taken over the conduct of the compaign on 17th November.

[9]*Biennial Report of . . . 1st July, 1941, to 30th June, 1943,* p. 12.

been built on them, a fighter link could be established between New Guinea and Guadalcanal, and, in consequence, the main northern entrance to the Coral Sea would then be commanded. Seven days later, Major-General O. W. Griswold, commanding the American XIVth Corps at Guadalcanal, occupied Rendova Island, from where he at once started shelling the enemy airfield at Munda in New Georgia. New Georgia was next invaded and the Munda airfield won on 5th August; fighting ending in that island on the 25th. By-passing the strongly held island of Kolombangara, the island of Vella Lavella was occupied on 9th October, and two islands in the Treasury group on 26th October.

Meanwhile, in order to gain a base of operations from which to invade the island of New Britain, on the northern extremity of which Rabaul was situated, MacArthur set out to win the Huon Peninsula. To accomplish this, on 29th-30th June, he first landed a force at Nassau Bay, which lies eleven miles south of Salamaua—a town situated on the southern side of the Markham River—and advancing on Salamaua he invested it from the south. Next, in order to isolate it from the north, he decided to take Lae, which lies to the north of Salamaua and on the northern bank of the Markham River, because, once he had done so, its occupation would automatically cut the supply line of Salamaua. To effect this, on 4th September, while the Japanese in Salamaua were being pressed from the south, an Australian force was landed east of Lae, and on the following day an American parachute regiment was dropped to seize the airfield of Nadzab, nineteen miles north-west of Lae. Of this daring manœuvre, which was eminently successful, General Arnold writes:

"The landing at Nadzab put an end to the carping at our early 'palm-tree-to-palm-tree' advance. Here was warfare at two hundred miles an hour. In less time than it takes to read this page, our Fifth Air Force landed 1,700 American paratroops, fully equipped and supplied, plus 36 Australian artillerymen with guns.

"These operations in the Markham Valley are well worthy of note. In front, forty-eight B-25's opened the fight by strafing Japanese positions and dropping fragmentation bombs. They were followed by six A-20's that laid the smoke screen which covered the landing of our paratroops from the ninety-six C-47's. Above these flew five B-17's carrying material, and three B-17's with Generals MacArthur and Kenney and their staffs. A fighter escort of 146 P-38's and P-47's covered the flight at various altitudes while at Heath's Plantation, half-way between Nadzab and Lae, four B-17's and twenty-four B-24's bombed and strafed the Japanese positions . . ."[10]

[10]*Report of 4th January*, 1944, pp. 37-38.

Salamaua fell on 11th September, and Lae was entered by Australian troops on the 16th.

A week after the occupation of Lae, MacArthur, employing mainly Australian troops, landed a force north of Finschhafen and took that town on 2nd October. Between then and the end of January he occupied Saidor and reduced the whole of the Huon Peninsula, consolidating his position for the next move. During these months extensive air attacks were made on the Japanese supply lines and air bases.

Meanwhile, in the Solomon Islands, preceded by diversionary landings on Choiseul Island, on 1st November American Marines landed on the west coast of the island of Bougainville.[11] This permitted of a naval base and three airfields being established within fighter aircraft range of Rabaul. Four days later, an American task force, built around aircraft-carriers, delivered an air attack on Rabaul, to be followed by a similar attack a week later. Lastly, on 14th February, an unopposed landing was made on Green Island, one hundred and fifty miles east of Rabaul. This, for strategical purposes, completed the campaign in the Solomons; for all that then remained to be done was to clean up some 20,000 Japanese by-passed and marooned in the islands.

While these conquests were being made, MacArthur, having completed his preparations, decided to move against the western end of the island of New Britain, in order to gain command of the Straits of Vitiaz and Dampier and establish air bases within closer range of Rabaul. To effect this, on 15th December the Japanese airfield on Cape Gloucester was neutralized by bombing and troops landed at Arawe on the south coast of the island. This landing was followed on the 26th by the occupation of the Cape Gloucester airfield by American Marines.

Because of the density of the jungle and the mountains, it was considered impracticable to advance along the coast to Rabaul, nor would it have fitted into MacArthur's scheme, even had this not been so, for his aim was not to occupy Rabaul but instead to neutralize it by air bombardment, and thus cut if off from succour. From now on, "round-the-clock raids on Rabaul, including mast-height attacks on shipping and installations" were made.[12] And on 29th January, 1944, a Tokyo broadcast stated: "The

[11]With reference to the landing on Bougainville, General MacArthur said: "My great need is airfields. My resources are limited. I have a shortage of means to hit the Japanese. We cannot mount fighter cover as we need to, but with an airfield at Empress Augusta Bay (on the west coast of Bougainville) we can put our fighter cover in range of New Britain. I have been able to neutralize Rabaul, but with my limited means I cannot keep the Japanese from syphoning in reinforcements." (*The Times*, 3rd November, 1943.)

[12]Rear-Admiral Robert Carnley, Chief of Staff of the South Pacific Command (quoted in *The Eighteenth Quarter*, p. 176).

situation at Rabaul has reached a serious stage for which we cannot hold even the slightest optimism . . . The enemy is directing attacks against Rabaul daily, with formations consisting on the average of 100 bomber and fighter aeroplanes."[13]

By 10th March a landing had been effected on the Willaumez Peninsula, half-way up the northern coast of New Britain, and an airstrip at the village of Talasea seized. This brought American aircraft to within one hundred and sixty miles of Rabaul.

It becoming now more and more apparent, because of heavy losses at sea, that Japanese shipping was inadequate to supply the numerous Japanese detachments scattered among the islands and along New Guinea, General MacArthur's plan was, as William Courtenay describes, "not to inch his way through jungles yard by yard or hop from island to island through a myriad atolls and island groups, but rather to make a series of what one might call kangaroo leaps of a few hundred miles at a time limited by the tactical radius of land-based fighters. If we wanted to jump further than that we should have to rely on carrier-borne aircraft—if we could get the carriers. He aimed at seizing places of value to him in the long westerly march towards the Philippines, leaving the rest of the Japanese behind the lines, strategically isolated and impotent. This would avoid making frontal attacks at those places where the enemy was established in strength, where there might be no prospect of securing a tactical surprise, and where we might suffer heavy casualties."[14]

The first of these leaps was to the Admiralty Islands, which lie west of the Bismarck Archipelago and two hundred and fifty miles north of New Guinea. Their importance lay in their airfields and roadsteads. It was initiated on 29th February by advance elements of the 1st Texas Cavalry Division embarked on high-speed transports to reconnoitre Los Negros Island. Little opposition being met with, the remainder of the division was landed on 6th March. Momote airfield was captured and a beach-head secured after a series of fanatical Japanese counter-attacks. During the rest of March and the first half of April, the occupation of Manus and the adjacent islands was completed. Of these Emirau, which was suitable for airstrips, was six hundred and ninety miles from Truk, which, in consequence, was brought within bombing range from the south.

The occupation of the Admiralty Islands still further weakened Rabaul, because they were the junction of the two main air lines leading from Japan. The one by way of the mandated islands including Truk, and the other by way of the Philippines and Wewak and Madang in New Guinea.

---

[13] *The Eighteenth Quarter*, p. 177.
[14] *Journal of the Royal United Service Institution*, February, 1945, p. 17.

The Japanese, therefore, realizing that their General Headquarters at Rabaul was now untenable, decided to move it westwards to Hollandia in Dutch New Guinea. But MacArthur, divining their intention, decided to forestall their move by making his next leap from the Markham Valley to

THE CONQUEST OF NEW GUINEA, SEPTEMBER, 1943-SEPTEMBER, 1944

Hollandia—that is, six hundred miles to the west—and, in consequence, by-pass the detachments of the Japanese Eighteenth Army, strung along the intervening coast. Never suspecting that so extensive a leap would be made, and imagining that their enemy's next objectives would be Madang and Wewak, the Japanese withdrew a number of their troops from the Hollandia area to those places and, thereby, unwittingly assisted their enemy in his daring manœuvre. So, once again, Napoleon's saying came true: "*Qui ne risque rien n'attrape rien.*" By accepting the risks MacArthur won the next round.

At Hollandia there were three good Japanese airfields, and Humboldt Bay, close by, was suitable for a naval supply base. But as the distance to Hollandia was beyond the range of army fighters, air support had to be provided by carriers.

On 22nd April the leap took place, Aitape, Humboldt Bay and Tanah-mera Bay—west of Humboldt Bay—were occupied. The Japanese were completely surprised, and by the 30th all the airfields were in Allied hands and more than 50,000 Japanese were cut off to the eastwards. On 12th July the Allied forces at Aitape were violently attacked, but by 2nd August the Japanese were finally repulsed.

In mid-May the advance westwards was continued, and on the 17th of that month an unopposed landing was effected at Arare, and a few days later the island of Wakde with its airstrip was occupied as well as Maffin Bay on the mainland. Ten days later, the U.S. 41st Division landed on Biak Island, three hundred and thirty miles still further west. The importance of this island lay in that it commanded Geelvink Bay. It was held by some 8,000 Japanese, who put up so fierce a resistance that it was not until 22nd June that the island was finally won and its three airfields put into use. After gaining Wakde Island, Noemfoor Island was invaded and occupied with little difficulty.

The last leap westwards in New Guinea took place on 30th July, an American force landing at Sansapor on the Vogelkop Peninsula to secure the air and naval base established there. Though there was a considerable Japanese force in garrison, it was so completely surprised that it offered little resistance. Sansapor was one hundred and twenty miles west of Manokwari, the headquarters of the Japanese Second Army, at which there were some 15,000 Japanese; but these could do nothing on account of the intervening swamps and jungle. Sansapor was also no more than six hundred miles from the south-east Philippines.

Thus, in a little over twelve months, the Allies had advanced one thousand three hundred miles and cut off no less than 135,000 Japanese beyond hope of rescue. "The operations had been conducted," writes General Marshall, "under adverse weather conditions and over formidable terrain, which lacked roads in almost every area occupied, and made troop movements and supply extraordinarily difficult. Malaria was a serious hazard, but with suppressive treatment and rigid mosquito control, it no longer was a serious limitation to tactical operations."[15]

Though the occupation of Sansapor brought the New Guinea campaign to an end, it is as well here to add to it as postscript the operation which immediately followed it; for though tactically it lay outside New Guinea, strategically it completed the New Guinea campaign. It was the occupation of Morotai, the most northern island in the Halmaheras group, on 15th September. "Here again," writes Mr. Courtenay, "the Japanese were completely out-manœuvred. They thought that our next objective would be the main island where they had a garrison of about 30,000 men, instead of which MacArthur went for Morotai where there were only about 200 to 500. We took the island with only five casualties, and the garrison in the main Halmaheras was simply left stranded; they could not get out and

[15]*Biennial Report . . . 1st July, 1943, to 30th June, 1945*, p. 70.

nothing could get in, for we had taken more airfields with the result that they could be neither reinforced nor rescued."[16]

Morotai brought MacArthur to within three hundred miles of the Philippines. Equally important, it lay in the focal area in which the second of the great Pacific campaigns, that conducted by Admiral Chester W. Nimitz along the central route since the spring of 1942, was to fuse with the first into a single offensive against the Philippines. This second campaign will be our next subject.

(4) *The Central Pacific Campaign*

Having now followed the course of General MacArthur's campaigns against the southern flank of the salient, up to the time that he gained a lodgment on its inner line of defence, next we will turn to the operations of Admiral Nimitz against its northern flank.

Though his problem, like MacArthur's, was largely one of winning local command of the air by gaining and neutralizing enemy air bases, unlike MacArthur, who was land-based, he had to move his base along with him. That is, at one and the same time, his fleet had to be his base of operations and his striking force: an instrument which had to gain command of the air, to fight battles at sea and to storm and occupy enemy islands. It was, therefore, a four-fold organization: a floating base, a fleet, an air force and an army. That it was designed, built and assembled within eighteen months of the Battle of Midway Island, is probably the greatest organizational feat in naval history. And it was only possible because of the enormous industrial power of the United States, which was the arbiter of the entire war.

During these eighteen months, a fleet was built which was more than a match for anything the Japanese could bring against it. Its unprecedented number of aircraft-carriers gave Admiral Nimitz a weapon of enormous striking power. By the autumn of 1943, as many as 800 carrier-borne aircraft were at his disposal, and in the following year, 1,000. As essential was his mobile base, which, by enabling him to overcome the vast spaces of the Pacific, completely upset the premises upon which his enemy's strategy was founded. Namely, that those spaces would prove insuperable to their enemy. "Each class of warship—battleship, cruiser, destroyer, aircraft-carrier and submarine—had a special type of supply and repair ship, vessels costing as much as a battleship and taking as long to build." These vessels were floating workshops with foundries, and carried hundreds of skilled workers. They could "undertake all repairs, including under-water

[16] *Journal of the Royal United Service Institution*, February, 1945, p. 18.

welding.''[17] Therefore, after an engagement, except for the heaviest repairs, ships could be restored to fighting condition on the spot. New units were also raised, such as the U.S. Navy Construction Battalions, popularly known as "Seabees." These units moved in on the heels of the landing forces to build wharves, barracks, roads, hospitals, as well as construct and repair airfields and establish radio communication. Besides this, vast numbers of marines and soldiers had to be trained for jungle and island warfare.

This great instrument of destruction enabled Nimitz and his subordinate Admirals to operate on so broad a front that the Japanese High Command were compelled to deploy their inferior strength—particularly their air force—over such wide spaces that they could seldom if ever concentrate it at any critical point. The consequence was that, because most of the Pacific islands are too small to be converted into really formidable positions, and are incapable of accommodating garrisons of sufficient strength to put up a prolonged resistance, they could be knocked out before aid could be brought to them. Further, that once one or more air bases in a group of islands had been seized and put into use, the remaining islands could be so completely cut off from succour that they could safely be by-passed and left to starvation. Thus, because the instrument was not only most powerful, but because it was self-sufficient to carry out all operations, including its own supply, maintenance and repair, and in consequence possessed an indefinite range of action, as we shall see, it rapidly knocked the bottom out of the defensive Japanese strategy by transforming the vastness of the Pacific from an ally into a deadly enemy.

In the summer of 1943, the attack on the northern flank of the salient was heralded by a series of preparatory operations. They consisted in carrier air attack on Wake Island on 24th and 27th July; on Marcus Island—an important Japanese air base serving as a relay point on the Japan-mandated islands supply line—on 31st August; as well as on key islands in the Marshalls. Baker Island, in the Phœnix group, and Nuku Fetau and Nanumea, in the Ellice, were occupied early in September. On 4th and 6th October Wake was again heavily bombed.

The initial phase of the campaign comprised the invasion of Makin Island, Tarawa Attols (Betio) and Abemama Atoll in the Gilbert Islands. Landings were successfully effected on the first and second on 1st November, and on the third on the following day. Makin was taken on the 23rd and Tarawa on the 24th, the landing on Abemama was unopposed.

On Tarawa was fought one of the bloodiest of the smaller battles of the entire Pacific war, for though the Japanese garrison consisted of no more

[17] *Ibid.,* p. 19.

than 2,700 regular soldiers and 1,200 armed workmen, they put up so fierce a fight that the Americans lost 1,026 in killed and 2,556 in wounded.[18]

The object of these operations was to relieve the Ellice Islands from further risk before the main central advance was made. It misled the Japanese into believing that their enemy's intention was to make his main thrust towards the Solomons and New Guinea in support of the Rabaul campaign. It was not until Admiral Nimitz struck his next blow that they began to discover their error.

This blow fell upon the Marshall Islands—five hundred miles north-west of the Gilberts. Again, the aim was not to occupy all the islands, instead only selected ones with good airfields. On 1st January, 1944, after a two days' intense bombardment, Majuro with its fine harbour was occupied without fighting; but Kwajanlein Atoll resisted stubbornly until 8th February. On 2nd February the 4th Marine Division invaded Namu and Roi, which were also reduced on the 8th. And between the 19th and 22nd, Eniwetok Atoll was taken.

Of these operations General Richardson wrote:

"As a result of air, naval and artillery bombardment, the scene at Kwajanlein was one of great devastation. The destruction was complete. Upon approaching it from the lagoon side, it gave the appearance of no-man's-land in World War I and was even greater, I think, than that of Betio or Tarawa. With the exception of rubble left by concrete structures, there were no buildings standing. All those which had been made of any other material except concrete had been completely burned or destroyed."[19]

Because Admiral Nimitz's intention was to by-pass the Caroline Islands and open the third phase of his campaign against the Marianas, and because the island of Truk in the Caroline group was one of the vital centres in the Japanese defensive scheme, which, as we have seen, was at this time about to be attacked from the Admiralty Islands, the control of the Marshalls enabled him very considerably to neutralize it by air bombardment, and at the end of January it was so heavily bombed that it was virtually put out of business. Other islands in the Carolines were also raided, and, on 29th March, a powerful force, including aircraft-carriers and battleships, attacked the Palau Islands.

The operations in the Marianas were directed against the islands of Saipan, Tinian and Guam. Between 10th and 12th June these three islands

---

[18]In these landings, "Amphibious tractors proved to be one of the effective assault weapons. They could be floated beyond the range of shore batteries, deployed in normal landing-boat formations, and driven over the fringing reef on and up the beaches." (*Biennial Report . . . 1st July, 1943 to 30th June, 1945,* General Marshall, p. 69.)

[19]*Ibid.,* p. 69.

were heavily bombarded, and, on the 15th, the 2nd and 4th Marine Divisions, followed by the 27th Infantry Division, landed on the first of them. It was the most important operation yet staged in the Central Pacific; for not only would the possession of the Marianas breach the enemy's inner line of defence, but it would enable the Americans to cut their enemy's direct line of communications with the Carolines as well as operate against the Bonin Islands, from where, once air bases had been established, the Japanese home islands could be readily bombed.

At the time of this landing, a powerful Japanese battle squadron, strong in aircraft-carriers, had entered the Pacific between the Philippines and Saipan. It would appear that its commander did not want to bring on a fleet action, for his plan appears to have been first to launch an air attack on the American fleet commanded by Admiral R. A. Spruance and then, after his bombers had re-fuelled on Guam and Rota, to attack the American beach-heads on Saipan. Unfortunately for him his enemy was prepared for such an eventuality. On 19th June, keeping his fleet off Guam, Admiral Spruance waited for the arrival of the Japanese, and so soon as they were reported he launched so violent an air attack on them that 353 of their aircraft were shot down; 335 by American carrier-borne machines and 18 by anti-aircraft fire. Next, on the 20th, Spruance launched his aircraft against the Japanese fleet, then some three hundred miles north-west of him, and inflicted heavy casualties on it. In importance the Battle of the Marianas ranks second to that of Midway Island.[20]

The fighting on Saipan lasted for twenty-five days, and it was not until 9th July, that organized resistance ceased, though mopping up continued, for several months. Of the Japanese garrison, estimated at 23,000, 21,036 were buried by the Americans. The American casualities were very heavy 15,053 in all, of whom 2,359 were killed, 11,481 wounded and 1,213 missing. The immediate result of this victory was the fall of General Tojo and his Government, and the formation of a new Japanese Cabinet under General Koiso.

The next island to be invaded was Guam. There, on 21st July, the 77th Infantry Division and the 3rd Marine Division landed and, on 10th August, organized resistance ceased. Lastly, the island of Tinian, after having largely been neutralized by air bombing and artillery fire from Saipan, was invaded by the 2nd and 4th Marine Divisions on 24th July, and after nine days' fighting was occupied.

[20]"The total of Japanese aircraft destroyed in the engagements of 19th and 20th June and in the other actions in the expedition against the Marianas was 848. Thirty ships had been sunk and fifty-one damaged. Against this the Americans had three warships slightly damaged and they had lost 151 aircraft and 98 airmen." (Admiral Nimitz's Report of 26th June.)

After the conquest of Saipan a pause in operations followed until 8th September. That day, the U.S. Third Amphibious Force, commanded by Vice-Admiral Wilkinson, appeared off the Palau Islands, and on the 15th American marines and infantry landed on the island of Peleliu. Thus, on the same day that General MacArthur invaded Morotai, the Central Pacific Fleet came up on his right flank. The stage was now set for the re-conquest of the Philippines.

Before we end this Section, it is as well to outline the tactics now generally applied in these many island assaults. In form they closely resemble those designed for the Battle of Cambrai in November, 1917, with the sea as no-man's-land. First, the objective to be assaulted was bombed and bombarded, and under this protective fire the assaulting forces moved across the water in three waves or echelons. First came a line of rocket-firing landing craft, which replaced the creeping artillery barrage of 1917. Next, behind them, in two or more lines, "alligators"—cannon-armed amphibious tanks—moved forward to seize the beaches. Lastly came the troop-carrying landing craft, bearing infantry, artillery and engineers, to give weight to the assault and to occupy, clean up and consolidate the ground gained. Though in idea these tactics were old, their novel application revolutionized amphibious warfare. In all probability, they were the most far-reaching tactical innovation of the war.

(5) *The Aleutian Islands Campaign*

Japanese strategy, as we have seen, was built upon space as a shock-absorber, triangular in form, with the line Burma-Paramushiro as its base. Therefore, in order that the sides of the triangle, though compressible, should not give way, it was essential that the base should hold firm; for, were it broken in the middle, the whole defensive system would collapse, and were its extremities driven in, to restore their solidity resources would have to be diverted to them, and, in consequence, the sides would be either directly or indirectly weakened.

The middle of the base comprised Eastern China and Manchukuo. In the one Japan was at war, and throughout the war China remained her main land problem. In the other, though at peace, its security depended on the outcome of the struggle between Germany and Russia. Were it to end in a Russian *débâcle*, its security would be unaffected, but were it to end in a German defeat, it would vanish. Further, there were two other alternatives. The first was that, with such slippery customers as Hitler and Stalin, there was no certainty that they might not compound their differences on the lines that were Russia to abandon the Ukraine, etc., to Germany, in return Russia would be granted a free hand in Asia. This possibility compelled the Japanese to lock up a huge army in Manchukuo, which clearly she would have preferred to employ in China. The second was that, in spite of Russia's neutrality, there was also a possibility that Stalin, without directly going to war with Japan, might agree to lease air

THE ALEUTIAN ISLANDS CAMPAIGN, 3rd JUNE, 1942-15th AUGUST, 1943

bases in Kamchatka and Primorskaya (north of Vladivostock) to the Americans. Were he to do so, this would bring the Japanese Islands within easy range—six hundred to seven hundred miles—of American bombers, and not only would Japan's industrial cities be attacked, but her sea communications with Manchukuo would be imperilled. Therefore, so far as the northern half of the base of the triangle was concerned, it was imperative for Japan to keep the Americans at arm's length. To do so without violating Russian neutrality meant the occupation of the Aleutians, a chain of volcanic islands one thousand two hundred miles in length, linking the Kurile Islands—the left extremity of the base—with Alaska.[21]

[21]In 1867 the U.S. bought Alaska and the Aleutian Islands from Russia for $7,200,000. Alaska is over two and a half times the size of France.

It is, therefore, highly probable that this was the reason why, on 3rd June, 1942, Japan launched a carrier-borne air attack on the U.S. naval base of Dutch Harbour. The attack failing, on the 14th the Japanese began to occupy the islands of Kiska, Attu and Agattu in the Western Aleutians. For the time being, having their hands full in the Central and Southern Pacific, the Americans could do nothing other than bomb Japanese ships bringing stores to these islands, and it was not until January, 1943, that action could be taken. During that month an un-opposed landing was made on Amchitka Island, seventy miles east of Kiska, and an advanced air base established there. Next, in the spring, more resources becoming available, it was decided to challenge the Japanese occupation, and, on 11th May, by-passing Kiska, which the Japanese expected would be attacked, a task force landed on Attu, and strongly supported by the Navy and Air Force it encircled and annihilated the 2,350 Japanese defenders of Chichagof Harbour. As this success ren-dered Kiska untenable, on 15th August the Japanese evacuated its garrison and abandoned the Aleutians altogether. Thereupon, the Americans built a number of air bases on the western islands from which they bombed the Kuriles, and in particular Paramushiro.

(6) *Defensive and Counter-Defensive in Burma,* 1942-1944

At the other extremity of the base lay Burma, and its maintenance by the Japanese as a defensive bastion was altogether a more difficult problem. Not only were they faced by the vast potential strength of India; but, except by sea, Burma was an all but ungetatable country. In order to protect their sea communications from Singapore, the Japanese had occupied the Nicobar and Andaman Islands; but on account of the strain their Pacific operations were putting on their fleet, merchant service and air force, and increasingly continued to put, they were never able to establish more than a nominal command of the Bay of Bengal.

For the time being their enemy was even more difficultly placed, and it was vital to Allied strategy that China should be kept in the field. Not so much because the war there pinned down a third of the Japanese land forces; but because, so long as it continued, the maintenance of these forces put an enormous strain on Japan's industrial resources and shipping. Therefore, in order to supply China, following the cutting of the Burma Road, General Stilwell "immediately initiated plans for an air-ferry service route over the Himalayas,"[22] which became known as "the Hump Route," because the transport aircraft had to rise to an altitude of 23,000 feet to clear the mountains.

[22]*Biennial Report . . . 1st July,* 1941, *to 30th June,* 1943, p. 23.

Except for this trickle of supplies, nothing else could be done for months, for as General Wavell, now Commander-in-Chief India, informs us: ". . . in March, 1942, India had not a single fully-trained division."[23] Further, ever since the spring of 1941, India had been treated as an emergency fund to draw upon in order to meet unexpected current expenses. Her troops had been sent to Africa and the Middle East. On Germany's invasion of Russia, Basra had been considerably reinforced, and in August Persia was invaded in order to open a supply line to Russia. After the fall of Singapore, Japanese activity in the Indian Ocean had, in May, led to the diversion of reinforcements and equipment for India to Madagascar, where a small war was started' with the French. In June, Rommel's advance to el Alamein did likewise, and in August the German advance into Caucasia caused a fresh demand to be made on India to send supplies to Russia via Persia. On top of these distractions, Congress agitation hindered training by scattering men on internal security. In fact, except for some minor skirmishing with the Japanese in the Naga Hills and desultory bombing of Japanese communications and posts,the sole military event of interest was the transportation by air of 13,000 Chinese troops to India, to make up the strength of the Chinese forces which had sought refuge there to two divisions. This took place between October and December.

In 1943 the stagnation of the war in Burma was only disturbed by two small campaigns, the one involving the 14th Indian Division in Arakan between December, 1942, and April, 1943, which ended in a fiasco, and the second initiating the first of the long-range jungle penetrations, which was remarkable in that it clearly proved that the solution of the jungle warfare problem was to be sought in the air more so than on the ground. This experimental expedition was placed under the command of Brigadier Orde C. Wingate, who had distinguished himself as a guerilla leader in Abyssinia. Operating in several columns, Wingate's force, known as the 77th Indian Infantry Brigade, set out in February, crossed the Chindwin and Irrawaddy rivers, and in the region of Katha cut the Myitkyina railway in many places. Having no transport, it depended almost entirely on air supply, which for three months maintained it in the field, giving it complete liberty of action. This conclusively proved that when soldiers are carefully trained for jungle fighting, by transferring their supply columns from the ground to the air the two main difficulties—lack of roads and need for an excessive number of lines of communication troops—in these operations could be avoided.

[23]"Despatches." *Supplement to the London Gazette*, 17th September, 1946, p. 4670.

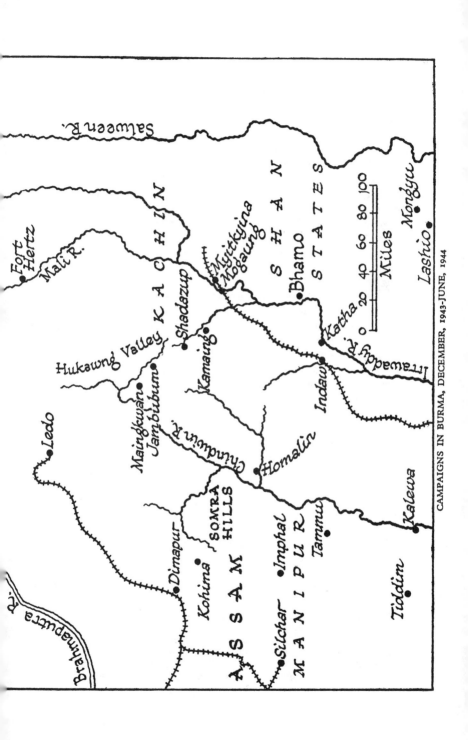

CAMPAIGNS IN BURMA, DECEMBER, 1943-JUNE, 1944

During the spring and summer of this year the situation in China so rapidly deteriorated that it became imperative that something should be done to come to her support, and, in August, at the first Quebec Conference the problem was fully considered.

It was decided to set up a separate South-East Asia Command (SEAC) under Vice-Admiral Lord Louis Mountbatten,[24] with Lieut.-General Stilwell as his deputy,[25] and to form all air forces in Burma into the Eastern Air Command under Major-General George E. Statemeyer. The task laid down was to re-establish land communications with China on the following lines: (1) An offensive on Northern Burma was to be undertaken during the winter of 1943-1944; (2) the Ledo Road from Assam, then under construction, was to be extended to meet the old Burma Road at Mongyu (Mong Yaw) near Lashio; (3) a pipe-line was to be built from Calcutta to Assam and another parallel to the Ledo Road; (4) the supply along the "Hump" route was to be raised from 10,000 to 20,000 tons a month; and (5) advanced air bases were to be established in China from which to strike at Japan and Manchukuo.

On these instructions the plan decided upon was based on three independent yet correlated operations, the main aim of which was to capture Myitkyina, because once in Allied hands the air route over the "Hump" would become unnecessary. The reason for this was that at Myitkyina there were three airfields, and by routing aircraft from India to China by way of them, not only would distance be shortened, but the 23,000 feet climb over the "Hump" would be avoided, and "with it some of the worst icing conditions in the world."[26]

The three operations were as follows:

(1) General Stilwell's Chinese-American Army (Chinese 22nd and 38th Divisions and Brigadier-General F. Merrill's U.S. Detachment) was to advance from the Hukawng Valley (headwaters of the Chindwin River) on Mogaung and Myitkyina, while Kachin levies from Fort Hertz (one hundred and twenty miles east of Ledo) co-operated with his left flank, and the Chinese forces under Marshal Wei Li Haung in the Salween Valley advanced westwards against the Bharmo-Lashio front.

(2) The 3rd Indian Division or "Wingate Force" was to be flown into the interior of Burma to play havoc with the communications along which the Japanese were operating against General Stilwell—that is, attack these

---

[24]At the same time, Lord Wavell was appointed Viceroy of India and General Auchinleck C.-in-C. India.

[25]General Stilwell was in command of the China-Burma-India U.S. theatre and also Chief of Staff of Generalissimo Chiang Kai-shek.

[26]"Air Aspects of the Operations in Burma," Air Marshal Sir John Baldwin, *Journal of the Royal United Service Institution*, May, 1945, p. 198.

forces in rear. Also it was hoped that the upset caused would disrupt the offensive it was known the Japanese were planning against the Manipur area.

(3) The XVth Indian Corps (5th and 7th Indian Divisions and the 81st West African Division), under the command of Lieutenant-General A. P. E. Christison, was to advance into Arakan with the object of clearing up the whole of the Maungdaw Peninsula and capture Akyab. It was hoped that this offensive, by containing large forces of Japanese in Lower Burma, would prevent their despatch to Upper Burma.

The campaigning season[27] was already far advanced, when early in January, 1944, the XVth Corps crossed the Burmese border and, on 11th January, recaptured Maungdaw. Early in February it was violently counter-attacked, and had it not been for a change in the British tactics, the campaign, like the previous one, would, in all probability, have ended in a severe repulse.

The tactics adopted were as follows: Instead of retreating when out-flanked in the jungle, divisional and brigade "boxes" on the Libyan pattern were formed and supplied by a fleet of air transports. This was rendered possible because complete air supremacy had been won. Meanwhile, the ground communications of the besieged Japanese forces were disorganized by bombing. The upshot was that the struggle became not so much one between the opposing armed forces, as between the maintenance of the opposing lines of supply. The British, having transferred theirs to the air and because of their command of the air—aerial lines of communication troops—were secure, whereas because the Japanese had lost command of the air, their ground supply lines were vulnerable. Thus it came about that it was not the static British who were starved into surrender, but instead it was the mobile Japanese who were starved into retreat.

The first call came from the 7th Indian Divisional "box" at Sinzweya on 6th February—ammunition having run short. Whereupon "Brigadier-General Old, the American officer commanding the troop-carrier command . . . boarded one of his aeroplanes and led the flight himself. The ammunition was delivered. During the twenty-one days' action British and American crews of this command dropped 1,500 tons of ammunition, food, petrol, oil and medical supplies, and lost only one Dakota aircraft."[28]

Though the campaign witnessed the first considerable defeat the Japanese had suffered at the hands of British and Indian troops in Burma,

[27]The monsoon season, which rendered the jungle all but impassable, began in May and ended in early October. In Assam the rainfall averaged about 150 inches. The campaigning season was, therefore, between October and May.

[28]*The Times*, 29th February, 1944. For a full account see *Campaign in Burma*, His Majesty's Stationery Office (1946), chapter 9.

the delay caused by the Japanese counter-thrust was so considerable, that with the coming of the monsoon in May it came to an indecisive end.

Meanwhile, five hundred miles to the north, General Stilwell, having for the first time since 1942 returned to Burma, in mid-January started to advance down the Hukawng Valley against the Japanese 1st Division, which had distinguished itself in the storming of Singapore. Progress was slow, for the country was extremely difficult and Japanese resistance stubborn, and it was not until 4th March that he occupied Maingkwan, from where he pushed on and took Jambubum on the 20th.

In April he worked down the Morgaung Valley from Shadazup towards Kamaing, while the Kachin levies advanced down the Mali Valley to within fifty miles of Myitkyina, and Marshal Wei Li Haung crossed the Salween from the east. The advance now speeded up, and on 17th May, as the monsoon broke, Merrill's "Marauders" attacked and seized the southern airfield at Myitkyina.

This speeding up was largely due to the operations of the 3rd Indian Division Long-range Penetration Groups ("Wingate Force," also called "Chindits"), which had set out by air on 5th March. Its first flight consisted of a party of Engineers which was dropped in the region of Katha to build airstrips for the landing of the main body. This work was completed in the remarkably short space of twelve hours, and directly the forces were grounded, operations against the rear of the Japanese 18th Division were undertaken. At that time it was withdrawing from before Stilwell's advance. Most unfortunately, on 24th March General Wingate was killed in an air crash. He was succeeded by Major-General W. D. Lentaigne.

In the Katha region the 3rd Indian Division threatened four Japanese supply lines—namely: (1) The road and railway from Mandalay to Myitkyina; (2) the road from Indaw to Homalin on the Chindwin River; (3) the road through the northern Shan States to Bhamo; and (4) the Irrawaddy, which was navigable by river steamers as far as Bhamo.

Thus the very centre of Japanese communications in Northern Burma was either threatened or attacked. It was this powerful distraction which eased the way for Stilwell's final advance, and though it was hoped that Myitkyina and its remaining two airfields would speedily pass into Allied hands, so stubborn was the Japanese defence that it was not until 4th August, after a siege of eighty days, that Myitkyina fell.

Neither of these remarkable campaigns would or could have been possible without air transport. In 1945, and while the war in the Far East was still being fought, General Marshall wrote:

"The re-entry into Burma was the most ambitious campaign yet waged on the end of an airborne supply line. From the first advance by the Chinese into the Hukawng Valley in October until after the fall of

Myitkyina town the next August, there were at all times between 25,000 and 100,000 troops involved in fighting and dependent largely or entirely on food, equipment and ammunition that could be air-supplied, either by parachute, free-drop, or air-landed."[29]

Besides General Stilwell's Army, the "Wingate Force" was entirely supplied by air. Thus:

"Night and day troop-carrier C-46's and 47's shuttled from numerous bases and airstrips in the Brahmaputra Valley to points of rendezvous with the Allied columns in the Burma jungles. Each trip had to be flown over one or more of the steep spines which the Himalayas shove southwards along the India-Burma frontier to establish one of the most formidable barriers to military operations in the world. The troop-carrier squadrons at the height of the campaign averaged 230 hours of flying time for each serviceable plane a month for three months."[30]

While these campaigns were being fought, the Japanese did not merely stand on the defensive, instead they boldly met attack by counter-attack, their aim being to prevent their enemy re-establishing land contact with China. To effect this, they launched two campaigns, the one eastwards across the Salween to drive back the Chinese in time to prevent the completion of the Ledo (Stilwell) Road; and the other, westwards against Imphal, the headquarters of the IVth Indian Corps in the Indian State of Manipur, in order to sever the Bengal-Assam railway on which the "Hump" route and General Stilwell's Army were based.

The weakness of the Imphal position lay in that its main supply line, the road leading from Dimapur on the above railway via Kohima to Imphal and thence southwards to Tiddim, ran parallel to the front of attack. Therefore, should this road be blocked north or south of Imphal, the garrison of that place would be forced to depend on the second-class road leading westwards to Silchar on a branch of the railway, and this road was not negotiable during the monsoon. Therefore the Japanese plan was to block the road to the north and south of Imphal and, if possible, starve the Imphal garrison out before the monsoon broke. Next, to occupy Imphal and from it operate against Dimapur and its airfields and thereby cut General Stilwell's line of supply and stop the "Hump" traffic.

On 15th March, the first Japanese move was made against Tiddim, about one hundred miles south of Imphal. Whereupon, after heavy fighting, Tiddim was evacuated by the 17th Indian Division, and Tammu, sixty miles north of Tiddim, which was evacuated by the 20th Indian Division, was reached by the Japanese on the 22nd. Simultaneously, an

[29]*Biennial Report . . . 1st July, 1943, to 30th June, 1945*, p. 58.
[30]*Ibid.*, p. 58.

advance through the Somra Hills on Kohima was made. On 2nd April the Imphal-Kohima road was severed, and five days later siege laid to Kohima. Meanwhile strong British and Indian forces were concentrated at Dimapur, the 5th Indian Division being flown from Arakan. From there they advanced on Kohima, and by re-opening the Dimapur-Kohima road they relieved the hard-pressed Kohima garrison. Nevertheless, the Japanese could not be so rapidly dislodged in the Imphal area, and in May, because of the blocking of the road, Imphal was in a state of siege, though by no means surrounded.

Once again the situation was saved by air transport. Not only during the worst period of the monsoon was the Imphal garrison supplied, but also it was reinforced by no less than two and a half divisions complete with their artillery.

"Use was made of helicopters," writes Air Marshal Sir John Baldwin. "The Dakota loads carried during our numerous operations varied from men and munitions, jeeps and guns, W/T equipment and petrol, to rations and constructional equipment, power boats and mules, beasts and pigs . . . Casualties were evacuated by returning supply aircraft. No special services were detailed, although returning aircraft were routed to airfields in close proximity to a hospital in order to save unnecessary road transport. A total of 30,000 casualties were air-lifted."[31]

Then, suddenly, on 7th June, Japanese resistance broke. Heavy losses, amounting to some 50 per cent of the attacking troops, coupled with the difficulties of road supply during the monsoon and the dangerous situation which was developing in the Myitkyina area, proved too much. The Japanese were in full retreat from the Imphal and Kohima areas. Their audacious campaign had failed; the air transport of their enemies had wrecked it. The initiative was no longer theirs.

(7) *The Meaning of Air Power*

The campaigns discussed in this Chapter scattered those verbal clouds in which the meaning of air power had been obscured by the so-called experts of 1919-1939, and brought it into the sunshine of the essentials of war.

These campaigns showed that the aeroplane was not primarily a bomb-carriage, but instead a new means of transportation around which warfare could be re-shaped. Had the experts, who for twenty years had so tediously discussed bomb *versus* battleship, bomb *versus* factory and bomb *versus* civil morale, been but historically-minded, they could not have failed to have seen that the influence of the aeroplane on war would not in any

[31] *Journal of the Royal United Service Institution*, May, 1945, p. 201.

essential respects differ from that of the horse when first used for military purposes. What was its *primary* influence?

It was not that it enabled the foot soldier to fight mounted. It was that it relieved him from the necessity of turning himself into a pack-animal. By increasing his means of supply, it revolutionized war logistically—that is, from the point of view of transport and supply—and in this *fundamental* revolution all other changes due to the horse had their roots.

Between 1919 and 1939 it should have been seen that the *primary* influence of the aeroplane would also be logistical, and that by relieving the soldier of the necessity of depending upon surface communications, in this all other changes it might introduce would have their roots.

The ability to dispense with roads, railways, rivers, canals and the surface of the earth itself as lines of communication, simplified war. Hitherto to the soldier it had been a problem of bases, communications and fighting forces, now it could become one of bases and fighting forces alone. As one writer, when considering the influence of air transport in Burma, says: "It freed unit commanders on the ground from the anxieties of covering their lines of communication and very greatly eased the problem of supply by limiting the necessity for large-scale construction of roads, which in any case were invariably swept away each year during the monsoon."[32]

Further, he writes:

"It is interesting to note that even on comparatively short lines of communication from railheads to the front, it may take a lorry some twelve days to complete a single turn round, and allowing for the petrol consumed by the motor transport, it is estimated that it requires eighteen lorries to deliver one lorry-load of material on the front per day. On the other hand, a transport aircraft carrying approximately three tons can deliver three loads per day, which, therefore, amounts to the work of some fifty-four lorries. Moreover, this single aircraft can evacuate up to sixty casualties during the day, whereas the return journey of the lorry is largely wasted, and certainly cannot be used for the evacuation of the wounded. Not only, therefore, is air transport the vital factor in the campaign in South-east Asia, but it has enabled us to achieve great economies in manpower, in motor transport and in the provision of road-making material, and has given our forces a flexibility which has allowed them to overcome all the disadvantages with which we were faced in the initial stages of the Japanese war. The technique of this form of warfare has developed far, but there are great possibilities yet to be explored."[33]

[32]"Air Transport on the Burma Front," "Aquila," *Journal of the United Service Institution*, May, 1945, p. 205.

[33]*Ibid.*, p. 206. Eighteen lorries would seem to be an exaggeration or misprint.

In all, during the Burmese campaigns, "Over 1,180,000 tons of supplies and equipment and 1,380,000 troops were transported by air. The air movement over the 'Hump' between India and China attained a peak rate of 71,000 tons in one month."[34]

Though the aeroplane could turn space into a supply line—as the above figures show—and could also cover the bases and fighting forces, it could not fashion space into a base of operations; for whatever the means of movement may be, the base must remain on the ground. Because this is so, at bottom war remains a struggle between bases; battlefields or fighting spaces being no more than the no-man's-lands which separate them and are contended for.

Again and again this is to be seen in the campaigns examined in this Chapter. Local command of the air, which was essential in order to establish a protective roof or covering to bases, communications and fighting forces, was gained not by careering about in the skies, and, like ancient Greek and Trojan heroes, challenging the enemy's air force to single combat—the conception of experts—but by depriving the enemy's air force of its bases and by winning new bases for one's own air force. The more air bases the enemy lost, the less mobile[35] did his air force become, and the more bases his adversary gained, the higher was his mobility in the air: not in terms of miles per hour, but in those of radius of action, and, therefore, in range of cover.

Once air cover over a given area was gained, the next two operations towards winning freedom of action were:(1)To strike at the enemy's basic (surface) mobility, and (2) to enhance one's own basic (surface) mobility by assisting one's armies and fleets to push their bases forward until ultimately they included the enemy's, when no-man's-land vanished.

The first of these operations was the primary duty of bomber aircraft; the second was the primary duty of transport aircraft; whereas the primary duty of fighter aircraft was to render these two duties possible for one's own side and impossible for the enemy's.

Such were the ingredients of the new form of war, whereas the form visualized by the 1919-1939 air experts was nothing other than the transference of the artillery battles of obliteration of 1916-1917 from the ground into the air.

Granted that this new form is true for jungle warfare, then, in principle, it is true for all warfare, in spite of the fact that each different sub-theatre of war will demand modifications in its application.

In the West, this was not understood, for there, as we shall see in the

[34]*United States Strategic Bombing Survey, Summary Report (Pacific War)*, 1946, p. 8.
[35]Better expressed by coining the word "locomobile."

three following Chapters, had but a fraction of the resources allocated to the construction of bomber aircraft been allotted to the construction of transport aircraft, the campaigns discussed in these Chapters would have been far more rapid, and immeasurably more profitable than they actually were, because the occupation and not the obliteration of the enemy's bases—ultimately of his entire country—is the strategic aim in war.

CHAPTER VII

ESTABLISHMENT OF ALLIED INITIATIVE IN THE WEST

(1) *The Strategic Bombing of Germany*, 1940-1944

If there is one strategical principle which throughout the history of war has been upheld by all great strategists, it is the principle of unity of command. Napoleon, possibly the greatest of them, was emphatic on this point; again and again in his *Correspondance* he returns to it. "*Un mauvais général,*" he said, "*vaut mieux que deux bons.*"[1] Writing to the Directory on 14th May, 1796, he pointed out: "*Si vous affaiblissez vos moyens en partageant vos forces, si vous rompez en Italie l'unité de la pensée militaire, je vous le dis avec douleur, vous aurez perdu la plus belle occasion d'imposer des lois à l'Italie.*"[2]

This principle, or rather fulcrum of all principles, was, as we have seen, set aside by the British Government in 1917, with the result that, in April, 1918, the Air Force was separated from the Navy and Army and formed into an independent fighting service under its own Ministry. The inevitable result was that unity of military thought was disrupted, and the upshot was that, in 1940, the command of the Air Force was so completely divorced from that of the Army that Lord Gort in France was placed in the fantastic position of having to obtain air support from the Air Ministry through the War Office in London.[3]

Throughout the first half of the war, the only co-ordinating link which existed was the British War Cabinet, and because it was dominated by Mr. Churchill, who was Minister of Defence as well as Prime Minister, he was the link.

As things stood in 1939, the rulings laid down by the 1922 Washington

[1] *Correspondance*, vol. I, No. 664, and vol. XXIX, No. 107.
[2] *Ibid.*, vol. I, No. 420.   On 25th February, 1798, writing to General Caffarelli, he said: "*Il faut que toute la marine qui est située dans l'enceinte de l'armée d'Angleterre soit absolument entre les mains du général qui commande l'armée, comme les autres armes.*" (*Ibid.*, vol. III, No. 2421.)
[3] "Despatches," *Supplement to the London Gazette* of 10th October, 1941, p. 5914. He writes: "From the 21st May onwards all arrangements for air co-operation with the B.E.F. were made by the War Office in conjunction with the Air Ministry at home."

Conference on the Limitation of Armaments, Article 22, Part II, "Rules of Warfare," remained valid. They read: "Aerial bombardment for the purpose of terrorizing the civilian population, of destroying or damaging private property not of a military character, or of injuring non-combatants, is prohibited."[4] Further, on 2nd September, 1939, the day after Germany invaded Poland, a declaration was made by the British and French Governments that only "strictly military objectives in the narrowest sense of the word" would be bombed, and a very similar statement was made by the German Government. Six months later this policy was reinforced by the British Prime Minister, Mr. Chamberlain, in a statement made by him in the House of Commons on 15th February, 1940. He said: "Whatever be the length to which others might go, the Government will never resort to blackguardedly attacks on women and other civilians for the purpose of mere terrorism."[5]

And thus the situation remained until 10th May, when Mr. Churchill becoming Prime Minister, strategic bombing was forthwith resorted to.

What actually is strategic bombing?

On 21st October, 1917, Mr. Churchill wrote a memorandum in which it is adequately defined:

"All attacks on communications or bases should have their relation to the main battle. It is not reasonable to speak of an air offensive as if it were going to finish the war by itself. It is improbable that any terrorization of the civil population which could be achieved by air attack could compel the Government of a great nation to surrender. Familiarity with bombardment, a good system of dug-outs or shelters, a strong control by police and military authorities, should be sufficient to preserve the national fighting power unimpaired. In our case we have seen the combative spirit of the people roused, and not quelled, by the German air raids. Nothing we have learned of the capacity of the German population to endure suffering justifies us in assuming that they could be cowed into submission by such methods, or, indeed, that they would not be rendered more desperately resolved by them. Therefore our air offensive should consistently be directed at striking at the bases and communications upon whose structure the fighting power of his armies and his fleets of the sea and of the air

_____

[4] The British, however, never adhered to it, and though the actual or alleged bombing of Guernica in Spain in April, 1937, caused such frenzied indignation in England that it nearly precipitated an Anglo-Spanish war, in a Despatch dated 11th November, 1925, from Air Vice-Marshal Sir S. Ellington to C.-in-C. India on air operations in Waziristan we read: "The targets in this campaign varied from good-sized villages . . . to purely cave dwellings" and "scattered huts and enclosures of the Guri Khel."

[5] *Hansard*, vol. 357, H. of C. Deb. 5s., col. 924.

depends. Any injury which comes to the civil population from this process of attack must be regarded as incidental and inevitable."[6]

But when this was written, Mr. Churchill, as Minister of Munitions, held but a subordinate position in the Government, whereas, in 1940, he was *de facto* if not *de jure* head of the British armed forces, and though he was unable to take the field, he forthwith overcame this difficulty by deciding to conduct a private war of his own,[7] with Bomber Command of the R.A.F. as his army. On 11th May, Freiburg in Baden was bombed. Thus, according to Mr. J. M. Spaight, "We (the British) began to bomb objectives on the German mainland before the Germans began to bomb objectives on the British mainland. That is a historical fact which has been publicly admitted . . . Yet, because we were doubtful about the psychological effect of propagandist distortion of the truth that it was we who started the strategic offensive, we have shrunk from giving our great decision of May, 1940, the publicity which it deserved. That surely was a mistake. It was a splendid decision. It was as heroic, as self-sacrificing, as Russia's decision to adopt her policy of 'scorched earth'."[8]

Thus, on Mr. Spaight's evidence, it was Mr. Churchill who lit the fuse which detonated a war of devastation and terrorization unrivalled since the invasions of the Seljuks.

At the time, with his hands full in France, Hitler did not retaliate. Yet there can be little doubt that the bombing of Freiburg and the subsequent attacks on German cities pushed him into his assault on Britain. This is borne out by his speech when opening the winter relief campaign on 4th September, 1940. In it he said: "For three months I did not reply," and then went on to say what he intended to do.[9]

Nevertheless, it may be said that, after the fall of France, the military situation bore no resemblance to that of October, 1917. Then the British and Germans were at clinch, whereas from the summer of 1940 onwards

---

[6] *The War in the Air*, Appendices (1937), Appendix IV, p. 19.

[7] On this very question, as late in the war as 3rd March, 1944, Captain Harry C. Butcher writes: "The Prime Minister had taken the position that either the R.A.F. Bomber Command should be independent of the Supreme Commander's (General Eisenhower's) control but to work in conjunction with him and his forces, or only a part of Bomber Command would be under his control. The Prime Minister wanted to conduct his own private war if he chose." (*Three Years with Eisenhower*, English edition, 1946, p. 427.)

[8] *Bombing Vindicated*, J. M. Spaight, 1944, pp. 68 and 74. Mr. Spaight speaks with authority, as he was Principal Assistant Secretary, Air Ministry.

[9] "*Wenn die britische Luftwaffe 2 oder 3 oder 4000 Kilogramm Bomben wirft, dann werfen wir jetzt in einer Nacht 150,000, 180,000, 230,000, 300,000, 400,000 und mehr Kilo! Und wenn sie erklären, sie werden unsere Städte in grossem Masstabe angreifen—wir werden ihre Städte ausradieren!*"

for three years, except for commando raids and the abortive expedition to Greece, there was no British army on the Continent of Europe. Was, then, the R.A.F. to do nothing during these one thousand days? Surely, if during them it could systematically destroy the industrial foundations of Germany's war might, even should this not in itself bring her to collapse, would it not make her eventual defeat more certain?

Clearly it would; therefore obviously it was the correct thing to do. The sole question was—how?

To destroy, with the means then existing, all or the greater part of German war industry, which was estimated to cover a target area of one hundred and thirty square miles, was manifestly impossible, and to render it, even in a period of years, possible, would require such an astronomical number of aircraft that the total industrial resources of Britain could not have supplied them. Therefore, it should not have been attempted as it was. Instead, had Mr. Churchill been strategically- instead of devastatingly-minded, it would have become clear to him that the objectives to strike at were not the industries themselves, but at coal and oil—the sources of their energy. Were they steadily reduced, then, eventually 90 per cent of German industry would be brought to a standstill.

There were only two possible arguments against this. The first was that coalfields are difficult to destroy; and the second, because oil targets were few in number, [10] they would, therefore, be strongly protected and attacks on them would be costly. The first was, however, no more than an apparent difficulty, because all that was needed was to keep the railways leading from and to the coalfields of the Ruhr and Saar—both close-range targets— under constant bombardment, when the coal, though it might be mined, could not have been distributed. The probability, however, is that none of these arguments was considered, and for the simple reason that industrial destruction was but part of a general scheme to devastate Germany and terrorize her civil population. This, anyhow, was borne out by events, which up to the spring of 1944 may be grouped under the headings: (1) The Economic Attack, and (2) the Moral Attack.

The first may be divided into two periods: May, 1940, to March, 1942, distributed and so-called "precision" bombing mainly by night by the R.A.F., and August, 1942, to March, 1944, daylight attacks on specific German industries by the U.S. Army Air Force.

During the first period, in spite of the damage done to built-up areas, the effect on German armament production was insignificant. Instead of it declining it increased by leaps and bounds. According to *The United States*

---

[10]There were only two oilfields of any size, the Rumanian and Hungarian, and ten main synthetic oil plants—namely, Leuna, Pölitz, Gelsenberg, Brux, Bohlen, Zeitz, Wesseling, Scholven, Magdeburg and Welheim.

Strategic Bombing Survey (European War)[11]: "Because the German economy throughout most of the war was substantially under-mobilized, it was resilient under air attack . . . The German experience showed," says the *Survey*, "that whatever the target system, no indispensable industry was put out of commission by a single attack. Persistent re-attack was necessary." Further, because Germany and the occupied countries were in extent twelve times that of Great Britain, the means the R.A.F. possessed in 1940-1942 were insufficient to attain remunerative results. This period was one of sheer waste of effort: it was one of "uneconomic" and not of "strategic" bombing.

The second period opened with the arrival of the U.S.A.A.F. in Europe. Holding that "specific industries and services were the most promising targets in the enemy economy," its Command believed that "if these targets were to be hit accurately, the attack had to be made in daylight." Nevertheless, as the *Survey* informs us, "no operations" carried out by the U.S.A.A.F. "during 1942 or the first half of 1943 had significant effect."

While these abortive operations were in progress, in January, 1943, it was decided at the Casablanca Conference that the objectives of the Anglo-American Strategic Air Force should be: "The destruction and dislocation of the German military, industrial and economic system and the undermining of the morale of the German people to the point where their capacity for armed resistance is fatally weakened." In June this decision was implemented, and for submarine bases the German aircraft industry was substituted.

The first of these attacks was made on the ball-bearing plants at Schweinfurt, and in a series of raids on them 12,000 tons of bombs were dropped. But in the attack on 14th October, the American losses were so costly[12] that further attacks on Schweinfurt were suspended for four months, during which recovery was so rapid that the *Survey* comments, ". . . there is no evidence that the attack on the ball-bearing industry had any measurable effect on essential war production."

After the above costly raid, daylight penetrations beyond fighter escort range were sharply circumscribed until the arrival of the P-51 (Mustang) long-range fighter in December, when again they were resorted to, the culminating attacks on the German aircraft industry opening during the last week of February, 1944. Nevertheless, says the *Survey*, "Production was not knocked out for long. On the contrary, during the whole year of 1944 the German air force is reported to have accepted a total of 39,807

---

[11]Published 30th September, 1945. An invaluable official publication. As I shall quote from it frequently, I will omit page references.

[12]Out of a force of 228 American bombers, 62 were lost and 138 damaged, some beyond repair.

aircraft of all types—compared with 8,295 in 1939, or 15,596 in 1942, before the plants suffered any attack ... acceptances were higher in March, the month after the heaviest attack, than they were in January, the month

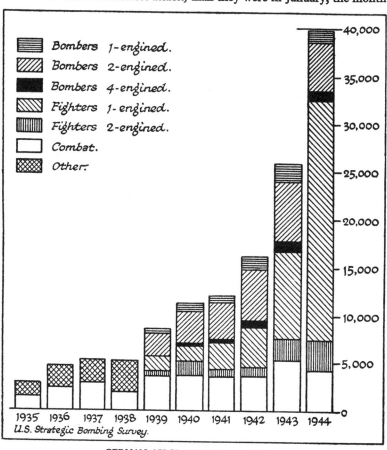

Bombers 1-engined.	
Bombers 2-engined.	
Bombers 4-engined.	
Fighters 1-engined.	
Fighters 2-engined.	
Combat.	
Other.	

1935 1936 1937 1938 1939 1940 1941 1942 1943 1944

U.S. Strategic Bombing Survey.

GERMAN AIRCRAFT PRODUCTION

before. They continued to rise . . . Recovery was improvised almost as quickly as the plants were knocked out."

These failures demanded a change in tactics. Thus far, the escort planes had protected the bomber force. Now they were instructed to incite opposition from the German fighter forces and to engage them whenever possible. The result was an ever mounting loss of German fighters and fighter pilots, until by the spring of 1944 opposition of the *Luftwaffe* ceased to be effective. Nevertheless, states the *Survey*, "German fighter production continued to increase during the summer of 1944, and acceptances reached a peak of 4,375 in September."

That, during these years, strategic bombing, from the point of view of the economic attack, was a grotesque failure is borne out by Senator Kilgore's *Statement on German Industry*,[13] based on "the official report of the Reich's Ministry for Armaments and War Production for 1944." The following extracts, a few out of many, from the *Statement* speak for themselves:

"The document shows graphically that in spite of Allied bombings Germany was able to rebuild and to expand its factories and to increase its war production until the final defeat of the German armies. German industry never lost its tremendous recuperative power."

"The report shows that three times as many armoured fighting vehicles were produced in the war-torn Germany of 1944 as were produced in 1942."

"More than three times as many fighter-bombers were built in Germany in 1944 as were built in 1942."

"Eight times as many night-fighter planes were produced in 1944 as in 1942."

"Not only were there increases in German war production in 1944 over previous years, but in a number of items there was an increase in the last quarter of 1944 over the first quarter of the year."

Next, from the economic attack, we will turn to its moral counterpart, the object of which was, as stated at the Casablanca Conference, "to undermine the morale of the German people." Officially it opened on the night of 28th-29th March, 1942, with a devastating raid on the city of Lübeck. It was then announced that an important change had been made in policy, in that "area" bombing as opposed to "precision" bombing was henceforth to be adopted. What it meant was this: Until then the forces sent out from England had been insufficient effectively to "brown" the target, but from now onwards they would be sufficiently powerful to do so. Therefore, there was no longer any need to aim at a military objective, for all that was necessary was to bomb the area in which it was located so intensely that everything in it would be destroyed.

Next Rostock was bombed and the centre of the town gutted, though the docks were barely touched. Then, on the night of 30th-31st May, came the first of the 1,000 bomber raids on Cologne. Actually 1,130 aircraft took part in it and 2,000 tons of bombs were dropped. After the attack it was announced that 250 factories had been destroyed;[14] but photographs

[13]Published by U.S. Office of War Information, London, 8th August, 1945.
[14]This was *pour faire rire*, because the factory area is outside the city.

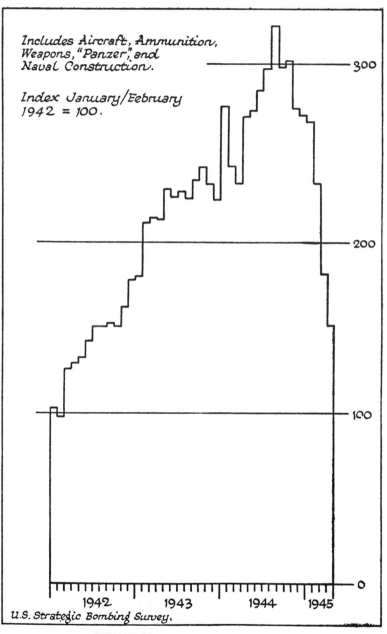

Includes Aircraft, Ammunition,
Weapons, "Panzer", and
Naval Construction.

Index January/February
1942 = 100.

300

200

100

0

1942   1943   1944   1945

U.S. Strategic Bombing Survey.

GERMAN COMBAT MUNITIONS OUTPUT

showed that the bull's-eye of the target was the centre of the city, of which some 5,000 acres were destroyed, and, according to German estimates, between 11,000 and 14,000 people were killed. It was, therefore, apparent that the main object of the attack was not to strike at the industries which circle Cologne, but at the inhabitants of the city. This was confirmed after the next 1,000 bomber raid on Essen; for when on 2nd June Mr. Churchill announced it in the House of Commons he said: "In fact, I may say that as the year advances German cities, harbours and centres of war production will be subjected to an ordeal the like of which has never been experienced by a country in continuity, severity and magnitude."[15] It will be noted that a distinction is made between cities and military objectives.

Of these attacks, that on Hamburg was the "star turn." During the last week in July, 1943, the city was raided six times by night and twice by day, and a weight of 7,500 tons of bombs was dropped. According to the *Survey*: 55 to 60 per cent of the city was destroyed; 75 to 80 per cent of this destruction was due to fire; 12.5 square miles were completely burnt out; 30 square miles damaged; 60,000 to 100,000 people killed; 300,000 dwelling units demolished, and 750,000 people rendered homeless. Of the conflagration we read:

"As the many fires broke through the roofs of buildings there rose a column of heated air more than two and a half miles high and one and a half miles in diameter, as measured by aircraft flying over Hamburg. This column was turbulent and was fed at its base by inrushing cooler ground-surface air. One and one and a half miles from the fire this draft increased the wind velocity from eleven to thirty-three miles per hour. At the edge of the area the velocities must have been appreciably greater, as trees three feet in diameter were uprooted. In a short time the temperature reached the ignition point for all combustibles and the entire area was ablaze. In such fires complete burnt-out occurred; that is, no trace of combustible material remained and only after two days were the areas cool enough to approach."[16]

These appalling slaughterings, which would have disgraced Attila, were justified on the plea of military necessity—only military objectives were attacked. In Britain, they were vindicated by the Archbishop of York, because they would "shorten the war and may save thousands of lives."[17]

[15]*Hansard*, H. of C. Deb., vol. 380, 5s., col. 553.
[16]Eyewitnesses described how the holocaust was so terrible that the air was sucked into it from outside the perimeter of the fire. Many were suffocated or shrivelled up by the intense heat. Others were drowned on throwing themselves into the canals that run through the city. Days later, when nearby cellars were opened, thousands were found to have perished as though cooked in an oven.
[17]*The Times*, 25th June, 1943.

Whereas, Mr. Attlee, Deputy Prime Minister, excused them by saying: "No, there is no indiscriminate bombing (cheers). As has been repeatedly stated in the House, the bombing is of those targets which are most effective from the military point of view (cheers)."[18] And four days later Captain Harold Balfour, Under-Secretary of State for Air, declared: "We are going right on to the end with our bomber attacks, just so long as the peoples of Germany and Italy tolerate Nazism and Fascism,"[19] which could only mean that the object of bombing was to make them revolt.

What does the *Survey* say on all this?

"It was believed that city attacks offered a means of destroying German civilian morale. It was believed that if the morale of industrial workers could be affected, or if labourers could be diverted from the factories to other purposes, such as caring for their families, repairing damage to their homes . . . German war production would suffer." Further, the *Survey* informs us that "24 per cent—nearly one-fourth of the total tonnage dropped, and almost twice the weight of bombs launched against all manufacturing targets together—was dropped in attacks against large cities . . . In sheer destructiveness these raids far outstripped all other forms of attack."

In spite of this, their moral effect was the very opposite to what Douhet and his followers had predicted. Instead of collapse being rapid, it was painfully slow. Bearing in mind that, of the sixty-one German cities of 100,000 inhabitants or more with a total population of 25,000,000 which were bombed, "3,600,000 houses were destroyed or heavily damaged—that is, 20 per cent of Germany's total residential area; 7,500,000 people were rendered homeless, about 300,000 killed and 780,000 injured . . ." the *Survey* continues: "The mental reaction of the German people to air attack is significant. Under ruthless Nazi control they showed surprising resistance to the terror and hardships of repeated air attack, to the destruction of their homes and belongings, and to the conditions under which they were reduced to live. Their morale, their belief in ultimate victory or satisfactory compromise, and their confidence in their leaders declined, but they continued to work efficiently as long as the physical means of production remained. The power of a police state over its people cannot be under-estimated."

Were these attacks of devastation and terrorization worth while? Otherwise put, were they strategic? They were not, because the entire strategic

[18]*Ibid.*, 28th May, 1943.

[19]*Ibid.*, 31st May, 1943. On the same day Air Chief Marshal Sir Arthur Harris said: "What she (Germany) has had in the past we can assure her will be chicken-feed compared with what she is going to get just as long as she persists in her aggression." (*Ibid.*, 31st May, 1943.)

problem was misread by Mr. Churchill and his advisers—if he had any.

In 1940, as we have seen, the German repulse was not due primarily to lack of air power or of land power, but of sea power. Hitler's problem was to span the English Channel. So was Mr. Churchill's from July, 1940, onwards, and, less excusably, he failed to turn the German error to his country's advantage. Every additional mile of foreign coastline the Germans occupied multiplied Britain's naval advantage by extending the target offered to her sea power. Simultaneously, it detracted from German military strength by enforcing dispersion. What depth was to Russia, breadth was to Britain; for as every mile added to land communications causes a weakening of the front, so also does every mile added to coastal protection.

Therefore, as a strategist, Mr. Churchill should have seen that the principal method of winning the war must be based on sea power, and that because sea power to make good its command of the sea demands air power, air power must come second to it. Further, because sea and air power to make good final conquest demand land power, land power must be bracketed with air power. In short, all three must be integrated in order to economize, mobilize and concentrate striking power.

Instead of this, air power was largely separated from sea and land power, and though the economic and moral air attacks made on Germany pinned down half her total aircraft strength on the defensive, and made a call on 1,000,000 men to man her anti-aircraft defences, and in consequence weakened her offensively, in order to accomplish this, England, according to the *Survey*, had to devote "40 to 50 per cent of her war production to her air forces" alone. This meant that only 50 to 60 per cent was devoted to sea and land power. In corroboration of this, when introducing the Army Estimates to Parliament on 2nd March, 1944, Sir James Grigg, Secretary of State for War, said: "The R.A.F. programme is already employing more workpeople than the Army equipment programme, and I daresay that there are, in fact, as many engaged on making heavy bombers as on the whole Army programme."[20]

[20]*Hansard*, H. of C. Deb., 5s., vol. 397, col. 1602. The same also applies to American aircraft production. "General Arnold, who headed the American air arm and was also a member of the Combined Chiefs of Staff, still believed that air power could bomb Germany into surrender—if only he could take enough men, *matériel* and priorities out of the rest of the war effort. He and his generals, and his public relations officers, fought the invasion (of Normandy) subtly and definitely—by pressing for ever greater expansion of the air arm. They stood constantly for delay and postponement, to give themselves time to get the fleets that were building and training into the air over Germany. Their motives seemed a mixture of sincere enthusiasm for their weapon (in the Billy Mitchell tradition) and intense personal ambitions. Playing military politics, they felt that if they could subdue Germany by

Had Mr. Churchill realized, as he should have, seeing that his great ancestor the first Duke of Marlborough in his day clearly did so, that Britain's strategical problem was initially a naval one and only subsequently a land one—that is, first a problem of crossing the sea, and secondly a problem of crossing the land—instead of allotting half the resources of his country "to make the enemy burn and bleed in every way,"[21] he would, in order of priority, have allocated them as follows: (1) To build up a sufficiency of fighter and fighter-bomber aircraft to win and hold command of the air, in order to secure the British Isles and cover naval and military operations; (2) to build up a sufficiency of landing craft, in order to exploit the command of the sea which was his; and (3) to build up a sufficiency of transport aircraft, in order to supply the land forces and maintain their mobility once they had been landed. Only after these requirements had been fully met, should resources have been allocated to his "well worth while experiment"—strategic bombing.

Because the second and third of the above requirements were insufficient, as we shall see, nearly every campaign following the final establishment of the Allied initiative in the West in November, 1942, was cramped by lack of landing craft or crippled by lack of transport aircraft. Therefore, the conclusion is that, as an experiment, the strategic bombing of Germany up to the spring of 1944 was an extravagant failure. Instead of shortening the war, its cost in raw materials and industrial manpower prolonged it.

(2) *The Battle of El Alamein and the Pursuit to Tripoli*

The first of the above mentioned campaigns arose out of the desperate situation in Russia. Early in July, 1942, thoroughly alarmed by the fall of Sevastopol and the German advance on Voronezh, in order to distract the German summer campaign, President Roosevelt insisted that an invasion of the Cherbourg Peninsula should be made in September. But this was out of the question, for by that date only sufficient suitable landing craft would be available to carry one division.[22] Therefore, on 24th July, it was decided to postpone the invasion of France until 1943, and instead, revert to the proposal first mooted at the Washington Conference in January, of

---

air alone, the air arm would automatically become the senior service." Though, according to Ingersoll, "The Air Force people never got more than a percentage of what they asked . . ." (*Top Secret*, Ralph Ingersoll, English edition, 1946, p. 52). Thirty-five to forty per cent of American war production was devoted to the building, etc., of aircraft.

[21] *The Times*, 2nd February, 1943.

[22] *Three Years with Eisenhower*, Captain Harry C. Butcher, p. 9.

invading North-West Africa[23] in conjunction with an advance westwards from Egypt. Meanwhile, as a good-will gesture to Russia, on 19th August an overseas raid in force was made on Dieppe, and with such disastrous results that it would seem to have strongly influenced Mr. Churchill against future cross-Channel operations. Also, about this time, twelve ships out of a convoy of thirteen bound for Malta were sunk.[24] In its turn this accentuated the danger of an African landing within fighter range of Sardinia and Sicily. Nevertheless, planning for the dual campaign was at once put into hand, and simultaneously changes in the Middle East Command were made: General Sir Harold Alexander succeeded General Auchinleck and Lieut.-General B. L. Montgomery was given the command of the Eighth Army.

In Egypt the immediate struggle was between communications; or, in other words, the question was—which side could re-equip itself the more speedily? In the long run, Rommel saw that the odds were against him. Therefore, in spite of being weaker[25] than his enemy, towards the end of August he decided to attack.

At this time, the front occupied by Montgomery's army was a novel one in desert warfare, because for the first time it rested on two unattackable flanks—the Mediterranean in the north and the Qattara Depression in the south. From the coast and a little to the west of el Alamein it ran southwards for forty miles to the Depression, which could not be negotiated by wheeled or tracked vehicles. On the British side of the front and about fifteen miles from the coast two ridges ran eastwards—namely, the Ruweisat and the Alam el Halfa—and wisely Montgomery, instead of attempting to hold the whole forty mile front in strength, deployed the bulk of his army from the coast to the western end of the Ruweisat Ridge and thence along the ridge itself to the Alam el Halfa Ridge. Therefore, the right half of his front was L-shaped, the horizontal stroke of the L flanking the northern side of the weakly held southern half of the front, the left flank of which rested on the Depression.

---

[23] The invasion of North Africa, writes Captain Butcher, was "Desired by the Prime Minister (Mr. Churchill) and not by the American military leaders" (*Ibid.*, p. 18). Throughout the war Mr. Churchill was, in the 1915 sense of the word, an "Easterner." That is, he was for decisive operations in the Balkans instead of in France; apparently, in order to deny them to Russia. But, ever inconsistent, in the end he and Mr. Roosevelt presented them and much else besides as a reward to Stalin for having remained loyal to the Allied cause, and by doing so lost the peace politically and strategically.

[24] *Ibid.*, pp. 45 and 63.

[25] In tanks he was markedly so. He had 230 to Montgomery's 390, of which 140 were Grants. (*Our Armoured Forces*, Lieut.-General Sir Giffard le Q. Martel, 1945, p. 198.)

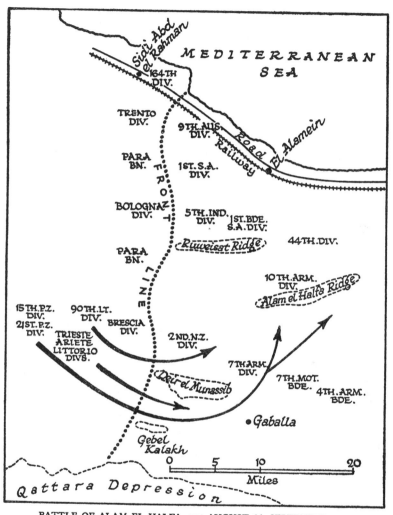

BATTLE OF ALAM EL HALFA, 31st AUGUST–6th SEPTEMBER, 1942

A little after midnight 30th-31st August Rommel attacked; his aim was to annihilate his enemy and win Egypt. He made three thrusts: a feint attack in the north, a holding attack in the centre and a main attack in the south, the last carried out by the Afrika Korps (15th and 21st Panzer Divisions and 90th Light Division) and the Italian XXth Corps (the Ariete and Littorio Armoured Divisions). Penetrating the British minefields north of the Qattara Depression, he swung northwards towards the Alam el Halfa Ridge in an attempt to break through the horizontal stroke of Montgomery's L formation and take the vertical stroke in rear. Had he succeeded in doing so, the bulk of the Eighth Army would have been trapped. However, he did not, and mainly on account of the admirable anti-tank and air tactics of his opponent. Failing, on 3rd September he began to withdraw, and on the 4th, 5th and 6th was heavily counterattacked. Wisely, on the 7th, Montgomery halted his army, because with Rommels' repulse the battle of communications had been won. He could now safely ignore his enemy until the Eighth Army was so powerfully reinforced that with it he could make mincemeat of him.

Though, as General Montgomery asserts, this skilfully fought defensive battle raised the morale of his men,[26] he gives little credit to his predecessors[27] for the excellence of the army he inherited from them. They had laboured under difficulties which he was never to be faced with—lack of experienced officers and trained men, lack of equipment and inferiority of weapons. All these defects had been made good, so good that, when on 30th August Rommel set out on his final gamble, the dice were already heavily loaded against him.

In October, when the Eighth Army was making ready to strike, Rommel's Army consisted of eight infantry and four armoured divisions: in all 96,000 men, of whom rather more than half were Germans, and between 500 and 600 tanks, of which more than half were Italian. With this force he faced Montgomery's three corps, the Xth, XIIIth and XXXth, respectively commanded by Lieut.-General Sir Herbert Lumsden, Lieut.-General B. C. Horrocks and Lieut.-General Sir Oliver Leese: in all seven infantry divisions, three armoured divisions and seven armoured brigades, together numbering 150,000 men and 1,114 tanks, of which 128 were Grants and 267 Shermans.[28] Numbers and armament

[26]*El Alamein to the River Sangro*, Field-Marshal Sir Bernard L. Montgomery (1946), p. 10.
[27]See *Three Against Rommel*, p. 306.
[28]Captain Butcher in his *Three Years with Eisenhower*, under date 25th October, writes: "Ike says that if quality and quantity of material and men can count in the desert warfare against the wily Rommel, then Montgomery should win. He has 300 new Sherman tanks with 75's in completely revolving turrets" (p. 131).

were, therefore, definitely against Rommel, and also was the position he occupied when compared to the one held by Montgomery on 30th August. There was no convenient ridge in its centre, and, in consequence, he could not shorten his front in the same way Montgomery had done. Further, though his flanks rested on the same impassable obstacles, 96,000 men were too small a force to hold forty miles of front securely even when elaborately mined. How Rommel would have attempted to hold it is unknown; for, some time prior to the attack, he temporarily handed his command over to General Stumme and went to Berlin. Once in command, knowing that the approaching attack would be frontal, Stumme committed the egregious error of spreading his troops evenly along the whole front, instead of holding it lightly and concentrating his armour well in rear in readiness to counter-attack.

Not possessing the means to turn his enemy's left flank by a sea-borne operation, Montgomery decided to penetrate that flank a few miles south of the coast; for though tactically it was stronger than Stumme's centre and right, strategically a successful penetration there would prove far more profitable, because it would cut the enemy's centre and right off from the coastal road—his sole line of supply and retreat. To confuse his enemy, Montgomery also decided to launch a subsidiary attack against Stumme's right flank, and prior to the attack, by means of dummy tanks and vehicles and a dummy pipe-line, he did all he could to mislead him.

The tasks laid down for his three corps were as follows: The XXXth in the north, on a front of four divisions, was to cut two lanes through the minefields. When cut, the Xth (1st and 10th Armoured Divisions and the 2nd New Zealand Division) was to pass through with the ultimate task of destroying the enemy's armour. Meanwhile, the XIIIth and the 7th Armoured Division were to attack in the south, contain the 21st Panzer Division and mislead the enemy. Directly the attack was launched, the whole of the bomber force was to switch on to the battle.

The battle, as planned, was built upon weight of striking power, and, therefore, closely resembled the battles of 1916-1917, and, as we shall see in his future battles, Montgomery was pre-eminently a general of *matériel*. Fortunately for him, he assumed his command at the very moment when munitions began to pour into Egypt; but had he done so earlier, it is difficult to imagine him fighting a Sidi Barrani or a Beda Fomm. "By the Montgomery method," writes Morehead, "the whole art of war was reducible to a pattern of a series of numbers; it was all based on units of manpower and fire power and so forth."[29] Later on, Captain Butcher says much the same—namely: ". . . but 'Monty' not satisfied. Essence of his

[29] *The End of Africa*, Alan Morehead (1943), p. 102.

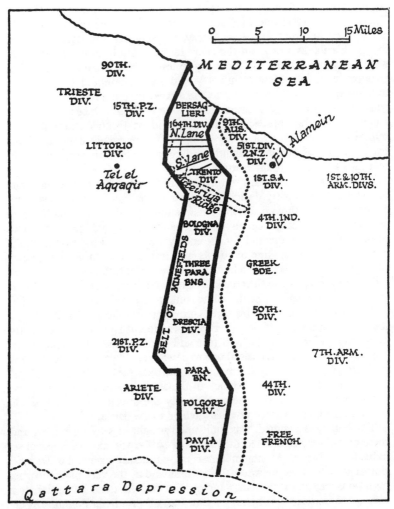

BATTLE OF EL ALAMEIN, 23rd OCTOBER-4th NOVEMBER, 1942

objections was that his part in HUSKY (invasion of Sicily) had to be so strong his risk of defeat would be nil."[30] Nevertheless, Morehead also says: "If his battles lacked genius, at least they were fought brilliantly and with good sound logic."[31]

Similar to so many of the battles of the First World War, Montgomery's attack was heralded by a long preliminary bombardment. This time, it was carried out by bomber aircraft instead of by artillery. On 9th October it opened and it lasted until the 23rd. Rommel's supply bases and ports in Italy were attacked from England, and his minefields, anti-tank batteries, airfields, dumps, transport columns and depots, including Tobruk and Mersa Matruh, were bombed from Egypt. No less than 700 bombers were employed, and by the 23rd the Axis air forces in Africa were grounded.

At 9.40 p.m. that day, 1,000 guns opened fire on a six miles front, and twenty minutes later, under a full moon, the infantry of the XXXth and XIIIth Corps, accompanied by engineers, advanced, and by 5.30 a.m. on the 24th on the XXXth Corps' front two lanes were pushed through the main mine belt. By 7 a.m. the first objective—the Miteiriya Ridge—was occupied; whereupon the 1st and 10th Armoured Divisions advanced up to it. Meanwhile, in the south, the attack of the XIIIth Corps failing, the 7th Armoured Division was ordered north.

On the 24th, the XXXth Corps consolidated its position; on the 25th General Stumme was killed, and on the 26th Rommel, returning from Germany, at once gathered together his armour and on the 27th launched a series of violent counter-attacks against the XXXth and Xth Corps, which at the time were held back by anti-tank fire. All these attacks were repulsed. Thereupon Montgomery re-grouped his army; the XIIIth Corps was placed on the defensive, the Xth withdrawn, and the XXXth was ordered to prepare to carry out a new infantry attack in order to deepen the salient.

On the 28th Rommel attacked again, and then swung half his armour north in order to relieve the 90th Light Division which had been surrounded by the 9th Australian Division. There heavy fighting continued until 1st November, on which day the XXXth Corps attack being ready, at 1 a.m. on the 2nd an advance on a 4,000 yards front was made, and by pushing forward a large number of cruiser tanks, the final minefield was penetrated at heavy cost. By 9 a.m. it became clear that Rommel was preparing to counter-attack with the 15th and 21st Panzer Divisions. Thereupon the Xth Corps ordered the 1st and 10th Armoured Divisions forward and a violent armoured battle was fought round and about Tel el Aqqaqir, which was lost to the Germans on the night of the 2nd-3rd.

[30] *Three Years with Eisenhower*, p. 248.   [31] *The End of Africa*, p. 103.

Recognizing that he was beaten, Rommel began to pull out, and abandoning the greater part of his right wing he retreated westwards. Mersa Matruh was re-occupied by the Eighth Army on the 7th-8th.

Thus ended the Battle of el Alamein, the most decisive land battle yet won for the Allied cause, and one of the mose decisive in British history. Rommel's losses were catastrophic: 59,000 killed, wounded and captured, of whom 34,000 were Germans; and 500 tanks, 400 guns and thousands of vehicles lost. The British losses were 13,500 killed, wounded and missing, and 432 tanks put out of action.

Though, as Clifford points out,[32] this battle could not have been won without the assistance of the American Grant and Sherman tanks, a more important point is noted by General Martel. It is that, in battles of assault against prepared positions, cruiser tanks are not sufficiently heavily armoured to work with infantry.[33] In the earlier campaigns the Matilda tanks had done well, but, as already noted, they were no longer proof against the German 50 mm. anti-tank shell, whereas the Churchill tank was. "There is no doubt," writes Martel, "that if a brigade of Churchill tanks had been available, they could have overrun . . . (the) 50 mm. anti-tank guns quite easily."[34] Only four Churchill tanks were used in this battle: "All . . . were struck many times by 50 mm. anti-tank guns, and there was only one penetration."[35] The conclusion is, therefore, as with artillery two categories of guns are required, one for field and the other for siege work, the same holds good with tanks, two types are required—a field tank and a siege or assault tank.

From Mersa Matruh to Tripoli, the Eighth Army's pursuit was, as Clifford remarks, "a dull and measured affair," and not "one of those mad, headlong, exciting chases."[36] And he adds: "Rommel was conducting a masterly retreat—a real textbook job. I do not suppose that ever in history has a withdrawal been so genuinely according to plan."[37]

The reason for this is to be sought in the faulty handling of the Desert Air Force more so than in administrative difficulties and in the badness of the weather. This is made clear by General de Guingand, Chief of Staff Eighth Army, who writes: "With the virtual air superiority we possessed, and the state of disorganization of the enemy, it looked to us in the Army that here was the 'dream target' for the R.A.F. In the event, the results

---

[32] *Three Against Rommel*, p. 359.

[33] Grant and Sherman tanks were of the cruiser type and the maximum thickness of their armour was 75 mm. The Matilda and Churchill were infantry tanks, and their maximum armour was respectively 78 mm. and 90 mm.

[34] *Our Armoured Forces*, p. 216.

[35] *Ibid.*

[36] *Three Against Rommel*, p. 319.

[37] *Ibid.*, p. 322.

appeared very disappointing. When setting out along the road between the Alamein battlefield and Daba, I had expected to see a trail of devastation, but the visible signs of destroyed vehicles were few and far between. After Daba much better results had been obtained, but even here a lot of the vehicles we found had stopped through shortage of petrol."

The reason he alleges for this is clearly the right one—namely, that the air force was so obsessed by air fighting and bombing, the pilots "were not allowed to come down low," and that in view of these activities, they "had not had the training in the low-flying type of attack with cannon." Further, he informs us: "After we arrived at Tripoli Air Vice-Marshal Harry Broadhurst, a famous 'Battle of Britain' pilot, took the matter in hand and carried out intensive trials and practice to get his force proficient at this low-flying technique. We were to reap the reward of all this during the Battle of Mareth."[38]

Tobruk was entered on the 13th, Gazala on the 14th, Benghazi on the 20th, Sirte on 25th December, and Tripoli on 23rd January, and all along the one thousand four hundred miles of retreat and pursuit there was little fighting, Rommel gaining in strength as he fell back.

It is true, as Morehead observes, that "Nine-tenths of desert warfare is the battle of supply."[39] Seeing that the same was doubly true in Burma, it makes it all the stranger that so little effort was made in the Middle East to overcome this supreme difficulty by air transport. Writing on this problem as it was in August, 1942, Morehead says: "The enemy could get all his replacements and reinforcements three times quicker than we could. Often he used aircraft to carry many of his supplies and reinforcements to the front. They arrived ten times quicker than by land and sea. We don't use troop-carrying aircraft to any extent yet."[40] And again: "Note that parachutists were not used at any time through these campaigns except in a limited way by the British."[41]

Only during the pursuit was an attempt made to remedy this oversight, for Clifford informs us that ". . . there was another thing—something which was nothing new to the Germans, but which no British army had ever done before. In this campaign, for the first time, air transport was used on a serious scale . . . The air force supply-lorries almost disappeared from the road. Nothing remotely resembling it had ever been seen before on our side of the front."[42]

[38]*Operation Victory*, Major-General Sir Francis de Guingand (1947), pp. 209-210.
[39]*The End in Africa*, Alan Morehead (1943), p. 104.
[40]*A Year of Battle*, p. 237.
[41]*Ibid.*, p. 244.
[42]*Three Against Rommel*, p. 318.

Why? There can be but one answer: Because the R.A.F. in England was so obsessed by strategic bombing that it was oblivious of the need for air transport. Yet it is unquestionable that, had Montgomery from the start had at his disposal an adequate force of transport aircraft, his major supply difficulties would have been solved. Further to this, had he had but one airborne division and a small number of landing craft, with the former he could have seized Halfaya Pass or some other point on the North African coastline, and with the latter have rapidly reinforced it. Had he been able to do these three things, by speeding up his advance and by blocking Rommel's retreat, he could have brought his pursuit to so rapid a termination that before the New Year he would have been able to overrun eastern Tunisia. What effect this would have had on the war will become apparent in the following Section.

(3) *The Invasion of North Africa and the Conquest of Tunisia*

Strategically, there can be little doubt that the invasion of North Africa should have preceded the Battle of el Alamein, because by directly threatening Rommel's base at Tripoli as well as his sea communications, it would have compelled him to look in two directions. Also, there can be no doubt whatever that the nearer to Tripoli the Allied forces landed, the more distracting would this threat become. Both these points were considered and both had to be abandoned because of shortage of landing craft. On this question General Marshall writes: "It was desired to carry out the operation early in the fall, but it was necessary to delay until November in order to receive a large number of craft from the shipyards . . ." Also: "It was urgently desired to make initial landings to the east of Algiers at Bone, Philippeville, and possibly Tunis, but the lack of shipping and of landing boats and aircraft-carriers at the time made the procedure impracticable."[43] In addition to this, the Royal Navy, which was to escort the expedition, fearing air attack from Sardinia and Sicily, was opposed to any landing being made east of Algiers. Therefore, it was decided to restrict the landings to Casablanca, Oran and Algiers. The first was to be carried out by an American force under Major-General George S. Patton, sailing direct from the United States, and the second, also American, and the third, part British and part American, respectively commanded by Major-General Lloyd Fredendall and Lieut.-General K. A. N. Anderson, by forces sailing direct from Britain. The last two were together to form the First Army under Anderson. Further, in order to facilitate the capture of the Oran airfields, it was decided to fly an American airborne force from England across Spain to them, in spite of the distance being one thousand

[43]*Biennial Report . . . 1st July,* 1941, *to* 30*th June,* 1943, p. 15.

five hundred miles. Finally, on 9th September, the date of the invasion was fixed for 8th November, and on 5th November, General Dwight D. Eisenhower, who had been selected to command the expedition, opened his headquarters at Gibraltar.

Though there were no Axis troops in Morocco, Algeria and Tunisia, the operation showed both originality and daring. First, there was no certainty what the French would do; would they submit or resist? Secondly, what would the Germans do; would they invade Spain and seize Gibraltar? This was the greatest danger of all; for with Gibraltar in their hands, communications with Algiers and Oran would be cut. At the time. this possibility caused much anxiety; but it is now known that, though Hitler contemplated the move, it was so strongly opposed by General Franco[44] that he set it aside. The truth is, Hitler had no longer the troops necessary to invade Spain.

On 25th October the forces from the British Isles sailed for Gibraltar, and, on 7th November, from the German look-out at La Linea, a report was sent to Berlin stating that a large convoy was heading for the Mediterranean. Yet, in spite of its size,[45] it does not seem to have aroused much interest; for on the next day Fredborg writes: "Then the 8th dawned. I shall never forget the complete surprise which the report of the Allied landings caused in Berlin. The amazement was as marked in the Wilhelmstrasse as among diplomats and journalists."[46] Next came an almost equally great surprise. Though the landings were opposed, but with unequal vigour, suddenly on the 11th Admiral Jean Darlan, Marshal Pétain's successor designate, who at the time happened to be on a visit in Algiers, ordered the cease-fire;[47] whereupon the Allied problem of invading Morocco and Algeria at once became one of invading Tunisia.

This also became Hitler's problem, and though completely surprised by the invasion, he acted with his accustomed celerity. He did two things. The first was the immediate occupation of Vichy France, which led to the

---

[44]See *Behind the Steel Wall*, Arvid Fredborg (1944), p. 149.

[45]In all 350 warships and 500 transports were required for the three forces.

[46]*Behind the Steel Wall*, p. 145. This is extraordinary, because on 9th October Ciano mentions Anglo-Saxon preparations "to land in force in North Africa," and on 4th November that the great convoy at Gibraltar "suggests the possibility of a landing in Morocco." (*Ciano's Diary*, pp. 508, 519.)

[47]This is all the more surprising, because ever since Mr. Churchill's impulsive raid on the French warships at Oran, on 4th July, 1940, Admiral Darlan had been violently hostile to England. Now Mr. Churchill is reported to have said: "Kiss Darlan's stern if you have to, but get the French Navy." (*Three Years with Eisenhower*, p. 151.) Throughout, he would seem to have been terrified lest the French fleet should fall into German hands. Why, it is difficult to imagine, because it was virtually inoperative. Darlan was murdered on 24th December, 1942, and his assassin hastily shot on the 26th.

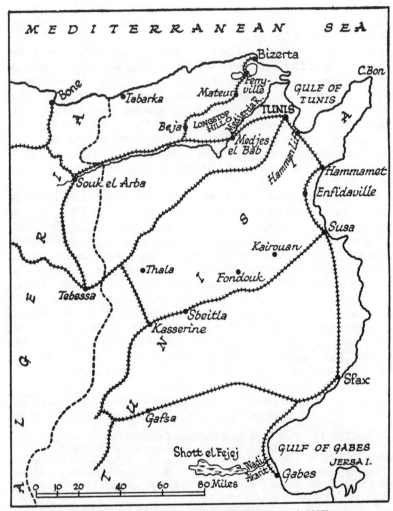

THE INVASION OF TUNISIA, 8th NOVEMBER, 1942-12th MAY, 1943

scuttling of the French fleet in Toulon Harbour on 27th November. The second was to rush troops by sea and air to Tunis and Bizerta, the first flights landing at el Aouana airport (Tunis) on the 9th. Without troop-carrying aircraft this amazingly rapid movement would have been impracticable. Soon troop-carriers were landing 1,000 men and more a day. This time it was the Allies who were surprised, for clearly, had they considered such rapid reinforcing possible, they surely would have risked landing even if only commando forces at Tunis and Bizerta on the 8th.

As from July to October the real battle between Alexander and Rommel had been one of supply, also was it one of supply from mid-November to mid-February between the Allied and Axis forces in Tunisia. If the advance of the former was to be methodical, delay was unavoidable, because the order of embarkation had been based on the likelihood of French opposition. Consequently, the assault parties with a minimum of transport were in the first wave of the invasion, and the administrative services and transport in the last. Therefore, before an organized advance could be made, the whole order of embarkation would have to be reversed. Were this done, the delay caused would enable the Axis to occupy Tunisia in strength.

Rightly, we think, Eisenhower decided on an immediate advance. Therefore, on the 11th, the leading troops of the First Army were hastily re-embarked at Algiers and landed at Bougie, from where they set out for Bone, which, on the 12th, was occupied by a seaborne commando and two companies of parachutists. On the 15th another party of parachutists was dropped near Tebessa to seize an airfield, and the next day yet another at Souk el Arba to cover the advance. This parachutist advanced guard was immediately followed by two infantry brigades of the 78th Division of the First Army, with such transport as was available. On the 15th it clashed with German patrols, and on the 25th occupied Medjez el Bab, thirty miles south-west of Tunis Three days later American parachutists reached the Sbeitla-Gafsa area.

The problem of Allied supply now became acute, and was worsened by torrential storm of rain and air attacks on shipping. By the 29th air supply had beaten road supply. From Algiers to Medjez el Bab was over three hundred miles and the best airfields were in Axis hands, and while the roads became rivers of mud, the German transport aircraft continued to pour troops into Tunisia. By Christmas the stalemate was complete Medjez el Bab, nevertheless, was held by the First Army, though the high ground to the north of it, in particular Jebel el Ahmera (Longstop Hill) was lost. To the south the line extended in a series of posts to Fondouk. Thus the situation remained until mid-February.

Meanwhile, in Tripolitania, the Eighth Army having occupied Tripoli,

Rommel fell back to the Mareth Line, a belt of French fortifications built to protect the Tunisian frontier, and on 13th February advanced troops of the Eighth Army came up with his rearguard at Ben Gardane.

With the entrance of the Eighth Army into Tunisia, according to the decision made at the Casablanca Conference in January, that army coming under General Eisenhower's command, Eisenhower decided on the following changes: General Alexander to become his deputy and command the 18th Army Group, comprising all land forces in Tunisia. All air forces to form the Mediterranean Air Command under Air Chief Marshal Tedder, with Lieut.-General Carl Spaatz as Commander of the North-west African Air Force. The strategic air force to be commanded by Lieut.-General Doolittle, and the light and medium bomber and fighter forces to be organized into a Tactical Air Force under Air Vice Marshal Coningham to lend close support to the fleet and army.

As the rainy season drew to an end, more and more precarious grew the situation of the two Axis armies in Tunisia, the one now under Field-Marshal Dietloff von Arnim, facing the First Army, and the other under Rommel, facing the Eighth. Rommel's was the more critically placed, because his line of retreat from the Mareth Line was directly threatened by the American 1st and 34th Divisions in the Sbeitla-Gafsa area, which at any moment might advance eastwards and bottle him up. Well placed to operate on interior lines, Rommel, knowing that Montgomery was not yet ready to advance, decided first to fall upon the Americans and next to attack the Eighth Army, not to win a decisive victory, but to gain time and keep the war going in Tunisia as long as possible.

Rushing a powerful force north, on 14th February he fell upon the Americans and broke through the Kasserine Pass on the 20th, from where, dividing his army into two columns, with one he advanced on Thala aiming at cutting the communications of the bulk of the First Army, and with the other he struck westwards at Tebessa, because it was the obvious point of junction of the First and Eighth Armies. Succeeding wonderfully at first, he was soon met by such fierce opposition that, on the 23rd, he was forced to withdraw. Next, on 6th March, he fell upon the Eighth Army at Medenine, a few miles east of the Mareth Line, but was severely repulsed and mainly by anti-tank fire, for in this engagement the Eighth Army tanks never came into action.

Thus the initiative in North Africa finally passed to the Allies. Nevertheless, in part, Rommel had succeeded in his purpose. For the time being his line of retreat was secure; therefore he decided to hold on to the Mareth Line as long as he could, and thereby prevent the junction of his enemy's two armies.

The position he held was an exceedingly strong one. Its left lay on the

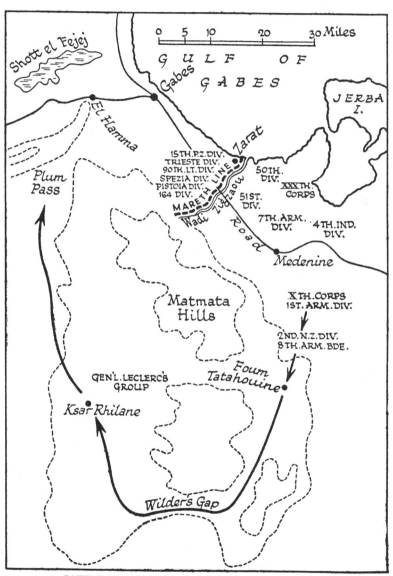

BATTLE OF THE MARETH LINE, 20th–27th MARCH, 1943

sea coast, along its front ran the Wadi Zigzaou, a formidable tank obstacle, in places fifty feet deep with an average width of eighty yards, and its right rested on the Matmata Hills, which were impassable for wheeled traffic. South of Medenine a pass crossed the hills at Foum Tatahouine, and forty miles due west of Mareth there was a gap in them called "Plum Pass," north of Bir Rhezane and south of El Hamma. The gap itself was fortified.

To outflank the Mareth front by way of Foum Tatahouine and "Plum Pass" entailed a journey of some one hundred and fifty miles over broken ground; nevertheless, Montgomery decided to attempt it. His plan was, while the XXXth Corps pinned the enemy down by a frontal attack against his left flank, to move the 2nd New Zealand Division and the 8th Armoured Brigade over the Foum Tatahouine Pass, link up with General Leclerc's small French force which had come up from Lake Chad, storm "Plum Gap" and then fall upon the enemy's rear. The Xth Corps was to be held in reserve. The whole operation is reminiscent of Chancellorsville at its best, though tactically very different.

It was also very different from any British battle hitherto fought by the Eighth Army, because at long last the heavy air support placed at Montgomery's disposal was used not only against the enemy airfields and in the preliminary bombardment, but in closest co-operation with the troops attacking the narrow frontage at "Plum Pass."

Immediately prior to the battle, de Guingand tells us that he had a long discussion with Broadhurst, A.O.C. the Desert Air Force, in which he pointed out to him that the Eighth Army "had always wanted to try out what is generally called a 'Blitz' attack as practised by the Germans." Broadhurst, he informs us, listened to his argument and then said: "I will do it. You will have the whole boiling match—bombs and cannon. It will be a real low-flying blitz . . ."

"The final air plan catered for a 'crump' by forty light bombers on the narrow frontage of attack, to take place just before it commenced. Then, with five Spitfire squadrons as top cover, sixteen Kittybomber squadrons would operate over the battlefield for two and a half hours, on an average density of two squadrons at any one time. These using bomb and cannon would shoot up everything they saw. In addition, a specially trained squadron of 'tank busters' were (*sic*) to go for the enemy armour when located."[48]

At 10.30 p.m. on 20th March, the 50th Division of the XXXth Corps, under cover of a tremendous artillery barrage, stormed the Wadi Zigzaou, gained a footing on its western side, but on the 22nd was driven back across it by the 15th Panzer and 90th Light Divisions.

---

[48]*Operation Victory*, pp. 256-257.

Next day, deciding to throw everything he could spare into the out-flanking movement, Montgomery ordered Xth Corps Headquarters and the 1st Armoured Division to move after dark on the 23rd and join the 2nd New Zealand Division, and reinforcing the XXXth Corps with the 7th Armoured Division, he ordered it, after withdrawing the 50th Division, to open a new attack against the enemy's centre.

Meanwhile, the 2nd New Zealand Division, having successfully crossed the Foum Tatahouine Pass, was unable to force "Plum Pass," a bottleneck some six thousand yards in width. On the Xth Corps Headquarters and the 1st Armoured Division coming up, a terrific air bombardment was opened on the pass, and on the evening of the 26th, under cover of a still more powerful air and artillery barrage, the attack on the defile was launched. "Never before," writes de Guingand, "had our Desert Air Force given us such superb, such gallant, and such intimate support."[40] The "Blitz" was an overwhelming success, and it was pushed until dark. Then a pause followed until the moon rose, when the advance was continued to a little short of El Hamma, where it was held up by a screen of anti-tank guns. Meanwhile, in spite of the XXXth Corps' second attack, Rommel had been steadily pulling out, and once again with high skill, on the night of the 27th, he succeeded in withdrawing his severely mauled army to the Wadi Akarit, at a loss of no more than 2,500 men captured.

A few days later he was ordered to hand his army over to General Messe, an Italian, and then to return to Germany. The reason for this probably was that, early in April, an all-out Allied offensive had been opened on the Axis air and sea communications, and it was thought as well to get Rommel home before they were completely closed. Between the 5th and the 19th 147 German air transports were shot down and 31 vessels sunk.

While this rear attack was under way, Messe, who on the 6th had at high cost to his army been driven out of the Wadi Akarit Line, rapidly fell back to Enfidaville, where towards the middle of the month he took up a

---

[40] *Ibid.*, p. 262. The sequel to this very proper use of air power goes to show how obsessed the R.A.F. Command was by its Douhet doctrines. De Guingand writes: "I feel it only right that I should mention certain repercussions that took place after the magnificent effort put up by the Desert Air Force in the El Hamma battle . . . Yet, in spite of its success, I happen to know that there was considerable anxiety shown by those in high R.A.F. places—from the Air Ministry downwards. Great efforts were made to write down the story . . . I suppose the idea behind all this was the fear that the Army would always ask for this kind of support, and that the result might be a heavy drain on our fighter strength, and therefore make the R.A.F.'s primary task of defeating the enemy's air forces more difficult . . . It is interesting to note that the losses for the day's operations were eight pilots killed or missing—by no means a heavy bill to pay . . ." (p. 264).

defensive position. Meanwhile, on the 7th, the First and Eighth Armies joined hands near Gafsa.

On the 19th, in order to pin the enemy down in the south, Montgomery was ordered to attack Enfidaville, which he did on the following day, carrying the town and gaining a few miles. Four days later the First Army attacked Longstop Hill, and on the 26th occupied it, and on 3rd May the 1st Armoured Division of the American IInd Corps took Mateur.

Thus, throughout April, blow had followed blow, but with the occupa tion of Longstop Hill, which opened the Medjerda Valley, Alexander determined to treat the Axis position as if it were a fortress, and first breach and then storm it at one point. In short, his idea was to return to the *blitz* attack on a narrow front.

First he regrouped his forces. On his left he assembled the whole of the American IInd Corps (1st, 9th, 34th Infantry and 1st Armoured Divisions); on his right he left the bulk of the Eighth Army where it was; and in the centre, then held by the 1st, 4th and 78th Divisions of the First Army—the point he intended for the main assault—he organized a new corps, the IXth, composed of the 4th Infantry Division and 6th Armoured Division of the First Army and the 4th Indian Infantry Division, 201st Guards Brigade and 7th Armoured Division of the Eighth, under the command of Lieut.-General B. G. Horrocks. To support it, an unpre cedented concentration of aircraft was placed at the disposal of Air Vice-Marshal Coningham.

Alexander's plan of attack was an exceedingly simple one. First, pressure was to be applied along the whole front of the Axis fortress, now about one hundred and thirty miles in length. Secondly, a concentrated attack was to be made up the Medjerda Valley direct on Tunis. The two infantry divisions of the IXth Corps were to break through on a frontage of three thousand yards, and to be followed by the two armoured divisions, which, once the enemy's anti-tank defences had been overrun, were to pass through the infantry and head straight for Tunis. The date fixed for the attack was 6th May.

Early that day the battle was opened by an intense bombing of the enemy's front and rear. ". . . during the final drive from Medjez el Bab to Tunis," writes General Arnold, "we flew 2,146 sorties, the great majority of which were bomber, fighter-bomber or strafing missions on a 6,000-yard front. We blasted a channel from Medjez el Bab to Tunis."[50]

While this attack of obliteration was being carried out, more than 1,000 guns pounded the enemy's defences, and at 3.30 a.m., under cover of their

[50]*Report of the Commanding General of the Army Air Forces,* 4th January, 1944, pp. 43-44.

fire, parties of sappers went forward to lift the mines and cut gaps in the wire. In rear of them came the infantry, who by sheer weight of numbers broke through the enemy's outpost line and by dawn reached his main defensive belt, which by 11 a.m. they penetrated at small loss. A breach having been made, the tanks of the 6th and 7th Armoured Divisions were ordered to advance. By nightfall they were well on the road and at 2.30 p.m. the next day they entered the suburbs of Tunis and occupied the town by nightfall. Thus the fortress was cleft in two. On the American front events moved with equal swiftness, Ferryville and Bizerta being occupied on the afternoon of the 7th.

In spite of these shattering blows, the greater part of the Axis forces was still intact, and in the general confusion these forces were making eastwards and northwards towards the Cape Bon Peninsula, an exceedingly strong position and the natural citadel of the Tunisian fortress. Like a double wall, across its base ran two lines of hills, with two main gates, one in the north and the other in the south at Hammam Lif and Hammamet respectively.

Giving his enemy no time to recover in and man this wall, Alexander ordered the 6th Armoured Division to force the Hammam Lif gate and then swing northwards in rear of the hills along the road leading to Hammamet and attack it in rear. Thus would both gateways be blocked.

At nightfall on the 8th, the 6th Armoured Division arrived outside Hammam Lif, and when the moon rose advanced. Of this extraordinarily audacious manœuvre Morehead gives the following graphic description:

"They broke clean through to Hammamet inside the next ten hours. They roared past German airfields, workshops, petrol and ammunition dumps and gun positions. They did not stop to take prisoners—things had gone far beyond that. If a comet had rushed down that road it could hardly have made a greater impression. The Germans were now entirely dazed. Wherever they looked British tanks seemed to be hurtling past . . . The German generals gave up giving orders since they were completely out of touch with the people to whom they could give orders, who were diminishing every hour . . . In a contagion of doubt and fear the German army turned tail and made up the Cape Bon roads looking for boats. When on the beaches it became apparent to them at last that there were no boats— nor any aircraft either—the army became a rabble."[51]

As Clifford points out: "The brain and nerve-centre of the army was paralysed, and nothing could function coherently any more."[52] It was the collapse of France over again.

---

[51] *The End of Africa*, p. 201.
[52] *Three Against Rommel*, p. 411.

On the 12th all was over; that day 252,415 Germans and Italians laid down their arms. Africa was won; once again the Mediterranean was open to Allied shipping; the French Army had been reborn, and the whole shore line of the Axis from the Pyrenees to the Aegean was now open to attack.

Thus ended the first of the great amphibious campaigns in the West: a campaign which conclusively showed that the strategical foundations of victory lay in sea power. It was the command of the Atlantic and not the so-called strategic bombing of Germany which rendered it possible. Quite otherwise, as we hope has been made clear, the latter actually impeded speedy victory; for had not a single German city been bombed, and instead had half the vast manpower employed on the building of heavy bombers been devoted to the production of landing craft and transport aircraft, there can be no shadow of doubt that, not only would Africa have been won months earlier, but, as will become apparent in the next Chapter, the war in Europe would have been won at least a year earlier than it actually was.

Also, this campaign showed that tactically, and because of ever-increasing Allied industrial power, battles of *matériel* were coming back into fashion. And though there is no reason to doubt that the great bombardments at el Alamein, Mareth and Medjerda were both right and profitable, there was a danger that once again, as in 1916-1917, the attack of obliteration would become a dogma, crowding out imagination and offering to the unimaginative a sealed-pattern solution for every offensive problem. This will also become apparent in the next Chapter, in which, in spite of brilliant exceptions, we shall see a steady decline of generalship into ironmongering.

(4) *The Catastrophe of Stalingrad and the German* 1942-1943 *Winter Retreat*

While in North Africa the initiative was systematically being wrested from the Axis, in Russia it was suddenly wrenched out of German hands. Not so much because the Russians were better winter soldiers, though they probably were; but because, on account of their superior organization and administration the Germans were more efficient summer soldiers, and that during the summer months of 1942, as of 1941, they so exhausted themselves that, when winter came, the Russian war potential was superior to their residual strength. This fundamental reason, due to the depth of Russia and the consequent difficulty of bringing the Russians to decisive battle, was vastly aggravated by faulty strategy and unimaginative tactics, as well as by two important developments: The first was that the Russians were increasingly becoming war experienced soldiers, and the second that their factories beyond the Volga and the Urals were increasingly approaching full production.

The side-tracking of Moscow after the first German summer campaign, and the abandonment of the advance on Saratov during the second, as we have seen, bereft that campaign of its strategic bottom. Simultaneously, by leaving Saratov in Russian hands, because it was a centre of communications, it enabled the Russians to concentrate against the left flank of the Stalingrad salient. Saratov was linked (1) to Moscow by rail; (2) to the Ural industrial region by rail and river; (3) to Astrakhan by rail; and (4) to Chkalov (Orenburg) by rail, nearby which town a pipe-line ran to the North Caspian oilfields. Troops, munitions, fuel and supplies could, therefore, be poured into the Saratov area from Moscow, Archangel, Siberia, Kazak, Caucasia and Persia.[53] That this was possible makes the German folly of staking nothing on Saratov and so much on Stalingrad all the more enormous.

South of Stalingrad, Astrakhan played a similar though subordinate role. By way of Saratov it was linked by rail to the whole of unoccupied Russia, and by way of the Caspian to Persia and thence to the outer world; the Persian Gulf playing the same strategical part in the south that the White Sea was playing in the north.

Tactically, the German errors were almost as great. During the winter of 1941-1942 their defensive system of "hedgehogs" had proved successful because Russian mobility—mainly due to lack of transport—had been low. Consequently, penetration between the "hedgehogs" had been hobbled. Thanks to increased home production, and also to American and British assistance, by the autumn of 1942 this limitation was nothing like so pronounced. Therefore, the Russians were in a position not only to carry out more rapid and deeper penetrations, but what was equally important, to mass stronger forces of artillery against the "hedgehogs." Further, because in 1941-1942 the Germans assumed an all-out defensive, their mobile forces were free to operate between the "hedgehogs," whereas in 1942-1943, because during the winter months considerable mobile forces were tied up in the Stalingrad and Caucasian offensives, this was no longer so fully possible. Hence the whole "hedgehog" system took on the form of a morcelated Maginot Line.

When examining the Battle of France, it will be remembered we pointed out that in itself there was little wrong with the Maginot Line, and what was wrong lay outside it—namely, lack of a powerful mobile force to act as sword to its shield. In the forthcoming campaign it will become apparent

[53]Further, the lateral railways Tula-Penza-Syzran, Michurinsk-Tambov-Saratov, Tambov-Balashov-Kamyshin, Voronezh-Borisoglebsk-Stalingrad, when coupled with the longitudinal railways Moscow-Voronezh and Gorki-Borisoglebsk, made the area north of the Don one of the best in Russia to concentrate and deploy troops in.

that the German error derived from a similar insufficiency of mobile forces to take advantage of the "hedgehog" system by stemming the Russian tide as it swept in between the "hedgehogs." This lack of mobility turned the "hedgehogs" into traps.

The gravity of these errors was magnified by psychological conditions. Within Russia the ever-increasing number of partisans struck terror into the hearts of the German soldiers scattered along the interminable lines of communication. In the vast spaces through which they ran guerilla bands played a similar part to that of U-boat packs in the Atlantic. "In daytime they were Russian workers in German service (under-water) and by night they were soldiers (on the surface)."[54] Without Russia, Spain was turning from a non-belligerent into a neutral; Turkey was adopting a more and more pronounced pro-Allied attitude; Italy, directly threatened by the invasion of North Africa, was sinking into complete defeatism; and the virtual disappearance of the Vichy Government was consolidating France. Within Germany conditions were rapidly worsening. People began to talk about the "*Teppichfresser*" ("the carpet-eater"), and "The police were compelled to take drastic measures to prevent the regime from being exposed to open criticism."[55] The concentration camps began to fill up, and with their over-crowding brutality became rampant. The manpower of Germany was again combed for recruits, and levies of forced labour imposed on the occupied countries.

Such was the intangible yet super-real background, which demanded only a cataclysm to push it into the foreground of the war. To this catastrophe we will now turn.

Early in November General Friedrich Paulus succeeded General von Hoth in command of the German Sixth Army. It consisted of twenty-two divisions, some 300,000 men in all, and the bulk of it, with its airfields and supply depots, was concentrated in a comparatively small area west of Stalingrad. To the north-west of it and for three hundred and fifty miles the defences of the Don were held by Rumanians and Italians, and to the south of it the Ergeni Hills were occupied by Rumanians. A further weakness was that the right flank of the Rumanians on these hills was in the air, because its sole link with the German army in Caucasia was the solitary German post of Elista, one hundred and seventy-five miles south of Stalingrad and about the same distance from Mozdok. Therefore, to all intents and purposes, the Germans in Caucasia were operating in a long and extremely narrow salient—Rostov-Mozdok-Novorossisk—the security of which depended entirely on the Stalingrad salient holding firm.

[54]*Behind the Steel Wall*, p. 154.
[55]*Ibid.*, p. 179.

This distribution of German forces automatically shaped the Russian plan of campaign. It consisted of two operations. The first was a distracting attack on the front Velikye Luki-Rzhev to pin possible German reinforcements down, and the second was to relieve Stalingrad by attacks of penetration against the flanks of the salient, which, if successful—as it was

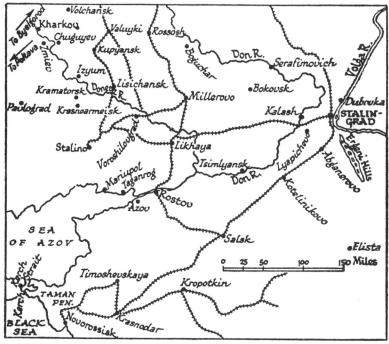

THE STALINGRAD CAMPAIGN, 19th NOVEMBER, 1942-2nd FEBRUARY, 1943

thought—would compel Paulus to raise the siege and retire. In its turn, this would automatically render the German position in Caucasia untenable. Once the flanks of the salient were pierced, the objectives were to be the Stalingrad-Stalino and Stalingrad-Novorossisk railways—Paulus's lines of supply. General Rokossovsky's army group was to cross the Don at Serafimovich, where the Russians held a small bridgehead, and advance on Kalash and cut the Stalingrad-Stalino railway. On his right, General Vatutin's army group was to cross the Don further to the west and direct its advance on the Stalingrad-Stalino railway at Likhaya; while in the south General Yeremenko's army group was to break through the Rumanians on the Ergeni Hills and occupy Abganerovo on the Stalingrad-Novorossisk railway. The idea that, in face of these three attacks on his communications, Paulus would continue the siege of Stalingrad very naturally never entered Marshal Zhukov's head, who, with General Vassilevsky, as his Chief of Staff, organized these vast operations.

On 19th November, and at the moment when the German situation in North Africa was critical, the offensives against the flanks of the Stalingrad salient were launched. In the north the Rumanians and Italians were scattered, Rokossovsky's armour forcing a passage of the Don at Kalash and penetrating to the Stalingrad-Stalino railway, while Vatutin, equally successfuly, moved on Likhaya. Meanwhile, in the south Yeremenko broke through the Rumanians on the Ergeni Hills, captured Abganerovo and pushed on to Lyapichevo, twenty miles south of Kalash.

These successful attacks placed the German Sixth Army in a critical situation, and though Paulus launched a series of vigorous counter-attacks, their aim was not to cover a withdrawal but to drive the Russians back!

The reason for this was political; for coming as the new crisis had on the top of Rommel's defeat at el Alamein and the Allied invasion of North Africa, a withdrawal might have been seized upon by the dissatisfied German generals to discredit Hitler and carry out a military *coup d'état.* Therefore, Paulus was ordered to hold on to Stalingrad while a force was organized for his relief. Thus it came about that, as early as the 28th, he was compelled to transfer his line of supply to the air, and at the very moment when heavy demands were being made for air transport in Tunisia. On the 30th no less than 50 German transport aircraft were shot down, and between 19th November and 10th January 600 in all were destroyed.

Where was a relief force to come from? At the time, the German general reserves in Russia were all but exhausted, and on the 25th the Russian attack on the Velikye Luki-Rzhev front immobilized such as still remained in the north. Nevertheless, with true German despatch forces were collected under von Manstein in the Rostov area. The 11th Panzer Division was withdrawn from Voronezh; the 17th from Orel; the 6th from France; and the 24th as well as a light division from the Caucasus.

Having assembled an army of about 150,000 strong, Manstein advanced up the Salsk-Stalingrad railway and on 12th December broke through the Russians between Tsimlyansk and Kotelinikovo, and after a violent battle took the second of these towns. But no sooner had he done so than, on the 16th, Vatutin struck at Bokovsk to the north of his left flank, and General Golikov's army group, which now appeared on Vatutin's right, took Boguchar on the Don and overran the Italian Eighth Army. Because this disaster exposed Manstein's left and left rear, the reserves intended for his front were switched northwards to stay the advance of Vatutin and Golikov on Millerovo, a station on the highly important Voronezh-Rostov railway. In part, at least, this diversion of reserves led to the defeat of Manstein's right wing by an armoured force under General Malinovsky on the 27th, and Kotelinikovo was lost. This spelt failure to the relief force. Meanwhile, Rokossovsky steadily pushed the German Sixth Army back towards Stalingrad.

This defeat precipitated the withdrawal of von Kleist's army in Caucasia, and on 2nd January, 1943, Mozdok was abandoned and occupied by the Russians. Thence von Kleist fell back on the Taman Peninsula commanding the Strait of Kerch, and on to a fortified area east of Rostov. Though the latter was later on abandoned, the former was held throughout the remainder of the winter and the spring.

Meanwhile, penned in between the Stalingrad garrison and Rokossovsky's army, the position of the German Sixth Army grew more and more critical. Its men were unprovided with winter clothes, short of food and munitions and ravaged by disease. According to Fredborg,[56] early in January Paulus flew to Hitler's headquarters and offered to break through the Russians at a loss of half his strength. The proposal was rejected, and by the 8th the position of the Sixth Army had become so hopeless that Rokossovsky called upon Paulus to surrender. This demand was also rejected, so the extermination of the Germans continued. On the 31st Paulus, now a Field-Marshal, with eight of his generals was captured. Two days later the end came, the final remnant of the Sixth Army, 22,500 officers and men, surrendered.

According to Russian claims, between 10th January and 2nd February 91,000 Germans had been captured and 100,000 had either been killed or died of disease. Disastrous though this loss of manpower was to the Germans, losses in *matériel* were even more so. Sixty thousand lorries are said to have been either destroyed or captured by the Russians between 19th November and the fall of the city, and, if all fronts are included, no less than 120,000, as well as 7,000 tanks and 5,000 aircraft.[57] If these are true figures, then they go far to explain the breakdown of the "hedgehog" system of defence.

The sole profit the German armies derived from this most disastrous campaign was the disappearance of Hitler from the direction of the war until about the middle of March, Field-Marshal von Manstein, assisted by General Halder, taking over supreme command of the German armies in Russia. But before we relate what followed, it is necessary to examine what was in progress on the other fronts.

[56] *Ibid.*, p. 175.   [57] *Ibid.*, p. 176.

Meeting with little opposition, by 19th January Vatutin had pressed forward to between Valuyki and Likhaya, and on 10th February, having established himself along the Donetz, he advanced on Chuguyev. Four days later, Voroshilovgrad and Rostov fell to Yeremenko. Meanwhile, on 22nd January, Grolikov routed the Second German-Hungarian Army in the Voronezh area, and four days later virtually annihilated it at Kastornaya. On 7th February the Kursk "hedgehog" was either abandoned or stormed, and two days later Byelgorod was occupied. This advance, coupled with Vatutin's, brought the Russians up against the "super-hedgehog" of Kharkov, and though the Germans made every effort to hold it, it was lost to them on 16th February.

Meanwhile, it had become clear to von Manstein that, if only to build up a striking force, it was imperative to shorten the front. Therefore, early in February, he ordered the evacuation of the Rzhev-Gzhatsk-Vyazma salient. This was completed by the 11th. About the same time Schlüsselburg was lost to the Germans and the road to Leningrad opened.

Manstein was too able a general not to realize that the aim, so persisted in by Hitler, was no longer to hold ground, but instead to sell it to his enemy at the price of his exhaustion. By the middle of February he reckoned that this aim had been achieved. The momentum of the Russians was slackening, and it was due not only to the advances they had made, but also to the dispersion of their forces, as well as to the thaw which had set in a month earlier than usual. Further still, the Russians had now driven a considerable salient southwards of Kharkov, and this gave him the opportunity he was waiting for—namely, to win a victory of sufficient importance to shake his enemy's command on all the Russian fronts.

Assembling in the neighbourhood of Dnepropeterovsk an army of twenty-five divisions, of which twelve were Panzer—the greatest weight of armour yet employed in any battle—on 21st February, Manstein launched the first of three co-ordinated attacks. First, he struck at the eastern haunch of the salient, and after a five days' battle drove the Russians out of Kramatorsk and Krasnoarmeisk. Next, halting this advance, he stormed the took Pavlograd and pushed on to Lozovaya. Lastly, he struck eastwards of Poltava. These three blows, coming in rapid succession, so completely unhinged the Russians that they forthwith fell back to the line Zmiev-Lisichansk, and, as von Manstein's pressure increased, to east of the Donetz. Instead of attempting to force the Donetz, von Manstein reinforced the most westerly of his three attacking forces, and on 8th March ordered it to advance on Kharkov. The town was entered on the 12th, and three days later was once again in German hands. From Kharkov he advanced on Chuguyev, extending his attack to Volchansk to the north of and to Izyum to the south of Kharkov. The thaw now set in without a break, and the winter campaign ended with this remarkable riposte.

From the point of view of armoured warfare, which, like cavalry warfare, should essentially be mobile warfare, this last operation of the 1942-1943 winter campaign, when coupled with the 1940 campaign in France and the various campaigns in Libya and Egypt, is highly instructive. What it showed was:

(1) That static defences in either the form of a continuous defended front or a morcelated front consisting of "boxes" or "hedgehogs" are valueless unless powerful mobile (armoured and motorized) forces are at hand to manœuvre from or around or between the defences. Defence does not reside in fortifications but in the mobile forces; the defended localities acting like groins which break the attacking forces up, and, in consequence, render them more vulnerable to counter-attack, and not like sea-walls to keep the attacker out.

(2) That in mobile warfare, when mobile forces are insufficient to endow either a continuous or morcelated defended front—should such fronts be possible—with defensive value, once the momentum of the attacker is exhausted, should the defender be in a position to counter-attack, the attacker should forthwith retire and draw his enemy after him, until he judges that his momentum has exhausted itself, when he should face about and counter-attack.

In the second winter campaign, once it became apparent, as it must have by mid-October, 1942, that the German momentum was petering out, and that, therefore, the initiative—freedom to attack or counter-attack—was passing to the Russians, there was only one manœuvre which should have occupied the German war brain. It was to retire as rapidly as possible, drawing the Russians after them, until the Russian momentum began to slacken, and only then to turn about and deliver a series of tremendous blows at prearranged points on the Russian front.

Had the Germans done this in 1941-1942, and again in 1942-1943, there can be little doubt that they would so completely have exhausted their enemy that an opening would have presented itself for a final knock-out blow. Fortunately, however, for the Russians, Hitler, who had solved the problem of the Maginot Line, had not solved the problem of Maginot-mindedness, and, in consequence, in spite of von Manstein's belated counter-attack, the initiative finally passed from the Germans to the Russians, as three months later it passed into Anglo-American hands at the Battle of Tunis; for the surrender of von Arnim's army in the Cape Bon Peninsula was the Stalingrad of North Africa.

Thus we reach the grand climacteric of the war. What were the Allied Powers going to do with the initiative which now was theirs?

It must have been clear to them that Germany could no longer win the war, and that, therefore, their problem was: What kind of peace did they themselves propose to win? To the world in general the answer had already been given in the Atlantic Charter, and now that Italy was on the point of collapse and German morale was tumbling,[58] the psychological moment had come wherein to elaborate its clauses into terms of peace profitable to the Allied Powers.

That Hitler would have agreed to them is unlikely, because the sixth clause of the Atlantic Charter demanded "the final destruction of Nazi tyranny." But that in the depths of their hearts the German people would eagerly have done so is highly probable, and, had they, the strength of their trust in them would have given to the powerful military faction which all along had opposed Hitler's war policy, enormous support. So great that the revolt of the Generals in July, 1944, would all but certainly have occurred a year earlier and have been successful, as it very nearly was, and without Allied moral support, when it was actually staged. Had this happened, then *National Socialism would have been destroyed by the will of the German people*, and replaced by the ideals of the Atlantic Charter.

Therefore, now that both in the West and the East the foundations of the Axis were sinking, the moment had arrived in which to launch a psychological attack on the cracking edifice erected on them.

What, at this crisis, President Roosevelt and Mr. Churchill should have asked themselves is, "What is the object of war?" And if, as in a moment it will become apparent, they were incapable of answering it, at least they might have requested their Combined Chiefs of Staff to provide them with the answer. Had they done so, they would surely have received the following: "To change the enemy's mind."

Instead, what did they do? At the Casablanca Conference of January, 1943, they made public that the war aim of the Allied Powers was the "Unconditional Surrender" of their enemies. Henceforth these two words were to hang like a putrifying albatross around the necks of America and Britain.[59]

---

[58] On this question Fredborg writes: "During the first half of 1943 moral disintegration reached such a point that hardly a single German remained quite loyal." And: "The Germans hate nothing so much as *die Partei*. The stories about it are innumerable. '*Es geht alles vorüber, es geht alles vorbei*,' sang the entire German people, until it was forbidden, because many went on: '*Zuerst fällt der Führer und dann die Partei*'." (*Ibid.*, pp. 209 and 229.)

[59] "There have been discussions with him (Roosevelt) as to the meaning of 'unconditional surrender' as applied to Germany. Any military person knows that there are conditions to every surrender. There is a feeling that, at Casablanca, the President a nd the Prime Minister, more likely the former, seized on Grant's famous term without realizing the full implications to the enemy. Goebbels has made great

What did these two words imply? First, that because no great power could with dignity or honour to itself, its history, its people and their posterity comply with them, the war must be fought to the point of annihilation.[60] Therefore, it would take upon itself a religious character and bring to life again all the horrors of the wars of religion. For Germany it was to become a question of salvation or damnation. Secondly, once victory had been won, the balance of power within Europe and between European nations would be irrevocably smashed. Russia would be left the greatest military power in Europe, and, therefore, would dominate Europe. Consequently, the peace these words predicted was the replacement of Nazi tyranny by an even more barbaric despotism.

capital with it to strengthen the morale of the German Army and people. Our psychological experts believe we would be wiser if we created a mood of acceptance of surrender in the German Army which would make possible a collapse of resistance similar to that which took place in Tunisia. They think if a proper mood is created in the German General Staff, there might even be a German Badoglio." (*Three Years with Eisenhower*, Captain Harry C. Butcher, p. 443.)

[60]Fredborg, writing in the spring of 1943, is illuminating: "The Germans of to-day are indeed in a terrible pass. Many of them know that a German victory would mean an unbearable strait-jacket for themselves and other peoples. They cannot, therefore, wholeheartedly wish for a German victory. But then there is a tragic conflict of conscience. It has been hammered into them that he who does not believe fanatically in the Führer is a traitor, and that National Socialism is *Germany*. Moreover, those who have experienced 1918 know what it means to be disarmed and exposed to enemy arbitrariness. They realize, too, that this time things might be sevenfold worse. The German people have begun to feel the heat of hatred that smoulders under the ashes throughout Europe and the threat from all the peoples of Europe—the Europe they wanted to unite *with* Germany, but which Nazism has united *against* Germany. They feel, too, the pressure of the Slav advance and the latent danger of the millions of foreign workers among them. They feel that they must play the game to its finish. Is there any way out except fighting? The Allies have, in point of fact, not given the German people any alternative but complete surrender. It is difficult for a people to accept such an alternative before the military situation has become catastrophic. *Actually the situation and Germany's adversaries are whipping the Germans together under the swastika.* 'Victory or Bolshevism' has become Goebbels' slogan. That is his way of telling the German people that there is no third alternative. The Nazis, in any case, know that their own fight is literally a fight of life and death." (*Behind the Steel Wall*, p. 239.)

CHAPTER VIII

INITIATIVE OF THE TWO FRONTS

(1) *The Conquest of Sicily*

Having decided upon unconditional surrender as their war aim, the next question which faced the Allied Powers was, how to implement it?

At the time, Marshal Stalin was angrily calling for the opening of a second front in Europe, and by it he meant a front in France which, strategically, would be complementary to the Russian front. But Mr. Churchill favoured an attack on Italy—"the soft under-belly" of the Axis, as he called it. And from all accounts it would seem that at this time he had some grandiose scheme in his head of equipping and bringing forty-five Turkish divisions into the war;[1] of pinching out the Balkans; of justifying his strategy of 1915,[2]; and of eating Christmas dinner with General Eisenhower in Rome.[3] The upshot was that his prestige as a strategist, backed by his forceful personality, carried the day, and at the Casablanca Conference, following on the conquest of North Africa, three courses of action were considered—the invasion of Southern France; the invasion of Greece to carry war into the Balkans; and the invasions of Sicily and Italy.

Strategy, as well as provision of air cover, pointed to the third as being the more practical, because the re-opening of the Mediterranean to Allied shipping was of real importance, and fully to accomplish it, it was necessary to occupy Sicily and Sardinia. But, as so often happens in war, politics intruded; whereupon this straightforward operation became confused. No longer was the aim solely to regain full command of the Mediterranean, but also to draw enemy strength away from Russia; to pin down German forces which otherwise might be transferred to France, when a second front was established there; to assist the forces of resistance in Yugoslavia, now strongly backed by Mr. Churchill; and to win the Foggia airfields in Italy from which to extend the strategic bombing of Central Europe.

Nevertheless, none of these objects demanded the conquest of the whole of Italy; at most of the foot only—that is, from the spur to Naples—which included the Foggia airfields. Yet, as we shall see, and mainly because of

---

[1] *Three Years with Eisenhower*, Captain Harry C. Butcher (1946), pp. 197-198.
[2] *Ibid.*, p. 317.
[3] *Ibid.*, p. 269.

Mr. Churchill's persistence that the conquest of Italy should be vigorously prosecuted after Sicily had been occupied,[4] the Allies' hard won initiative was in part squandered on a campaign which for lack of strategic sense and tactical imagination is unique in military history.

The initial step taken towards the invasion of Sicily was the reduction of the islands of Pantellaria and Lampedusa, which lay in the Sicilian Channel. The first possessed an airfield considered to be useful for Allied fighter aircraft, and the island was garrisoned by some 11,000 second line Italian troops. Both islands were already neutralized by Anglo-American air and sea power and were completely cut off from all succour. Nevertheless, it was decided to reduce them by "saturation" bombing, and between 18th May and 11th June 6,570 tons of bombs were dropped on Pantellaria alone. Apparently, the main object of this terrific assault was to determine the effect of "mass air bombardment on heavily defended fortifications,"[5] or as Air Marshal Coningham described it, it was "a test tube experiment of the effect of intense and prolonged bombing."[6] If so, then the results were purely negative; for it was not until 11th June, when a "formidable armada"[7] was seen approaching the island, that its garrison hoisted the white flag. Further, on the invaders landing, it was discovered that the garrison's casualties "were surprisingly light"; that "undamaged aircraft reposed in underground hangars that were almost intact"[8]; and that "of fifty-four shore batteries on the island, only two were completely knocked out."[9] Therefore, what the experiment clearly proved was that "saturation" bombing, on account of its extreme inaccuracy, was a complete failure. Nevertheless, we are told that "The information obtained proved of immense assistance in the planning of future operations."[10] We shall see!

The truth is, now that Allied ammunition production was approaching its peak, tactics were fast retrogressing to battles of attrition based on weight of metal and high explosives, in contradistinction to battles of movement based on imagination and audacity. In 1915-1917 the saying was: "Artillery conquers, infantry occupies"; now it read: "Bombing conquers, all else follows up."

[4] *Ibid.*, pp. 267-268.

[5] "Air Aspects of the Campaigns in Italy and the Balkans," Air Vice-Marshal J. H. D'Albiac, *Journal of the Royal United Services Institution*, August, 1945, p. 325.

[6] *Road to Rome*, Christopher Buckley (1945), p. 13. Buckley was war correspondent to the *Daily Telegraph*.

[7] *Three Years with Eisenhower*, p. 278.

[8] *Report of the Commanding General of the Army Air Forces to the Secretary of War*, 4th January, 1944, p. 46.

[9] *Three Years with Eisenhower*, p. 279.

[10] *Journal of the Royal United Services Institution*, August, 1945, p. 326.

Clearly, instead of these four weeks' experimental bombing, Sicily should have been invaded immediately after the occupation of Tunis. This, we are told, General Eisenhower wanted to do, but found it to be impossible because of "the scarcity of landing craft."[11] In consequence, a two months' delay occurred.

THE INVASION OF SICILY, 10th JULY-16th AUGUST, 1943

The forces to be employed were the American Seventh Army of two and a half divisions under General Patton, and the British Eighth Army of four and a half divisions under General Montgomery, both under General Alexander. The Seventh was to land between Licata and Scoglitti, advance across the island to Palermo, and then swing eastwards on Messina; while the Eighth was to land between a point a little to the south of Syracuse and Cape Passaro, seize Syracuse, next Catania, and finally move on Messina. The two armies were to be transported in from 2,600 to 2,800 ships and

"*Three Years with Eisenhower*, p. 257. "The Prime Minister has been rather critical of Ike and the Allied Command here (Algiers, 27th May) for failing to be prepared to follow up quickly on our Tunisian victory with the invasion of Sicily. Beetle (Lieut.-General Walter Bedell Smith, Eisenhower's Chief of Staff) said he seemed completely to overlook our continued shortage of landing craft." (*Ibid.*, p. 265.)

assault craft, and sail from points as far spaced as Gibraltar and Suez, and the landings were to be preceded by a six week's preliminary bombing of enemy airfields, ports, communications, etc., and immediately heralded by paratroops landings. At the time, Sicily was garrisoned by five Italian infantry divisions, five Italian coastal divisions, which were distributed along the coastal defences, and two German divisions—the 15th Panzer Grenadier and the Herman Goring—in reserve in the western part of the island.

On 9th July the British and American airborne forces, carried in 400 transport aircraft and 137 gliders, set out from Kairouan in Tunisia for Sicily, protected by fighters and bombers of the Tactical Air Force; but on account of the wind and insufficient training, not a few of the gliders fell into the sea, whereas many of the parachutists were dropped miles away from their objectives. Following on this unfortunate performance, the seaborne landings were made at 2.45 a.m. on the 10th. The Eighth Army met with next to no opposition, and the Seventh with some in places. The reasons for this were that the Italian coastal defence troops abandoned their positions and fled, and that Anglo-American command of the air was so unqualified that tactical surprise was complete.

The focal point of the advance was Messina, protected on the south by Mount Etna—10,758 feet in altitude—which stood like a castle overlooking the three practical lines of approach: the road from Catania along the eastern Sicilian shore; the road from Cefalu along the northern; and a road in between, which by way of Centuripe, Agira, Regalbuto, Randazzo and Castiglione, wound round the western flank of Etna.

On 22nd July Patton's advanced troops entered Palermo, and wheeling eastwards, the Seventh Army occupied Termini on the 25th, Cefalu on the 27th and Nicosia on the 29th. Meanwhile, on the 11th, a boldly executed landing by the British 11th Parachute Brigade secured for Montgomery the important bridge of Primo Sole over the Simeto river, after which for nearly three weeks the Eighth Army was held up in the Catanian plain. To break the deadlock, Alexander brought the 78th Division, the most experienced mountain fighters in the Mediterranean, over from Tunisia, so that he might outflank the German opposition by moving on Centuripe and operate by the central road. There then followed a series of blasting operations mixed with night attacks, in which by sheer weight of metal the Germans were pushed back from village to village towards Messina. These "poliorbuster" operations showed that in a mountainous country, where the employment of tanks is limited, tactical bombing as an accelerator of ground movement is of little value. Also, what is more remarkable, is the all but complete immunity of the German withdrawal in face of their enemy's absolute command of the air. As Christopher Buckley points out:

"They retreated very much at their own speed and with insignificant losses."[12] Further, by 16th August, when the Americans entered Messina and the campaign ended, the Germans carried over the Strait not only the bulk of what remained of the 15th Panzer Grenadier and Herman Göring Divisions, but also much of their heavy equipment. According to Air Vice-Marshal D'Albiac, this was due to "the orderly and methodical order of the evacuation, the heavy scale of the anti-aircraft and coastal gun defences, the good morale of the German troops and their callous use of their Italian allies to screen their own movements."[13] How this last item was carried out is not stated, and it would seem highly improbable that even a far more warlike people than the Italians could, in their highest fanaticism, turn themselves into bomb-proof umbrellas. It appears more likely that someone in the Allied Air Forces had blundered.

Nevertheless, in spite of this successful retreat, the campaign was the last straw which broke the Axis' back.[14] On 25th July Mussolini resigned, the King handing the government over to Marshal Pietro Badoglio. On the following day the once mighty Duce was clapped into jail, but some six weeks later he was rescued from a crag among the Abruzzi Mountains in perfect Hollywood style.

Unfortunately, the fruits of this as yet most decisive Allied political victory were allowed to rot. General Eisenhower wanted a quick peace, which meant reasonable terms, and then an immediate move on Naples. Three things, however, stood in his way: British caution;[15] lack of landing craft;[16] and unconditional surrender.[17]

From 27th July to 2nd September a wrangle with Badoglio took place over the meaning of these two words. Under cover of this casuistry the Germans poured thirteen divisions into Italy. Field-Marshal Rommel took command in the north, and Field-Marshal Albert Kesselring—who had been commanding in Sicily—in the south. Risings in Milan and other industrial cities were at once quelled, and were in no way assisted by violent Allied strategic bombing. Rome was occupied and then Naples, and even had the Italians had the heart to resist, the sole alternative to German

---

[12]*Road to Rome,* p. 143.

[13]*Journal of the Royal United Service Institution,* August, 1945, p. 328.

[14]The losses during it were: Axis, 167,000 killed, wounded and prisoners, of whom 37,000 were Germans; and Allied, 31,138 killed, wounded and missing, as well as 85,000 tons of shipping sunk.

[15]*Three Years with Eisenhower,* p. 316.

[16]*Ibid.,* p. 316.

[17]"The British public . . . seems rather tired of the war but, oddly, is insistent on 'unconditional surrender.' The two simply do not fit. We can shorten the war by giving Italy honourable terms, not to mention the lives that would be saved." (*Ibid.,* pp. 332-333.)

occupation was war up and down the length of Italy. At last, on 2nd September, Badoglio accepted unconditional surrender, and on the 8th the terms of the armistice were publicly announced, whereupon, according to Clause 4, the Italian fleet sailed to Malta.

As we shall soon see, this foolishness, conceived by President Roosevelt and Mr. Churchill at Casablanca, trapped the British and Americans into tactically the most absurd and strategically the most senseless campaign of the whole war. Unconditional surrender transformed the "soft under-belly" into a crocodile's back; prolonged the war; wrecked Italy; and wasted thousands of American and British lives.

Though it lasted but thirty-eight days, the Sicilian campaign is peculiarly instructive, and mainly because it was the first truly integrated combined operation carried out in the West against the Germans. Its base was sea power and not air power; yet without the latter it could not have been attempted. Again, as its object was the conquest of Sicily, it could not have been effected without land power, which, in its turn, could not successfully operate without air power. Because its first requirement was sea power, and because the flexibility of sea power confers on its holder ability to strike wherever he lists, and, by keeping the defender guessing, compels him either to disperse his forces or else concentrate them to meet a number of hypothetical contingencies, with the high probability that they will eventually find themselves in the wrong place, on the face of it it is obvious that, could more use have been made of sea power, the campaign would have ended even quicker than it did.

For instance, once a stalemate set in on the Catania front, had sufficient landing craft been at hand, it would have been possible to turn the position by sea, instead of by moving round the Etna massive. Again, once it became apparent that the Germans were withdrawing by the Strait of Messina, by landings in Italy it would have been possible to block their retreat. Yet none of these things was practicable because the two greatest sea powers in the world, having become air-minded, had ceased to be sea-minded. Landing craft in sufficiency was impossible with bombing craft in superfluity. Such was the crux of the problem.

Granted that at sea it was lack of shipping which hamstrung Anglo-American strategy, equally so on land it was lack of imagination which emasculated Anglo-American tactics. On this question, and so far as the British were concerned, Christopher Buckley—an eyewitness—is illuminating. He writes: "Each operation tended to be a repetition of its predecessor, and the preliminary bombardment from the air grew heavier and heavier. Villages like Regalbuto, and later Randazzo, were blotted out by bombing from the air on a scale unprecedented in the history of war."[18]

[18]*Road to Rome*, p. 107.

Further, he points out, as a rule the Germans "seldom established their defensive positions in the villages themselves, but normally a short distance to the rear. That meant that these bombings, though they frequently killed large numbers of Italian civilians, as a rule did no harm to the German soldiers. Secondly, and still more important, our objective, which was to block the roads with rubble and render the retreat of German wheeled vehicles impracticable, was largely frustrated because it was not necessary for the Germans to retreat through the villages. Instead, we found that when our troops entered these places they had to spend hours clearing away the rubble in order to continue the advance. Our own bombing was piling up obstacles in the way of the advance of our ground forces. Nor was the occupation of these villages eased by the necessity for coping with the scores of homeless inhabitants and the hundreds of dead and wounded civilians. The danger of the rapid spread of disease under those conditions was a very real one."[19] Further still, writes Buckley: "I could not help feeling that our pursuit tactics resembled the employment of a ponderous sledge-hammer to crush a small but alert reptile which slips away time after time just as the hammer ascends. The Germans lost few men in the process; nor did it prove so exhausting an experience as the hard fighting of the middle phase of Sicily, since on these narrow fronts it was possible for them to rest battalions by leapfrogging them backwards."[20]

Was this a proof of the inapplicability of tactical air power to the needs of the battlefield? In this question we strike the root of the problem. It was not tactical air power that was at fault; instead, it was that the tactics applied by means of tactical air power were asinine, because in these battles of obliteration all that took place was the transference of the psychology of strategic bombing from the enemy's cities to the battlefields. Though the target differed, the idea was the same: to drop an overwhelming weight of metal upon it—it was bulldozing with H.E.!

Because, as Air Marshal Coningham stated at a Press Conference "the German air force had been shot out of the air," surely it should have occurred to him that low-flying attack with cannon and machine-gun fire would have caused the Germans incomparably more damage than this insensate bombing of villages? Yet the fact remains that the most economical solution was seaborne attack, because in coastal operations he who commands the sea can nearly always find an open flank leading to the enemy's rear—the decisive point in every battle. This was *the* lesson of the Sicilian campaign, and it was not learnt.

(2) *The Invasion of Italy*

Of all the greater Continental Powers, strategically, Italy is the nearest to being an island. Size for size, her coastline is the longest and her land frontier the securest of any; therefore she is more open to sea than to land attack. Clearly, then, if invaded by a sea power operating from the west or south, it is more profitable for the invader to land in Liguria than in

THE INVASION OF ITALY, 3rd SEPTEMBER, 1943-4th JUNE, 1944

Calabria, because the sole great natural obstacles protecting the Valley of the Po—Italy's vital area of operations—are the Ligurian and Etruscan Apennines, some thirty miles in breadth; whereas an invasion by way of Calabria means that the invader will have to advance up the entire length of the Apennines, a distance of six hundred miles. Further, as nearly every river, gully, ravine and spur runs at right angles to this central backbone, each forms a natural line of defence, which, if held, will have to be stormed frontally.

Though it would appear that General Eisenhower realized the advantages of the Ligurian line of approach,[11] shortage of aircraft-carriers and landing craft forced the Calabrian line upon him. Even then, as General Marshall informs us, throughout the campaign which followed, "shortage of assault shipping and landing craft continued to haunt operations."[12] The result was, not a speedy but a long drawn out and exhaustive campaign, which may be divided into three stages:

(1) The reasonable, to the capture of Naples and Foggia.
(2) The political, to the occupation of Rome.
(3) The daft, from the occupation of Rome onwards.

General Alexander was given command of the expedition, which comprised two armies, the Eighth, of British troops under General Montgomery, and the Fifth, part British and part American, under Lieut.-General Mark W. Clark. The former was to land at Reggio, and when it had drawn the Germans into the toe of Italy, the latter was to land behind them at Salerno and cut them off. Salerno was selected because it lay just within range of fighter air cover. Had a sufficiency of aircraft-carriers been available, the whole operation could have been rendered far more elastic; but as this was not the case, the upshot was that the Germans could not fail to gauge their enemy's plan. Once again the entire operation, based though it was on sea power, was largely dominated by land-based aircraft, and, in part at least, on account of this, as Morehead points out: "At every point, from the long-range selection of Italy as the route, down to the tactics of landing at Salerno, imagination and risk were sacrificed to security."[13]

The invasion of the Eighth Army, which was prepared by a sustained air assault on the enemy's lines of communication and railway stations, was fixed for one hour before dawn on 3rd September, and was immediately preceded by one of General Montgomery's now customary "colossal cracks." But as there were no Germans to crack, for having fathomed their enemy's plan, they were by then rapidly retreating up the toe—a fact which could easily have been ascertained—this, "the biggest bombardment since Alamein," was a quite unnecessary waste of metal. Buckley, present at the time, states that the voyage across the Strait "was just about as hazardous an undertaking as the crossing from Southsea to the Isle of Wight in

---

[11] *Three Years with Eisenhower*, p. 362.

[12] *Biennial Report of 1st July, 1943, to 30th June, 1945*. Writing on 6th September, 1943, Captain Butcher comments: ". . . no one seems to emphasize the bitter truth, which is that troops do not have that mysterious power attributed to Jesus when he walked across the water. We still have to rely on landing craft and, unfortunately, we didn't have enough to continue to supply Sicily and conduct two other large-scale operations at the same time" (p. 348).

[13] *Eclipse*, Alan Morehead (1945), p. 22.

peace-time."[24] The point to note is that, irrespective of circumstances, the "colossal crack" had now become a fixed convention, and, as in the years 1915-1917, tactical imagination was petrified.

The Italian fleet having sailed to Malta on 8th September, Taranto was occupied by the British 78th Division and the 1st Airborne Division on the 9th. And at 4 a.m. the same day, after a heavy preliminary bombardment and strongly supported by aircraft and naval gunfire, the Fifth Army began to land on the Salerno beaches. On the 11th it was heavily attacked by the Germans powerfully supported by the *Luftwaffe*, and the situation became critical; the American cruisers *Philadelphia* and *Savannah*, and the British battleship *Warspite* were hit by glider bombs.[25]

One reason for this failure was that fighter planes based on Sicily could carry only sufficient petrol to permit them fighting for fifteen minutes over the beach-heads. Another, that "the shortage of shipping made it impossible for General Alexander to bring his own heavy armour into the fight until the British 7th Division started to unload on D+5 (14th)."[26] At this time, General Eisenhower informed General Marshall, "We are very much in the 'touch and go' stage of this operation . . . We have been unable to advance and the enemy is preparing a major counter-attack . . . I am using everything we have bigger than a row-boat . . . In the present situation our great hope is the Air Force . . ."[27]

During the next three days—12th-14th September—the entire tactical and strategical air forces were turned on to the enemy. His troop concentrations were broken up and his columns raked by machine-gun fire. On the 15th the crisis was over, and it is not too much to say that air power saved the Fifth Army. On the 16th the Eighth Army linked up with the Fifth at a point some forty miles south-east of Salerno.

On the 27th Foggia was captured, and on 1st October Naples was occupied. Thereupon Field-Marshal Albert Kesselring withdrew his army to the Volturno. On 20th September Sardinia was evacuated by the Germans, as was Corsica on 4th October. In the middle of the latter month, abandoning the Volturno, Kesselring fell back on the Garigliano river.

From now onwards the campaign developed into a "slow, painful advance through difficult terrain against a determined and resourceful enemy, skilled in the exploitation of natural obstacles by mines and demolitions";[28] and the main reason was the inability on the part of the

[24] *Road to Rome*, p. 158.
[25] A radar-controlled rocket bomb launched from an aeroplane outside the anti-aircraft defence area.
[26] *General Marshall, Biennial Report of 1st July, 1943, to 30th June, 1945*, p. 18.
[27] *Ibid.*, p. 19.
[28] *General H. Maitland Wilson's Report to the Combined Chiefs of Staff on the Italian Campaign, 8th January, 1944, to 10th May, 1944*, p. 1.

Allied armies to turn their enemy's flanks. On this question, General Wilson writes: "After the juncture of Fifth and Eighth Armies below Salerno, several small amphibious operations to turn the enemy's flanks had been considered; one such operation executed on the Eighth Army front at Termoli had proved encouragingly successful"; but "The position of landing craft within the Theatre was most difficult. Distribution and availability of craft had by now become a permanently limiting factor in planning all amphibious operations, not only in the Mediterranean but throughout all the Allied Theatres of War."[29]

Also, there was another reason for this stalemate. Two campaigns were being fought at the same time, one on the ground and the other in the air. The building-up at Foggia of the strategic bombing force, which was not under the command of General Eisenhower, consumed approximately 300,000 tons of shipping, during what General Marshall points out "were the most critical months of the Italian campaign. So heavy were the shipping requirements of the Fifteenth Strategic Air Force . . . that the build-up of our ground forces in Italy was considerably delayed."[30]

Further still, the situation was in no way improved by the command having now become so habituated to the Montgomery tactics that it overlooked that the problem was one of mountain warfare. These tactics consisted in: (1) The building-up of such a superiority in every arm that defeat would become virtually impossible; (2) the amassing of enormous quantities of munitions and supplies; (3) a preliminary air and artillery bombardment of obliteration; (4) followed by a methodical infantry advance, normally begun under cover of darkness; and (5) followed by tanks, used as self-propelled artillery, to provide the infantry with fire support.

So long as the Germans did not intend to do more than delay their enemy, position after position was methodically taken by these tactics. First the Volturno, next the Trigno, then the Sangro, until on the Garigliano Kesselring decided to stand.

The position he occupied was one of the strongest in Italy, and rightly General Eisenhower decided, while the Germans were pinned down by a frontal attack on the Garigliano, to turn their position by landing the American VIth Corps in the Anzio-Nettuno area, some thirty miles south of Rome. From there a successful advance inland would cut Kesselring's communications, and force him either to retire or surrender. Then, on 24th December, Eisenhower, as well as General Montgomery, Air Chief Marshal Tedder and General Bradley were ordered to England to take

[29] *Ibid.*, pp. 1 and 2.
[30] *Biennial Report of 1st July, 1943, to 30th June, 1945*, p. 19.

over preparations for the invasion of France. Eisenhower was replaced by General Sir Henry Maitland Wilson; Lieut.-General Sir Oliver W. H. Leese assumed command of the Eighth Army; and Lieut.-General Ira C. Eaker of the Mediterranean Allied Air Forces.

On the night of 17th-18th January the Battle of the Garigliano was launched, and soon after the river was crossed the left of the attack petered out around the village of Castelforte, and the right, finding it impossible to establish its bridges, failed altogether.

On the 22nd, when the battle was in its last stage, virtually unopposed, the VIth Corps—50,000 American and British troops—under command of Major-General Lucas, landed on the Anzio beaches at 2 a.m. The invasion came as a complete surprise; for though Kesselring knew that an expedition was in preparation at Naples, apparently he thought it was destined for Civita Vecchia, Gæta or Terracina. In this landing, air support followed the normal pattern; but the preliminary naval bombardment was dispensed with, except for two rocket ships which put down a barrage on the beaches immediately before the troops landed. One thing alone was lacking, and that was audacity. Instead of pushing on towards the Alban Hills, in order to magnify the initial surprise and create a scare epidemic in rear of the German front on the Garigliano, like Stopford at Suvla Bay in 1915, Lucas set to work to consolidate his beach-heads. The inevitable result was that Kesselring, realizing that his communications were not immediately threatened, contained the flanks and spearheads of the VIth Corps and built up a strong counter-attack force. Thus, within a few days of its landing the expedition was bunkered for months.

This dismal failure was followed by a series of Somme-Ypres battles, among mountains instead of swamps. Of these there were three, all fought to gain the small town of Cassino, which was dominated by Monastery Hill, upon which stood the famous Abbey of St. Benedict.

The first of these battles was launched on 29th January, and by 4th February was fought to a standstill. The blame for the failure was debited to the Abbey, instead of to the hill upon which it stood; therefore it was decided to destroy the building. Instead of keeping this decision secret, it was made public and freely discussed, with the inevitable result that, when the blow fell, the Germans were fully prepared to meet it. Because the Abbey was so obviously a bomb trap and because Monastery Hill provided the Germans with innumerable observation posts, it is highly improbable that Kesselring—an able soldier—would occupy the Abbey itself, and since then it has been stated by the monks who lived there that it was never used as an observation post.

On 14th February Allied aircraft dropped leaflets on the Abbey, warning the monks and refugees to leave it. The next day 229 bombers dropped

453 tons of bombs upon the Abbey and it was destroyed. But all that this destructive bombing did was to turn the Abbey from a building into a fortress, because the defence of a rubble heap mixed with ruins is an easier and more comfortable operation than the defence of a building. Not only is material at hand to construct strong points with, but there are no roofs and floors to fall upon the defenders. Therefore, the bombing of the Abbey was not so much a piece of vandalism as an act of sheer tactical stupidity.

Next day Cassino and its surroundings were bombed again; yet it was not until the early hours of the 18th that the infantry attack was launched. The artillery bombardment opened at 9 o'clock on the night of the 17th-18th, and for five hours shells were poured on the rubble heaps at the rate of 10,000 the hour. At 2 a.m. the infantry went forward, and making little progress, on the 19th General Alexander wisely decided to cut his losses and break the battle off.

Had the lesson of Pantellaria been learnt that saturation bombardments are seldom a short cut to victory? No! For as Buckley informs us: "The air attack on the Abbey had failed to produce the expected results, therefore the number of bombers and the weight of the bomb-load must be increased ... The sledge-hammer must be larger this time. Like the plagues of Egypt our assault upon Cassino was to gather in intensity until Pharaoh-Kesselring saw fit to yield."[31] This is corroborated by General Wilson himself. He states that, ". . . the Combined Chiefs of Staff were concerned over the influence which prolongation of the present situation in Italy might have on the overall strategic position. They felt that the concentration of nearly 3,000 bombers and fighters on vital restricted areas would have a determining effect on the enemy provided it was related to vigorous offensive action on land."[32] Therefore, in the face of all evidence, the dogma that weight of metal could so stun the defenders that all the ground forces would have to do was merely to occupy the paralysed target held the field. This is endorsed by General Eaker, for on 15th March, the day upon which the third battle of Cassino was launched, he is reported to have said: "The efficiency of the bombing would be determined by the extent of the ground forces' advance." And not waiting for proof, he added: "Let the Germans ponder that what we have done on the Ides of March to the fortress of Cassino we will do to every stronghold where they elect to stand."[33]

This time we will leave it to Lieut.-General Jacob L. Devers, Deputy Allied Commander, to describe in a letter, written on 22nd March, the attack which took place on the 15th:

[31]*Road to Rome*, p. 300.   [32]*General H. Maitland Wilson's Report*, p. 37.
[33]*Daily Mail*, 16th March, 1944.

"On 15th March I thought we were going to lick it by the attack on Cassino and advance up the Liri Valley. We used air, artillery and tanks, followed closely by infantry. I witnessed the attack from across the valley. It got off to a start with excellent weather. The bombing was excellent and severe, and the artillery barrage which followed it and lasted for two hours was even more severe and accurate, with 900 guns participating. Two groups of medium bombers, followed by eleven groups of heavies, followed by three groups of mediums, started on the minute at 8.30 a.m. and closed at 12.00 noon, the groups coming over every ten minutes up to 9.00 o'clock and thereafter every fifteen minutes. In spite of all this and with excellent support all afternoon with dive-bombers and artillery fire, the ground forces have not yet gained their first objective . . . These results were a sobering shock to me. The infantry had been withdrawn in the early morning hours five miles to the north of Cassino. When they arrived back in the town of Cassino at approximately 1.00 o'clock close behind the barrage, the Germans were still there, were able to slow up their advance and even to reinforce themselves during the night by some unaccountable means."[34]

Let us now turn to some explanatory detail.

One of the main items in the plan was to drop during the first three hours 1,400 tons of bombs in an area of about a square mile; but such is the inaccuracy of bombing on even so large a target that the Eighth Army commander's caravan headquarters, standing in the vicinity of Venafro, was demolished. More extraordinary still, an entire formation of heavy bombers dropped the whole of their load on the French Corps head-quarters at Venafro, which it mistook for Cassino, though the two towns are twelve miles apart!

Within a few hours of the infantry assault having been launched, in came tumbling reports such as these: "Armour supporting our infantry was delayed by rubble" . . . "Early reports state that the advance is restricted by terrible devastation" . . . "Remnants of buildings and masses of debris have been transformed by the enemy into strong points." And General Wilson says: "Although our infantry was able to advance, no tanks could get through to give them support because of bomb craters, which measured some forty-fifty feet in diameter and quickly filled with water. Tanks were unable to follow the infantry into the town until thirty-six hours later, when a path had been cleared by bulldozers."[35] Yet this is what happened at Pantellaria, the harbour could not be entered until bulldozers had cleared a road; it had happened also at Palermo, at Regalbuto and at Randazzo, and also at the Battle of Passchendæle in 1917!

[34]*General Marshall's Report*, p. 22.
[35]*General H. Maitland Wilson's Report*, p. 39.

For eight days the battle continued. Then, little having been accomplished, a halt was called.

This fiasco was followed by a period of true strategic bombing, directed by and in the main carried out by the Tactical Air Force, against the German road and rail communications. By the end of March, on an average, twenty-five cuts were made daily, which by mid-May rose to seventy-five and even more. There can be no doubt that this sustained attack on the enemy's supply system, which not only interrupted his traffic but restricted him to night movements, did him far more damage than had any of the "colossal cracks."

Under cover of the bombardment of interruption, instead of obliteration, the second battle of the Garigliano was mounted and launched on 11th May. This time Cassino itself was severely left alone.

The battle was opened by a night artillery bombardment of forty minutes of extreme intensity on a front of from thirty to forty miles. This time the infantry assault succeeded, partly on account of the air preparation and partly because the German winter line had now served its purpose, and no longer supported by his ally, bad weather, Kesselring saw that the time to withdraw had come. On the night of the 16th he began to disengage his army; on the 17th Cassino, turned from the rear, passed into British hands; and on the 18th Monastery Hill was occupied by the Poles. On 4th June, in spirit if not in body, Mr. Churchill—the presiding deity throughout this "soft under-belly" campaign—like a second Alaric led his armies into Rome, and two days later the news was flashed around the world that France had been invaded by the Americans and the British. But before we describe that decisive event—the opening of a strategic second front—we must return to the first front in Russia.

(3) *The Russian Summer and Autumn Campaigns of* 1943

On Hitler's resumption of the supreme direction of the war in mid-March, 1943, it must have been clear to him that the war could no longer be strategically won, and that the sole chance of preventing it being irretrievably lost was to fight it politically. What did this mean?

In spite of the complexity of the situation, to a mystic like Hitler, the answer was simple and direct. It was to turn the whole German war problem upside down and invert everything he had hitherto held to be essential. Instead of imposing his will on Europe in order to establish a German *Lebensraum*, he would champion European freedom against the establishment of a Russian *Lebensraum*. He knew that, at bottom, every Continental nation was terrified by the prospect of a Russian victory. He knew that the age-old policy of Britain was antagonistic to a hegemony of any one nation over the rest. Further, he knew that the Russians were well aware of these sentiments, and that, therefore, there was a possible opening for him to play upon European fears and Russian suspicions. Could he draw the war out by replacing the strategy of annihilation by the strategy of exhaustion, or what he and his propagandists called "Frederician strategy," a time might come when Russia would agree to a separate peace. But to persuade Russia to consider such a proposal, all signs of German moral weakening must sedulously be avoided.

This is not pure assumption, because once the forthcoming campaign began to fail, the psychological war initiated by Dr. Goebbels clearly disclosed this policy. The worse the German situation grew in Russia, less and less was heard of the Germanic New Order. By the end of the summer campaign, *Lebensraum* had given way to *Festung Europa*. Then a summons went forth to man the Eastern Wall, and once again a crusade was proclaimed against Asia. Added to this, the Allied policy of unconditional surrender, by deliberately preventing the surrender of Germany on terms, could mean but one of two things to every German—either victory or annihilation. Therefore, unconditional surrender crippled opposition to Hitler within Germany and, like a blood transfusion, gave two years of further life to the war.

Nevertheless, war cannot be reduced to a purely psychological contest, and the situation facing Hitler in the summer of 1943 was still predominantly a physical one. To prolong the war, it was imperative for him to hold the Russians back, and to do so meant that the wastage of the winter campaign must be made good. From where was the necessary fighting power to come? Though he could skim the garrisons of the occupied countries, there was a point beyond which they could not be reduced, because, ever since the invasion of North Africa, the sea power of his western enemies had hung like the sword of Damocles over his head. It was this threat which already, potentially, had established a second front, for it forced him to pin down the best part of one hundred divisions outside the Russian sub-theatre of the war. In short, the whole of the general reserve which should have been in Russia, or at the call of the Germans in Russia, was riding at anchor elsewhere, and in face of Allied sea power its cables could not be cut.

Because the policy Hitler had now adopted did not warrant a shortening of the front and its communications in order to accumulate reserves—for a purely voluntary withdrawal would have shown fear—he determined to continue to show strength. Though both his previous summer offensives had failed strategically, both had opened with overwhelming tactical successes. Therefore, why should he not be tactically successful again?

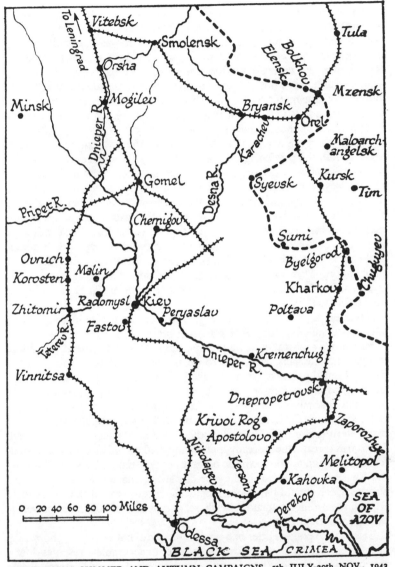

THE RUSSIAN SUMMER AND AUTUMN CAMPAIGNS, 5th JULY–30th NOV., 1943

This time, all he wanted was a resounding tactical victory in order to re-fortify German morale and upset the offensive he knew the Russians were planning.

The pattern of the front fitted this project, for the winter campaign had left the Russians in a great blunt-nosed salient west of Kursk, with its haunches resting between Orel and Byelgorod, both still in German hands. Could this salient be cut off and the forces within it annihilated, the Russian offensive would be delayed by months.

Always a gambler and never backward in accepting risks, Hitler decided on this operation, and though it was destined to end in disaster, in the political circumstances in which he was placed, it is difficult to say that he was wrong. Merely to fall back before mounting Russian manpower and mounting Anglo-American munitions, could lead nowhere other than to ultimate defeat. Further, because at the time it must have been apparent to him that the Americans and British were unlikely to open their second front campaign during 1943, a violent Russian setback before it opened might lead to the political end he had in sight.

To carry out this daring project, seven Panzer, two Motorized and nine Infantry Divisions were assembled at Orel, and ten Panzer, one Motorized and seven Infantry Divisions at Byelgorod. Both these forces, together numbering some 500,000 men, were placed under the command of Field-Marshal von Kluge, and the point of junction of the two attacks was fixed at Tim, a town to the east of Kursk.

Both attacks were launched at 5.30 a.m. on 5th July on strictly conventional *blitz* assault lines—identical to those laid down in the German textbooks of 1939. Further, they were directed at the haunches of the salient which, though earlier in the war were tactically the most profitable points to strike at, had long since and because of their tactical importance become the most strongly defended sections of every salient. In spite of this lack of imagination, the northern flank penetrated ten miles and the southern between thirty and forty, but at such cost in men and tanks that by the 22nd both attacking forces had to be withdrawn. Nevertheless, these penetrations show that, had less obvious points in the salient been assaulted, the probability is that the attack would have succeeded. As it was, the Russians were so confident that their deep defences would hold that, on the 15th, they attacked the Orel salient which flanked the northern side of the Kursk salient, and which had been weakened in order to provide troops for von Kluge's attack. Striking it from the north at Elensk and from the south-east at Maloarchangelsk, and carrying Mzensk and Bolkhov by storm between the 19th and 21st, on 4th August they forced the Germans to evacuate Orel. On the same day in the south, by a surprise attack, General Vatutin drove them out of Byelgorod.

Thus the German offensive ended in a decisive defeat, in which the loss of tanks was so serious that the bottom was knocked out of Hitler's defensive strategy, which depended on powerful mobile forces for its execution. It is in no way an exaggeration to say that the defeat at Kursk was as disastrous to the Germans as had been their defeat at Stalingrad.

Immediately following the capture of Orel and Byelgorod, a Russian drive westwards began, Sokolovsky's and Popov's army groups moving towards the upper, Rokossovsky's, Vatutin's and Koniev's towards the middle, and Malinovsky's and Tolbukhin's towards the lower Dnieper. On 11th August Chuguyev was occupied, and four days later Koniev's advance was approaching Kharkov. Simultaneously from Orel the advance was pushed, and on the 16th Karachev on the Bryansk-Orel railway was occupied. Next, on the 23rd, Kharkov fell, and a general retreat of the Germans in the Donetz area followed. Whereupon Tolbukhin advanced west of the Mius river in the Rostov area. Taganrog was stormed on the 30th and Stalino occupied on 8th September. Meanwhile, in the Kuban, von Kleist, in command of the 1st Panzer and 17th Armies, in all probably fourteen divisions, began to pull out of his bridgehead and cross the Strait of Kerch into the Crimea. This withdrawal led to the occupation of Novorossisk by General Petrov's army group on 15th September.

Meanwhile, in the centre steady pressure was maintained. Pushing forward west of Kursk, Rokossovsky directed his advance towards the north of Kiev, while to the south of him Vatutin moved towards the south of the same city. These advances cut the Gomel-Kremenchug and Gomel-Odessa railways, severing the main links between the northern and southern German groups of armies east of the Dnieper. On 22nd September Poltava was occupied, and three days later so was Smolensk.

Throughout the whole of this period—5th August to 22nd September—there would appear to have been little fighting of a serious nature. The German retreat was methodical, the daily withdrawals averaging from one and a half to three and a half miles, according to localities. It would seem to have been little harried, except possibly by guerillas, and, in consequence, ample time was gained by the Germans in which to leave a "scorched" area behind them. This is all the more astonishing, seeing that they were suffering from a shortage of mobile arms, due not only to their losses in the Kursk offensive, but also to events in Sicily and the threatened invasions of Italy and Southern France. That the Russian pursuit was not more rapid was probably due to difficulties of supply.

By the end of September the Germans were back on the line of the Dnieper and the fortified barrier they had constructed from Zaporozhye southwards, passing eastwards of Melitopol to the Sea of Azov. Though they called the Dnieper their "Winter Line," the Russians had no intention of it becoming such; for now that they had their enemy on the move, they intended to keep him moving. Therefore, instead of halting to regroup and refit, they pressed on. On 7th October they announced that a general offensive was in progress along the whole front. In the north on the Volkhov river, which links Lakes Ilmen and Ladoga, Kirishi was taken, and on what the Germans called the "Fatherland Front" and the Russians the "White Russian Front," Nevel was occupied on the 11th and Gomel also. But it was to the south of this front that the main blow was struck by the army groups of Rokossovsky, Vatutin and Koniev. On 5th and 6th October the first crossed the Dnieper north of Kiev between the Teterev and Pripet rivers; the second crossed at Peryaslav; and the third a few miles to the south-east of Krememchug.

The bridging of this great river is described by General Martel as follows:

"The majority of the bridges constructed across the Dnieper were pile or trestle bridges made from trees felled locally. The Russian sappers were exceptionally good at this work. A body of men would arrive at the river bank and every man had an axe, no doubt they used other tools as well, but nearly everything seemed to be done with the axe. Some officers and non-commissioned officers would go out in boats and measure the depth and take a 'section' of the river. They made some rough sketches and sharpened their pencils, using the same axe for this purpose. The party would then disperse to the woods and, in a very short time, the local trees were being converted into very practical trestles and timber piles for bridging. The average time required to build one of these bridges was four days, and they carried ten-ton lorries. The river was some 1,500 feet wide. Special bridges were built for tanks. The bridging of this river was a very fine feat."[36]

As these central operations were in progress, on the 10th Tolbukhin started to attack the barrier line north and south of Melitopol. Whereupon the Germans launched a tank counter-attack from their bridgehead of Zaporozhye. This was beaten back by Malinovsky's group, which after three days of fierce fighting carried Zaporozhye by storm. Meanwhile, though Tolbukhin's men pierced the first line of the barrier defences and reached the outskirts of Melitopol, they were unable to capture the town. But by now operations within the Dnieper bend were rapidly influencing the situation to the south of it. On the 17th, Koniev, having pushed south of his bridgehead near Kremenchug, started an attack in the direction of Krivoi Rog, and by the 21st had advanced to within twenty miles of that town. Two days later Manstein abandoned Melitopol in order to avoid being left in an ever-narrowing salient, and two days later still Malinovsky

[36]*Our Armoured Forces*, p. 270.

took Dniepropetrovsk. On 2nd November Tolbukhin's advance entered Kahovka, less than fifty miles east of Kerson, which placed the Germans in the Crimea in a critical position, for their sole line of retreat lay by way of Perekop-Kerson.

These several advances of Koniev's, Malinovsky's and Tolbukhin's groups, now named the Second, Third and Fourth Ukrainian Groups, was rapidly placing the Germans within the Dnieper bend in a similar position to the one the German Sixth Army had been forced into at Stalingrad. Therefore, in order to keep the sole remaining railway, Zaporozhye-Apostolovo-Nikolayev, open, von Manstein, then commanding the resuscitated German Sixth Army in the Dnieper bend, linking up with von Kleist's Fourth Panzer Army, launched a powerful counter-attack on the Russians at Krivoi Rog and drove them back as they were on the point of storming the town. Baulked within the bend, to the north of it the First Ukrainian Group under Vatutin, now on the outskirts of Kiev, on 4th November fell upon the city. Whereupon the Germans abandoned it and Kiev was occupied by the Russians on the 6th. On the 7th Vatutin occupied Fastov, on the 12th Zhitomir, and on the 17th Korosten and Ovruch. The last two on the vital Leningrad-Odessa railway.

To stabilize the position, the Germans began to move several of their Panzer and motorized divisions from the Krivoi Rog front by way of Vinnitsa northwards to halt Vatutin, and on the 12th—the day the Russians occupied Zhitomir—von Manstein having assembled six Panzer and six infantry divisions,[37] some 150,000 troops in all, advanced on the Russians at Fastov, Zhitomir and Korosten. On the 19th he re-took Zhitomir and on the 20th Korosten, and by December drove the Russians out of Radomysl, twenty miles south of Malin, as well as pushing them back towards Fastov.

Winter had now set in, and, so far as climatic conditions were concerned, the summer and autumn campaign ended; but, tactically, there was no pause in the operations.

(4) *The Russian Winter and Spring Campaigns of* 1944

The remarkable Russian successes of 1943, coupled with the collapse of Italy, the sinking morale of the Satellite Powers, the rising resistance in the

---

[37]This army was commanded by General von Hoth. Its Panzer composition is interesting, for it shows how the Germans were compelled to skim the other fronts. He had three Panzer divisions of his own, the 7th, 8th and 12th. He was reinforced by the 25th from Norway, the Adolf Hitler Division from the Balkans, and the 1st Division from Greece. Later the 16th and 24th came from Italy, where, owing to the unfavourable terrain, they had been employed as infantry.

occupied countries, the waning of the U-boat campaign in the Atlantic,[38] and above all the ever-increasing threat of an Allied invasion of Western Europe, showed conclusively that the war in the West was entering its final lap. Consequently, it is not surprising that the close of the year saw the assembly of a number of important inter-Allied conferences to consider the future.[39] But what is surprising is that, by the time they were concluded, except for the extirpation of Hitlerism, everything the Western Allies had thus far fought for was jettisoned. The Atlantic Charter was thrown overboard, Poland and the Baltic States were abandoned, and the gates of Eastern Europe opened to the Russians. Symbolic of the last concession, appropriately on 29th November at Teheran, Mr. Churchill, to the strains of the *Internationale*, presented Marshal Stalin with a Crusader's sword.

Though the political consequences of this unconditional surrender of the United States and Great Britain to Russia do not concern us here, the strategical consequences do. Hence onwards the Soviet war aim was rapidly expanded from the defeat of Germany into the conquest of Eastern Europe, the strategic key of which is Vienna and not Berlin. Therefore, the first step to be taken by the Russians was to orient their winter campaign in a south-easterly direction, not only in order to liberate the Ukraine, but also to gain a springboard from which the Balkans could be invaded and the road to Vienna opened. Bearing this in mind, and it had a prodigious influence on the succeeding operations as well as on the outcome of the war, we will first outline the situation as it was in Russia when the winter campaign opened.

At the close of the autumn fighting there were three German Army Groups extended between the Baltic and Black Sea: the Northern, Central and Southern. The first consisted of three armies, the second of four and the third of six, respectively commanded by Field-Marshals Küchler, Busch and von Manstein. The front of the first extended from the south of Leningrad to west of Nevel; of the second from west of Nevel

[38]In a broadcast on 9th November Mr. Churchill said: "The ratio of U-boat to merchant ship attrition during October was more satisfactory than in any previous month." And on 9th December, in a statement issued by President Roosevelt and Mr. Churchill: "The number of merchant vessels sunk by U-boats in November is smaller than in any other month since May, 1940."

[39]The Moscow Conference, 15th–30th October; the First Cairo Conference, 22nd–26th November; the Teheran Conference, 29th November–1st December; and the Second Cairo Conference, 4th–6th December. On 12th December, 1943, the Soviet-Czechoslovak Pact was signed at Moscow. Of it *The Times* Special Correspondent in Moscow wrote: "Like the decisions of the Moscow and Teheran Conferences, this treaty marks for the Russians another stage towards entry into a full share in European affairs, and makes a popular appeal to the reviving sense that Russia has a great mission to play on the Continent." (*The Times*, 13th December, 1943.)

to west of Ovruch; and of the third from west of Ovruch to the Black Sea, including the Crimea. Since the loss of Nevel and Ovruch, the main railway linking the three army groups—namely, the Leningrad-Odessa line—had been blocked; therefore, except for the round-about way of Dno-Vilna-Sarny-Rovno-Sheptovka-Proskurov-Zhimerinka-Odessa, there was no rail connection. This separation was strategically a serious handicap.

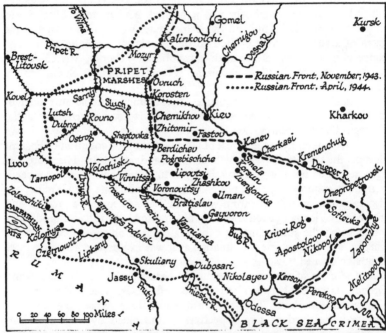

THE RUSSIAN WINTER AND SPRING CAMPAIGNS, 24th DEC., 1943-15th APRIL, 1944

Defensively, the northern and central sectors were stronger than the southern, not only topographically but also artificially, because their long occupation had given the Germans ample time to fortify them. Further, whereas the fronts of the northern and central sectors were without pronounced salients, the southern formed one vast salient running south-east of Korosten to the Dnieper south of Kiev, and thence within the Dnieper bend to Kerson. Therefore, irrespective of political aims, the existence of this salient clearly pointed to the next Russian offensive being directed against it, and more particularly against its northern flank, with the aim either of enveloping the whole of the German forces within the Dnieper bend, or by driving them over the Southern Bug, Dneister and Pruth into

Rumania, create a wide gap in the German front between the Pripet Marshes and the Carpathians, the focal points within which gap were Rovno (Równe), Tarnopol and Czernowitz (Cernauti).

To accomplish the first of these aims, which, if successful, would automatically achieve the second, the army groups of Vatutin, Koniev and Malinovsky were set the task of enveloping von Manstein's group. But for reasons which are by no means clear and which may have been due to climatic causes—for the winter of 1944 was an unusually erratic one—or to supply difficulties, particularly south-west of Kiev, a region much devastated, or to a definite plan to distract the Germans in other areas before delivering the main blow, the grand offensive was preceded by four limited offensive operations: one in the centre, one in the north and two in the south. These operations absorbed the first two months of the winter campaign.

The first was carried out by Vatutin's group, and judging from results its aim was two-fold: First to win more room for its strategic flank to manœuvre in before it swept south; secondly, by pushing out westwards, to gain the cover of the Pripet Marshes in its rear as well as to block the German rail communications running eastwards from Brest Litovsk to Kiev.

On 24th December Vatutin moved against von Manstein, and on the 29th wrested from him Korosten and Chernikov to the north of and Berdichev to the south of Zhitomir. Whereupon von Manstein, in order to prevent the encirclement of its garrison, abandoned Zhitomir on the 31st. This retrogressive move would appear to have created a gap south of the Pripet Marshes. Seizing on the opportunity, Vatutin pushed mobile forces into it, and on 13th January occupied Sarny on the Vilna (Wilno)-Lvov railway. At the same time, and very opportunely for Vatutin, Rokossovsky to the north of him took Mozyr and Kalinkovichi on the Leningrad-Odessa railway, which considerably added to the security of the rear of Vatutin's strategic flank.

This attack made it clear to von Manstein that, in order to keep open the Odessa-Tarnopol railway, it was imperative to stop the Russians moving south of Berdichev on Vinnitsa and Zhmerinka. For some days he was unable to do so, with the result that, on 7th January, Vatutin took Liportsi and on the 11th Voronovitsy, the first twenty-eight miles east of and the second fifteen miles south-east of Vinnitsa. On the 18th Manstein was ready, and that day he launched a powerful counter-attack to the north and east of Vinnitsa, and drove his enemy back to Pogrebischche and Zhashkov, the one forty-five miles north-east of and the other sixty-five miles east of Vinnitsa.

Thus ended the first limited or preparatory Russian offensive, and while it was in its final stage the second was opened against the northern sector of the German front, held by the Fifth, Eighteenth and Sixteenth Armies of Field-Marshal von Küchler's group. The Fifth was holding the front south of Leningrad; the Eighteenth the Volkhov river and Lake Ilmen front; and the Sixteenth the front from Staraya Rusa to Novo-Sokolinki.

The Russian plan was to envelop the northern half of Küchler's front by an attack from Leningrad under General Govorov, combined with an attack from the east of Novgorod under General Merezkov, with subsidiary attacks further to the south. The date of launching was fixed by the freezing of the Volkhov and Lake Ilmen, and it was not until 15th January that the ice was sufficiently thick to warrant an advance. That day, both attacks were made, and on the 17th Govorov broke through to Krasnoe Selo, and two days later Merezkov took Novgorod. On the 29th Novo-Sokolniki fell, whereupon Küchler ordered a general withdrawal. On 12th February Luga was captured by the Russians. Two days later the Germans withdrew from their "hedgehog" at Staraya Rusa (south of Lake Ilmen) and on the 23rd Dno was abandoned. From there von Küchler fell back to the line Pskov-Ostrov-Opochka, which had been organized by General Model, the front running eastwards of Nevel and thence to the east of Vitebsk. The freeing of Leningrad and Kronstadt was thus completed.

While von Manstein was stabilizing his position north and north-east of Vinnitsa, the third Russian limited offensive was initiated by an order to Vatutin, in conjunction with General Koniev, to encircle a group of eight German divisions in the area Kanev-(on the Dnieper)-Smela-Korsun, which divisions formed the greater part of the German Eighth Army under General Wöhler. Early in February this operation started, and though the Germans made a determined attempt to relieve the encircled divisions and evacuated a considerable number of officers by air, on the 17th the remnants surrendered. During the operation, which was mainly being carried out by Koniev, Vatutin suddenly pushed southwards from Sarny and drove the Germans out of Rovno and Lutsk, and later advanced towards Kovel and Dubno. This bold move, carried out by mobile columns, compelled Manstein to shift troops westwards to cover the approach to Galicia.

The last limited offensive which preceded the main winter campaign was made by Malinovsky. On 2nd February, he attacked on a front of forty miles to the south of Dniepropetrovsk between the Dnieper and the town of Sofievka, and on the 7th captured Apostolovo Junction. This advance cut the German forces into two; whereupon Malinovsky pushed one half towards Nikopol and the other towards Krivoi Rog. Co-operating with Malinovsky from the south, Tolbukhin took Nikopol on the 8th, and during the second half of February the much-fought-for town of Krivoi Rog was occupied by Malinovsky.

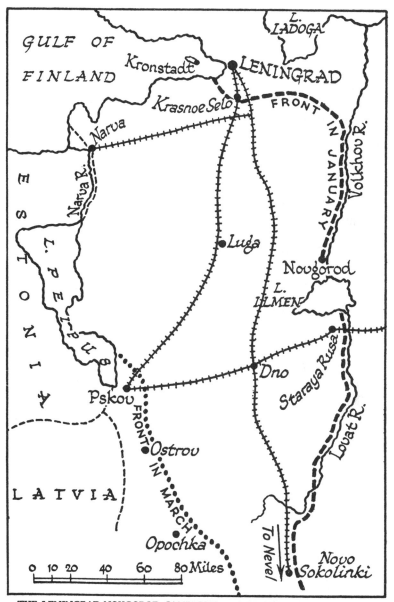

THE LENINGRAD-NOVGOROD CAMPAIGN, 23rd FEBRUARY-15th APRIL, 1944

Prior to launching the great offensive against the Germans within the Dnieper bend, Marshal Zhukov, deputy to Stalin, replaced General Vatutin in command of the First Ukrainian Group, and Marshal Vasilevssky, Stalin's Chief of Staff, was given the task of co-ordinating the operations of the Third and Fourth Ukrainian Groups, those of Generals Malinovsky and Tolbukhin.

Zhukov's group occupied a front of about two hundred and fifty miles from the outskirts of Kovel to the north-east of Vinnitsa. On his left came the Second Ukrainian Group under Koniev, recently promoted to the rank of Marshal. The first objective of the two groups was the Odessa-Lvov railway, which roughly ran parallel to their fronts.

The offensive was opened by Zhukov on 4th March between Ostrog in the west and the River Sluch in the east on a front of about sixty miles, and during the first two days a penetration of over fifty miles was made, and Volochisk on the Odessa-Lvov railway was captured. On the 9th Zhukov's advance reached the outskirts of Tarnopol.

Two days after this offensive began, Koniev started to attack south of Zvenigordka, twenty-five miles to the south of Korsun, and rapidly driving westwards, on the 10th he surprised and captured the great German base at Uman, where he seized 500 tanks and 12,000 lorries. This swift and sudden blow so overwhelmed the Germans that they broke back in panic. Such was the disaster that the situation along the whole of the southern front was changed. Following as it did on the heels of the Korsun surrender, the Germans were left with totally inadequate forces and means to stem Koniev's advance. On the 12th he took Gayvoron, and on the 15th his tanks captured Vapniarka Junction (Peschanka) on the Odessa-Lvov line, some thirty miles from the Dniester and the Rumanian frontier.

Following on this success, Zhukov turned southwards and advanced on Czernowitz (Cernauti), the last rail link between the German armies in Poland and those in Southern Russia. Advancing west of the Zbruch river—on the south of the 1939 Polish frontier—between 21st and 24th March German resistance was shattered, and the Dniester was reached and crossed at Zaleschiki—north of Kolomya. By the 25th the Dniester had been crossed on a front of fifty miles, and on the 27th Zhukov closed in on Czernowitz and three days later occupied the city.

Meanwhile Koniev's right had crossed the Southern Bug near Bratislav, and in virtual rout the Germans abandoned Zhmerinka on the 18th, Vinnitsa on the 22nd, Proskurov on the 25th and Kamenets Podolsk on the 26th, and retreated southwards.

On the 27th Koniev reached the Pruth on a front of seventy-five miles between Skuliany (fifteen miles north of Jassy) and Lipkany (thirty-five miles east of Czernowitz). Thus at the end of March Zhukov and Koniev stood on the Pruth, and by the middle of April their two fronts were stabilized on a line running from a little east of Kovel to the eastern extremity of Czechoslovakia, thence to Jassy (Iasi) and on to the Dniester at Dubosari.

While these great operations were under way, Malinovsky also advanced, and on 13th March captured Kerson, and next, after a fierce struggle, Nikolayev on the 28th. Odessa was not defended, and on 10th April was entered by the Russians, and a few days later Malinovsky reached the Dniester and linked up with Koniev's left at Dubosari.

One further operation remains to be described—namely, the re-conquest of the Crimea.

The peninsula was occupied by the German Seventeenth Army under General Jänecke, consisting of five German infantry divisions and seven weak Rumanian divisions, and to hold it the Germans had considerably strengthened the defences of the isthmus of Perekop and the Akmanal Line, built by the Russians in 1942 across the narrowest section of the Kerch Peninsula. Also, they had strongly fortified the town of Kerch and in part had repaired the defences of Sevastopol. But it would appear that they failed to pay much attention to the shallow lagoons, called Sivash, which lie to the east of the isthmus of Perekop, and which, if the winter is severe, become frozen, when they can be crossed on foot.

The conquest of the Crimea was the principal task of the Fourth Ukrainian Group, commanded by General Tolbukhin. Realizing that the weak point in his enemy's defences was the Sivash, he planned to cross the lagoons directly they were frozen over, and simultaneously assault the Perekop Lines and reinforce two small bridgeheads he had already established on the mainland to the north and south of Kerch; from them pinch out the town and then advance against the Akmanal Line.

Unfortunately for Tolbukhin the winter was exceptionally mild, and by March it was certain that the Sivash would remain unfrozen. Undaunted by this, he decided to ford it where its waters were shallowest, and move the bulk of his troops and their heavy equipment over it in barges, pontoons and on rafts.

Early on the morning of 8th April, and mainly to distract his enemy, he opened his attack with a concentrated artillery bombardment of the Perekop defences, and on the 9th, when Kerch was being attacked, he broke through the first Perekop line, but was halted by the second at Yushun, Meanwhile, the crossing of the Sivash was accomplished with unexpected ease, because as it was unfrozen, except for a few posts, the four Rumanian divisions, detailed to hold its southern shore as well as the Arabat sand-bank, were resting twenty miles inland at Dzhankoi.

This surprise attack, threatening as it did the lines of supply and retreat of the German forces at Yushun and Kerch, so completely unhinged General Jänecke that instead of ordering the Rumanians at Dzhankoi boldly to counter-attack, he instructed them to hold their ground and ordered the Kerch garrison to withdraw to the Akmanal Line. The result was that, on the 11th, Tolbukhin, having by then ferried a considerable force over the lagoons, advanced on Dzhankoi, scattered the Rumanians

RE-CONQUEST OF THE CRIMEA, 8th APRIL–12th MAY, 1944

and occupied the town. Thereupon Jänecke ordered a general retreat of all his troops in the northern and eastern Crimea on Simferopol. What for, it is difficult to imagine, because this retrograde movement carried with it the abandonment of the Yushun and Akmanal Lines, and threw open the front and back doors of the Crimea. But before this concentration could be effected, Simferopol was in Russian hands. Then followed a German *sauve qui peut* towards Sevastopol.

Because Sevastopol could not be stormed until Tolbukhin had brought up his siege artillery, it was not until 6th May that the bombardment of the fortress opened. Meanwhile, three of Jänecke's Rumanian divisions, as well as some other troops, were shipped to Rumania. Attacking from the north and east against the Mackenzie and Sapun Heights, Tolbukhin rapidly drove what remained of the German Seventeenth Army back into Sevastopol. Lastly, General Allmendingen, who had replaced Jänecke, was ordered by Hitler to abandon the fortress and concentrate his troops at Cape Khersones. There, on 12th May, he surrendered. Thus the Russian winter offensive of 1944 was ended by one of the most brilliantly conceived and executed campaigns of this remarkable year.

(5) *The Allied Invasion of Normandy*

On 24th December—the day the Russian winter offensive opened—as previously mentioned, General Eisenhower and his chief lieutenants were ordered to return to London to take over the plans for the invasion of France, which ever since the Casablanca Conference Lieut.-General Sir Frederick E. Morgan had been engaged upon. Their basis was an initial landing by three divisions; but since both Eisenhower and Montgomery considered this insufficient the number was increased to five. This increase in strength demanding considerable alterations in detail, D-Day was put forward from 1st May to 5th June.

These changes were agreed to on 21st January, at the first meeting held by Eisenhower[40] and his three Commanders-in-Chief, Admiral Sir Bertram H. Ramsay, Commander of the Allied Naval Expeditionary Force, Air Chief Marshal Sir Trafford Leigh-Mallory, Commander of the Allied Expeditionary Air Force, and General Montgomery, Commanding General of the Allied Land Expeditionary Force, which consisted of the United States First Army, including the 82nd and 101st Airborne Divisions, under General Omar N. Bradley, and the Twenty-First Army Group, comprising the First Canadian Army, under Lieut.-General H. D. G. Crearar, the British Second Army, under Lieut.-General Sir M. C. Dempsey, the 6th Airborne Division, under Lieut.-General F. A. M. Browning, and various Allied contingents.

The invasion area decided upon was the Bay of the Seine, because it was protected against the prevailing westerly winds by the Cotentin Peninsula, and because by bombing the bridges over the Seine and the Loire the north-western quarter of France could, strategically, be isolated. Two large ports—Cherbourg and Havre—lay on its flanks; both, as well as the Bay, were within easy fighter range of England, and as Cherbourg was situated at the tip of the Cotentin Peninsula, once the peninsula was overrun, it could be completely invested.

In all, the frontage was some seventy miles in extent, stretching from the small town of Quinéville, south of Barfleur, to the estuary of the River Orne. The Americans were to land on its western half, the British on its eastern, and the objective for the first day was the line St. Mère Eglise-Carentan-Bayeux-Caen. The last mentioned town was a useful port linked by canal with the sea.

In brief, the plan of attack was as follows: First to secure a lodgement

[40] Air Chief Marshal Sir Arthur W. Tedder was appointed Deputy Supreme Commander to General Eisenhower.

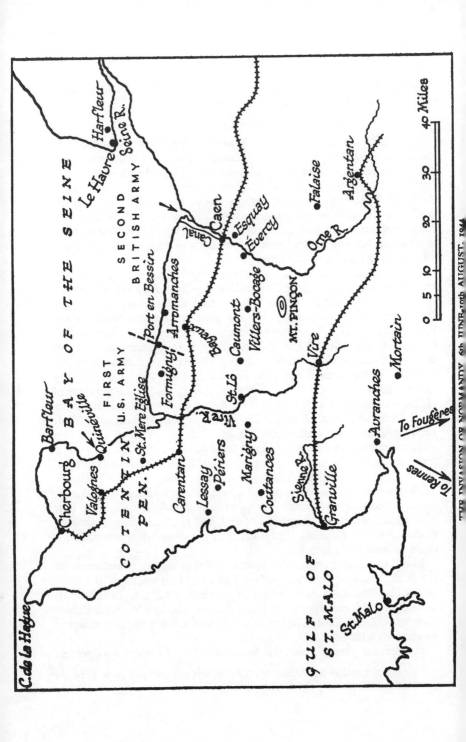

C. de la Hague

BAY OF THE SEINE

Cherbourg
Barfleur
Valognes
Quinéville
St. Mere Eglise
FIRST U.S. ARMY
COTENTIN PEN.
Carentan
Lessay
Périers
Marigny
Coutances
Sienne R.
Granville
GULF OF ST. MALO
St. Malo
Avranches
Mortain

Le Havre
Harfleur
Seine R.
SECOND BRITISH ARMY
Port en Bessin
Aromanches
Formigny
Bayeux
St. Lô
Caen
Canal
Esquay
Évercy
Caumont
Villers-Bocage
MT. PINÇON
Vire
Orne R.
Falaise
Argentan

To Rennes
To Fougères

0 5 10 20 30 40 Miles

area, including Cherbourg, Caen and airfield sites. Next "to advance on Brittany with the object of capturing the ports southwards to Nantes." Lastly, "to drive east on the line of the Loire in the direction of Paris and north across the Seine with the purpose of destroying as many as possible of the German forces in this area of the west."[41] "This," writes General Montgomery, "would cut off all the enemy forces south of the Seine, over which river the bridges were to be destroyed by air attack."[42] During these operations the American Seventh Army, under Major-General Alexander M. Patch, was to land in the South of France and advance up the Valley of the Rhône.

Opposed to General Eisenhower was Field-Marshal von Rundstedt, Commander-in-Chief of the West. Realizing that throughout the whole theatre of war the German armies were over-extended and that air superiority was the enemy's absolutely, Rundstedt held that France should be evacuated and its garrison withdrawn to the German frontier. Though Hitler would on no account listen to this, he, nevertheless, kept von Rundstedt in overall command, but in February he appointed Field-Marshal Rommel to command the troops in France. This gave Rommel Army Group B, which consisted of the Seventh Army in Normandy and Brittany, and the Fifteenth Army in the Pas de Calais and Flanders, with the LXXXVIIIth Corps in Holland. Besides Group B, von Rundstedt also had Group G, composed of the First and Nineteenth Armies under Field-Marshal Jacob Blaskowitz, stationed on the Biscay coast and in the Riviera. In all, von Rundstedt had fifty infantry and ten Panzer divisions, of which thirty-six infantry and nine Panzer were located from Holland to Lorient on the Bay of Biscay; the greater part in the Pas de Calais, with nine infantry and one Panzer divisions in Normandy.

For the Germans, Rommel's appointment was a most unfortunate one; for though he and von Rundstedt were agreed upon holding the French ports to the last man, in order to deny their use to the enemy, the two Field-Marshals disagreed on the manner the invaders should be met. Whereas Rommel favoured fighting them on the beaches, and, therefore, advocated strong beach garrisons with reserves close in rear, von Rundstedt favoured diametrically the opposite; for his idea was to let the enemy gain a footing and then counter-attack him in force before he could consolidate it. This meant keeping the bulk of the troops well in rear of the coastal

[41]*Report by the Supreme Commander . . . 6th June, 1944, to 8th May, 1945* (English edition, 1946), p. 9. This was to be done by the American Third Army under General Patton. He was to move his headquarters to France about D plus 30, and first reduce the Brittany peninsula.

[42]Field-Marshal Montgomery's "Despatch." *Supplement to the London Gazette,* 3rd September, 1946.

defences. These divergent views led to a compromise, generally the very worst thing in war: the infantry were kept forward and the bulk of the armour was kept back. The result was that when the crisis came there was little co-ordination between the two.

Added to this faulty arrangement, the very nature of the German coastal defences exaggerated it; for in form they were linear, with little or no depth. They consisted in a chain of works running along the coast linked together by obstacles both under-water and on the beaches. In rear of them there was no secondary defensive line; therefore the whole system was, in fact, a Maginot Wall, and astonishing as it may seem, both Hitler and Rommel had the same confidence in it as the French had had in the actual Maginot Line in 1940.

Further still, the Germans made a grave miscalculation. They were convinced that the main landing would take place in the Pas de Calais, and, therefore, not only did they defend its coastline far more strongly, but allotted to it far more powerful garrisons than on any other sector. Knowing of this, General Eisenhower did all in his power to encourage their error by distributing his shipping as if he intended to land there. Of this ruse he says: "I cannot over-emphasize the decisive value of this most successful threat, which paid enormous dividends, both at the time of the assault and during the operations of the two succeeding months."[43]

Once it was decided to increase the initial wave of the invasion from three to five divisions, Eisenhower's problem became one of finding the additional shipping. He writes: "Even with the extra month's production of craft . . . it became necessary . . . to consider drawing craft from either the Mediterranean or the Pacific to round out the figure needed."[44] General Marshall says exactly the same. He points out that "the Allies were beset by innumerable specific problems of implementing the desired strategy," and that "The greatest of these by far was the critical shortage of landing craft."[45] Though, as he informs us, an attack in the South of France was considered essential to the invasion of the North of France, sixty-eight landing ships were withdrawn from the Mediterranean "to meet the requirements of the cross-Channel assault as then planned." The upshot was that "The operations in Southern France, which were originally to be made simultaneously with the attack on Normandy, were delayed

[43]*Report by the Supreme Commander*, p. 35. That the Normandy Sector was as strongly held as it was, was due to Hitler's insistence that the invasion would be attempted in that locality. (See *Defeat in the West*, pp. 96 and 98.)

[44]*Ibid.*, p. 8.

[45]*Biennial Report*, 1st *July*, 1943, to 30th *June*, 1945, p. 27. Commander Kenneth Edwards in *Operation Neptune* notes the same: "The cry was for more landing craft and yet more landing craft" (p. 52). So does Ingersoll in *Top Secret*, see pp. 24, 25, 31, 37, 38 and 50.

months so that landing craft could be used first in the Channel, then rushed to the Mediterranean to do double duty . . ."[46]

Besides landing craft there was a shortage of tugs, ferry craft and ammunition lighters, and, in addition to all these ships, a vast naval armada was required to convoy and cover the landings. Eventually 702 warships and 25 flotillas of minesweepers were used for this purpose. That in the end over 5,000 ships and 4,000 additional "ship-to-shore" craft were employed in crossing the Channel, makes the possibility of a German invasion in 1940 look somewhat ridiculous.

In order to facilitate the landings, all mechanical vehicles and tanks were water-proofed in order that they could be driven through deep water, or, if necessary, when submerged. And as the landings were to be made on open beaches, this problem was prepared for by designing five shelter harbours, known as "Gooseberries," formed by sinking sixty blockships, and by the building of two prefabricated ports which could be towed over the sea in sections. These were known as "Mulberries," each roughly the size of Dover Harbour. Besides these, a submarine pipe-line (eventually several) to carry petrol across the Channel, known as Pluto, was prepared for.

The air plan was in two parts, the preparatory and the assault phases. The aim of the first was to restrict enemy mobility: (1) by crippling the French and Belgian railways; (2) by demolishing bridges in North-western France; and (3) by attacking enemy airfields within one hundred and thirty miles radius of the battle area. The first was to begin on D-60; the second on D-46; and the third on D-21. The total fighter aircraft allocated for the second phase was: Beach Cover, 54 squadrons; Shipping Cover, 15 squadrons; Direct Air Support, 36 squadrons; Offensive Fighter Operations and Bomber Escort, 33 squadrons; and Striking Force, 33 squadrons. Making a total of 171 squadrons.

In the attack on railways and bridges the underlying idea was not only to isolate the landing area, but also the whole of the forward area of operations between the Seine and the Loire by demolishing the rail and road bridges over these rivers. Should this be successful, the enemy would be impeded moving the Fifteenth Army westwards of the Seine, and his troops in the South of France northwards of the Loire. In fact, except for the gap between Orléans and Fontainebleau, these demolitions would turn

[46]*Biennial Report, 1st July, 1943, to 30th June, 1945*, pp. 27 and 30. General Eisenhower says, that it was hoped the landing in the South of France would be made with three or "at the worst" two divisions, building up to ten; but that by 23rd January, on account of shortage of assault craft for the enlarged Normandy operation, it became necessary to reduce it to one division. (*Supreme Commander Report*, pp. 15-16.)

the whole forward area into a strategic island. Beyond the above two rivers lay another line of "interdiction" along the River Meuse and the Albert Canal, the crossings over which were vital to the supply of the German Fifteenth Army. Therefore, were these crossings demolished, that army would be strategically bottled up. On the one hand, its supply lines would be crippled, and on the other its westward lines of advance would be restricted. This meant that the German Seventh Army, west of the Seine, could not be rapidly reinforced.

In the attacks on railways the primary object was the destruction of rail motive power through the bombing of the locomotive depots. Eighty of these "nerve centres" were selected, and by D-Day more than fifty were so heavily damaged that, whereas "Before the bombing, the total of all military traffic into France had exceeded one hundred trains per day . . . By the end of April the average had been reduced to forty-eight trains, and by the end of May it had fallen to twenty trains per day."[47] And no wonder, for no less than 62,000 tons of bombs were dropped on the above centres—mostly in France.

Besides these attacks on communications, other preparatory operations were undertaken by the Allied Air Forces, the more important being attacks on enemy coastal batteries and defences, radar stations and airfields.

Though coastal defences were bombed for several weeks before D-Day, the day previous to it ten super-heavy radar-sighted batteries on the Normandy coast were bombed as well as the whole of the northern coast of France. This was done in order to confuse the Germans as to the actual locality which was to be invaded. In all, more than 14,000 tons of bombs were dropped on these targets.

The whole of this bombing, whether termed "strategic" or "tactical," was preparatory, and as directly related to the coming battle—the invasion—as were the preliminary bombardments of the artillery battles of 1916-1917 to the infantry going over the top. That it was somewhat overdone, and more especially so as regards the destruction of bridges, seems probable; but as to its effectiveness there can be no doubt.

June opened with high winds and rough seas, and on the 3rd meteorological predictions were so unfavourable that Eisenhower decided to postpone the invasion for twenty-four hours. Though on the 5th conditions had but slightly improved, at 4 a.m. he made the bold decision to launch the cross-Channel assault on the following day. Little was it realized at the time, but as events proved, the decision to launch the assault when the weather was so unsettled was largely responsible for the surprise achieved.

[47]"Air Attack on Communications," Air Marshal Sir Robert Saundby, *Journal of the United Service Institution*, November, 1945. p. 478.

The time table was as follows: Airborne troops, utilizing 2,395 aircraft and 867 gliders, to land at 2 a.m.; the aerial bombardment, for which were allotted 2,219 machines, to open at 3.14 a.m., and to be augmented by a naval bombardment at 5.50 a.m. The first wave of the invading five divisions, carried in 4,266 landing ships and landing craft, to land at 6.30 a.m.

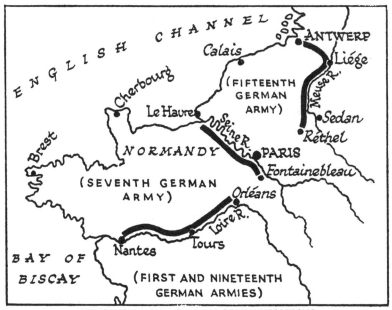

INTERDICTION OF GERMAN COMMUNICATIONS

The task of the airborne forces was to protect the flanks of the assault. The British 6th Division was dropped precisely on its objectives along the estuary of the Orne, but, unfortunately, a considerable proportion of the American 82nd and 101st Divisions was scattered over an area of twenty-five miles by fifteen in extent in the Carentan region.

Because the air and naval bombardments intermingled, it is as well to consider them together. The bombardment was opened by an intense bombing of the enemy's coastal defences and beach obstacles, 7,616 tons of bombs being dropped upon them, whereas the landing itself was directly supported by the 2nd British and 9th U.S. Tactical Air Forces. While the first of these operations was under way, the combined fleets with their heavy guns bombarded the enemy's fixed batteries and concrete defences.[48] Next, closing range, the lighter defences were bombarded by the lighter ordnance. Finally, as the first wave of the assault neared the shore, a standing barrage was placed on the beaches, which was timed to lift immediately the troops landed. For this, Commander Edwards informs us, destroyers and L.C.G's (landing craft guns)—the modern equivalent of the old floating batteries—literally "drenched" every yard of the beaches with high explosives. In order further to increase the density of the "drenching fire," rockets were used from landing craft—L.C.R's. "For purposes of short-range 'drenching fire'," he writes, "one such craft has a fire-power equivalent to over 80 light cruisers or nearly 200 destroyers."[49]

These operations were covered by a standing patrol of ten fighter squadrons, consequently German fighter reaction was negligible.[50] But probably the main factor in the landing was the amphibious tank. Of this weapon, Eisenhower writes: "The use of large numbers of amphibious tanks to afford fire support in the initial stages of the operation had been an essential feature of our plans, and, despite the losses they suffered on account of the heavy seas . . . It is doubtful if the assault forces could have firmly established themselves without the assistance of these weapons."[51]

Though in places strong ground opposition was met with and Caen was not occupied, within twenty-four hours of the landing taking place a secure footing in France was established. On the 10th the first airfield in France was in operation; by the 11th the beach-heads were linked up into a continuous front; by the 12th 326,547 men, 54,186 vehicles and 104,428 tons of stores were landed; and during the first week 35,000 sorties were

[48]"Despite the massive air and naval bombardments . . . the coastal defences in general were not destroyed prior to the time when our men came ashore. Naval gunfire proved effective in neutralizing the heavier batteries, but failed to put them permanently out of action, thanks to the enormous thickness of the concrete casements. Air bombing proved equally unable to penetrate the concrete . . ." (*Supreme Commander's Report*, p. 27.)

[49]*Operation Neptune*, Commander Kenneth Edwards (1946), p. 89.

[50]On D-Day the Germans had only 160 aircraft in the invasion area.

[51]*Supreme Commander's Report*, p. 30. Of the assault of the VIIth U.S. Corps, General Montgomery writes: "The progress of the assault was greatly assisted by thirty amphibious tanks, launched five thousand yards offshore, which arrived on the beach with the loss of only one" ("Despatches," p. 4438). He also mentions: ". . . assault engineer tanks, tank-carried bridges for crossing anti-tank ditches, mat-laying tanks for covering soft clay patches on the beaches, ramp tanks over which other vehicles could scale sea-walls, flail tanks for mine clearance . . ." (*Ibid.*) p. 4435). I first proposed the use of amphibious tanks in a lecture given at *The Royal United Service Institution* on 11th February, 1920, entitled "The Development of Sea Warfare on Land and its Influence on Future Naval Operations."

made. "So complete was our air mastery," writes Eisenhower, "that in fine weather all enemy movement was brought to a standstill by day."[52]

Meanwhile, the synthetic ports were towed over the Channel and built; one "Mulberry" in the American zone, and the other at Arromanches in the British. Unfortunately, between the 19th and 22nd landings were severely interrupted by a gale which completely destroyed the American "Mulberry," and wrecked or damaged 415 vessels. Therefore, it was fortunate that Cherbourg fell before the month was out. On the 26th-27th it was stormed and occupied by the Americans; but on account of the damage done the port could not be used for about a month.

The fighting in the British half of the bridgehead showed how little had been learnt from campaigning in Italy. Twenty-one miles south of Bayeux rose a height 365 feet above sea level, called Mount Pinçon, and because it dominated the greater part of the bridgehead, it was of importance that the Germans should be driven from it. This led to a series of battles around Villers-Bocage. The country being enclosed and the British tanks inferior both in armour and gun power to the German, "The plan was," writes Alan Morehead, "Let us bomb the crossroads town of Villers-Bocage. Let us knock the houses into the streets, and then the Germans will not be able to get their supplies through to their forward troops." After which, he adds: "It was early in the campaign, much too early for the commanders to pause and remember Cassino, and all the useless battering down of the villages in Sicily and Italy."[53]

Thus it came about that "On the 30th June, the heavy bombers were first used on the actual battlefield of Normandy ... The risks," we read in an official report, "were obvious; the bomber crews were to bomb little more than a mile away from our own troops, and the chances of error, especially when the whole target area became covered with dust and smoke, needed no emphasis."[54]

This is an interesting statement, because, if in broad daylight errors of a mile are to be expected, in the night bombings of military objectives in German cities they certainly cannot have been less.

[52] *Supreme Commander's Report*, p. 36.
[53] *Eclipse*, Alan Morehead (1945), p. 112.
[54] "Strategic Bombing in Europe." A statement issued by the Air Ministry and U.S. Strategic Air Forces in Europe on 30th April, 1945, *Journal of the Royal United Service Institution*, August, 1945, p. 369. According to Montgomery, the first time the assistance of Bomber Command was called upon was 7th July, when "the bomb line would not be brought nearer than six thousand yards from our leading troops" (*Normandy to the Baltic*, p. 73). De Guingand also says so (*Operation Victory*, p. 401). Nevertheless, in "Strategic Bombing of Europe" it is definitely stated that "The first attack of this kind was made in daylight on 30th June. The target Villers-Bocage ..." (p. 369).

The results of this attack are described by Morehead. "The bombers came low over the bridgehead from England," he writes. ". . . It was all over in twenty minutes. In went the ground attack and came under precisely the same opposition it had struck before. The Germans had simply withdrawn out of Villers-Bocage and taken cover in the surrounding fields. Eventually, after many days, when we got into Villers-Bocage there was nothing you could really recognize any more. The bulldozers arrived and drove new roads through the twenty-foot deep rubble . . . The bombing of Villers-Bocage accomplished nothing, unless you count the delay caused to our subsequent advance."[55]

If this repetition of the Monte Cassino fighting is excusable on the grounds that the country was too enclosed for tanks to manœuvre in, no such plea can be urged in the battle for Caen, for the country surrounding it is open plainland. Nevertheless, the same tactics are to be seen there. On 7th July the city was mercilessly bombed, and, when carried on the 9th, "The final assault," writes Morehead, "was preceded by an immense aerial bombardment, which wrecked large areas of the town without hitting the Germans or discouraging them seriously." Two thousand two hundred bombers were employed in this attack, and 7,000 tons of bombs were dropped on the city.

Should it be thought that Morehead is prejudiced, here is what another war correspondent wrote:

"Caen, when I went in, was the scene of the most appalling devastation . . .

". . . I understand very fully indeed military necessity, but I am not convinced that the indiscriminate bombing of French cities and large towns such as Caen was necessary, and it was most certainly not desirable. Take Caen as a test case. All the evidence I gathered was, that the Germans were not in the town on 'D' Day, when we blasted the place and killed, according to estimates which I averaged out, some 5,000 civilians, men, women and children.

"In the final bombing (9th July), when the Lancasters came in very low to plaster the defences outside the northern suburbs of Caen, they blasted them so thoroughly that another 2,000 civilians were killed. The Germans, when we pressed them close, passed rapidly through the town to the other side of the river. They did not attempt to stay and fight in the town itself . . . The bombing was supposed to be on military objectives, but the result had been to devastate a city, and the bombing, so far as military objectives were concerned, was thoroughly inaccurate . . . I confess frankly I was horrified at the bombing of Caen, not because of the destruction of buildings but because of the terrible loss of life amongst innocent people . . .

[55] *Eclipse*, p. 112.

The bombing of Caen was wrong militarily and morally ... My opinion was shared by others, and I knew of no War Correspondent who was not ashamed of what he saw at Caen."[56]

While Montgomery was hammering at Caen, the need to re-group the American forces after the occupation of Cherbourg delayed General Bradley striking southwards until 3rd July, and then, owing to the close nature of the country and the bad weather, his advance was slow. Nevertheless, progress was made, and towards the middle of the month Eisenhower decided on the following offensive plan.

By means of a vigorous feint thrust, delivered by the Second Army in the Évrecy-Esquay area on the 16th-17th, to draw the enemy's armour westwards. Next, on the 18th, "the main British-Canadian thrust was to take the form of a drive across the Orne from Caen towards the south and south-east, exploiting in the direction of the Seine basin and Paris." Lastly, on the 19th, General Bradley was to launch his major attack across the line Périers-St.-Lô. and should a break-through be achieved, "he was to swing his spearheads westward to Coutances, in order to isolate the enemy divisions between St.-Lô and the coast and then strike down through Avranches, creating, if possible, an open flank." By this means the Brittany Peninsula could be opened and its much needed ports occupied, "while the German Seventh Army and at least parts of the Panzer Group West[57] could be encircled and crushed between U.S. forces to the west and the British and Canadians to the east."[58]

From this it will be seen that the manœuvre intended was to be on the Cannæ lines: a double envelopment and not a break-through on the western flank alone, which actually happened and turned the manœuvre into an Arbela one.

The Second Army feint attack on the night of the 16th-17th was successful in deceiving the enemy, and was notable in that a novel expedient, called "artificial moonlight," was for the first time employed. It was produced by focusing the beams of massed searchlights on the clouds; from them the light was reflected back on the ground.[59] According to General Montgomery it proved of great assistance to the infantry.[60]

[56]*European Victory*, John D'Arcy-Dawson (1946), pp. 87-88. Reference the bombing of Caen, de Guingand writes: "The trouble then was that *too much disruption* was caused, and our advance was impeded by the effects of the bombing." (*Operation Victory*, p. 396.)

[57]The Panzer Group West, commanded by General von Schweppenburg, was responsible for the administration of all Panzer formations.

[58]*Supreme Commander's Report*, p. 45.

[59]See *European Victory*, pp. 98-99.

[60]"Twenty-First (British) Army Group in the Campaign in North-West Europe, 1944-1945," Field-Marshal Sir Bernard L. Montgomery, *Journal of the Royal United Service Institution*, November, 1945, p. 450.

The attack on the 18th was a super-Montgomery operation. The plan was to bridge the Orne Canal, pass three armoured divisions (the Guards, 7th and 11th) with supporting tanks and infantry over, and then, under cover of a "super-colossal crack" swing south towards Falaise and cut off and destroy three German divisions.

To clear a lane for the tanks, the heavy bombers were to bomb on each side of an area 4,000 yards wide, in order to silence the enemy anti-tank guns on the flanks of the attacking armour, while between these two walls of bursting bombs lighter machines were to drop fragmentation (non-cratering) anti-personnel bombs, so as not to render the ground impassable. The tanks were then to advance through the bomb-swept lane under cover of a creeping artillery barrage.

On the evening of the 17th, Air Vice Marshal Broadhurst informed a gathering of war correspondents that "One thousand Lancasters and Halifaxes would be coming over early the next morning, fifteen hundred Fortresses and Liberators of the U.S. 8th Air Force would be following them in; six hundred British and American medium bombers; the whole of the American 9th Air Force fighters, and the whole of our own Tactical Air Force. 'They began forming them up back in England this morning,' Broady said. 'I don't really know what bit of air will be left unoccupied when the show starts'."[61]

Eisenhower corroborates this, for he informs us that the attack was preceded "by what was the heaviest and most concentrated air assault hitherto employed in support of ground operations"; 12,000 tons of bombs were to be dropped, 5,000 "in less than forty-five minutes . . . At the same time, a strong naval bombardment was made to supplement the air effort."[62]

The Germans, however, had seen through these clumsy tactics. They withdrew their troops and prepared a zone of anti-tank defences on a line a few miles in rear of the prospective lane. In this zone their gunners remained underground until the bombing was over. Then they emerged and opened fire "on the hundreds of vehicles deployed across the plain." They knocked out between 150 and 200 of the attacking tanks, the 11th Armoured Division losing over 100, after which some fifty German aircraft heavily bombed the division during the night. Next day the weather broke, and the plains of Caen becoming a sea of mud, the battle ended.[63]

---

[61]*First Tide*, Alan Melville (1946), p. 101. Montgomery says: "About 1,100 heavy bombers of Bomber Command and 600 of Eighth United States Air Force, together with 400 medium bombers of Ninth United States Air Force, were to be employed." (*Normandy to the Baltic*, p. 81.)

[62]*Supreme Commander's Report*, pp. 45-46.

[63]This is Eisenhower's reason in his Report. But, according to Butcher, other reasons are alleged—namely: 19th July, "Around evening Tedder called Ike and

According to D'Arcy-Dawson, "The German was much more quick moving than we were, and senior officers taken prisoner said frankly . . . if they had the same weight of air support, guns, tanks and material as we, they would have pushed us out of France within eight days. 'You have tremendous fire power,' said one High German officer, 'but you have no movement'." This writer attributes Montgomery's slowness to over caution. "Caution," he writes, "was necessary and praiseworthy, but the difference between a good sound general and a brilliant commander is that flash of genius which tells him when to take risks and when to go forward slowly."[64]

The break in the weather—possibly also the failure on the 18th— persuaded General Eisenhower to postpone General Bradley's attack until the 25th, when the plan to be put into force was: To advance on a three divisional front west of St. Lô with the line Marigny-St. Giles as the primary objective. Next, with three fresh divisions, leapfrogged through the first three, to turn westwards and strike for Coutances and Granville.

On this occasion the air tactics were as follows: First, fighter-bomber attacks were made on all enemy bridges over the River Vire south of St. Lô, in order to isolate the area of advance. "At 10.40 hours," writes General Arnold, "P-47 Thunderbolts with bombs and incendiaries crossed east to west in seven waves, two or four minutes apart. Then for an hour more than 1,500 Fortresses and Liberators dropped 3,431 tons of explosives. P-48 Lightnings followed in eight waves lasting twenty minutes, laying more incendiaries. Then 400 medium bombers attacked the southern end of the area with 500-pound bombs, concentrating on crossroads and the German concentration of tanks and troops in the village of St. Giles. Incendiaries started flames that swept unchecked over German bivouac areas and dug-outs."[65]

Once again, as in the Caen attacks, this mighty air blow "did not cause a large number of casualties to the enemy, but it produced great confusion." And, "Again, as at Caen, this stunning effect was only temporary . . . The

---

said Monty had in effect stopped his armour from going south. Ike was mad. Monty always wants to wait to draw up his 'administrative tail'." 20th July, "Then he (Eisenhower) appeared . . . blue as indigo over Monty's showdown." 22nd July, Eisenhower wrote to Monty to "push on with every ounce of strength and zeal." (*Three Years with Eisenhower*, pp. 529, 530, 531 and 532.) According to General Theodor Wisch, commander of the 1st Panzer Division, on the evening of 18th July his Panther tanks surprised approximately 100 British tanks in leaguer and knocked out 40 during the night and another 40 next morning. (*Defeat in the West*, pp. 140-141.)

[64] *European Victory*, p. 113.
[65] *Second Report*, 27th February, 1945 (English edition, 1945), pp. 11-14.

advance was met with intense artillery fire, from positions not neutralized by the air bombing."[66]

The infantry attack was made on a four mile front, with tanks in support, and the most interesting thing about it was the air co-operation. "As our ground troops went forward," writes General Arnold, "fighters and fighter-bombers in closest communication and under common direction ranged ahead of them destroying military targets . . . Fighters in direct communication with tanks by radio flew constantly alert over our armoured columns. Ground officers called on the fighters to bomb or straf artillery or armour in their path. Pilots warned tank commanders of troops at crossroads or woods. German armoured units, without aerial eyes, fought at a disadvantage."[67] This was *blitzkrieg* on the grand scale.

During the 27th the towns of Périers and Lessay were taken, and on the 28th the escape route through Coutances was closed and 4,500 Germans captured. Meanwhile, to the east, the Canadian IInd Corps' advance towards Falaise had been halted by a strong defensive belt of anti-tank guns, dug-in tanks and mortars.

Five days later, the U.S. Third Army, composed of the VIIIth, XIIth, XVth and XXth Corps, under General Patton, officially came into existence; Lieut.-General C. H. Hodges was given the command of the U.S. First Army (Vth, VIIth and XIXth Corps), General Bradley becoming 12th Army Group Commander. This left Montgomery in command of the Canadian First Army and the British Second Army; nevertheless, until September, he continued to act as Eisenhower's army representative.

Following the capture of Coutances, the plan was for the Third Army to drive south, break through Avranches into Brittany and seize the area Rennes-Fougères. Thence turn westwards and secure St. Malo and Brest, while the First Army advanced south to seize the Mortain-Vire area. At the same time the Second Army was to thrust forward in the Caumont area. This time, whatever the weather conditions might be, Eisenhower decided "to indulge in an all-out offensive and, if necessary, throw caution to the winds."[68] It was certainly high time to do so, seeing that he had absolute command of the air, a personnel superiority of at least two to one, and a tank and gun superiority of about three to one in his favour.

On the 29th, Patton's leading armour crossed the Sienne, south of Coutances, and two days later Avranches was entered. "No effective barrier," writes Eisenhower, "now lay between us and Brittany, and my expectations of creating an open flank had been realized. The enemy was

[66]*Supreme Commander's Report*, pp. 47-48.
[67]*Second Report*, 27th February, 1945, p. 14.
[68]*Supreme Commander's Report*, p. 50.

in a state of complete disorganization . . ."[69] At the same time Montgomery launched his thrust south of Caumont "preceded by another smashing air bombardment" by 1,200 aircraft. Évrecy and Esquay, south-west of Caen, were stormed on 4th August, and Villers-Bocage occupied on the next day.

Following the capture of Granville and Avranches, Patton met with negligible resistance. On the 2nd Rennes was entered and St. Malo by-passed. By the 6th, the line of the Vilaine River was held from Rennes to the sea, thus completing the cutting off of the Brittany Peninsula. Nantes fell on the 10th, and that same day the U.S. 6th Armoured Division stood before Brest.

Thus was the greatest seaborne invasion in history brought to a decisive end. Hence onwards final victory was assured irrespective of what happened on any other front. Yet it was more than a victory; it was a revolution which cracked the age-old foundations of maritime security. Conclusively, it showed that, granted the necessary industrial and technical resources, no coastline, whether of a Continental or an insular power, even when strongly defended, henceforth was secure. It proved that, had Hitler allotted but a fraction of the resources at his disposal between the years 1933 and 1939 to solving the problem of the English Channel, he would have won the war. Therefore, it showed that, never again, unless insane, would a would-be master of Europe repeat this mistake.

Of the campaign itself, the outstanding factor was air power—its uses and abuses. The first—the enormous power command of the air endows an attacker with when he uses it strategically to impede his adversary's movements. The second—the enormous waste of power which results when command of the air is utilized to accelerate tactical movements by obliteration bombing.

The reason for this is that bombing, in spite of scientific sighting, still remains so inaccurate that it demands a fixed object as its target. Thus, the "interdiction" of the French and Belgian railways was successful because their depots, their bridges, their signals and their lines could not be shifted from place to place, whereas attempts to "interdict" the enemy's troops in the field normally ended in failure because they could be moved from place to place.

This question of inaccuracy is so important, and has been so little reckoned with by tacticians, that we will quote a few examples to drive the fact home.

In one of the Normandy attacks, Alan Morehead states that he saw "one great salvo fall five or six miles inside our own lines."[70] The same appears

[69] *Ibid.*, p. 50.
[70] *Eclipse*, p. 125.

to have happened on 25th July, when General McNair was killed.[71] On 8th August, Alan Melville was an eye-witness of the bombing of the Canadians by the U.S. 8th Army Air Force. He says: "The road back into Caen was impassable because of burning transport."[72] D'Arcy-Dawson also witnessed this mishap. His description runs:

"The first wave went on and dropped its bombs just outside the suburbs of Caen. I rubbed my eyes and looked. Yes, I was right, the bomb line was a good four miles farther on. Worse was to come, as the following planes . . . dropped their thousand-pounders right back in our reserve area. Unfortunately, they hit our enormous reserve dump of ammunition and the lot went up with a roaring explosion . . . So it went on until our back areas were a mass of smoke and flame from bursting bombs and vehicles set alight . . .

". . . Everybody had come out to see the bombers come in, and as they were seven miles behind the line it was unimaginable that the Americans would miss their bomb line . . . One of the Canadian Divisional H.Q. which was putting in the attack received direct hits and was put out of action . . . while close-support bombing is not accurate, to be seven miles out was a shocking error."[73]

Later on in the same battle the same thing happened again. This time by Bomber Command R.A.F., and from an altitude of 10,000 feet! On this occasion the error was only three miles, and the same Canadian Divisional H.Q. which had been hit by the Americans was hit once more.

The truth is that, whereas the Allied planning of the campaign was brilliant; the invasion itself was brilliant; and the use put of command of the air to impede German movement was brilliant; the insistence on attempting to achieve tactical mobility by means of "colossal cracks" was asinine. Further, it was totally unnecessary, because Generals Eisenhower and Montgomery had at their disposal a complete tactical organization which, if used—and it was not—would almost certainly have solved their problem for them. It was the use of what were called "C.D.L.'s."—tanks equipped with powerful projectors especially designed to carry out *blitzkrieg* warfare under cover of darkness.[74] Why this novel and powerful weapon was never used is a mystery. And we believe that, had it been, it would have solved the tactical problem which was never efficiently and seldom effectively solved by "colossal cracks," and thereby have shortened the war by months.

[71] *Supreme Commander's Report*, p. 47.
[72] *First Tide*, pp. 127-130.
[73] *European Victory*, pp. 136-137.
[74] See Appendix: "The Attack by Illumination."

(6) *The Russian 1944 Summer Campaigns*

In so vast a theatre of war as Russia, where continuity of front is impracticable, the initiative—freedom of movement from a secure base—depends upon two main factors: the one is good lateral communications and the other adequate reserves. Granted these, then the tactical gaps in the front itself are not necessary points of weakness. The reason is that, should an enemy attempt to exploit them, by moving reserves laterally against him, he can be attacked in flank and forced to fight at a disadvantage, because his communications will run parallel to his line of advance. Conversely, should lateral communications be poor and reserves weak, or should both be non-existent, then the gaps will offer the enemy every chance of carrying out a series of Cannæ operations by pinching out in succession the occupied sectors of his adversary's front.

This was the unenviable position the Germans found themselves in as summer approached. Their reserves were pinned down in France, Italy and the other occupied countries, and in Russia such as they had had, had been absorbed, whereas their lateral communications had largely been lost, and markedly so on the southern sector of the front. There, von Manstein's group of armies had been split in half; the left wing, under his own command, having been driven north of the Carpathians, where it was covering Lvov and the approaches to Silesia, and the right wing, under von Kleist, having been driven into Rumania, where its task was to hold back the Russians from the lower Danube. Between these two wings communications were so indifferent that, strategically, they were separated; therefore, tactically, they could not co-operate.

Thus it came about that there were now four main groups of German armies instead of three: General Lindemann's on the Northern or Baltic Front; Field-Marshal Busch's on the Central or White Russian Front; Field-Marshal Model's—he had replaced von Manstein—on the Lvov Front; and Field-Marshal von Kleist's on the Rumanian. All these armies were woefully under establishment, and though they were reinforced before the summer campaign opened, the troops they received were of poor fighting quality. Nevertheless, every step was taken to meet the emergency, and it was held that the next blow would fall on the Rumanian Front in order to seize the Ploesti oilfields—a major vital area in the German war economy.

While the Germans were making bricks without straw, the Russians were mixing more and more political straw with their military clay. Unlike their allies in the West, whose one controlling idea was to win the war unconditionally, the Russians, being realists, intended to win the peace as well as the war. Therefore, from now onwards their operations began to diverge from those of their allies, and the position the Germans were in, coupled with Russian tactical theory, gave the Russians every chance of attaining their political aim—a *Lebensraum* in Eastern Europe. The difference in tactics is worth noting.

Whereas Western European nations had adopted the Napoleonic theory of striking at their enemy's main forces and continuing to strike until they were annihilated, the Russian theory was to strike until either the momentum of their attack was approaching exhaustion, or the resistance of their enemy had so far stiffened as to make continuity of attack un-remunerative, when at once it was slowed down to be re-opened on some other front. The Russian tactical aim was, therefore, to exhaust their enemy and not to annihilate him, unless annihilation were cheap. Space and a long front permitted of these tactics in Eastern Europe, whereas lack of space and a far shorter frontage restricted their application in Western.

Though, for the Russians, the political direction of the war was to become more and more oriented on Vienna—the key to Central Europe and, therefore, to Eastern also—they did not select the southern line of advance until towards the end of the summer campaign, and clearly for the following reasons: (1) Their communications on the Baltic and White Russian Fronts were far shorter than on the Ukrainian and Rumanian, also they were in better order because no great advance on these fronts had been made; and (2) knowing that the last of the above four fronts, on account of its isolation, could be overrun at will, they considered it advisable to exhaust their enemy on his stronger fronts before striking at his weakest—they wanted to gain a clear road to Vienna.

When the blow fell, their order of battle was as follows: Karelian Front, General Meretskov's Group; Leningrad Front, General Govorov's; 1st Baltic Front, General Bagramyan's; 2nd Baltic Front, General Yeremenko's; 3rd Baltic Front, General Maslennikov's; 1st White Russian Front, General Rokossovsky's; 2nd White Russian Front, General Zakharov's; 3rd White Russian Front, General Chernyakhovsky's; 1st Ukrainian Front, Marshal Koniev's; 2nd Ukrainian Front, General Malinovsky's; 3rd Ukrainian Front, General Tolbukhin's; and 4th Ukrainian Front, General Petrov's. In all, at least, 300 divisions 4,500,000 strong, or ten times the force Napoleon carried into Russia in 1812. Opposed to this mighty array were, possibly, 200 German divisions, but many were mere cadres and most were under-strength. In all, their manpower was probably under rather than over 1,500,000. If in personnel the Russian superiority was three to one, in *matériel*—tanks, guns, aircraft, etc.—it must have been about five to one. Nevertheless, the Russians were nothing like so highly equipped as their allies. Consequently, the war in the East of Europe continued to remain more primitive than in the West.

THE RUSSIAN SUMMER CAMPAIGN, NORTHERN FRONT 10th JUNE-16th AUG., 1944

In brief, the Russian programme for the summer was to demolish each German sector in turn, starting with the Finnish Front, in order to clear their right flank and release the Baltic Fleet. Waiting until France had been invaded, on 10th June General Govorov, commanding the Leningrad Group, attacked the Karelian Isthmus, broke through the Mannerheim Line, and on the 20th captured Viborg. This virtually brought the campaign to an end; for although hostilities did not cease until September, negotiations to terminate the Russo-Finnish War were already secretly being discussed.

Three days after the fall of Viborg the main Russian offensive was opened by the three White Russian and the First Baltic Groups, over 100 divisions in all, under cover of a tremendous artillery bombardment. The attack was directed on Field-Marshal Busch's Fourth and Ninth Armies holding the "hedgehogs" of Vitebsk, Orsha, Mogilev and Zhlobin and the intervening defences. The Russian plan was to envelop the whole area in the triangle Vitebsk-Zhlobin-Minsk, as well as pinch out the "hedgehogs." General Bagramyan's First Baltic Group burst through the German defences north of Vitebsk, Chernyakhovsky's Third White Russian Group penetrated those to the north of Orsha, while Zakharov's Second White Russian Group broke through north of Mogilev, and Rokossovsky's First White Russian Group stormed Zhlobin. All four "hedgehogs" fell: Vitebsk on the 26th, Orsha on the 27th, Mogilev on the 28th, and Zhlobin on the 29th. On the 30th the Russian advance was threatening Minsk from the east of Borisov and from Osipovichi, where a considerable part of the German Ninth Army was encircled and annihilated.

The second phase next opened with the crossing of the Berezina, the aim now being to pinch out Minsk. After a fierce engagement Borisov fell on 1st July; whereupon the Germans evacuated Minsk, which was entered by the Russians on the 3rd. This success was followed on the 4th by the storming of Polotsk by Bagramyan's Group, and on the same day the 1939 Polish frontier was crossed.

After the capture of Minsk, Rokossovsky moved on Baranovichi, fought his way into that town on the 7th, and then advanced on Bialystok, while to the north of him Chernyakhovsky moved on Riga. On the 10th the latter surrounded Vilna and took it on the 13th. Three days later his mobile columns broke into Grodno and established a bridgehead over the Niemen at Olita (Alytus), opening the road to East Prussia.

By mid-July, communications having enormously lengthened, the momentum of the advance began to slacken; whereupon the Russian High Command shifted the weight of the offensive to the Latvian and the Lvov fronts.

The first was launched on 12th July by Yeremenko's Second Baltic

Group. Swinging in to the north of Bagramyan's Group, it broke through the German defence at Opochka and outflanked the fortified area of Ostrov, which fell to Maslennikov's Third Baltic Group on the 21st. Next Pskov was taken on the 23rd. In the meantime Yeremenko captured Ludza and reached the main Ostrov-Dvinsk (Daugavpils) road. Then on the

THE RUSSIAN SUMMER CAMPAIGN, SOUTHERN FRONT, 16th JULY–16th SEPT., 1944

26th and 27th came the fall of Dvinsk, Rezekne, Shavli (Siauliai) and Narva; the first two to Yeremenko, the third to Bagramyan, and the fourth to Govorov.

The capture of Shavli, nearly one hundred and fifty miles west of Dvinsk, was made by a mobile tank column under General Obukhov, who directly after moved due north and, on the 31st, surprising the Germans at Mitau (Jelgava), drove them out of that important rail centre. Pressing further north still, on 1st August he occupied Tukum, and thus cut Lindemann's sole remaining railway to Germany. Simultaneously, Bagramyan captured Bausk and Birzha to the south of Riga.

This bold advance led to the replacement of Lindemann by General Schörner, who on 16th August struck at Shavli with three Panzer and one infantry divisions. Though he failed to retake Shavli, he forced the Russians out of Tukum, but could not dislodge them at Mitau. Wisely, he then began to pull out of Estonia and Latvia.

Meanwhile, on the Lvov front a more extensive offensive had started. Its primary aim was to pinch out Lvov by a double envelopment from Zlochov—due east—and from the direction of Kamenka and Rava Russka—due north. These operations were initiated by Marshal Koniev's First Ukrainian Group on 16th July. Both Kamenka and Zlochov were taken on the 17th, and though the Germans made every effort to hold Brody, it fell on the 18th, as did Rava Russka on the 20th.

Sixty miles north of Kamenka, columns on the right of Koniev's advance had moved westwards of Vladimir Volynsk on 20th July. Reaching the River San, they crossed it at Rudnik and Lezajsk and thence moved on Sandomeirz, bridging the Vistula on 2nd and 3rd August at Baranow. On the 10th they were heavily attacked, but held their ground. Sandomierz was taken on the 18th, and a bridgehead established there and linked up with Baranow.

Meanwhile Rokossovsky, who was already in occupation of Kovel, sent out from there a strong mobile column which surprised the German Second Army, and on 21st July reached the River Bug on a wide front. This column, which was commanded by General Kolpakchi, crossed the river at Opalin, captured Kholen (Chelm) on the 22nd and Lublin on the 23rd.

While this most important advance was under way, Koniev pushed on towards Lvov. On the 24th the Lvov-Przemysl road was reached at a point some fifteen miles west of Lvov, and on the next day Lvov was taken. This loss resulted in the disappearance of Field-Marshal Busch and his replacement by Field-Marshal Model.

From Lvov Koniev pressed on westwards and took Yaroslav on 28th July, whereupon Model abandoned the San. Next, Koniev advanced on Rzeszow and occupied it, while south-west of Lvov Sambor was taken and contact made with General Petrov's Fourth Ukrainian Group, now operating on the left of the First Ukrainian. Petrov had taken Dolina on the 29th, and on 5th August he captured Stryi, which led to the occupation of the oilfield towns of Drohobycz and Borislav on the 7th and 8th.

Operations on the White Russian Front were now begun again by Zakharov's Second White Russian Group moving on Bialystok, which he took on 28th July, while Rokossovsky moved against Brest-Litovsk, and after severe fighting occupied it on the same day. While this latter advance was being made, Kolpakchi, moving from Lublin, took Deblin (Ivangorod) on the 26th, and from there he rapidly advanced north and seized Otwock and Radzimin, the first a few miles to the south-east of and the second a few miles the north-east of Warsaw. This happened on the 31st. The next day the Polish Underground Army, commanded by General Bor-Komorowski, thinking that Warsaw was about to fall, rose against the Germans. This same day Chernyakhovsky's Third White Russian Group forced the Niemen and took Kovno.

Because Rokossovsky's columns were now much scattered, Model seized upon the opportunity thus offered, and between 1st and 10th August he counter-attacked them in the neighbourhood of Siedlce, but with no great success. Threatened on his left flank by Zakharov, who on 30th July had taken Belsk and was advancing west, Model fell back on Praga, the eastern suburb of Warsaw, and on the 15th started a series of vigorous counter-attacks against Zakharov. By these means he delayed his enemy for a month, during which Rokossovsky captured Tluscz, to the north-east of Warsaw, and Zakharov, Ostrow. At the beginning of September Zakharov moved against the Ostrolenka-Wyszkow line, captured Wyszkow on the 3rd, and on the 12th completed his operations by storming Lomza, while on the 15th Rokossovsky established himself in Praga. Thus ended the summer campaign in the centre.

By mid-August the German situation was desperate in the extreme. In Poland her enemy stood on the borders of East Prussia, in the eastern suburbs of Warsaw and on the Central Carpathians; in France her Seventh Army and much of the Fifteenth which had reinforced it were being pounded to pieces in the Falaise pocket, and on the coast of the Riviera the Seventh American Army was disembarking; while in Italy the German army was retiring from Florence. Total collapse seemed imminent, total collapse was expected and predicted; yet hedged in by unconditional surrender, total collapse demanded total ruin. Therefore, the war continued, and the Russian armies on the Polish front having run their course, the next blow in the East fell upon Rumania.

There the German Eighth and Sixth Armies were deployed across Moldavia and Bessarabia. Together, they numbered some twenty-five divisions, each probably less than 6,000 strong, supported by fifteen or sixteen Rumanian divisions, now utterly unreliable. They could not be reinforced, for not only did communications prohibit this, but there were no reinforcements.

Once again the Russian plan was a double envelopment. From the north of Jassy Malinovsky's Second Ukrainian Group was to smash through the

German Eighth Army and move southwards against the left rear of the Sixth Army, while Tolbukhin's Third Ukrainian Group was to cross the lower Dniester, break through the right of the Sixth Army and join hands with Malinovsky. In brief, the Sixth Army was to be encircled.

Tolbukhin had already established two small bridgeheads west of the Dniester at Grigoriopol and opposite Tiraspol. These he skilfully reinforced, and on 20th August launched his attack, making his main thrust from the latter bridgehead. Success was immediate, for the Rumanians broke and fled. Whereupon, all but unopposed, Tolbukhin's column swept north-westwards and south-westwards. Meanwhile, Malinovsky struck at the Eighth Army, drove the Germans out of Jassy and occupied the town on the 23rd.

These blows brought to an end Rumanian resistance; for on the day Jassy fell King Michael of Rumania by a *coup d'état* arrested Marshal Antonescu; abolished his government; formed a new one under General Sanatescu, and pledged his support of the United Nations on the condition that Transylvania be returned to Rumania. There can be little doubt that this *coup d'état* had been pre-arranged with the Allied Powers; for so far back as the previous March contact had been made between the King's representative—Prince Barbu Stirbey—and Allied representatives at Cairo. And on 2nd April Mr. Molotov had stated in a broadcast that ". . . the Soviet Government declares that it does not pursue the aim of acquiring any part of Rumanian territory (other than Bessarabia), or of altering the social structure of Rumania as it exists at present. The entry of Soviet troops into the boundaries of Rumania is dictated exclusively by military necessities, and the continuing resistance of enemy troops."[75]

Though this was far from being unconditional surrender, the statement "was warmly welcomed in London and Washington."

From Jassy, Malinovsky advanced on Husi, cutting the line of retreat of the Sixth Army. At Leovo he linked up with Tolbukhin's right wing, and by the 25th the bulk of the Sixth Army was encircled about Kishinev (Chisinau) and soon after liquidated. Whereupon King Michael declared war on Germany. The next day Tolbukhin's left wing entered the fortress of Ismail on the delta of the Danube, and on the 27th occupied Galatz (Galati).

Meanwhile, Malinovsky pressed south, and on the 29th reached the oil regions of Buzau; on the 30th he occupied Ploesti and on the 31st entered Bucharest. Thus, more effectively than could have been accomplished by any strategic bombing, Germany lost the bulk of her natural supply of oil and all her Rumanian wheat.

[75]Quoted from *The Nineteenth Quarter*, p. 136.

In the meantime, on the 26th, Bulgaria had withdrawn from the war. Whereupon the Germans hastily began to evacuate Greece. On 16th September Sofia was occupied by the Russians, and thus having gained complete control of Rumania and Bulgaria, they next initiated "a separate and independent campaign up the Danube Valley, with the subjection of Hungary and the invasion of Austria as its ultimate objectives."[76]

(7) *The Strategic Bombing of Germany* 1944-1945

Immediately after General Eisenhower opened his headquarters in London to organize the invasion of France, the whole problem of what may be called the "Third Front" came under his review. Because he did not believe that Germany could be reduced to submission by air bombing alone, he was in no way satisfied that, during the preparatory period and the invasion itself, strategic bombing should remain under a separate command and continue as a separate front.

On 20th January, when this important question would appear to have first cropped up, strategic bombing from the United Kingdom was under the direction of the Combined Chiefs of Staff,[77] and still largely influenced by the strategy of the British War Cabinet, its primary aims, as we have seen, being the destruction of German industry and the demoralization of the German people.

To the proposal Eisenhower now made to bring strategic bombing under his own control, it would seem that he met with considerable opposition from the British Air Ministry.[78] Nevertheless, supported by General Marshall, in the end a compromise was arranged, for though Bomber Command, R.A.F., and the U.S. Strategic Air Force were not actually handed over to him, he was granted authority to control both forces as he pleased directly the plan of invasion had been settled on and thence during the invasion itself.[79]

The next problem was: What would be the most profitable air targets? To go on slaughtering German civilians, smashing up cities and striking at industrial centres was manifestly ridiculous; for as General Arnold wrote at about this time: "Contrary to prevailing beliefs, all industry is not absolutely essential to every belligerent country. Industrial damage, even on a very large scale, might have absolutely no effect on the front-line

---

[76]*The Twentieth Quarter*, p. 135.

[77]In the U.K. the senior members of each of the three Services were called the Chiefs of Staff and in the U.S. the Joint Chiefs of Staff. Together they were known as the Combined Chiefs of Staff.

[78]*Three Years with Eisenhower*, p. 405.

[79]*Ibid.*, pp. 427 and 450.

strength of a warring nation for twenty years or longer."[80] At length it was decided that priority should be given to transportation and synthetic oil plants. Lieut.-General Carl Spaatz, Chief of the U.S. Strategic Air Force, advocated concentrating on oil, whereas Air Chief Marshal Tedder favoured attacking the German railways. His argument ran as follows: By disrupting rail movements, the Germans would be compelled to move by road, which was much slower, and on roads they would offer admirable air targets to strike at. Bombing transportation offered the only reasonable prospect of disorganizing the enemy in the time available, whereas the effects of bombing oil plants might not be felt for months. On 30th March Tedder's argument was accepted, and undoubtedly it was the right one; transportation was to come first and synthetic oil plants second on the strategic bombing list. At long last, strategic bombing was, for the time being at least, to become strategic.

As we have seen, during the preparatory period and the invasion the main air object was to disrupt all rail traffic between Germany and Normandy, and as the front moved eastwards so was the attack on the railways and waterways extended into the Reich, until by October Western German traffic was all but paralysed. This also had a catastrophic influence on the distribution of coal, which constituted about 40 per cent of the traffic carried by the German railways. We read in the *U.S. Strategic Bombing Survey:*

"Essen Division car replacements of coal, which had been 21,400 daily in January, 1944, had declined to 12,000 in September, of which only 3,000-4,000 were for long haul traffic. Coal placements in the Cologne Division were virtually eliminated. Progressive disruptions in other divisions outside of the Ruhr early prevented the return of coal cars into the loading territory. By November deliveries of coal to factories in Bavaria had been reduced by nearly 50 per cent, and the situation deteriorated further during the winter. The north continued to be moderately well supplied. By January, 1945, coal placements in the Ruhr district were down to 9,000 cars per day. Finally, in February well-nigh complete interdiction in the Ruhr district was obtained. Such coal as was loaded was subject to confiscation by the railroad to supply locomotive fuel coal. Nevertheless, coal stocks of the Reichsbahn were reduced from eighteen days in October, 1944, to four and a half days in February, 1945. Some divisions in the south had less than one day's supply on hand by March, and locomotives were standing idle because of the shortage of coal in districts where additional traffic could otherwise have moved."[81]

[80]*Report to the Secretary of War*, 4th January, 1944, p. 47.
[81]*United States Strategic Bombing Survey, Over-all Report (European War)*, 30th September, 1945, pp. 63-64.

The two main sources of German oil were: (1) The Rumanian and Hungarian oilfields, and (2) eighteen synthetic home plants.[82] The Ploesti refineries were first attacked by U.S. bombers in August, 1943, and again in April, 1944, but only with limited effect. As we have seen, in August, 1944, they were occupied by the Russians; consequently, from then on German dependence on synthetic production became more vital than ever.

A preliminary attack was made on the synthetic plants at Leuna, Bohlen, Brux (near Prague) and Pölitz on 12th-13th May,[83] and another on those at Leuna, Zeitz, Lutzhendorf and Königsborn by an immense force of U.S. bombers escorted by nearly 2,000 fighters on 28th May; but it was not until after the Normandy landings that the main blow was struck. By July every major plant had been hit. In May these plants had been producing 316,000 tons a month; in June this output fell to 107,000 tons, and by September to 17,000. Also, the output of aviation petrol dropped from 175,000 tons in April to 30,000 in July and 5,000 in September. Though with remarkable rapidity these plants were brought back into partial production, it was the persistence of the attacks which told. For example, to keep the capacity of the great Leuna plant down to 9 per cent of its full output, twenty-two attacks were made on it, twenty by the U.S. 8th Air Force, and two by the R.A.F., in which 6,552 bomber sorties were flown and 18,328 tons of bombs dropped.

"The loss of oil production," states the *Survey*, "was also felt in many other ways. In August, 1944, the final run-in time for aircraft engines was cut from two hours to half an hour. For lack of fuel, pilot training, previously cut down, was further curtailed. Through the summer the movement of German panzer divisions in the field was hampered more and more seriously as a result of losses in combat and mounting transportation difficulties, together with the fall in fuel production. By December, according to Speer, the fuel shortage had reached catastrophic proportions. When the Germans launched their desperate counter-offensive on 16th December, 1944, their reserves of fuel were far from sufficient to support the operation. They counted on capturing Allied stocks. Failing in this, many panzer units were lost when they ran out of gasoline.

. . . .

"The results of the oil shortage made themselves felt also on the eastern front. The Russian victories in Silesia in February and March, 1945, was

---

[82] In 1938 Germany consumed 7,500,000 tons of petroleum. In 1943 6,180,000 tons were produced in Germany and 2,000,000 imported from Hungary and Rumania.

[83] Speer, German Armaments Minister, said after this attack: "The happenings of the 12th of May had been a nightmare to us for over two years." (*U.S. Strategic Bombing Survey*, p. 41.)

(*sic*) hastened by the German lack of fuel. At the Baranov bridgehead 1,200 tanks, which had been massed by the Germans to hold the line, were immobilized for lack of gasoline and overrun. On the testimony of Marshal Stalin, bombardment of oil played an important part in the sweeping Russian victories."[84]

The attacks on German synthetic oil plants also vastly reduced the supply of synthetic nitrogen and methanol—both used in the manufacture of high explosives, and the former in that of fertilizers—and synthetic rubber, which was reduced to about one-sixth of its war-time peak of 12,000 tons a month.

What, however, is strange is, as the *Survey* points out: There was but one operative ethylene dibromide plant in Germany which produced ethyl fluid, "an indispensable constituent of high-grade aviation gasoline . . . so beneficial that no modern aircraft is operated without it." Nevertheless, this solitary plant was never bombed, and in spite of it being "highly vulnerable to air attack."[85]

Accepting this as correct, then more damage could have been done to the *Luftwaffe* by bombing this unique target than was effected by all the other devastating aircraft plant attacks combined. Ethyl fluid was "the centre of gravity" of the whole problem; yet it was missed. This suggests that in a technical age, unless soldiers and airmen are technically-minded, they are more of a liability than an asset.

Anyhow, from what we have now written and quoted, it is to be clearly seen that the economic attack only became a true strategical operation of war when it was directed against the sources of industrial and military energy and the means of distribution. Had Mr. Churchill and the Air Ministry founded their bombing policy on these obvious facts, far greater assistance would have been rendered to the Allies as a whole than by the insensate bombing of cities and industrial centres. Nevertheless, even in the last year of the war how little did those in control appreciate what strategic bombing really meant, for during it area bombing became universal,[86] apparently because the output of aircraft was by then so immense that their use became irresistible. It vastly exceeded that needed to paralyse the enemy's transportation and neutralize his production of synthetic oil. For instance, when during the last four days of October, 1944, 9,000 tons of bombs were rained on the rubble heaps of Cologne, the R.A.F. bombers "were crowding each other so closely that there seemed more danger of a collision than of being hit by flak."

---

[84] *Ibid.*, p. 44.   [85] *Ibid.*, p. 45.
[86] Of the total tonnage dropped in Europe by the R.A.F. and the U.S.A.A.F. 83 per cent was dropped after 1st January, 1944. Of the total tonnage dropped in Germany, 72 per cent was dropped after 1st July, 1944.

Thus devastation continued, reaching its climax on 13th February, 1945, when Dresden was destroyed. That night, in two attacks, 800 R.A.F. bombers showered 650,000 incendiary bombs mixed with 8,000 lb. and 4,000 lb. high-explosive bombs on the centre of the city. On the following day the greater part of 1,350 American bombers, escorted by 900 fighters, continued the attack which, on the 15th, was taken up by 1,100 American bombers. At the time the city was crowded with scores of thousands of refugees fleeing from before the advance of Marshal Koniev's armies. Therefore, the slaughter was appalling: 25,000 people were killed and 30,000 injured; six square miles of the inner town were reduced to ruins; and 27,000 houses and 7,000 public buildings were completely destroyed.

The excuse for this act of vandalism was that, because Dresden was a rail and road centre, it was essential to prevent the Germans using it to rush troops through to stay the Russian advance. Yet, in order to neutralize these communications, all that was necessary was to keep their exits from the city under continuous air bombardment—that is, lay the city under air siege instead of storming it with bombs.

While Dresden was being annihilated, many other raids were in progress. In fact, during the last thirty-six hours of the catastrophe 14,000 tons of bombs were dropped by 12,000 to 13,000 aircraft based on Britain, Italy, Holland, Belgium and France. And so on until the war ended.

And what was the final result of this Mongoloid destructiveness? That, while the First and Second Fronts were advancing to win the war, the Third Front was engaged upon blowing the bottom out of the peace which was to follow its winning; for cities and not rubble heaps are the foundations of civilization.

(8) *The Advent of the Flying Bomb and Long-range Rocket*

Taken as a whole, the German strategic bombing of the United Kingdom was as fatuous as was the British and American strategic bombing of Germany up to the spring of 1944, and it only warrants the name "strategic" during the period of the Battle of Britain. Though the damage done to private and public property was considerable, except in the seaports, few military objectives were hit, and even in the port areas the damage done was in no sense crippling. For the months of August-December, 1940, 22,744 people were killed and 30,498 injured, and for those of January-May, 1941, 19,576 and 19,177 respectively. After June, 1941, during which month only 399 were killed and 461 injured, the Germans were too busily engaged in Russia to waste good projectiles on unremunerative targets. Thus it came about that, except for an occasional raid and the so-called "Baedeker" raids of April and May, 1942, against Exeter, Bath, Norwich, Canterbury and York, in retaliation for the bombing of Lübeck, Rostock, etc., there was virtually no strategic bombing until the arrival in England of the first V1 (*Vergeltungswaffe Ein*) projectile on the night of 12th-13th June, 1944.

Though this novel weapon was, for purposes of propaganda, pooh-poohed by the English press, it initiated a tactical revolution as important as those following the invention of the aeroplane and the tank. Writing on this type of projectile in 1931, I pointed out that "The central problem in future warfare is not even electrification. Instead it is elimination, the elimination of the human element . . . The whole history of weapon development is one in which the aim has been to reduce to a minimum the human element, and its goal would appear to be the Robot obedient to a distant mind." Picturing these Robots, I wrote: "They will be wirelessly directed . . . Only direct hits will bring them to earth. Otherwise, soulless, nerveless and without fear, they will move swiftly onwards, and, as their target is reached, without a tremor they will dip and rush upon it. To be attacked by such monsters will be fearful in the extreme. Monsters blind, deaf and dumb. Monsters of steel and high explosives, who can neither curse nor cheer and who, nevertheless, are the incarnation of destruction."[87]

As predicted, the effects of the V1 were largely moral, the chief one being the instinctive dread of a machine divorced from human control, a weapon which cannot be terrorized. Such an instrument is uncanny. Man has grown so accustomed to fight man that he is apt to feel impotent when faced by a bloodless and nerveless "creature," which, though it can be destroyed, cannot be killed.

In spite of its belittlement by the British press—*The Times* described it as "the last exhibition of venom against the island which has stood between the aggressor and his plans," and the *Daily Mail* as a "blood-curdling bogey"—the British Government were exceedingly perturbed by its arrival. So much so that, as early as 18th June, when the invasion of Normandy was less than a fortnight old, the bombing of V1 sites was given priority over all other air targets.

The V1, or flying bomb, as it was generally called by the Americans and British, was a pilotless, jet-propelled, gyro stabilized aeroplane mechanically and not radar controlled. It had a wing span of sixteen feet, its overall length was twenty-five feet four inches, and its width two feet eight and a half inches. It had a warhead carrying 1,000 kgs. of high explosive; its maximum velocity was from three hundred and fifty to four hundred miles per hour and its radius one hundred and fifty miles.

It was not used against the invasion ports, but primarily to demoralize

[87]From an unpublished article based on a previous one called "The Day of Electrical Battles," which appeared in *Radio Times* of 6th July, 1928.

the British and moralize the Germans. Between 12th June and September, when the launching sites in France were captured, about 7,400 V1's were launched from France against England, and subsequently some 800 were launched from Holland or from Heinkel bombers against the same target. Of the 7,400, some 2,300 got through to the London region. Between October, 1944, and March, 1945, about 7,800 were launched against Continental targets, chiefly Antwerp. The casualties suffered in England from June to September were 5,649 people killed and 16,194 injured.

Less formidable psychologically, because its arrival was unheralded by either sight or sound, but with greater future possibilities than the flying bomb, was the V2 or long-range rocket, which the Germans had been experimenting with from about 1927 onwards. Its length was forty-seven feet, its weight fifteen tons, its warhead carried 1,000 kgs. of explosive; its maximum velocity was declared to be three thousand five hundred miles per hour, and its maximum range was two hundred miles, its trajectory rising to an altitude of seventy miles. It was a complicated projectile and erratic, sometimes missing the centre of the area it was aimed at by as much as fifteen miles. The output of this weapon was from fifty to three hundred per month from January to August, 1944, and then onwards about seven hundred a month. The fuel used in both the V1 and V2 was concentrated hydrogen peroxide, liquid oxygen and hydrazine hydrate.

The first rocket fell at Chiswick in England on 8th September, and the last at Orpington, south of London, on 27th March, 1945. In all, approximately 1,100 reached England, chiefly London, and 1,675 reached Continental targets, principally Antwerp. In England, the casualties ascribed to V2's were 2,754 killed and 6,524 injured.

Allied bombing counter measures began in August, 1943, on V1 launching sites and storage depots in France, and approximately 100,000 tons of bombs were dropped on them during the thirteen months which followed, that is, 9 per cent of the total bomb tonnage dropped by the Allied Air Forces during this period. Also, in August, 1943, the experimental V1 and V2 station at Peenemunde was raided, but the experimental work was unaffected. A year later, three further attacks were made, and though the station was seriously damaged, by this time in would appear that the development of the V1 had been completed.

"Only two of the ten German plants making dilute hydrogen peroxide were bombed. These attacks caused the loss of only a few days' production. The big plant for concentrated hydrogen peroxide at Bad Lauterberg was not bombed. Likewise, the important plant for hydrazine hydrate at Gersthofen was not bombed. All these plants were extremely vulnerable. The industry was unusually concentrated in a few plants."[88]

[88] *The United States Strategic Bombing Survey*, p. 88.

Once the V1 attack was launched, besides bombing the launching sites, the tactics of defence were built around anti-aircraft artillery, fighter air-craft and a balloon barrage. The first was established on the coast of Sussex and Kent, the third lay from twenty to twenty-five miles south of London, and the second worked in between. During the first week of the attack 33 per cent of the flying bombs was destroyed *en route*, and during the last week 70 per cent.

Though these two weapons were nothing more than explosive pro-jectiles, their introduction constitutes a revolution in the art of war; for in their employment the human element is virtually reduced to its irreducible minimum. Further, the fighting man is replaced by the technician, who, in complete safety, can operate these weapons hundreds of miles behind the battle front or from the target aimed at. Such a man is neither soldier, sailor nor aviator any more than is a far-away broadcaster.

Further still, once a more economical fuel than any of those experi-mented with or used is discovered, the revolution the V2 will effect is to be sought not so much in its forms of a projectile, as in that of a reaction propulsion engine, which acting purely by recoil does not require air to "push against" or to sustain it. Therefore, it adds a new sphere of move-ment to those existing: movement in a vacuum. This possibility is as great if not a greater revolution than that introduced by the aeroplane, because it raises war into pure space.

CHAPTER IX

CONSUMMATION OF ALLIED INITIATIVE IN EUROPE

(1) *The Invasion of Southern France and the War in Italy*

It will be remembered that the invasion of Normandy was planned as the major half of a combined operation, the minor half of which was the invasion of Southern France, the idea being that the second would draw opposition away from the first, and were both successful a double envelopment of the German forces in France would follow.

When at the Quebec Conference of August, 1943, this dual operation was first suggested, Italy had not yet been invaded, and when at the Cairo Conference, during the following November, it was finally decided upon, it was expected that the Italian campaign would be finished before 1st May, 1944, the date upon which the invasion of France was to take place. But, as we have seen, this did not happen, and the result was that in February, 1944, it became apparent that resources were inadequate to permit of a full-scale campaign in Italy and simultaneously mount two full-scale invasions of France. First, there were not sufficient landing craft, and, secondly, there were not sufficient troops. Already, on account of the promise made by President Roosevelt and Mr. Churchill to Marshal Stalin at Teheran that nothing would be diverted from the Second Front, a proposed amphibious operation in the Bay of Bengal had been cancelled in order to economize in landing craft. And, on top of this, as already related, it was decided to withdraw the bulk of the landing craft in the Mediterranean to the Channel. Thereupon, General Wilson, who as Supreme Commander in the Mediterranean was responsible for the prospective invasion of Southern France, proposed that it should be abandoned and that, instead, the war in Italy be pressed to the full. Further, once Rome and its airfields had been taken, that he should be given sufficient means to carry out amphibious operations along the shin of Italy in order to obviate frontal attacks up the Apennines.

Next, it became apparent that the advance on Rome was going to be a more lengthy operation than at first thought, and, in consequence, Wilson informed the Combined Chiefs of Staff that the invasion of Southern France could not take place until 15th August, and that this postponement increased his doubt as to the wisdom of committing his command to "that particular operation as the best service to the invasion of France from the United Kingdom."[1]

The whole problem soon became completely confused, and because of Italy. And though the campaign there was still in middle course, on 14th June—ten days after the occupation of Rome—Wilson was instructed to order Alexander to withdraw the U.S. VIth Corps (3rd, 36th and 45th Divisions), the French Expeditionary Force (seven divisions), a considerable part of the air forces, as well as other units, in order to build up the U.S. Seventh Army, under the eventual command of Major-General Alexander M. Patch, for the invasion of Southern France. Yet nobody could possibly know what the general situation would be like two months later—that is, on 15th August.

The upshot was that three alternative operations were next suggested by the Combined Chiefs of Staff: (1) Against Southern France; (2) against Western France; and (3) at the head of the Adriatic Sea.

Arising out of this, Wilson and his Commanders-in-Chief arrived at a fourth. They suggested that all existing and prospective resources be allotted to General Alexander, in order (1) to continue his offensive through the Pisa-Rimini (Gothic) Line into the Po Valley, and (2) to support this offensive with an amphibious operation against the Istrian Peninsula "for exploitation through the Ljubljana Gap into the plains of Hungary." "It was possible," writes Wilson, "that such a course might achieve decisive results by striking at the heart of Germany and thereby provide the most powerful kind of indirect support to General Eisenhower's operation in France by inducing the Germans to withdraw formations from the west to meet the new threat . . ."[2] But, he continues, "General Marshall informed me that General Eisenhower required operations to clear additional French ports in order that Allied formations might be deployed in France more rapidly and on a broader front, that there were between forty and fifty divisions in the United States which could not be introduced into France as rapidly as desired or maintained there through the ports of North-west France . . ."[3] In short, what Eisenhower now wanted was the capture of a major port. On this, General Wilson comments: "I admitted that General Marshall's emphasis on the necessity of seizing a major port in Southern France was to me a new factor of paramount importance, but a shift of our operations for that purpose seemed to me to imply a strategy

---

[1]*Report by the Supreme Allied Commander Mediterranean to the Combined Chiefs of Staff on the Operations in Southern France*, August, 1944 (1946), p. 18. (General Wilson's Report.)

[2]*Ibid.*, p. 22.

[3]*Ibid.*, p. 23.

aimed at defeating Germany during the first half of 1945 at the cost of an opportunity to defeat him (*sic*) before the end of 1944 . . . Although the British Chiefs had originally supported my recommendation, General Eisenhower's requirements were naturally decisive, and on 2nd July I received a directive . . . to carry out the assault on Southern France on the target date 15th August if possible."[4]

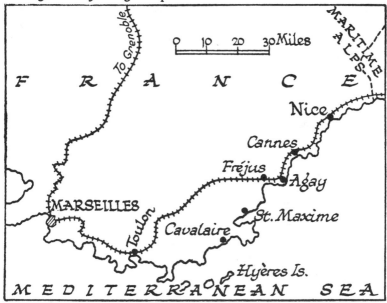

THE INVASION OF SOUTHERN FRANCE, 15th AUGUST–11th SEPTEMBER, 1944

The beaches selected for this assault were those between Cavalaire and Agay, and much assistance was expected from the Maquis (F.F.I.), of whom there were about 24,000 in the South of France; and an additional 53,000 were to be armed by 1st August. Opposed to the invaders were ten German divisions, of which only three were on the coast. The Seventh Army also numbered ten divisions, the U.S. VIth Corps and two French Corps, and the former was to lead the assault, with the 36th Division on the right, the 45th in the centre at St. Maxime, and the 3rd on the left. The total air force at General Wilson's disposal numbered 5,000 aircraft, 44 squadrons of which were based on fourteen airfields in Corsica. The main ports of embarkation were Naples and Oran, and in all 2,110 ships were needed to carry the invaders.

[4] *Ibid.*, p. 24.

The preparatory air operations were opened as early as 28th April and lasted until 10th August, between which dates 12,500 tons of bombs were dropped on Southern France. During the last five days of these operations the Strategic Air Force concentrated on the enemy communications along the line Valence-Grenoble-Montmelian, and the Tactical on the Rhône bridges south of Valence.

On the 15th at 12.30 a.m. the invasion began. At that hour pathfinders took off from the airfields in the Rome area and executed their drop at 2.15 a.m. Later they were followed by 396 troop-carrier aircraft, which dropped their loads very accurately at 4.15 a.m. Next, at 7.10 a.m., a violent air and naval bombardment was opened on the beaches, in which the planes of nine aircraft-carriers took part. Lastly, at 8 a.m., the first seaborne wave landed.

The landing was eminently successful and the enemy was surprised. By noon D+1 day all three assault divisions were ashore, when the immediate objectives became Toulon and Marseilles. By the end of the first week both were sealed off, and on 28th August both were occupied. Meanwhile, the advance up the Rhône Valley was being pushed at full speed.[5] On 3rd September the 36th Division approached Lyons; on the 8th the 3rd Division cleared Besançon; and on the 11th the French 1st Armoured Division took Dijon and in the vicinity of Sombernon linked up with the right of Patton's Third Army. On the 15th General Wilson transferred operations to Eisenhower, and by the 20th, in all 400,614 officers and men, 65,480 vehicles and 360,373 tons of cargo had been landed.

Technically and administratively, the invasion of Southern France was an overwhelming success; strategically, it was a blunder. The war was in its last lap, as to this there could be no possible doubt, and because war is the instrument of policy, then the nearer the termination of the war was approached, the more should its political end have been considered by the Americans and British, if only because for months past it had been by the Russians. This was essential, because the political aim of the Russians differed diametrically from that of their two major partners.

General Wilson and his Commanders-in-Chief would appear to have seen this when they suggested the Ljubljana operation; but General Eisenhower did not, because, so it would seem, he was too much of a soldier and too little of a statesman to realize that already for months past the war problem had shifted from a tactical on to a political basis. The defeat of Germany was now certain in any realizable set of circumstances; therefore the political problem had become paramount. Yet he still thought

[5] So rapid was the advance that A-20 bombers, B-24 Liberators and C-47 transports had to be utilized to bring up petrol and oil. (*General Arnold's Second Report*, 27th February, 1945, p. 47.)

in terms of France as the decisive theatre of the war,[6] and of building up overwhelming strength at what, though still strategically the decisive point in the West, had long ceased to be politically the decisive area. This area was Austria and Hungary, for were the Russians to occupy those two countries—the strategic centre of Europe—before the Americans and British could do so, then the two Western Allies would have fought the war in vain; for all that would happen would be the establishment of a Russian *Lebensraum* in Eastern Europe instead of a German.

Granted that the means did not exist for a campaign in Hungary, which is hard to grant, seeing that those employed in the invasion of Southern France would have been more than ample, then, strategically, the next best course of action would have been for the American Seventh Army, once it had landed and had occupied Toulon and Marseilles, to have turned eastwards instead of northwards, and, following in the footsteps of Hannibal and Napoleon, to have crossed the Maritime Alps, and by descending into the plains of Piedmont and Lombardy have turned the Apennines from the north while Alexander pushed his way through them from the south. This could not have failed to have cleared the Germans out of Northern Italy before winter set in, and have placed so formidable an Allied force in Venezia that the Ljubljana-Vienna campaign could have followed during the late autumn and winter months.

Instead, what do we see? A campaign with inadequate means; with no strategic goal and with no political bottom. The war in Italy becomes senseless; for after the occupation of Rome there "began the process which Winston Churchill once described as 'dragging the hot rake of war up the length of the Italian peninsula'."[7] Briefly, we will follow this senseless campaign of destruction up to the early spring of 1945.

After the occupation of Rome there followed a rapid Allied advance northwards. Next, the Germans rallied, and as they did so, Alexander lost ten divisions! Later on he was reinforced with Greeks, Italians and Brazilians, until eleven nations were represented in his two armies—the Fifth and Eighth. Next followed what Morehead rightly describes as "the insensate battering of the Gothic Line."[8] The assault on it was opened by General Leese's Eighth Army, on the Metauro—south of Rimini—on 26th August, and Leese describes the fighting which followed "as some of the bloodiest in the history of the British Army."[9] Then the Fifth Army attacked south of Pisa, and by 29th September the entire defensive zone, except for a fraction in the west, was penetrated. Yet, well may it be asked,

[6] *General Wilson's Report*, p. 24.
[7] *Eclipse*, Alan Morehead (1945), p. 71.
[8] *Ibid.*, p. 73.
[9] *The Times*, 18th October, 1944.

what for? Should the answer be, to pin Field-Marshal Kesselring down and so prevent him sending reinforcements elsewhere, then this could have been more effectively accomplished by keeping him closer to Rome, because then his lines of communications would have been longer, and the longer they were, the bigger the target they would offer to air attack, and the more difficult would it have been for him to move. By merely holding him north of Rome he could have been pinned down more completely than by driving him north. With his longer western and eastern sea flanks, ever open to amphibious attack, he could not have spared a man for any other front.

In December units of the Eighth Army were sent to Greece, and in February, 1945, four British and Canadian divisions were withdrawn, three to be sent to France and one to the Eastern Mediterranean. This further accentuates the senselessness of the Gothic Line slaughterings. Well may it be said that seldom if ever in the history of war has a general had so raw a deal meted out to him as Alexander.

(2) *The Re-Conquest of France*

At the time when Alexander with inadequate means was planning how to penetrate the Gothic Line, Eisenhower with a superfluity of means was faced by so complete a penetration in Normandy that, in spite of his need for the Brittany ports, he decided not to detach major forces for their capture, but instead to press the opportunity created by Patton's breakthrough of encircling the German Seventh Army. As he writes, "it was decided virtually to turn our backs on Brittany"[10]—that is, to reverse the western move in the original plan.

Though there can be little doubt that this change was correct, it at once introduced the problem of supply, for so long as the Brittany ports remained uncaptured, all supplies had to be brought forward from the beaches, the "Mulberry" and Cherbourg, and those for the American Third Army through the Avranches defile. This difficulty, as Eisenhower points out, "dictated the enemy's strategy."

During the latter part of July German reinforcements had been pouring in west of the Seine, and the arrival of a number of infantry divisions enabled Field-Marshal von Kluge, who had replaced von Rundstedt on 2nd July (Rommel had been severely wounded on the 17th) to relieve his armour and mass it in the vicinity of Mortain. There he assembled the greater part of five Panzer divisions (about 400 tanks), supported by infantry, and a not inconsiderable force of bomber aircraft.

With this formidable force, on 7th August, under direct orders from

[10] *Supreme Commander's Report,* p. 53.

Hitler, he struck westwards towards Avranches, his aim being to cut Patton's communications. It has been called a "gamble," and gamble it was; but war is largely made up of gambles, and at the time the Germans were in so critical a situation that, however risky the move, it was justifiable. At Mortain, von Kluge was but twenty miles from Avranches, and could he occupy that town and hold it for only a few days, except by air, Patton's supplies would have been cut off. Had he succeeded in this, there can be little doubt that his attack would have gone down to history as a classical example of bold generalship.

That he failed was largely due to the staunchness of the U.S. VIIth Corps, as well as the weather, which being fine enabled an attack by rocket-firing Typhoon aircraft to be made on him. ". . . in a few hours," writes Alan Melville, "the Typhies . . . won a major tank victory. If there was any doubt about the deadliness of the rocket, it was settled once and for all that morning . . . It is difficult to imagine how anything can make much impression on the hide of a Panther tank, but there they were—strewn all over the fields like leaves tossed about in the wind . . . More than ninety of them had been completely wiped out . . . The plates of the tanks were split and ripped wide open or torn off and flung down on the fields fifty yards away from the rest of the body . . . The whole place was a scrap-heap."[11]

On the 7th the First Canadian Army also attacked—towards Falaise. The attack is interesting in that the infantry "were moved by night a distance of five miles" in armoured transporters (Kangaroos), "the last three miles of this advance were actually within the enemy positions, and the troops debussed almost on the edge of the enemy gun areas."[12] Also D'Arcy-Dawson informs us that "The confidence which the armoured 'bus' gave to the men was tremendous, and we developed the technique later on so that it became part of our routine for frontal attacks."[13]

The mistake Hitler made was not so much to order the attack, as to refuse to allow von Kluge to withdraw once he was decisively checked. He waited until the 12th, but then it was too late, for on the 10th orders had been issued by Montgomery to encircle his forces. The Canadian First Army was instructed to attack towards Falaise and the XVth Corps of the U.S. Third Army from Alençon towards Argentan, while the U.S. First and British Second Armies pressed in from the west and north-west of Mortain.

[11]*First Tide*, Alan Melville (1946), p. 124.

[12]"Twenty-First (British) Army Group in the Campaign in North-West Europe, 1944-1945," Field-Marshal Sir Bernard L. Montgomery, *Journal of the Royal United Service Institution*, November, 1945, p. 450.

[13]*European Victory*, John D.Arcy-Dawson (1946), p. 135. It is strange that these vehicles were not used earlier, for armoured infantry transporters were built in 1918.

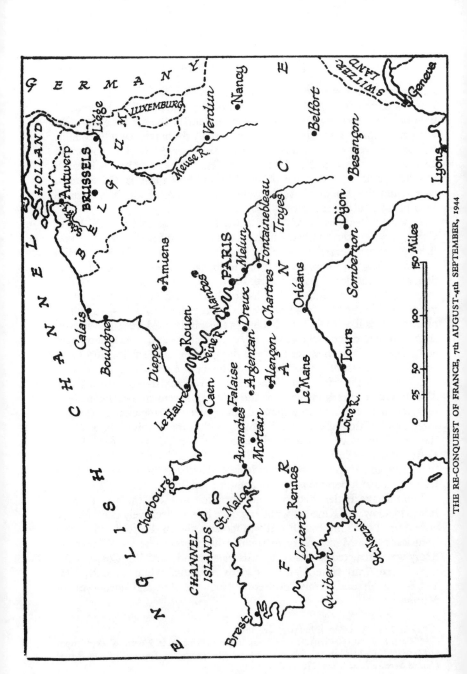

THE RE-CONQUEST OF FRANCE, 7th AUGUST–4th SEPTEMBER, 1944

On the 13th the German withdrawal was under way, von Kluge's Panzer divisions being pushed out on each flank to hold the sides of the pocket he was now in, while the infantry escaped through its neck. But on the 16th, Falaise falling to the Canadians, he withdrew his armour, and the retreat, which so far had been orderly, rapidly degenerated into a rout. Eight infantry divisions and parts of two Panzer divisions were trapped when on the 19th the mouth of the pocket was finally closed, and on the 22nd their remnants surrendered. The remnants of the fourteen divisions (some 80,000 men) which escaped, now under command of Field-Marshal Walter Model, who on the 17th had relieved von Kluge, headed in complete disorder towards the Seine.

In this notable and decisive battle, "P-47 Thunderbolts," writes General Arnold, "caught German tanks and trucks in column moving three abreast, bumper to bumper, on three highways of Argentan. The planes bombed the leaders of the columns, blocking the roads, and then roamed over them strafing and bombing . . . A.A.F. Fighters kept up the attack all day despite intense flak and foul weather. The smoke was so thick along some roads that pilots could not tally the destruction exactly, but they estimated 1,000 vehicles destroyed. Next day in the Royal Air Force area, Spitfires, Mustangs and Typhoons destroyed another thousand."[14]

Though the disaster at Falaise did not destroy the entire German forces in Normandy, it unbarred the roads across France, and nothing now, except inadequacy of supply, could prevent a stern chase of the disorganized enemy to the Rhine. Realizing that, so long as they could hold fast to the Brittany ports there was still a chance of stemming the Allied advance, the Germans defended them with the utmost stubbornness. St. Malo was not cleared until 2nd September, and Brest held out until 18th September. When occupied, it was found to be so completely wrecked that Eisenhower did not consider it worth while to attempt to carry Lorient, St. Nazaire and Quiberon Bay by storm. Handing their investment over to the French, he transferred the VIIIth Corps, which had been operating against Brest, to the newly-created American Ninth Army under the command of Lieut.-General W. H. Simpson.

While the VIIIth Corps of the Third Army was occupied in Brittany and the XVth Corps was operating against the Falaise pocket, the XIIth and XXth Corps advanced eastwards north of the Loire, their primary objective being the denial of the communications through the Paris-Orléans gap to the enemy. By 17th August Chartres and Dreux were captured and the roads south of Paris blocked. Two days later the XVth Corps, having joined in the advance, reached the Seine at Mantes and

[14]*General Arnold's Second Report*, pp. 14 and 28.

severed the roads leading from Paris to Normandy—below Mantes no bridges remained intact. Meanwhile the XIIth Corps, on the right flank of the Third Army, took Orléans on 17th August. North of it the XXth Corps entered Fontainebleau on the 20th. Next, sweeping east of Paris, by the 25th the head of the XIIth Corps was forty miles east of Troyes. Thus the pursuit continued until on 3rd September it had advanced in the south to within sixty miles of the German frontier.

An interesting tactical point in this rapid pursuit was the use Patton made of his air power. To each armoured division he attached a fighter-bomber group "providing the 'eyes' of the columns and smashing the enemy's troop concentration, armour and supply systems in advance of the ground forces. The closeness of the air-ground liaison in this work was one of the remarkable features of the advance and produced extraordinary successful results."[15] A further use was the tactical employment of aircraft as a flank guard. As Patton's intention, once turned eastwards, was to develop the highest possible mobility, he handed the protection of his strategic flank over to Brigadier-General Weyland, Commander of the 19th Tactical Command.[16] South of the Loire were some 30,000 Germans who, unless watched and held, might drive northwards and interrupt the Third Army's supply communications.

"For three weeks," writes General Arnold, "the German commander below the Loire tried to move his divisions by night to attack, but he could not, and it became obvious that to save his own organization he must retreat. In desperation he began moving by day, and the incessant air attacks broke up his forces. Although at no time had he been engaged by any sizeable element of our ground forces, his position became hopeless and he surrendered, in fact, to an air force."[17]

An interesting point in this aerial flank guard is its close resemblance to cavalry flanking protection in past wars, such as J. E. B. Stuart's cavalry corps in the Gettysburg campaign of 1863.

When the Third Army reached Melun and Mantes, the German position in Paris became untenable, with the result that the Germans withdrew from the capital, and on 25th August General Leclerc entered the city. Meanwhile, following on the elimination of the Falaise pocket, the U.S. First Army, the Second British Army and the First Canadian Army closed

---

[15] *Supreme Commander's Report*, pp. 59-60.
[16] For a full account of General Weyland's operations see *Air-Ground Teamwork on the Western Front*, published by Headquarters, Army Air Force, Washington, D.C.
[17] *General Arnold's Second Report*, p. 30. Also a point of vital importance was that during his advance Patton was assisted by the Maquis (F.F.I.), who not only operated against the German lines of communication, but provided him with full information of his enemy's whereabouts and movements.

in on the Seine, occupying its entire length north of Paris. Nevertheless, many Germans escaped over the river by the aid of ferries and pontoons.

On 26th August, General Montgomery issued orders for the advance north of the Seine, and on 1st September, promoted Field-Marshal, he handed the command of the land forces over to General Eisenhower, retaining direct command of the British and Canadian armies. Thenceforth the mission of his Army Group became the isolation of the Ruhr. The First Canadian Army was to move along the coast and the Second British Army on central Belgium, while the U.S. First Army advanced on the line Duchy of Luxembourg-Liége and the Third on Nancy-Verdun, with a column directed on Belfort to link up with the Seventh Army.

Amiens was reached on 31st August, Brussels on 3rd September, and the next day Antwerp was entered.

By 25th August the Germans had lost since 6th June 400,000 in killed, wounded and captured—half being prisoners. Also 1,300 tanks, 20,000 vehicles, 2,000 guns, and 2,378 aircraft destroyed in the air and 1,167 on the ground. Nevertheless, writes General Eisenhower, despite these losses, the German Army as a whole "had clearly not yet reached the stage of mass morale collapse . . . In fact, although we might have reached the military condition of 1918, the political conditions which produced the German collapse in that year were still remote."[18]

The reason for this was that, whereas in 1918 President Wilson's Fourteen Points offered a fire-escape to the beaten Germans, in 1945 President Roosevelt's Unconditional Surrender offered nothing less than total incineration. Added to it, at this critical moment in the war, instead of the Allied Powers attempting to bring the conflict to a sane political end by astute psychological attack, no effect was missed to stimulate German resistance. Lists of so-called war criminals were issued, whole organizations, such as the German General Staff and the Nazi Party, were proscribed, and at this crucial moment the Morgenthau Scheme was published, which demanded that Germany should be partitioned, devastated, pillaged and pastoralized!

The sole thing which could have mitigated this political blunder was a continuation of the pursuit. This, however, was impossible because these actions, by remoralizing the demoralized Germans, demanded that the pursuit should be in such strength that the critical condition which supply had now reached prohibited it.

The supply crisis had begun to take form when von Kluge had thrust at Avranches. Then, writes Eisenhower, "If our planes had been grounded, the enemy might have succeeded in reaching Avranches in his first thrust,

---

[18] *Supreme Commander's Report*, p. 64.

and this would have forced us to depend for a time on air supply to our troops south and east of the Avranches corridor . . ."[19] The words "forced us" indicate that Eisenhower did not welcome this method of supply. Later on, when Patton was nearing the Seine, "truck transportation became utterly inadequate to cope with the situation," and, in consequence, aircraft had to be withdrawn from the newly-created First Allied Airborne Army as well as from the Strategic Bombing Force in order to supply Patton with 1,000 tons of petrol a day, a figure which soon had to be doubled.[20]

When, on 5th August, Eisenhower changed the original invasion plan by turning his back on the Brittany ports, logistically, he unbalanced his army. Had he had an adequate number of supply aircraft at his disposal, this would not have happened. But he had not, hence the growing crisis. And so it came about that once Patton cleared Paris, priority of supply (P.O.L.—petrol, oil and lubricants) had to be given to the left wing of the advance under Montgomery in order that he might gain Antwerp and open an additional major port. Next, when Antwerp was taken, because the Germans held fast to the Scheldt Estuary fortifications, it could not be used as a port until 26th November. Up to this date the main supply lines of the armies ran back to the Normandy beaches and Cherbourg. Because of this, "In order to sustain the advances of the A.E.F. (Allied Expeditionary Force) towards the Siegfried Line, three American divisions had to be 'grounded' near Cherbourg, all their transport being diverted to assist the victorious armies forward."[21]

"To meet the full needs of our troops," writes General Arnold, "truck convoys poured down the Red Ball highways[22] night and day from Cherbourg. It was not enough. American tanks were consuming thousands of gallons of gasoline every hour. With every mile of our advance, supply became more critical."[23]

---

[19]*Ibid.*, p. 54. During the initial stage of Patton's advance petrol became short. Thus Ingersoll mentions that when his 6th Armoured Division reached Brest and his 4th Armoured Division neared Lorient and St. Nazaire, both pulled up "screaming bloody murder on the radio for gasoline and ammunition which they never got. Communication lines had long since stretched to absurdity and here they snapped clean." (*Top Secret*, p. 142.)

[20]*Ibid.*, p. 60. Air Chief Marshal Sir Trafford Leigh-Mallory writes in his "Despatch" (see *Fourth Supplement to the London Gazette*, 31st December, 1946) that "In the critical 25-day period from 9th August to 3rd September, no less than 13,000 tons of supplies were flown to forward positions," and during the full month of September 30,000 tons.

[21]"The Influence of Logistics on Operations in North-West Europe, 1944-1945," Brigadier C. Ravenhill, *Journal of the Royal United Service Institution*, November, 1946, p. 499.

[22]Roads for petrol supply only, marked by red balls.

[23]*General Arnold's Second Report*, p. 30.

Rightly, General Martel points out that this was the one problem which had not been sufficiently considered, and the result was that by 30th August petrol convoys had to be switched over to the American First Army, whereupon the armour of the American Third Army became grounded. "Quite early on in the operations," writes Martel, "it became clear that there would be a shortage in petrol supply, and last-minute plans were made to drop less essential commodities such as reserve clothing and load up petrol instead. In addition, petrol-carrying trucks were loaded up to carry 1,300 gallons instead of the normal load of 650 gallons. The divisional echelon which normally carried fuel for one hundred miles now carried enough for two hundred miles. This type of last-minute planning is not the way to organize these vitally important administrative arrangements in fast mobile warfare."[24]

Why had this oversight occurred? The answer is, because air power had been so fully exploited strategically and tactically that, when supremacy in the air was assured, it was found that its administrative possibilities had been overlooked. In fact, it had not been grasped that, because the aeroplane can dispense with roads and because it is the most mobile vehicle in existence, it is the ideal supply transporter when cost does not enter into the question. Had fewer bombers been built, and in their stead had General Eisenhower had at his call, say, two thousand flying four-ton-tankers, there need have been no pausing west of the Rhine, because the northern thrust could have been made in spite of Antwerp,[25] and its flanks could have been protected by aircraft, as Patton's right flank had been in his advance on Paris.

Along the entire Anglo-American front, with over half the world resources of oil behind it, in September, for lack of a sufficiency of air transport, petrol supply became almost as decisive a factor for the two Western Allies as for the Germans, who since August had been restricted to an ever-dwindling synthetic production.

To supplement road and rail supply, air transport, not having been organized, had to be improvised. General Arnold tells us that "C-47 transports and troop-carriers took off from England, filled with five-gallon gasoline cans. Heavy bombers were pressed into transport service. Ordinary values in air transport were turned upside down. Gasoline was first priority. Ammunition came second. Food was third."[26] Yet, "Even with these and many other expedients," writes Morehead, "Eisenhower found that his rate of build-up was not sufficient to launch all his armies into

[24]*Our Armoured Forces*, Lieut.-General Sir Giffard Martel (1945), p. 325.
[25]Even after the port of Antwerp was opened, so intense was the V1 and V2 fire that it became doubtful whether unloading could be continued.
[26]*General Arnold's Second Report*, p. 30.

Germany before the winter set in. It was a most dangerous period of delay. Every hour, every day, the German morale was hardening. As the broken remnants of the Fifteenth and Seventh Armies struggled back to the Reich they were re-grouped into new formations."[27]

Thus, the Second Battle of France, which had been opened by petrol, was closed by lack of petrol. Complete command of the air had been won and held for months; yet after an astonishing advance, at the very moment the German frontier was crossed by the U.S. First Army on 11th September, and in spite of the devastation Germany was being subjected to, because the most important potential of air power had not been sufficiently developed, a halt had to be called, and under cover of it the Germans shook themselves together and formed phalanx facing west.

(3) *The Russian 1944 Autumn Campaigns*

The conquest of the Danubian region, which followed on the defection of Rumania, was accomplished in three campaigns. The first was preparatory and consisted in the occupation of Transylvania and the crossing of the River Tisza (Theiss); the second culminated in the fall of Budapest; and the third brought the Russians to Vienna.

When the first, which immediately followed on the occupation of Bucharest, opened, Marshal Malinovsky's Second Ukrainian Group was deployed from Northern Bukovina to Turnu Severin, close by the Iron Gate of the Danube, on a front of over four hundred miles. On his right lay General Petrov's Fourth Ukrainian Group extended west of Cernowitz along the Carpathians to the Uzhok Pass, and well to the south of his left Marshal Tolbukhin's Third Ukrainian Group was operating in Bulgaria. Opposed to Malinovsky were no more than from three to five German divisions and possibly eight Hungarian. But Hungary was so important to German economy and security that there could be little doubt that Hitler would make every endeavour to hold it. Moreover, Rumania was now at war with Hungary, and this in its turn would stiffen Hungarian resistance. Nevertheless, and in spite of the exceptional difficulties of the terrain, Malinovsky determined to push on while resistance was weak. This he did by advancing a number of columns, the two main ones from Brasov (Kronstadt) and Sibiu (Hermannstad) in the direction of Cluj (Koloszvar), the capital of Transylvania.

On 10th September Alba Julia (Karlsburg) was occupied, and from it a tank column proceeded westwards and on the 12th entered Deva, eighty miles east of Arad and Temesvar (Timisoara). Next, it occupied Temesvar

<hr>

[27]*Eclipse*, p. 170.

on the 19th and, after some fighting, took Arad on the 21st. This advance brought Malinovsky to within a few miles of the Hungarian frontier.

Meanwhile Tolbukhin—now also a Marshal—having settled with the Bulgarians in a three days bloodless war, turned northwards towards

THE DANUBIAN CAMPAIGN, 10th SEPTEMBER-3rd DECEMBER, 1944

Belgrade, and late in September, crossing the Danube at Kladovo—south of the Iron Gate—occupied Negotin on 1st October, where he linked up with forces of Marshal Tito's Yugoslav partisans.

This advance brought him into contact with Malinovsky's left at Turnu Severin. Thereupon Malinovsky advanced westwards and on 5th October occupied Pancevo, a few miles to the north-east of Belgrade. Five days later Tolbukhin's columns reached Vel on the Morava, and on the 15th entering the outskirts of the Yugoslav capital, four days later drove the Germans out of it.

While this operation was under way, Malinovsky opened yet another offensive. On the 5th his columns crossed the Hungarian frontier west and north of Arad, and on the 11th forced a passage over the Tisza at Szeged.

On the same day another of his columns took Cluj, the Germans and Hungarians rapidly withdrawing towards Budapest, because at this time Petrov's Fourth Ukrainian Group was increasing its pressure on the Galician front. Thus far, the advance of this group had been slow, not only was the terrain it was advancing through exceedingly broken, but well-equipped German divisions were beginning to appear. Nevertheless, in the middle of October Petrov moved on the important railway junction of Cop, and, therefore, was approaching the main road and railway linking Cluj and Budapest. On the 28th he took Cop, but was immediately counter-attacked and driven out of the town, which was only recaptured by the Russians after prolonged fighting.

After occupying Szeged, Malinovsky paused on the lower Tisza until the 20th. That day he moved forward and occupied Baja and Sombor, and on the 25th attacked and took the towns of Apatin, Palanka and Novi Sad on the Danube, the last of which faced the old Austrian fortress of Peter-warden. Next, on the 29th, he broke through the German position at Kecskemet, captured the town, and then advancing north on 1st November took Nagy Koros, and on the following day Czegled, forty miles south-east of the Hungarian capital. On 11th November his advanced guards reached its southern and eastern suburbs, but advanced no further because the Germans had occupied the region of Jaszbereny and were holding it with three Panzer and two Panzer Grenadier divisions, which threatened his right flank at Czegled. To meet this difficulty, already on the 9th he had crossed the Tisza at Tiszafured and Tiszapolgar—thirty-five miles south-east of Miskolcz—and on the 12th he occupied Mezokovesd. Because this manœuvre turned Jaszbereny from the north, on the 14th the Germans withdrew their armoured forces, occupying the line Godollo-Hatvan-Gyongyos-Eger, which forthwith Malinovsky attacked, taking Gyongyos on the 18th, Eger on the 21st, and Hatvan on the 25th. Next he moved on Miskolcz and encircled it, but was unable to occupy it until 3rd December. This led to his gaining contact with Petrov's Group, which had already captured Kosice, the last German stronghold in Eastern Slovakia.

These various movements resulted in the clearance of the Germans and Hungarians from the plain between the Tisza and the Danube, except for a small area to the east and north of Budapest, running from Monor by way of Godollo to Vac. In this area the Germans had concentrated two Hungarian armies and some fifteen German divisions, including a considerable amount of armour. Because this force was considered too strong for Malinovsky to attack single-handed, Marshal Tolbukhin was directed to advance north and assist him. Thus ended the first Danubian campaign.

While this campaign was in progress, another was being fought in the Baltic States, the aim of which was to isolate General Schörner's forces as a preliminary step to an offensive on East Prussia. On 15th September it was opened by Govorov's Leningrad Group in Estonia. Six days later Tallinn (Reval) was taken, and by 5th October the islands of Muhu (Moon), Dago and Oesel were occupied. In the meantime Maslennikov's Third Baltic Group took Valk (Valga), driving the Germans back towards Riga, while

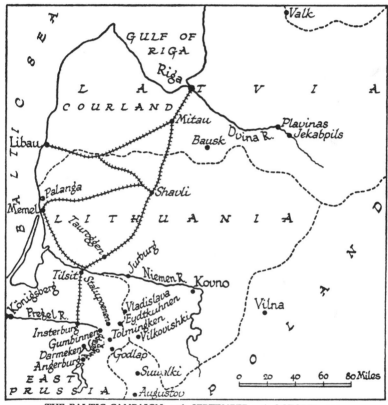

THE BALTIC CAMPAIGN, 15th SEPTEMBER–24th OCTOBER, 1944

Yeremenko's Second Baltic Group occupied Plavinas and Bagramyan's First Baltic Group forced the River Aa, captured Bausk, crossed the Nermunek, took Jekabpils (Friedrichstadt), and advanced to within fifteen miles of Riga.

With the Russians already at Mitau, these advances decided Schörner to pull out of Latvia as speedily as he could and withdraw his forces into Courland and Western Lithuania, where they could establish contact with those in East Prussia. This the Russians wanted to prevent, so as to avoid a large concentration of German troops flanking the north of the Warsaw area. Therefore it was decided that, while Maslennikov and Yeremenko moved on Riga, Bagramyan should advance on Libau (Liepaja) and cut Schörner's line of retreat.

Bagramyan's offensive began on 3rd October, and, little opposed, on the 10th his advanced guards struck the Lithuanian Baltic coast at Palanga, a few miles north of Memel, while another of his columns captured Tauroggen (Tauragé) twenty miles north-east of Tilsit on the East Prussian border. At the same time a column of Chernyakhovsky's Third White Russian Group captured Jurburg (Jurbarkas) on the Niemen east of Tilsit. About the same time Maslennikov and Yeremenko pierced the Riga defences and entered the city on 13th October. Thus was Schörner encircled on his landward side. At the opening of the offensive, in all he probably had thirty divisions of various strengths. Some of these had, however, slipped through to East Prussia and others had escaped by sea. Therefore, when the net closed on him, he may have had some twenty divisions in Courland and the Memel area, many of these during the winter months were also withdrawn by sea.

The last phase of this campaign was taken up by Chernyakhovsky's Group. Ordered to attack in the direction of Gumbinnen and force the Insterburg Gap to the east of Königsberg, after massing a vast number of guns, on 16th October he opened a terrific bombardment on the first line of the German defences west of Vladislavo-Vilkovishki, and captured Eydtkuhnen. Next, between the 18th and 20th, he extended the battle to the forest of Augustov, south of Suvalki, attacking the German second line of defences at Stalupoenen, Tolmingken and Goldap. The third of these towns was taken after fierce fighting, as was Suvalki, and on the 21st Stalupoenen was stormed. Driving west from Goldap, Russian tanks reached the River Angerapp between Angerburg and Darmeken on the German third line. Blocked in front and met by powerful enemy forces, including five Panzer divisions, intense fighting took place between the 22nd and 24th. By the 25th the Russians were so severely hammered that they broke off the attack and went on the defensive. Thus ended the autumn campaign in the Baltic.

(4) *The Battles of the German Western Frontier*

When in a state of rout the fragments of the Seventh and Fifteenth German Armies were pouring over the Seine, rightly General Eisenhower decided to continue the stern chase towards the Rhine. But, as we have seen, even before the Anglo-Americans crossed the Seine, supply began to dominate the pursuit. To push everything simultaneously forward was no longer feasible; therefore, either the pursuit would have to be abandoned or else continued on a more limited scale. As Ingersoll points out: "All the situation called for was a co-ordinated push behind *one* army, giving it all the nourishment, all the rich blood of supplies, that the arterial Red Ball highways could carry, and then, after it had gone through into Germany, while the weather was still good in the early fall, it could be fed from the air . . . In the situation," he continues, "history called for a Supreme Allied Commander—not necessarily a brilliant one, but a bold and forceful man, making at least good horse sense. Such a commander would have . . . seen that a single army could have been driven into Germany through the military chaos that was the Reichswehr then . . . and that such an army now, rammed home, could in a fortnight wholly destroy the usefulness of both the West Wall and the Rhine as military obstacles and, capitalizing further on confusion, had at least an even chance of taking Berlin and forcing peace in another."[28]

This possibility led to two proposals, one put forward by Montgomery and the other by Bradley. The first was to allot all available supplies to the Twenty-First Army Group, so that it could drive northwards and cross the Rhine between Arnhem and Düsseldorf, because a crossing between these cities would not only lead into the plains of Northern Germany and towards Berlin, but also into the Ruhr, the industrial heart of the Reich. Further, immediately behind this front lay Antwerp, the third greatest port in the world. The second was to allot all available supplies to the Twelfth Army Group, and by advancing eastwards through the Frankfurt Corridor cut Germany into two halves at the waist, and, "if the Combined Chiefs of Staff so desired, take Berlin from the south after reaching Central Germany."[29]

As regards the first, the sole limiting factor was that Antwerp was still blocked. Yet, in spite of this, Montgomery vigorously urged an all-out advance northwards, and we think that the dictum of history will be that he was right. Not only was it strategically the soundest course to take, but also politically the soundest, because were the Western Allies to occupy Berlin well ahead of the Russians, at the termination of hostilities their political position would be a far stronger one than should the reverse be the case. This time, throwing caution to the winds, Montgomery urged the following audacious course:

"My own view, which I presented to the Supreme Commander," he writes, "was that one powerful full-blooded thrust across the Rhine and

[28] *Top Secret*, Ralph Ingersoll (1946), pp. 164-165.
[29] *Ibid.*, p. 168.

into the heart of Germany, backed by the whole resources of the Allied Armies, would be likely to achieve results . . . The project therefore involved calling upon combined Allied resources in the widest sense, and would have entailed reverting sectors of the Allied front to a purely static role."

Next, pointing out that there were two feasible axes of advance, the northern axis through Belgium to the Rhine north of the Ruhr, and the southern axis through Metz and the Saar leading into Central Germany, he continues:

"I favoured the northern route . . . If we could maintain the strength and impetus of our operations beyond the Seine sufficiently to keep the enemy on the run straight through to the Rhine, and 'bounce' our way across that river before the enemy succeeded in reforming a front to oppose us, then we should achieve a prodigious advantage."

The alternative course on crossing the Seine, "was to drive to the Rhine on a broad front . . . it clearly involved a slower and more deliberate campaign . . . our available administrative resources would be spread accordingly, and in my opinion would not stand up to the strain.

"Apart from the administrative difficulties, my objection to the broad front policy was that nowhere should we be strong enough to get decisive results quickly; the Germans would thus have time to recover, and we should become involved in a long winter campaign."[30]

Nevertheless, Eisenhower decided on the broad front policy, either because he was a timid strategist or because he did not possess a strong enough personality to order one or other of his Army Group Commanders to assume for the time being a passive defence and subsist on the minimum of supplies. Therefore, he decided "that the Allied Armies should line up along the River Rhine, establishing bridgeheads wherever feasible, and that operations could not be developed further east until the port of Antwerp was opened and functioning. Meanwhile, a firm link-up was to be made with Sixth United States Army Group[31] advancing from the

---

[30]*Normandy to the Baltic*, Field-Marshal the Viscount Montgomery (1947), pp. 119-120. Also see "Twenty-First (British) Army Group in the Campaign in North-West Europe, 1944-1945," Field-Marshal Sir Bernard L. Montgomery, *Journal of the Royal United Service Institution*, November, 1945, p. 437. De Guingand holds that Eisenhower was right and Montgomery wrong. He says: ". . . if this gamble had not come off. The Supreme Commander would have been in for a very difficult time. What would his commanders and troops who had been 'grounded' say about it? . . . Even more important was the matter of national opinion and national pride; what would the people of America have said if Montgomery had been given these resources and yet failed?" (*Operation Victory*, p. 413.) But what about Bradley? De Guingand completely overlooks his proposal.

[31]The U.S. Sixth Army Group consisted of the U.S. Seventh Army and the First French Army. It was commanded by Lieut.-General Jacob L. Devers.

Mediterranean, in order to complete our front from Switzerland to the North Sea."[32]

Commenting on this episode, Ingersoll writes: "I believe that in August

THEATRE OF OPERATIONS IN WESTERN EUROPE, SEPTEMBER-DECEMBER, 1944

of 1944, a Supreme Allied Commander with the qualifications set down above could have ended the war by Christmas by decisively backing *either* Montgomery or Bradley. But there was no such Supreme Allied Commander. There was no strong hand at the helm, no man in command. There was only a conference, presided over by a chairman—a shrewd,

[32]*Normandy to the Baltic*, p. 121.

intelligent, tactful, careful chairman."[33] We believe that history will support this contention.

In spite of Eisenhower's decision, Montgomery did not altogether abandon what he held to be the correct course; he writes: "Although the broad front policy restricted our present aims to reaching the Rhine, I continued to plan the concentration of such resources as I had into a drive that would hustle the enemy straight through to that river: in order to jump it quickly before the Germans could seriously oppose us."[34] This plan led to one of the most surprising battles of the whole war. Though Montgomery was a cautious soldier, none of his great battles, not even el Alamein, is likely to lend greater lustre to his generalship than the epic failure of Arnhem; for in audacity of conception and execution it stands in a class of its own.

By the first week in September, briefly the situation in Belgium was as follows: The Second British Army was faced by determined German resistance along the Albert Canal from Antwerp to Maastricht. After severe fighting this resistance was overcome and a foothold gained on the northern side of the Escaut Canal, fifteen miles south of Eindhoven. At the time there were between 300,000 and 400,000 German troops in Western Holland, with their lines of communications running eastwards between the Zuider Zee and the Escaut Canal. Therefore, could a sudden thrust of some seventy miles be made northwards—that is, from the Escaut Canal to Arnhem—all communications south of Arnhem would be severed, and to all intents and purposes the Germans in Western Holland would be trapped. Further, and even more important, once Arnhem was occupied, the whole of the Rhine and the fortifications of the West Wall would be turned and the plains of Northern Germany opened to an Allied advance.

The sole means of effecting this deep thrust in a minimum of time in order to gain maximum surprise were airborne troops, and those involved were the 1st British Airborne Division, the U.S. 82nd and 101st Airborne Divisions, and a Polish Parachute Brigade. The operation was to be carried out in daylight under powerful fighter and bomber protection. Lieut.-General F. A. M. Browning was given the command, and on the first two days of the operation 2,800 aircraft and 1,600 gliders were used.[35]

---

[33] *Top Secret*, p. 169.

[34] *Normandy to the Baltic*, p. 122.

[35] "Between 17th-30th September, 20,190 troops had been dropped from aircraft by parachute, 13,781 had landed in gliders, and 905 were air-landed on a strip made ready by the preceding airborne troops. In addition to this total of 34,876 troops, 5,250 tons of equipment and supplies, 1,927 vehicles and 568 artillery pieces were transported by air." (*Supreme Commander's Report*, p. 84.)

The aim of the operation is outlined by General Browning as follows:

"The opening up and holding open of the corridor Eindhoven-Veghel-Grave-Nijmegen-Arnhem, and the capture of the bridges *en route*, notably those at Grave over the Maas, over the Maas-Waal Canal west of Nijmegen, the great road bridge over the Waal at Nijmegen and the bridge over the Neder Rijn at Arnhem.

"Immediately the corridor was established, the centre corps of the Second Army was to break out along the corridor and drive at high speed to link up with and pass through the airborne forces. The flank corps were to advance with all speed, but of necessity more slowly, to protect the flanks of the corridor and to reinforce the airborne troops holding it."[36]

The snag in the operation was that the resources in transport aircraft demanded four separate lifts. This, in view of the uncertainty of the weather, was a tremendous handicap; for had sufficient been available to permit of but two lifts, the probability is that the operation would in the full have succeeded. Therefore, once again, because air force was in superabundance, air power was at a deficit.

On 17th September the first lift landed in Holland, the 101st Airborne Division clearing the Eindhoven-Grave corridor; the 82nd captured Grave and set to clearing the Nijmegen area; and the 1st landed west of Arnhem and advanced on the bridge.

On the 18th the second lift landed in face of considerable opposition. German resistance increased, and the Guards Armoured Division, which was rushed up the corridor, was held up south of Eindhoven, but on the 19th it crossed the Grave bridge and linked up with the 82nd Airborne Division. Then the weather broke and the third lift was unable to fly in. On the 20th the Nijmegen bridge was taken intact and the Guards Armoured Division crossed the Waal, and on the evening of the 21st the 43rd Division reached the southern bank of the Neder Rijn opposite the 1st Airborne Division. During the next three days every effort was made to link up with that division but without success, and so desperate was its situation on the 24th, that on the 25th it was decided to withdraw it. This was successfully done under cover of night, after it had lost some 7,000 men in killed, wounded and missing.

It has been said that, but for the weather, which from the 19th onwards was abominable, Arnhem would have been strongly reinforced and permanently held. Though this is probable, man has no command over the winds. Nevertheless, the British and Americans had command over the waters. Therefore, it may be asked why was not this audacious and

---

[36]"Airborne Forces," Lieut.-General F. A. M. Browning, *Journal of the Royal United Service Institution*, November, 1944, p. 356.

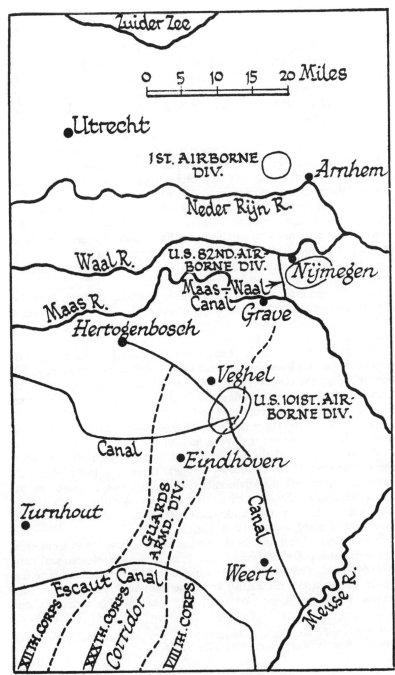

BATTLE OF ARNHEM, 17th-25th SEPTEMBER, 1944

obviously hazardous operation supported by a landing in Friesland? Even had but fifteen to twenty thousand troops, immediately prior to the air-borne attack, been put ashore there, seeing that the German garrisons in Northern Holland were negligible, would not such a "surprise packet" have compelled the Germans to operate in two directions instead of one? Was it because the Normandy landing craft had returned to the Medi-terranean and that there were not sufficient remaining in home waters to effect such an operation? In other words, was not it once again deficiency in landing craft, as much so as bad weather, which lost the Allies Arnhem? They had integrated ground and air, but once again they had overlooked the sea, or were incapable of calling it to their assistance.

Though Arnhem was abandoned, the corridor was held against repeated attacks, and this in itself was a considerable achievement, because it included the important bridges over the Maas and Waal, as well as adding considerably to the security of Antwerp.

Following on this notable battle, the next major problem was the clearance of the Scheldt Estuary defences by the First Canadian Army. This exceptionally difficult task, involving amphibious operations against the islands of Beveland and Walcheren, was not finished until 9th November, and it was not until the 26th that the first Allied ships began to unload in Antwerp, which by then was being subjected to a heavy VI and V2 bombardment.

Meanwhile the American armies south of the Twenty-First Army Group had been pressing slowly on. Already by 12th September the First Army had crossed the German frontier in the Trier (Treves) and Aachen areas, and on 15th September the Third Army had entered Nancy. South of the Third, the U.S. Seventh and First French Armies were, step by step, advancing towards the Belfort Gap. After very heavy fighting, Aachen—now reduced to ruins—was entered on 13th October and cleared a week later. This was the first great German city to fall.

These various advances, limited by supply difficulties, at length led up to a general offensive in November, the aim of which was to occupy the left bank of the Rhine from its mouth to Düsseldorf, or if possible to Bonn or even Mainz. It was opened by the Twenty-First Army Group on 15th November; but on account of the atrocious weather it was not until 4th December that the last pocket on the west bank of the Maas was cleared. At the same time, the First and Ninth Armies, covered by intensive air and artillery bombardments, attacked west of Düren, and advancing slowly reached the Roer River on 3rd December, the fighting closely resembling the Battles of the Somme and Ypres in 1916 and 1917.

South of the Ardennes the Third Army offensive, which had opened on 8th November, made more rapid progress. Metz was taken on the 22nd, though seven of its forts continued to hold out until 13th December, and bridgeheads were established over the Moselle near Saarlautern. On the Sixth Army Group front, the First French Army attacked on 14th November and cleared Belfort on the 22nd; whereupon the Germans fell back from the front of the Seventh Army, which, pushing on, occupied Sarreburg on the 21st. Six days later Strasbourg fell to the French. By 15th December the Seventh Army had penetrated deeply into the Siegfried defences north-east of Wissembourg; but the French failed to drive the Germans out of Colmar. Then, once again, the unexpected happened; suddenly on 16th December Field-Marshal von Rundstedt launched a violent counter-offensive in the Ardennes.

Though, from the first, the odds against this blow succeeding were probably in the neighbourhood of ten to one, the German position was so desperate and the Anglo-American armies so over-extended, that the one demanded almost any risk and the other offered at least a remote chance of success.[37]

The German plan[38] was by means of a *blitz* attack to break through their enemy's weakly held front between Monchau and Echternach, drive towards Namur, seize Liége, the main communication centre of the Twelfth Army Group, and then advance on Antwerp and occupy or destroy it. Could this be accomplished, not only would the Allied line of armies be cut in half, but the northern half would be severed from its supply bases, when anything might happen. Gamble though this plan was, because all alternatives must inevitably lead to defeat, it was strategically justified. Whether it was politically so, is another question.[39]

To carry out this imaginative and daring plan, the Fifth and Sixth Panzer Armies, as well as the Seventh Army, were placed at von Rundstedt's disposal. They consisted of ten Panzer and Panzer Grenadier divisions and fourteen or fifteen motorized and infantry divisions, supported by 3,000

---

[37] "'I fully agreed with Hitler that the Antwerp undertaking was an operation of the most extreme daring,' said Colonel-General Jodl, in explaining his acceptance of the plan. 'But we were in a desperate situation, and the only way to ease it was by a desperate decision. By remaining on the defence, we could not expect to escape the evil fate hanging over us. By fighting, rather than waiting, we might save something'." (*Defeat in the West*, p. 226.)

[38] The plan was Hitler's. Göring said: "The Führer planned it all himself. His alone was the plan and the idea." (Quoted by Lieut.-General Bedell Smith in *Saturday Evening Post*, 22nd June, 1946.) Though there was nothing wrong in this, throughout the battle Hitler conducted the operations by wireless orders.

[39] Politically, the best course would probably have been to have abandoned the Western Front altogether and have concentrated everything against the Russians. This would have handed the whole of Germany and Austria over to the Americans and British and have dealt a crushing blow to Russian prestige.

aircraft, all of which was to be used tactically to co-operate with the armour and infantry.

In face of his enemy's command of the air, how was it that von Rundstedt was able to assemble so great a force? In all, it probably numbered at least 1,000 tanks, 250,000 men, and many thousands of vehicles.

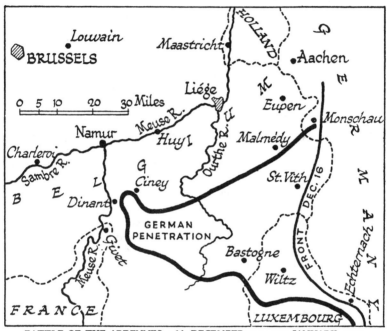

BATTLE OF THE ARDENNES, 16th DECEMBER, 1944-31st JANUARY, 1945

Several items make up the answer: (1) Allied intelligence would appear to have been indifferent; (2) bad weather made air reconnaissance difficult; and (3) though it was known that von Rundstedt had something up his sleeve, emulating the French in 1940, it was not believed that during the winter he would plunge into so broken a region as the Ardennes.

What von Rundstedt needed was a moderately clear day for the start and then foggy weather, and on 16th December he got what he wanted. That day he struck in strength between Monschau and Echternach, the main blow falling on the front St. Vith-Wiltz. The initial attack carried all before it, and the German tanks swept on towards the Meuse.

At once Eisenhower ordered the cessation of all attacks along the whole front, and moved every available reserve towards the haunches of the deepening salient. Next, he ordered Patton's army to attack in the direction of Bastogne, which was held by the American 101st Airborne Division,[40] and placing the U.S. First Army and part of the Ninth under Montgomery, left it to him to deal with the northern flank of the salient.

On the 18th a dense fog settled over the battlefield; yet already on the 17th the battle had reached its critical stage, because the U.S. 101st Airborne Division in Bastogne—a vital road centre—held firm, and because the haunches of the salient were so staunchly defended that the Germans could not widen their base of operations, and, thereby, gain room to manœuvre in as well as increase their communications.

On the 24th the weather cleared. This spelt the German doom, for an Anglo-American fleet of some 5,000 aircraft swept over the battlefield and fell upon the German supply columns. As General Arnold writes: "The A.A.F. took to the air with enormously superior strength. We headed, with hundreds of planes, for the supply lines through which the vital means for Rundstedt to go on, or even to stay where he was, would have to move. From then on there was no let-up. We prepared to isolate the battlefield."[41]

Thus, having effected a penetration of some fifty miles, von Rundstedt was compelled to pull out. By 1st January he was in full retreat, and, to cover it, on that day he sent over 700 aircraft to attack his enemy's airfields in France, Belgium and Holland, which, as Arnold points out, showed that the *Luftwaffe* was not to be underestimated—they destroyed nearly 200 Allied machines. On the 22nd the combined Anglo-American air forces destroyed 4,200 pieces of heavy equipment, including locomotives, railway trucks, tanks, motor and horse-drawn vehicles. By the 31st the salient was eliminated.

After the war, Speer, the German Minister of Munitions, is reported to have said: "Transport difficulties were decisive in causing the swift breakdown of the Ardennes offensive . . . the most advanced railheads of the Reichsbahn were withdrawn further and further back during the offensive owing to the continuous air attacks."[42]

The losses suffered in this battle were considerable for the Allies and catastrophic for the Germans. The former lost approximately 50,000 men and the latter 70,000 in killed, wounded and missing, as well as 50,000 captured, 600 tanks, 1,600 aircraft and countless vehicles.

To the military student this battle clearly shows: (1) The enormous

[40]Immediately after the Germans attacked, Eisenhower sent the U.S. 101st Airborne Division by road to hold Bastogne. General McAuliffe commanded the 101st. When surrounded and asked to surrender, his answer was a single word—Nuts!" For a full account of the remarkable defence of Bastogne, see *Bastogne*, Colonel S. L. A. Marshall and others (1946).

[41]*General Arnold's Second Report*, p. 36.

[42]See "Air Attack on Communications," Air Marshal Sir Robert H. M. S. Saundby. *Journal of the Royal United Service Institution*, November, 1945, p. 481.

influence of weather on tactical flying; (2) the power air supremacy places in the hands of the defender (or attacker) to destroy the administrative foundations of his enemy's army; (3) the importance of shaping tactics according to each tactical situation; and (4) the futility of the cordon system in attack or defence, which so long ago was proclaimed by Napoleon to be good only against smugglers.

Finally, it proved that the "broad-front" distribution, decided upon by Eisenhower, in spite of Montgomery's warning, was a faulty one. Had the northern offensive front ended at Mainz, and had the front south of Mainz been solely occupied by a line of observation, and had the U.S. Seventh Army and the bulk of the First French Army been held in general reserve in the neighbourhood of Sedan, there would have been no Ardennes battle, nor would there have been any worth-while eruption of the Germans south of Mainz. Though, as things were in December, 1944, no great military damage was done, six very important political weeks were lost. The enormity of Eisenhower's distribution can be measured by supposing that it had been made in May, 1940. Had it been, then there can be little doubt that his armies would have suffered a similar fate to Gamelin's. To say that, had he been faced by the May situation he would have made some other distribution is no apology, because whatever the situation is the principles of war should not be violated.

(5) *The Russian 1945 Winter and Spring Campaigns*

In the circumstances created by the invasion of France, it is strange that nothing of importance occurred on the Russian-Polish front from mid-August, 1944, until mid-January, 1945. If this long halt were due to difficulties of supply, then the same did not hold good on the Danubian front; for in spite of communications there being far longer, the offensive was continuous. Whatever the reason was, whether political or logistical, the five months' rest was spent in re-grouping the Russian armies. By January, their distribution was as follows:

(1) In the north, two groups of armies, General Chernyakhovsky's and Marshal Rokossovsky's. The former operating from the Memel southwards and the latter from the Narew northwards against East Prussia.

(2) In the centre, two groups of armies, Marshal Zhukov's and Marshal Koniev's. The one to assault Warsaw and advance due westwards on Berlin, and the other to invade Upper Silesia and force the upper Oder.

(3) In the south, two groups of armies, Marshal Malinovsky's and Marshal Tolbukhin's, to clear Slovakia, occupy Budapest and advance on Vienna.

(4) Linking Malinovsky's right with Koniev's left was General Petrov's group, its main aim being to clear the Northern Carpathians.

In all, these seven groups were composed of at least 300 divisions and 25 tank armies, followed by numerous Cossack forces.

Having already made so strong an effort to resist in East Prussia and in

BUDAPEST AND VIENNA CAMPAIGNS, 29th NOVEMBER, 1944-12th APRIL, 1945

Hungary, the German armies opposing the Russian centre were totally inadequate. In all, they would seem to have numbered seven armies in Slovakia and Hungary, of which three were Hungarian; four on the Upper Vistula and four in East Prussia. In addition, and largely on paper, there was a considerable number of recently raised *Volkssturm* units, of little fighting value. Excepting these and purely garrison troops, it is doubtful whether the German field armies numbered more than 100 weak divisions, with practically no reserve of petrol for their aircraft, tanks and transport.

In the south, the winter campaign was opened on 29th November by Marshal Tolbukhin's advance on Budapest. Setting out from south of Mohács, from where Solyman the Magnificent had marched on Budapest in 1526, his columns moved westwards towards Lake Balaton and north-wards towards Lake Valencze, and by 8th December he had deployed his main strength between Lepseny on the northern end of Balaton and Ercsi to the south of Budapest. Meanwhile, Malinovsky advanced on the east of the Hungarian capital, his northern columns directed on Vac, situated on the elbow of the Danube. Forcing a crossing over the River Ipel, he advanced on Komarno, the main German base on the Hungarian front.

In order to secure his depots there, as well as shorten his front, General Friesner, in command of the German and Hungarian armies, decided on a bold and imaginative plan. It was to hold the fronts along the Hron river and between the River Drava and Lake Balaton defensively; strongly garrison Budapest and abandon the city; and lastly establish a striking force behind the sector linking the above defensive fronts—namely, between Komarno and Lake Balaton. His idea was to be in a position to strike at any attempt to turn or assault the Buda half of Budapest from the north, south or west. The weak point in his plan was that he had not sufficient force to hold the Hron line in strength.

On 20th December, Tolbukhin took Szekes Fahervar on the west of Lake Velencze, and crossing the Vertesz Hills captured Esztergom on the Danube. Next, in co-operation with Malinovsky, he completed the encirclement of Budapest. This presented Friesner with the opportunity he was waiting for. On 2nd and 3rd January he launched two violent counter-attacks; the one between Komarno and Esztergom and the other between Komarno and Bicske. Re-taking Esztergom on the 5th, he next swept the Russians off the Vertesz Hills, but was unable to re-take Bicske, because on the 10th Malinovsky had broken through the Hron defences and had advanced to within two miles of Komarno. This attack brought Friesner north of the Danube, and though he checked Malinovsky's advance, the shift of strength enabled Tolbukhin to close in on Buda.

Pest was completely subdued by 18th January. But these successive offensive operations had so exhausted Friesner's striking force that he was compelled to leave Buda to its fate. Early in February Malinovsky opened his last assault on the city, and after a desperate struggle stormed its final strongholds on Gelerthegy and Palace Hills on the 13th. Thus the second phase of the Danubian campaign ended by opening the road to Vienna. Meanwhile to the north the road to Berlin was being cleared.

West of the Vistula, between the River Pilica and the Carpathians, the four German armies commanded by General Harpe were struck two terrific blows. One was delivered by Marshal Koniev, starting from the Sandomierz-Baranow bridgehead, and the other by Marshal Zhukov from his two main bridgeheads, the one west of Magnuszew and the other at Kazimierz. At the same time, to the south of Koniev, General Petrov's

THE ODER AND LOWER VISTULA CAMPAIGNS, 12th JANUARY-8th APRIL, 1945

Group moved on Jaslo, north of the Dukla Pass leading through the Carpathians.

Koniev's attack was launched on 12th January, Zhukov's on the 14th. Both were preceded by violent artillery bombardments, and both resulted in an immediate break-through. On Koniev's right the Germans fought desperately to hold on to Kielce, while his left swept forward at great speed. With Zhukov it was much the same. His right fought its way across the Pilica, gained the Warsaw-Radom road, and turning northwards up it approached the Polish capital from the west. This led to its evacuation by the Germans, and it was occupied by the Russians on the 17th. At the same time Zhukov's left pinched out Radom. Other disasters immediately followed: Petrov took Jaslo, and the Germans abandoning Cracow, Koniev's left wing occupied the city on the 19th. Equally important, on the same day Zhukov took Gostynin, Kutno and Lodz.

Meanwhile, on the 14th, Chernyakhovsky and Rokossovsky had fallen upon East Prussia; the first advancing from south of the River Memel, crossed the frozen marshlands and moved on Tilsit and Insterburg. Tilsit was entered on the 19th, and from it the defences of the Insterburg Gap were turned from the north. The second crossed the Vistula north and south of Pultusk and advanced on Osterode and Deutsch Eylau. On the 20th Rokossovsky captured Neidenburg. Crossing the 1914 battlefield of Tannenberg, his left linked up with Zhukov's right in the neighbourhood of Plock. On the 22nd Osterode, Deutsch Eylau and Allenstein were occupied, and on the 26th Marienburg was taken and the Baltic coast reached near Tolkemit, north of Elbing. Thus, except by sea, East Prussia was severed from Pomerania. Meanwhile, Chernyakhovsky was breaking through the Masurian defences.

The eastern half of Western Poland having now been overrun, the sole obstacle of any size which lay between the Russians and Berlin was the River Oder, a strong natural defensive line strengthened by a chain of old and modern fortresses, the more important being Küstrin, Glogau, Breslau, Oppeln and Ratibor. Between Thorn and Breslau there were no natural obstacles, and even had there been the Germans would not have had strength enough to hold them.

On 20th January Koniev's group crossed the German frontier north and south of Breslau, and four days later took Oppeln. Outflanking the industrial towns of Upper Silesia from the south and west, one after the other was taken, while bridgeheads over the Oder were established at Oppeln and in the vicinity of Brieg and Steinau. On 4th February Koniev, having completely surrounded Breslau, crossed the Oder at Steinau, Brieg and Oppeln, and by the 15th had advanced to Bunslau, sixty miles west of Breslau and seventy east of Dresden. There his momentum petered out.

Pushing west of Bromberg (Bydgoszez), Zukhov encircled Posen (Poznan), at which town the Germans, after leaving a strong garrison to hold it, fell back on Schwerin on the Warta and thence on Frankfurt on the Oder and Küstrin. Soldin was lost by them on 2nd February, and the same day, Zhukov occupied Bärwalde. By the 10th Zhukov's central advance came to a stop. Having crossed the 1759 battlefield of Kunnersdorf he reached the Oder opposite Lebus. In rear of him the fortresses of Schneidemühl, Deutsche Krone, Posen and Arnswalde were still holding out, and they crippled his communications.

Zhukov's right flank ran from Soldin—twenty-five miles north of

Küstrin—to Thorn, which fell on 9th February. North of it, in Pomerania, increasing numbers of German units were coming in by sea from East Prussia, and as these forces threatened his communications, Zhukov decided first to take the above mentioned fortresses, and, secondly, cut the Germans in Eastern Pomerania off from those in Western. On 11th February he took Deutsche Krone, next Schneidemühl on the 14th; then Arnswalde on the 22nd, and lastly Posen on the 23rd; after which he advanced between Wangerin and Falkenberg towards the Baltic, reaching the coast near Kolberg on 9th March; but Kolberg itself was not occupied until the 18th.

While Kolberg was being besieged, and on account of Rokossovsky's advance on Gdynia, the Germans began to evacuate Danzig by sea. On 23rd March Rokossovsky reached Zoppot, immediately to the south of Gdynia. This enabled him to attack Danzig from the north—its most vulnerable flank—and on the 30th the city was stormed. Thus for Rokossovsky the Baltic campaign ended. He was now free to relieve Zhukov's right wing on the Lower Oder.

Meanwhile, early in March, Zhukov worked his way into Küstrin, and except for some island forts which held out until the 30th, he occupied the whole of the old fortress on the 12th. This enabled him to throw two bridges over the Oder, one to the north and the other to the south of the town.

While these several operations were being undertaken, the Germans put up a fierce struggle in East Prussia, where they still had some twenty weak divisions. Königsberg was fanatically defended and was not entirely isolated, for by way of Pillau its sea communications still remained open. Advancing westwards, Chernyakhovsky had taken Friedland on 1st February and Preussisch Eylau on the 9th. On the 17th he was mortally wounded and replaced by Marshal Vassilevsky, who early in March invested Königsberg, but it was not until 8th April that he finally assaulted the fortress, which surrendered to him the next day.

When Zhukov's and Koniev's offenseives were nearing their end, the Danubian campaign entered its third and final phase, and during the third week in February it was opened by a German and Hungarian offensive against the Russians on the line of the Hron and between the Drava and Lake Balaton. These operations were so encouraging that General Friesner was reinforced by the Sixth Panzer Army, which had recently taken part in the Ardennes offensive, and on 3rd March he launched a powerful attack, strongly supported by the *Luftwaffe*, between Lakes Balaton and Valencze, and advancing on Herczeg-Falva came within a few miles of the Danube. There, as had happened in the Battle of the Ardennes, his tanks ran out of fuel, and by the 15th such as could move were forced back towards their starting points.

This failure was rapidly followed up by his enemy. On the 18th Tolbukhin struck south of the Vertesz Hills and Malinovsky north of them, the one re-taking Szekes-Fehervar and the other capturing Esztegom. Next came a blow against the German-Hungarian flanks. On the 27th Malinovsky forced the Hron and three days later took Komarno, while Tolbukhin, striking between the Drava and Lake Balaton, captured Zala-Egerszeg and a large number of Hungarians. The whole German-Hungarian front now began to crumble, and on the 29th Tolbukhin's advance crossed into Austria at Koszeg.

From then onwards the Russians closed in on Vienna; Tolbukhin from the south by way of Weiner Neustadt, and Malinovsky from the east along the Vienna-Budapest road and by way of Bratislava (Pressburg), which was abandoned by the Germans on 3rd April. On the 7th Malinovsky penetrated into the eastern suburbs of the Austrian capital, and the next day neared its centre. On the 11th and 12th the Germans and Hungarians were driven over the Danube, and on the following day the city was completely in Russian hands.

Thus was the Russian political objective gained, and as Dr. Benes and Marshal Tito were already in the Soviet pocket, Russia had now pushed her political frontier right across the southern half of the waist of Central Europe from Prague to Trieste. Therefore, all that now remained for her to do, was to advance from the Oder to the Elbe, when provisionally, if not actually, her Western *Lebensraum* would be established.

(6) *The Conquest of Germany*

In a sane war, Rundstedt's defeat in the Ardennes would have brought hostilities to an immediate end; but because of unconditional surrender the war was far from being sane. Gagged by this idiotic slogan, the Western Allies could offer no terms, however severe. Conversely, their enemy could ask for none, however submissive. So it came about that, like Samson, Hitler was left to pull the edifice of Central Europe down upon himself, his people and their enemies. The war having already been irretrievably lost, chaos was now his political aim, and thanks to unconditional surrender he was in a position to achieve it.

The war, in fact, had ceased to be a strategical problem, and having entered upon its purely political course, the race was no longer between armed forces, but instead between two political systems: on the one hand that of the Western Allies, and on the other that of Russia. Which of these two would dominate Eastern and Central Europe—this was the question?

Because by the end of January the Russians had advanced to Budapest and were standing on the Oder, politically Eastern Europe had already been lost to the democracies. And as nothing could now prevent the Russians from occupying Vienna, the sole possibility left of salvaging what then would remain of Central Europe lay in the occupation of Berlin by the Americans and British in advance of their Eastern Ally. Nevertheless, at this critical moment, instead of acting with boldness, General Eisenhower

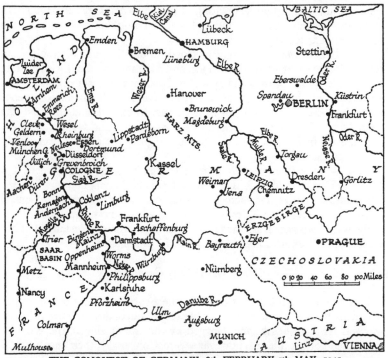

THE CONQUEST OF GERMANY, 8th FEBRUARY-5th MAY, 1945

displayed ultra caution. The whole problem in his mind was still a strategical one—the conquest of Germany—when it clearly should have been a political one—the occupation of Berlin. To win the war strategically and lose it politically was from the point of view of the Western Allies to declare it null and void; this he or his masters showed no signs of realizing.

His plan was to continue the "broad front" policy and advance to the Rhine along its entire length in three methodical stages. First, the Twenty-First Army Group and the U.S. Ninth Army were to occupy the Rhine below Düsseldorf; secondly, the Twelfth Army Group was to clear the Saar Basin and occupy the Rhine between Düsseldorf and Mainz; and, thirdly, the Sixth Army Group was to clear the Colmar pocket and advance to the Rhine between Mainz and Switzerland.

The first stage was opened by the First Canadian Army on 8th February. The weather was appalling, and, in consequence, the advance was slow, "the fighting," writes Eisenhower, "soon developed into a bitter slugging match in which the enemy had to be forced back yard by yard."[43] Cleve was taken on the 12th, and on the 14th the Rhine was reached opposite Emmerich. Meanwhile, the U.S. Ninth Army, which should have opened its offensive between the 10th and 15th, was delayed by the enemy breaching the Roer Dams, and it was not until the 23rd that the floods had sufficiently subsided to permit of an advance northwards towards the Canadians. In the Jülich sector the River Roer was crossed and Düren cleared on the 25th. By 1st March München Gladbach had been gained, Grevenbroich had fallen, Neuss had been entered, and Venlo reached. Two days later contact was made with the Canadians at Geldern. Thus was the whole of the western bank of the Rhine between Düsseldorf and the sea, except for an enemy bridgehead at Wesel, occupied by the Allies, and this bridgehead was cleared on the 10th. During these operations Montgomery states that the Germans put up an intense and fanatical opposition.[44]

The second stage opened with the drive of the U.S. First Army towards Cologne. By 10th February the River Erft was gained, and on the following day its western bank was cleared. Bridgeheads were then established, and on 5th March advance elements of the VIIth Corps entered Cologne, and two days later the whole of the city west of the Rhine was occupied. Further to the south the advance was even more spectacular. On 7th March the IIIrd Corps drove the enemy back towards Remagen, and by a stroke of luck seized the bridge spanning the Rhine there before the Germans could fire the demolition charges. At once a lodgement on the eastern bank was made, and by the 24th it had grown into a bridgehead twenty-five miles long and ten deep. From it the Ruhr was threatened from the south.

Meanwhile, during February, the U.S. Third Army was engaged in preparing to move west. By the 23rd resistance in the Saar-Moselle triangle was overcome. Trier fell on 2nd March, and on the 9th the advance reached the Rhine at Andernach, where contact was made with the First Army. The next day the western bank of the Rhine from Coblenz to Andernach was cleared, and by the 19th this clearance was extended to Bingen. Then followed another dramatic surprise; on the night of the 22nd, without any special preparations, Patton effected a crossing of the Rhine near Oppenheim, south of Mainz. This same day resistance ceased in Mainz, and on

---

[43] *Supreme Commander's Report*, p. 107.
[44] "Despatch," *Supplement to the London Gazette*, 3rd September, 1946, p. 4446.

the following day Speyer was reached and the German forces west of Karlsruhe placed in a hopeless position.

In the south, the third stage was opened in the middle of March. Having between 20th January and 3rd February eliminated the Colmar pocket, on 15th March the Sixth Army Group began its advance to the Rhine, and by the 25th all organized resistance on its western bank had ended.

Of these operations Eisenhower writes:

"No defeat the Germans suffered in the war, except possibly Tunisia, was more devastating in the completeness of the destruction inflicted upon his (*sic*) forces than that which was suffered in the Saar Basin . . . The whole operation was characterized by boldness, speed and determination, and the victory was so complete that when General Patton thrust a division across the Rhine on the night of 22nd-23rd March he was able to do so with almost no reaction from the enemy."[45]

Vast though the above operations were, they were no more than the curtain-raiser of the main event—the crossing of the Rhine north of the Ruhr, supported by a secondary thrust from the bridgeheads in the Frankfurt area in the direction of Kassel, the object of which was to envelop the Ruhr from the east. The plan was given the somewhat ominous code name of "Plunder," and in more detail for the Twenty-First Army Group was as follows:

The crossing of the Rhine north of the Ruhr was to be carried out between Rheinburg and Rees by the Twenty-First Army Group and the U.S. Ninth Army, both under command of Field-Marshal Montgomery; the Ninth Army on the right and the Second British Army on the left, the one south of and the other north of Wesel. To assist the advance of the latter, the First Allied Airborne Army was to drop the U.S. 17th and the British 6th Airborne Divisions north of Wesel, this time immediately following the ground assault in order that it might come as a surprise. On its left the Second Army was protected by the First Canadian Army.

Long before the operation was launched, on lines very similar to those employed prior to the invasion of Normandy, the Ruhr had been isolated by air attack. The programme of interdiction had opened on 21st February, and a vast tonnage of bombs was rained down on the German railways, bridges and vital points. For example, on 11th March 5,000 tons were dropped on the Essen rail centre, and on the following day 5,487 tons on Dortmund. Between 21st and 24th March no less than 42,000 sorties were made against Germany.

The width of the Rhine on Montgomery's front was between four hundred and five hundred yards, liable to increase to from seven hundred to one thousand two hundred yards at high water, and the mean velocity of the current was about three and a half knots. With this breadth of water to cross, the whole operation was organized on amphibious lines—it was an inland water-borne invasion.

At 8 p.m. on 23rd March the crossing of the Rhine was heralded by a violent artillery barrage of one hour's duration; immediately followed by a Commando assault on Wesel. Next, the main attacks went in over the river, and meeting with slight opposition secure lodgements were established on the eastern bank. As these crossings were being made, the U.S. 17th and British 6th Airborne Divisions—the one flown from the Paris area and the other from East Anglia—dropped on the eastern bank within artillery supporting distance of the western. The two divisions were carried in 1,572 planes and 1,326 gliders, and were protected by 2,153 aircraft of the Tactical Air Forces. The casualties suffered were insignificant.

Meanwhile, in the central sector, the Oppenheim bridgehead was extended to nine miles long and six miles deep, and on the 25th Darmstadt was taken and the bridges over the Main at Aschaffenburg seized. While this advance was under way, the U.S. First Army bridgehead at Remagen was expanded, and on the 26th the Germans were forced out of the Sieg river line. Further to the south Limburg was reached.

On the 29th the U.S. Third Army took Frankfurt and advanced on Kassel. Meanwhile, on the 26th the U.S. Seventh Army had established its first bridgehead near Worms, and on the following day had linked up with the Third Army south of Darmstadt. On the 28th the Seventh Army crossed the Neckar, and on the 29th occupied Mannheim. Three days later the First French Army crossed the Rhine at Philippsburg. Thus, between 23rd March and 1st April, the Rhine had been breached along its entire course, and, as Eisenhower says, at fantastically small cost. This success resulted in von Rundstedt being removed from his command for the last time, the command of his beaten armies being given to Kesselring, who was recalled from Italy.

Within a week of crossing the Rhine the German forces were in complete disintegration. All organization on the Western Front had collapsed; yet the fighting went on so that unconditional surrender might receive its belly full.

In the north the first objective now became the envelopment of the Ruhr by the Twenty-First Army Group from the north and the Twelfth Army Group from the south, the point of junction between the two being fixed in the Kassel-Paderborn area, not far from where Varus in A.D. 9 lost his legions. The Sixth Army Group was ordered to protect the right flank of the Twelfth.

This double envelopment—one of the greatest Cannæ operations ever undertaken—was successfully accomplished on 1st April, the Ninth Army from the north linking up with the First from the south near Lippstadt. Inside the pocket formed were trapped the whole of German Army Group B and two corps of Army Group H, with Field-Marshal Model in command. For twelve days Model put up a stiff fight in the industrial towns; but on the 13th resistance began to disintegrate, and on the 18th he surrendered with thirty general officers and 325,000 men.

While this vast encirclement was in progress, Eisenhower decided on his final plan to bring the war to an end. What was it? The answer is one of the strangest in military history, and the gist of it we will give in his own words. In his *Report* he writes: "Berlin, I was now certain, no longer represented a military objective of major importance . . . Military factors, when the enemy was on the brink of final defeat, were more important in my eyes than the political considerations involved in an Allied capture of the capital. The function of our forces must be to crush the German armies rather than to dissipate our strength in the occupation of empty and ruined cities."[46] If at the eleventh hour of a war political considerations are less important than military factors, well may it be asked, *when are they more important?* And, if they are never so, then war cannot possibly be a political instrument.

[46]*Ibid.*, p. 131. On this question Ralph Ingersoll is illuminating, he writes: "In seeking to win the war, the United States of America had no regard . . . for political considerations . . ." (p. 46). War to them "was like football . . . It was a game played for cheers from the grandstand . . . a game in which people get hurt and a grim game which is taken seriously—but still a game" (p. 244). "British objectives were not strictly military, but included political objectives as well. They wanted Berlin and the north coast of Germany as insurance that in the event of the German collapse they should not fall into the hands of the Russians" (p. 168). And again: "During the war, the British attempted to manipulate our (American) military policy so that we would fight the war the way they wanted it fought—which was an anti-Russian way. They did not succeed" (p. 271). According to Ingersoll, it was General Bradley and not Eisenhower who was responsible for the lack of political insight in not marching on Berlin. With high approval Ingersoll affirms that it was Bradley's idea, and that "Bradley was so completely the boss that Eisenhower had no choice but to approve—and forwarding Bradley's plan, he got approval back from Washington" (p. 246). Next he writes: "Within twenty-four hours after Bradley's plan hit Washington and was read by the British representatives of the Combined Chiefs of Staff, the lid went right off Anglo-American relations . . . The British blast was that Bradley had no right to drive due east to the Elbe, but should join Montgomery to force the way to Berlin. The British Chiefs accused Marshall and the other American Chiefs of breaking a firm agreement to back Montgomery to take Berlin . . . The spirit of the reply which came boiling back from the American Joint Chiefs of Staff was in the idiom of General McAuliffe's famous 'Nuts!' at Bastogne. The chapter and verse, spelled out, was that there had been no agreement, written, oral and implicit—and that there would be no change whatever in Bradley's plans, which promised the surest, quickest, most decisive total victory over the German

His reasons for adopting this extraordinary outlook are equally strange. There were two. One was that the Russians were then thirty miles from Berlin and that an entanglement with them was to be avoided, and the other was that the Germans might concentrate in what was called the "National Redoubt"—the mountainous area in Southern Germany, the Tyrol and Western Austria—100 divisions and up to 30 Panzer divisions! Though at one time this was possible, it was so no longer, because the stupendous air power of the Allies prohibited it.

Abandoning a move on Berlin, Eisenhower decided on an offensive in the centre by the U.S. First and Third Armies from Kassel towards Leipzig, and to assist in this the Ninth Army reverted from the Twenty-First Army Group to the Twelfth on 4th April. And while this operation was under way, those of the Twenty-First and Sixth Army Groups were to be of a limited nature. Of these two groups the first was to strike towards the Elbe, and the second to protect the southern flank of the central drive. "When the central thrust had achieved its object, the principal task was to be an advance to the Baltic and the cleaning out of the whole northern area from Kiel to Lübeck westward by the Twenty-First Army Group."[47]

Kassel was cleared by the Third Army on 4th April; Weimar was reached on the 11th; Jena and Chemnitz on the 13th; and the frontier of Czechoslovakia was crossed on the 18th. Meanwhile, the Ninth Army pushed on towards Brunswick, reaching the Elbe south of Magdeburg on the 11th. It entered Brunswick on the 12th, and after severe fighting took Magdeburg on the 18th. On the 11th the First Army offensive south of the Harz Mountains got under way and made rapid progress, reaching Dessau on the 14th, and clearing the whole of the Harz area by the 21st.

While the Twelfth Army Group was pushing eastwards, the Twenty-First advanced on Bremen and Hamburg, the First Canadian Army clearing North-east Holland. The Second British Army crossed the Weser

State . . . The next blast was neither pure nor military. Winston Churchill's hat sailed into the ring . . ." (p. 248). "Mr. Churchill apparently said everything but the truth, which was that the military situation had nothing to do with it—Bradley being militarily one thousand per cent sound—but that, the quick defeat of Germany be damned, the British Empire wanted British troops in Berlin before the Russians got there and, *en route*, wanted British troops in Hamburg and Bremen, which it was feared the Russians might occupy and try to hold at the conference table. President Roosevelt said NO—and the war and the President's life ended with very bad blood between the two great leaders of the Western Powers" (p. 249). The truth would seem to be that throughout the war the Americans were such military amateurs that they failed to realize that war is a political instrument, and that the defeat of the enemy is but a means to a political end. Looking upon war as a game, they imagined that once it was won both sides would disperse and, like Candide, go home and cultivate their gardens.

[47] *Supreme Commander's Report*, p. 131.

on the 5th. Lüneberg was reached on the 18th and, while Hamburg was masked, the Elbe was crossed on the 29th and the advance pushed forward on Lübeck. During these advances the Sixth Army Group moved on Bayreuth. There it linked up with the Twelfth, and on the 16th Nürnberg was entered. At the same time the First French Army captured Karlsruhe and Pforzheim.

These astonishing advances, some opposed and some not, and not a few covering one hundred miles in a day, were only possible because preparations had been made to supply the armoured columns by air. "In executing this task," writes Eisenhower, "the carrier planes accomplished remarkable feats, and, invaluable as they had proved throughout the campaigns in North-west Europe, the 'flying boxcars' were never more essential than in these concluding stages of the war. Landing on improvised airfields close to the front line and sometimes within pockets temporarily surrounded by the enemy, 1,500 IX Troop-Carrier Command C-47's, supplemented by heavy bombers stripped for the purpose, flew over 20,000 sorties during April to carry nearly 60,000 tons of freight (including 10,255,509 gallons of gasoline) to the forward elements of the ground forces . . . Without such assistance it would have been impossible for the armoured divisions to achieve the sweeping successes which attended their operations."[48]

At length the lesson had been learnt, and it was the principal lesson of the war on land: *That, once superiority in the air is assured, the primary military purpose of aircraft in war lies in the logistical and not in the tactical sphere.* Though soldiers must still fight on the ground, they can now be supplied by air. This is the *fundamental* difference between present-day and past land warfare. Dropping high explosives is altogether secondary to it.

While Western Germany was being conquered, the final battles for Eastern Germany and Northern Italy were fought, and by mid-April from west, east and south the Third Reich was rapidly compressed into chaos.

In the East, as we have seen, "political considerations" had for long been steadily supplanting "military factors." The Russians were not only waging war to defeat their enemy, but to win something they held was worth while—a political, social, economic and strategical *Lebensraum* in Eastern and Central Europe. Therefore, on 17th April, four days after their occupation of Vienna, they set out to conquer Berlin, then the point of greatest political importance, and also to establish their western frontier on the Elbe, because they understood its strategical value as the great thoroughfare linking the northern half of Central Europe to the southern and the Danube.

[48]*Ibid.*, p. 137.

The advance on Berlin was undertaken by Zhukov's and Koniev's groups of armies, the one advancing from the Oder westwards, and the other from the River Niesse northwards. Opposed to them were four German armies, the Twenty-First between Stettin and Eberswalde, the Twelfth, with the Third Tank Army in support, from Eberswalde to Frankfurt, and south of Frankfurt the Ninth on the Niesse. In Berlin there may have been 250,000 armed men. If so, then such a force was inadequate to garrison so large a city, which was almost impossible to defend should the Russians gain the Ring Autobahn which encircled it.

On the 17th the curtain was raised for the final act in the World's Tragedy. On the morning of that day Koniev moved forward from his bridgeheads on the Niesse, and directing his left on Dresden and Torgau, he swung his centre and right northwards towards Berlin, scattering the German Ninth Army. Simultaneously, Zhukov unleashed his armies from their bridgeheads north and south of Küstrin, broke through the strong fortifications of the German Twelfth Army, and on the 22nd reached the Ring Autobahn and moved westwards along it towards Spandau, while Koniev gained it from the south.

On the 25th two events of outstanding importance occurred: (1) Berlin was completely encircled, and (2) the van of the Russian 58th Guards Division of Koniev's group linked up with the advanced patrols of the 273rd Regiment of the U.S. First Army at Torgau on the Elbe.

In Berlin ferocious street-fighting had already broken out, and by the 29th it was carried into Charlottenburg, Wilmerdorf, Moabit, Shöneberg and other quarters of the capital. Soon, nothing was left to the Germans but the Inner Stadt, the whole of which was raked by gunfire. On the 30th Hitler shot himself, and on 2nd May what remained of the Berlin garrison surrendered.

Meanwhile, in Italy collapse was equally rapid. On 10th April Field-Marshal Alexander set out on his final offensive between Faenza and Lake Commachio. Bologna was taken on the 21st, the River Po was crossed and Verona entered on the 26th. Two days later, as they were attempting to cross into Switzerland, Mussolini and his mistress, Clara Petacci, were assassinated by Italian partisans at Dongo near Lake Como, and on the 29th, at Caserta, General Heinrich von Vietinghoff-Scheel, now commanding the German forces in Italy, unconditionally surrendered to Field-Marshal Alexander with close on 1,000,000 men.

Once a junction had been made with the Russians, Eisenhower halted his armies on the Rivers Elbe and Mulde and on the Erzgebirge. Orders were then issued for the Twenty-First Group to continue its advance on Lübeck; the Twelfth to move on Linz; and the Sixth to be prepared to operate against the "National Redoubt" should the Germans occupy it.

As to Berlin, Eisenhower writes, that it would have "to await the development of the situation following the accomplishment of (these) more important tasks."[49]

While these movements were under way, on 3rd May Admiral Friedeburg, now head of the German Navy, accompanied by three officers, presented themselves at Montgomery's Headquarters near Lüneberg and asked to be allowed to surrender the Third Panzer, Twelfth and Twenty-First Armies which had been fighting against the Russians. Montgomery refusing to discuss capitulation on these terms, on the 4th Friedeburg returned and announced that he had received authority unconditionally to surrender all German armed forces in Northern Germany, Holland, Schleswig-Holstein and Denmark. This was agreed to as a local tactical measure, and accordingly the instrument of surrender was signed, and at 8 a.m. on 5th May the "cease fire" sounded along the front of the Twenty-First Army Group. Two days later the instrument was signed again at Supreme Allied Headquarters in Rheims, and on the 9th it was ratified in Berlin. Thus, the war in Europe was concluded by the victors accepting unconditional responsibilities.

[49]*Ibid.*, p. 138.

CHAPTER X

CONSUMMATION OF ALLIED INITIATIVE IN THE PACIFIC

(1) *The Re-conquest of Burma*

With the defeat of Germany, the strategical position of Japan became a hopeless one, and in a normal war her capitulation would rapidly have followed. But this was not to be, for once again unconditional surrender barred the road to peace. Therefore, in this chapter of anti-climax, we must first return to the summer of 1944, when the great salient Japan had thrust into the Pacific was caving in and when its southern haunch in Burma was about to collapse.

The defeats the Japanese had sustained in Arakan, at Kohima and at Impal, together with General Stilwell's advance to Myikynia, had handed the initiative they so far had held over to their adversaries. Hence onwards it was the Allies who were to be on the offensive. Nevertheless, their aim remained exactly what it had been—the development of overland communications with China. Its attainment demanded two things: First, the conquest of Northern Burma, and, secondly, of Southern Burma; for as Admiral Mountbatten has since pointed out, he "did not feel it was militarily sound to remain poised in mid-Burma without any firm surface lines of communications, particularly during the monsoon."[1]

To gain this vast end—the re-conquest of the whole of Burma—Mountbatten planned two closely related operations; the one from the north, the other from the south. In accordance with the first, the Fourteenth Army (IVth and XXXIIIrd Corps) under Lieut.-General Sir William Slim, was to advance from Manipur across the Chindwin into the Yeu-Shwebo area north-west of Mandalay, where airfields existed, while General Stilwell's and Marshal Wei-Li-Huang's armies advanced on Bhamo from the north and east. This triple operation would place the Japanese in Northern Burma between three fires. The second was to recapture the Rangoon area by a combined airborne and seaborne assault, and then advance north, driving the Japanese towards the Fourteenth Army and away from their

---

[1]"The Strategy of the South-East Asia Campaign," Admiral the Viscount Mountbatten. *Journal of the Royal United Service Institution.* November, 1946, p. 479.

main communications with Siam. To carry out this operation six additional divisions, including an airborne division, and a large number of landing craft would be required from the United Kingdom, and as they could only be provided should Germany be defeated by October, they were never forthcoming. Therefore, this part of the plan had to be scrapped, and it meant that Southern Burma would have to be conquered from the north.

At once the problem became one of how to supply the Fourteenth Army once it moved south of the Shwebo area. It depended almost entirely upon air transport, which was based on Assam, and at Shwebo the useful radius of action of the Dakota supply aircraft, which was two hundred and fifty miles, would be fully attained. Therefore, to supply the Fourteenth Army during its advance on Rangoon, it was essential to establish air bases closer in. This could best be done by occupying the islands of Akyab and Ramree. Consequently, it was decided to push on with operations in Arakan and secure these two islands by seaborne landings. In order to prepare this amphibious operation, Admiral Sir Arthur Power was instructed to collect all available craft. In fact, the whole operation had to be improvised upon what was at hand and what could be found.

Though this plan could not be fully implemented until the monsoon was over, there was no pause in operations, and on the withdrawal of the Japanese from Imphal and Kohima they were hotly pursued until on 19th August they were driven over the India-Burma frontier. Nevertheless, such were the difficulties of the road that it was not until 3rd December that the Fourteenth Army established its main bridgehead on the Chindwin at Kalewa. Meanwhile, the XVth Corps in Arakan slowly advanced down the Mayu Peninsula towards Akyab.

In November an extensive reshuffle of the higher appointments was made. General Stilwell returned to America and was replaced by Lieut.-General R. A. Wheeler as Deputy Supreme Allied Commander, by Lieut.-General D. I. Sultan as Commander of the Chinese armies in India and Burma, and by Major-General A. C. Wedemeyer as Chief of Staff to Chiang Kai-shek. In addition to these changes, Lieut.-General Sir Oliver Leese, who had been in command of the Eighth Army in Italy, was appointed Commander-in-Chief Allied Forces, South-East Asia, which included the Eleventh Army Group (Fourteenth Army and XVth Corps), and Sultan's Northern Combat Area Command (N.C.A.C.)—in all some twenty divisions.

The N.C.A.C. now consisted of five Chinese divisions, a mixed American and Chinese brigade known as Mars Task Force, which had replaced Merrill's, also the British 36th Division commanded by Major-General F. Festing.

When General Sultan took over his command, he found its advanced

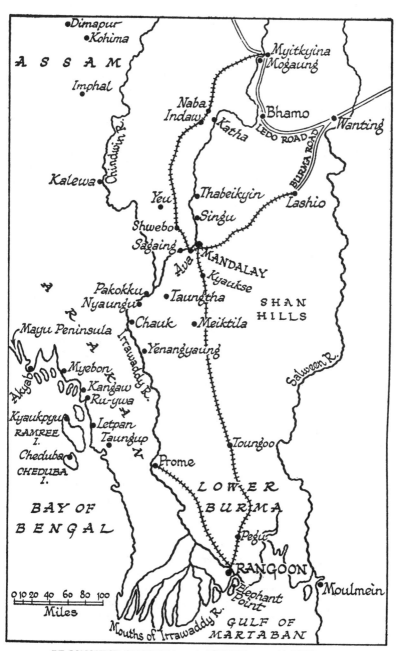

RE-CONQUEST OF BURMA, 19th AUGUST, 1944–6th MAY, 1945

troops well to the south of Myitkynia. At the time the 36th Division was moving down the railway from Mogaung, and on 16th December it contacted the 19th Indian Division of the IVth Corps of the Fourteenth Army at Naba, a little to the north-west of Katha on the Irrawaddy. On 2nd January, 1945, the Fourteenth Army occupied Yeu and on the 7th Shwebo. Meanwhile, the Chinese Sixth Army (22nd and 50th Divisions) under Lieut.-General Liao Yo Hsiang, advanced on the left of the 36th Division, and on its left moved the Chinese First Army (30th and 38th Divisions) under Lieut.-General Sun Li-jen, with the Mars Task Force and Kachin Levies. Their goal was Bhamo, which was occupied by the Chinese 38th Division on 16th December. At the same time Marshal Wei-Li-Huang's army pushed on westwards of the Salween, and on 27th January, linking up with the N.C.A.C., the Burma Road was at length re-won. The next day the first convoy from Ledo crossed the Burma-China frontier at Wanting on its way to Chungking.

These operations were almost entirely dependent upon air supply, and by the New Year, 7,500 tons were weekly being forwarded from Assam. This, however, was not enough, and more transport aircraft were required; one hundred for the troops and forty to feed the civil population. These were authorized by the Chiefs of Staff and sent to India.

Then, writes Mountbatten, ". . . we gradually built up the largest-scale air supply that has ever been seen. It was not just a question of auxiliary air supply, because 96 per cent of our supplies to the Fourteenth Army went by air. In the course of this campaign we lifted 615,000 tons of supplies to the armies, three-quarters of it by the U.S. Air Force and one-quarter by the Royal Air Force; 315,000 reinforcements were flown in, half by the British and half by the Americans; 110,000 casualties were flown out, three-quarters by the British and a quarter by the Americans. In our best month—March, 1945—we actually lifted 94,300 tons. During that time the American Air Transport Command were building up their 'Hump' traffic, so that by July they had reached their peak of 77,500 tons per month." Nevertheless, as he points out: "We had not really got the aircraft to do this, at all events on paper. In fact, we had only about half the aircraft that were really required, but we made up the other half by the expedient of flying almost double the number of hours allowed for sustained operations . . . Although there was the gravest risk that the whole of the air transport arrangements might break down . . . This went on day after day, week after week, and month after month."[2]

While Sultan and Wei-Li-Huang were re-opening the Burma Road, Slim was faced by the formidable problem of carrying the Fourteenth

[2]*Ibid.*, p. 481.

Army over the Irrawaddy, a river nearly seven times the normal width of the Rhine at Wesel.

The first step taken was on 14th January. That day the 19th Indian Division on the northern flank of the XXXIIIrd Corps established two small bridgeheads on its eastern bank at Thabeikkyin and Singu, against which General Kimura, commanding the Japanese Fifteenth and Thirty-Third Armies, at once began to mass strong forces.

In order to avoid a frontal assault against strength, Slim decided on an extremely audacious manœuvre. Knowing that Kimura was aware that the 19th Indian Division formed part of the IVth Corps, he reckoned that its presence at Singu, coupled with the advance of strong columns from the west, north-west and north towards Mandalay, would in all probability lead Kimura to assume that the IVth Corps was reinforcing the XXXIIIrd in order to strike the main blow north of Mandalay. Therefore, he decided to turn this assumption to his advantage by switching the IVth Corps, less the 19th Division, from the left of the Fourteenth Army above Mandalay southwards to Pakokku, and from there, while Kimura was massing his troops against the Singu bridgehead, seize a crossing over the Irrawaddy and strike at Kimura's rear in the Meiktila region, in which his main depots were established, and where there were eight good airfields.

This daring project entailed a march of three hundred miles across the rear of the XXXIIIrd Corps. "To supplement his tenuous road supply, already four hundred miles distant from railhead at Dimapur," writes Colonel Frank Owen, "the Fourteenth Army Commander turned to the resources at hand. These were the Chindwin River and the timber that grew upon its banks. The sappers became lumberjacks and shipwrights, and soon they were turning out hundreds of boats . . . Outboard engines and even tugs in sections were flown in from Calcutta and assembled on the river bank. Two naval gunboats, mounting Bofors and Oerlikon guns, were built and launched to patrol the river . . . By one means or another the river route was established and IVth Corps, with its necessary supplies, assembled in the assault area on time."[3]

On 14th February the 7th Indian Division of the IVth Corps seized a crossing over the Irrawaddy at Nyaungu, ten miles south of Pakokku. Even then Kimura was still misled, and doubly so because on the 11th the 20th Indian Division had effected a crossing in the west of Myinmu, not far from Mandalay, which suggested that the Nyaungu operation was a feint.

All was now ready for the combined operation which was to open the road to Rangoon. The 19th and 20th Divisions were over the river to the

[3] *The Campaign in Burma*, Lieut.-Colonel Frank Owen (1946), p. 122.

north and west of Mandalay, with the British 2nd Division in rear of the latter, and the 7th Division was at Nyaungu, one hundred miles south-west of Mandalay, with the 5th and 17th Indian Motorized Divisions and the 255th Indian Tank Brigade in rear of it.

On 19th February the offensive was initiated by an advance of the 19th Division from its bridgehead. This led to two weeks of fierce fighting, and it was not until 7th March that the 19th gained Mandalay Hill overlooking the city. So soon as the hill was cleared, the attack was pressed into the city and against Fort Dufferin, which was strongly held by the Japanese.

While the 19th was thus engaged, the 20th Division was repeatedly attacked by three Japanese divisions, because Kimura appreciated that its crossing, as well as that of the 2nd Division at Ngazun on the 24th, were a greater threat to his plan than the crossing of the 7th Division at Nyaungu.

Meanwhile, in the south, where the decisive blow was to be struck, on 20th February the 17th Indian Motorized Division advanced from the Nyaungu bridgehead, and meeting with little opposition, on the 24th gained Taungtha, forty miles to the north-west of Meiktila. On the 27th one of the eight airfields was won and at once brought into use. This success was followed by a furious battle for the remaining seven, which lasted until 5th March, when Meiktila was finally taken by the 255th Indian Tank Brigade. Thereupon Kimura determined to retake it and the whole Meiktila area in order to clear his communications.

Striking at the Nyaungu bridgehead to cut the 17th Division off from its base, Kimura might well have succeeded in his object; but, as Colonel Owen points out, "He could not contest the air route, and Allied transport planes, flying twelve hours a day, continued to land on the airfields and unload supplies and men even while the Japanese artillery ranged on air-craft already on the strip."[4] Thus the Meiktila "box" was able to hold out while other factors intervened.

While the 17th and 5th Divisions were battling in Meiktila, the 19th Division took Maymyo, and after heavy fighting Mandalay. The 2nd Division advanced against slight opposition and seized Ava, while the 20th moved with great speed and after a week's heavy fighting took Kyaukse. Heavily mauled the Japanese 15th, 53rd, 31st and 33rd Divisions were forced off the main Mandalay-Meiktila road and into the hills. Thus the XXXIIIrd Corps effectively removed all opposition to the IVth Corps to the north of Meiktila, where by 10th March the Japanese were so badly beaten that they abandoned their guns and transport and withdrew into the Shan Hills east of the Mandalay-Rangoon railway.

[4] *Ibid.*, p. 124.

Thus the road to Rangoon was won, but as that city lay over three hundred miles to the south and the monsoon was due in mid-May, the race now became one against the rains, a race which would have been impossible but for the capture of the Arakan airfields, which enabled the Fourteenth Army supply base in Assam to be shifted five hundred miles to the south. This part of the problem of the re-conquest of Southern Burma was solved by Lieut.-General Sir Philip Christison's XVth Corps, which consisted of two Indian divisions, two West African, an East African brigade and a tank brigade, and was supported by the 224th R.A.F. Group and a naval force under Rear-Admiral B. C. S. Martin. Its opponents were the Japanese 5th and 6th Divisions.

On 10th December the campaign opened by an advance astride the Mayu Ridge. On the 25th the tip of the Mayu Peninsula was gained; whereupon the Japanese, being too weak to hold the island of Akyab, abandoned it, and it was occupied by the XVth Corps on 3rd January. Next followed a series of amphibious operations, which included seven separate landings. At Myebon on 14th January; at Kyaukpyu on Ramree Island on 21st January; at Kangaw on 24th January; at Cheduba Island on 26th January; at Ru-ywa on 17th February, and at Letpan on 20th February. The whole of Ramree Island was cleared by 8th February, and the tactical importance of its occupation was that the XVth Corps was placed within easy striking distance of the road from Prome on the Irrawaddy to Taungup—the Japanese line of retreat.

The fighting at Kangaw and Myebon was savage, but when Kangaw fell on 30th January, the Japanese forces to the north of it, having lost their only road, were compelled to abandon their guns and transport and escape over the mountains. By the end of February the whole coastline had been cleared, and airfields were being established from which the Fourteenth Army could speedily and economically be supplied during its advance on Rangoon.

When Japanese resistance around Meiktila was finally broken, the XXXIIIrd Corps was directed to move against the enemy in the Chauk-Yenangyaung oilfields, and then advance down the Irrawaddy on Prome, while the IVth Corps followed the metalled road to Rangoon by way of Toungoo and Pegu.

In order to speed up the IVth Corps' advance to its maximum, its Commander, Lieut.-General F. W. Messervy, "reorganized it on the basis of one airborne and two motorized brigades a division,"[5] and placing his tank brigade in the van, the 5th and 17th Divisions followed, forging straight ahead and leaving any small parties of Japanese on their flanks to

[5] *The Twenty-Third Quarter*, p. 276.

be dealt with by the 19th Division in rear. After little fighting on the way, Pegu was entered on 1st May, three hundred miles having been covered in sixteen days.

Meanwhile the XXXIIIrd Corps, after some considerable resistance, took Chauk on 18th April and Yenangyaung on the 22nd, from where it struck southwards to reach Prome on 2nd May. Next day the monsoon broke—about fourteen days earlier than normal. However, this did not delay operations, for on the same day Rangoon was occupied by the XVth Corps.

For this bold venture the 26th Indian Division had been selected. It embarked at Akyab, and though it was known that the Japanese were withdrawing from Rangoon, its approach up the Irrawaddy was a hazardous one, for its channels had not been dredged since the Japanese occupation, and the mouth of the river at Elephant Point was protected by powerful batteries and minefields.

Under the protection of the fleet and air force, Elephant Point was taken by Gurkha paratroops, who found it held by no more than thirty-seven of the enemy. Next, the main landings followed, and Rangoon was discovered to have been meanwhile evacuated. On 6th May the port was once again open to shipping.

Thus, except for the clearing up of a considerable number of Japanese detachments, Burma was re-conquered in one of the most remarkable campaigns of the entire war. Remarkable in that few other theatres of the war presented so many obstacles to organized fighting. Heat, rain, tropical diseases, mountains, rivers, swamps, and an all but total lack of roads seemed to have marked out Burma as one of the few regions in the world where powerful and highly equipped armies could not fight. Yet, in this last campaign, half a million men were employed, and, as we have seen, armies of considerable size freely moved from north to south and west to east over high mountain ranges, broad rivers, and through dense forest and jungle at no mean speed. That this was possible was due to many factors, and, besides leadership and soldiership, the three outstanding were air power, medical care and engineering.

Of the first we have written fully; yet the other two were as important. Of the second it is astonishing to read that, whereas in 1943 "for every man who was admitted to hospital with wounds there had been one hundred and twenty who were casualties from . . . tropical diseases . . . By 1945 the rate had dropped to ten men sick for every one battle casualty, and during the last six weeks of the war these ten had been reduced to six."[6] And of the third, that to keep the Fourteenth Army and XVth Corps on the move,

72,000 engineers and 130,000 labourers were needed, and mainly for the construction of roads and airfields—the maintenance of mobility.

(2) *The Re-conquest of the Philippines*

As related in Chapter VI, the campaigns in New Guinea and the Marianas had, by mid-September, 1944, led to a junction of General MacArthur's and Admiral Nimitz's forces on the inner line of the Japanese defences at the islands of Morotai and Peleliu. North-west and west of them lay the Philippines, a great bastion protecting the South China Sea, the command of which was vital to the security of the whole of the Japanese conquests south of the island of Formosa.

Prior to their occupation, the American advance on the Philippines had been projected as a series of short jumps, each kept "within range of fighter support from airfields established at the last position occupied."[7] The first jump was to be made to the Talaur Islands, and the next to Mindanao, the most southerly of the Philippine Group. But on 13th September—that is, two days before the landings on Morotai and Peleliu were made—Admiral Halsey, in command of the U.S. Third Fleet,[8] who with his carrier force had been operating against the Philippines, Formosa and the Ryukyus Islands, having destroyed a large number of Japanese aircraft, and having encountered surprisingly little air opposition in the Leyte-Samar area of the Philippines, suggested that the projected advance could be stepped up by making the next jump from Morotai to Leyte in the Central Philippines. This meant the by-passing of Mindanao.

When this was reported by Admiral Nimitz to General MacArthur, together they agreed to advance the planned date of the assault on the Philippines from 20th December to 20th October, and strike direct at Leyte. Further, it was decided that, meanwhile, the extensive cleaning-up of marooned Japanese detachments in the Solomons, New Britain and New Guinea should become the responsibility of the Australian forces.

This was not only tactically a bold decision, for all air cover would have to be provided by carrier aircraft and the Japanese navy was still intact; but strategically it was a brilliant one, because a successful landing on the Central Philippines would split the Japanese forces, reckoned to be 250,000 strong under General Yamashita, into two main groups, one in Luzon and the other in Mindanao. Further, once Mindanao was by-passed, its garrison would be marooned, and should the Japanese attempt to

[7] "The Victory in the Pacific," Admiral Raymond A. Spruance, U.S.N. *Journal of the Royal United Service Institution*, November, 1946, p. 551.

[8] When Admiral Halsey was in command, this fleet was called the Third, and when Admiral Spruance was in command—the Fifth.

re-establish a "continuous front," they would be compelled to bring their fleet into action, the one thing above all others which Nimitz most desired. Should they do so, and should it be defeated, then the Japanese forces in Luzon and Mindanao could be dealt with in detail and "rolled-up" in turn. In fact, the assault on Leyte closely resembled a *blitz* attack on land with fleets replacing tank forces.

In order to prepare the way, on 10th October powerful carrier-borne aircraft attacks were made on the airfields in the islands of Okinawa and Formosa, the main links between Japan and the Philippines. Next, between the 13th and 15th, they were followed up by similar attacks on Luzon, in which a large number of Japanese aircraft was destroyed. And lastly, on the 18th and 19th, violent air attacks were made on airfields and shipping in the Visayan Sea.

On the second of these days, when the U.S. Third and Seventh Fleets, under Admiral Halsey and Vice-Admiral Thomas C. Kinkaid, were escorting Lieut.-General Walter Krueger's Sixth Army towards Leyte, a Japanese reconnaissance plane, discovering the expedition, reported its approach to Admiral Soemu Toyoda, Commander-in-Chief of the Combined Japanese Fleet. Immediately Toyoda put into operation what was known as the *Sho* plan, which comprised the following fleets: (1) Vice-Admiral Takeo Kurita's of five battleships, twelve cruisers and fifteen destroyers, based on Singapore; (2) Vice-Admiral Tokusaburo Ozawa's of two battleships, three cruisers and ten destroyers, based on Japan; (3) Vice-Admiral Shoji Nishimura's of two battleships, one cruiser and four destroyers, based on Singapore, and (4) Vice-Admiral Kiyohide Shima's of three cruisers and four destroyers, based on the Pescadores. The first became known as the Central Force; the second as the Northern, and the last two as the Southern. The plan itself was one of the most remarkable in naval history.

The Northern Force, with very few aircraft aboard its carriers, was to steam north of Luzon, at Cape Engaño turn south, and, *acting as a bait*, draw Halsey's fleet towards it. Meanwhile the Central and Southern Forces were to enter the Sulu Sea, the former passing through San Bernardino and the latter through Surigao Straits, and strike at the northern and southern flanks of the invaders.

On 18th October Kurita and Nishimura stood out from Singapore and Ozawa and Shima got under way, and on the 22nd the first two were reported by American submarine scouts nearing Palawan Island. Thereupon Halsey, sending one of his four task groups (Vice-Admiral John S. McCain's) back to Ulithi (near Yap) to reprovision, moved the remaining three east of Leyte to engage any enemy ships attempting to force the San Bernardino Strait. On the 24th, information coming in that a strong Japanese fleet was moving eastwards through the Sibuyan Sea, Halsey violently attacked it with his carrier aircraft. Though actually only one Japanese ship was sunk and one damaged, the air reports received were so exaggerated that Halsey was given the impression that Kurita's fleet had been virtually placed *hors de combat.*

While this attack was in progress, at 4.40 p.m. U.S. search planes, which had been sent north, reported a strong enemy force with carriers one hundred and thirty miles east of Cape Engaño. Halsey, considering that the Japanese Central Force was now of little consequence, decided to leave the San Bernardino Strait unguarded, strike at the Northern Force, annihilate it and then return and deal with the Central Force should it continue on its course. But, apparently, he failed to make the abandonment of the San Bernardino Strait clear to Admiral Kinkaid; for the latter continued to believe that it was blocked.

Three actions now followed: one in Surigao Strait; one off Cape Engaño, and one off Samar Island. Together they resulted in the greatest naval battle of the war—the battle for Leyte Gulf.

To deal with the Japanese approach through Surigao Strait, Admiral Kinkaid, holding back his aircraft carriers and their escorts, ordered Rear-Admiral Jesse B. Oldendorf to block the strait with the remainder of the Seventh Fleet; in all, six battleships; eight cruisers; twenty-six destroyers and thirty-nine motor torpedo boats. To effect this, Oldendorf deployed the last two mentioned craft across the narrowest stretch of the Strait, holding back his battleships and cruisers in rear.

At midnight the 24th Nishimura's fleet was sighted, and at 2.30 a.m. the 25th a series of torpedo attacks was made on it. At 3 a.m. the main action opened, and half an hour later, when the Japanese were more than twenty miles within the strait, they were annihilated by "A wall of 16-in., 8-in. and 6-in. gunfire,"[9] only one destroyer, the *Shigure* escaping. Admiral Shima then came up, and after an abortive torpedo attack turned about and headed south.

While the battle of Surigao was being fought, the U.S. Third Fleet was steaming north, and at 8.25 a.m. the 25th Admiral Halsey received an urgent message from Kinkaid informing him that Japanese battleships were firing on his carriers north-east of Leyte Gulf. Message after message followed, nevertheless, except for calling back McCain's task group, Halsey kept on his course until 11.15 a.m. At that time, leaving the Third and Fourth Task Groups to deal with Ozawa's fleet, which they later on

[9]"The Battle for Leyte Gulf," Captain K. M. McManes, U.S.N. *Journal of the Royal United Service Institution*, November, 1945, p. 495. The battle was fought entirely during the night. The American guns were radar-controlled; the Japanese relied on searchlights.

did, sinking his four carriers, he turned his battleships and Second Task Group about, and made southwards at high speed.

What had happened? Admiral Kurita, finding the San Bernardino Strait unguarded, had passed through it during the night of the 24th-25th. Then, turning south, at 6.53 a.m. had opened fire on Kinkaid's carriers. Surprised by this attack, Kinkaid ordered Oldendorf, who with the bulk of the Seventh Fleet was still deep in Surigao Strait and short of ammunition, to turn

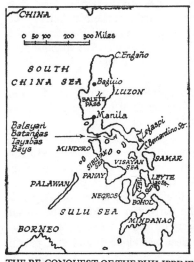

THE RE-CONQUEST OF THE PHILIPPINE   LEYTE ISLAND CAMPAIGN,
ISLANDS, OCTOBER, 1944-JULY, 1945   20th OCTOBER-31st DECEMBER, 1944

about; simultaneously, he sent his first urgent message to Halsey. "No match for the guns of the Japanese battleships and cruisers," writes Captain McManes, "our carriers took evasive action covered by smoke screens laid down by a destroyer escort and two destroyers, which then, in one of the most gallant actions of the war, dashed in to launch torpedo attacks on the enemy."[10] Pressing home his attack, Kurita sank two U.S. escort carriers and three destroyers, and seriously damaged seven escort carriers and one destroyer. Then, suddenly, at 9.25 a.m., when it seemed that an American defeat was imminent, and apparently because his destroyers were short of fuel, he broke off the action and retired northwards, passing back through the San Bernardino Strait before Halsey could come up.

Thus the Battle of Leyte Gulf ended in a decisive American victory.

[10]*Ibid.*, p. 497.

Never again did the Japanese navy put to sea as a fleet. The Japanese lost three battleships; four carriers; ten cruisers and nine destroyers, and the Americans three carriers and three destroyers.

Meanwhile, on the 20th, the Xth and XXIVth Corps of the U.S. Sixth Army disembarked; whereupon General Krueger pushed inland and soon penetrated to Dagami and Burauen in the centre of the island, and by mid-November approached Limon, to be held up by the Japanese 1st Division. During this period, effort after effort was made by the Japanese to reinforce their garrison, but on 11th December their losses at sea became so heavy that further attempts were abandoned. By then, however, the decisive blow had been struck. On 7th December the U.S. 77th Division was taken by sea round the southern end of the island and landed three miles south of Ormoc. This new thrust placed the Japanese forces in the Limon-Ormoc area between two fires. On 10th December Ormoc was stormed and taken, and by the end of the month the whole island was cleared. Shortly before this occurred, an American force landed on the island of Mindoro, cleared it by the 28th, and established on it a fighter air base within seventy-five miles of Manila Bay.

No sooner had organized resistance ceased on Leyte than a new assault was mounted to re-conquer the island of Luzon from Lingayen Gulf. Early in January, in 850 ships the U.S. Sixth Army, now composed of the Ist and XIVth Corps, slipped through Surigao Strait and passing into the Mindanao and Sulu Seas turned northwards.

Every effort was made to conceal the destination of this new invasion from the Japanese. Their attention was distracted by guerilla demonstrations in the southern extremity of the island, while the navy swept the minefields in Balayan, Batangas and Tayabas Bays and transports approached their beaches. Also dummy parachute descents were made in their neighbourhood.

On the 9th, unopposed by aircraft, the landing was made under cover of concentrated air attacks on roads, bridges and tunnels in order to prevent Yamashita moving his forces in time to meet the assault. The result was that the "Japanese forces on the land, harassed by guerillas and by air, drove north, south-east and west in confusion, became tangled in traffic jams on the roads, and generally dissipated what chance they might have had to repel the landing force."[11] By nightfall the 9th 68,000 troops were ashore, and a beachhead fifteen miles long by over three deep had been established.

At the time, Yamashita had at his immediate disposal the 10th and 105th Divisions in the Manila area and the 2nd at Clark Field, north of

[11]*General Marshall's Biennial Report*, 1st July, 1943, to 30th July, 1945, p. 78.

the Bataan Peninsula. Caught unprepared, he was forced to commit his troops piecemeal, with the result that, by the 15th, the forward elements of the Sixth Army advanced rapidly.

Because the American left flank was the most exposed, General Mac-Arthur deployed his strongest forces towards Rosario and Urdaneta, and

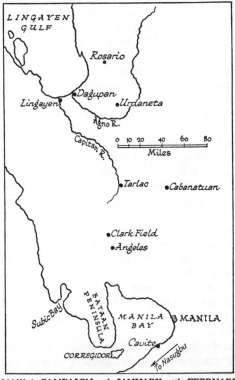

THE MANILA CAMPAIGN, 9th JANUARY-25th FEBRUARY, 1945

under their cover struck straight across the Agno River towards Manila. Little resistance was met with until Clark Field was approached. Meanwhile stiff fighting was taking place on the left, but on the 20th Japanese resistance began to slacken, and five days later Clark Field, the chief air base in Luzon, with its five neighbouring airfields and the town of Angeles, were in American hands.

In order to turn the Japanese position from the south, on the 29th the XIth Corps was landed a few miles to the north of Subic Bay, and meeting with little resistance, it advanced rapidly inland and cut off the Bataan Peninsula, so that the enemy might not withdraw into it as MacArthur had done three years before. Next, on the 31st, the U.S. 11th Airborne Division made an unopposed amphibious landing at Nasugbu to the south of Manila Bay, and as it closed in on Manila, the Sixth Army advanced on the city from the north. This double envelopment placed the Japanese in Manila in a hopeless position; nevertheless, they put up so fierce a resistance that it was not until 23rd February that the city was cleared.

Meanwhile, between late January and 13th February, air and naval forces had bombarded the entrance to Manila Bay and the island fortress of Corregidor, 3,128 tons of bombs being dropped upon it. On 16th February it was attacked from the air by the 503rd Parachute Regiment and invaded by the 34th Infantry Regiment. Fighting in its underground galleries next followed and continued for nearly a fortnight. Eventually the Japanese brought this operation to an end by firing the main magazine and destroying both the galleries and themselves.

The Manila area having been cleared, late in February troops were landed on Palawan Island, and during the first half of March on Mindanao, Panay, Cebu and Negros Islands, while the Sixth Army met with fanatical resistance between Baguio and Balete Pass, in the centre of Luzon. Lastly, Luzon was invaded at Legaspi in its southern extremity. Much irregular warfare followed these events, and it was not until July that the campaign ended.

In all, the re-conquest of the Philippines cost the Americans 60,628 in killed, wounded and missing, and the Japanese 317,000 in killed (probably an exaggerated number) and 7,236 in prisoners.

Not only did this campaign clear the way for the assault on the Japanese Islands, but it so completely exhausted Japan's resources as to render any hope of resisting it highly problematical.

The campaign had cost Japan over 9,000 aircraft, and more than half her remaining fleet. Her industries and communications were inoperative through blockade and crumbling under air attack; her coal, oil, steel and other raw materials were severed from her by lack of shipping, and her cities were progressively being reduced to ashes. In Burma Admiral Mountbatten was preparing to invade Malaya; in China Chiang Kai-shek had assumed the offensive; and in April Russia had renounced the Neutrality Pact made with her four years before. Nevertheless, the Japanese determined to fight it out to the death. Faced by unconditional surrender, there could be no surrender and moral survival. Therefore, like Macbeth, they cried:

> "Ring the alarum-bell! Blow wind! come wrack!
> At least we'll die with harness on our back."

Thus it came about that the war senselessly continued.

(3) *The Assault on the Outworks of Japan*

When Manila was being battered and stormed, a more direct line of approach than by way of the Philippines was being pushed against the home islands of Japan, so that airfields might be gained from which to prepare the way for their eventual assault. Already the occupation of Saipan, Tinian and Guam in the Marianas had enabled shore-based aircraft to bomb Tokyo. But because the distance from Guam was 1,565 miles—3,130 there and back—clearly, if it were reduced, not only could heavier bomb loads be carried, but attacks could be more continuous; also, on the return journey, many damaged aircraft would be saved.

Three islands were suitable for advanced bases—namely, Formosa, Okinawa (the largest in the Ryukyu Archipelago), and Iwo Jima in the Volcano Group. The first was large—13,500 square miles in area—with mountains rising to 14,000 feet above sea level, and it was strongly garrisoned; therefore its reduction was likely to be slow. Okinawa, sixty-seven miles long and seven to eight wide, was a less formidable proposition, and it possessed two good airfields. But, strategically, it was strongly placed. It lay centrally between Formosa, south-eastern China, Kyushu and Iwo Jima; therefore an expedition approaching it from any direction might expect to be attacked from one or more of these localities. Besides Okinawa was more distance from the Mariana bases than Iwo Jima, and nearer ones to it could not be established until the airfields in northern Luzon were in American hands.

It was, therefore, decided first to neutralize Formosa and Okinawa by bombing, and next to invade and occupy Iwo Jima, which was seven hundred and seventy-five miles distant from Honshu, the largest of the Japanese home islands, and slightly less distant from Saipan. The operation was to be carried out by the Vth Marine Corps (4th and 5th Marine Divisions), some 60,000 officers and men carried in 850 ships and supported by Admiral Spruance's Fifth Fleet. It is of interest to learn that 220,000 naval personnel were engaged in this operation[12]—that is, nearly four for each Marine.

Though Iwo Jima was but five miles long and less than three wide, its importance was so considerable that it was exceedingly strongly fortified and garrisoned by slightly over 20,000 Japanese under the command of Lieut.-General Tadamichi Kuribayashi. Possessing but two landing beaches, it could not easily be surprised. The date for its invasion was 19th February.

---

[12]*Second Official Report*, Fleet-Admiral Ernest J. King, C.-in-C. U.S. Fleet, 1st March, 1944-1st March, 1945, p. 26.

For seven months prior to that date, the island had been subjected to aerial and surface bombardments, which early in December were stepped up. Thence onwards for seventy days the bombing of the island was continuous.[13] Also, during January neutralizing attacks by carrier-borne aircraft as well as by the U.S. 14th Air Force in China were made on

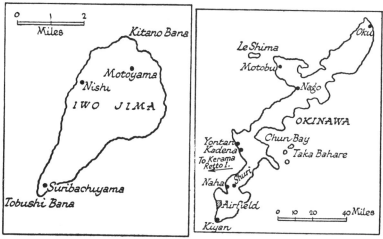

IWO JIMA CAMPAIGN, 19th FEBRUARY-
16th MARCH, 1945

OKINAWA CAMPAIGN, 1st APRIL-
21st-JUNE, 1945

Okinawa and Formosa. Simultaneously, the Japanese home islands were heavily bombed. Finally, on 16th February, the pre-invasion bombardment and bombing were opened on Iwo Jima, while strong forces of carrier-borne aircraft attacked Tokyo.

At 9 a.m. on 19th February the invasion began, and though at first little resistance was met with, it soon stiffened and eventually became fanatical. On the 20th the Motoyama No. 1 airfield in the north of the island was occupied by the American Marines; but it was not until the 27th, and after having been reinforced by the 3rd Marine Division, that the 4th and 5th cleared approximately half the island, which in all was less than eight square miles in area. On the 28th, in the extreme south, the summit of Suribachiyama was taken; nevertheless, it was not until 10th March that the fanatical resistance of the Japanese began to slacken, and only on the 16th, four weeks after the first landings were made, that fighting ceased.

Of all the land actions fought during the Pacific War, in proportion to numbers engaged, that of Iwo Jima was the most costly. The American

[13]*General H. H. Arnold's Third Report*, 12th November, 1945, p. 56.

losses totalled 4,189 killed, 15,305 wounded and 441 missing, or nearly one for each of the Japanese garrison, of which close on 21,000 were killed and less than 100 taken alive.

The strategic gain was, however, considerable; for as General Marshall points out: "The Iwo fields saved hundreds of battle-damaged B-29's unable to make the full return flight to their bases in the Marianas . . ."[14] Further, a fighter base was at once established on the island, from which the bombers from the Marianas could be escorted on their way to Japan.

Within ten days of the conquest of Iwo Jima, a preparatory offensive was started against the Ryukyu Islands, the ultimate object of which was the occupation of Okinawa. On 26th March, the U.S. 77th Division landed on Kerama Retto Island, immediately to the west of Okinawa. The strategic position of the latter was of great value, not only because it was no more than three hundred and twenty-five miles south of Kyushu, but because, as Admiral Spruance points out. ". . . it commanded the East China Sea, which in turn gave access to the Yellow Sea and to the Straits of Tsushima. It provided a base for further operations against either south-western Japan or positions on the coast of China north of Formosa. Physically, it had sites for a considerable number of airfields, as well as space for extensive shore installations. It had one small protected harbour and two large bays, fairly well enclosed and suitable for use as fleet anchorages."[15] Against these advantages must be set that it lay in the track of many of the late summer and autumn typhoons, and that it was known to be exceptionally strongly garrisoned.

On 1st April, the U.S. XXIVth Corps and IIIrd Marine Corps, transported in 1,400 vessels and under cover of an intense naval bombardment and a realistic feint attack against Kiyan on the southern tip of Okinawa, landed on the island. It was the largest amphibious operation yet made in the Pacific. Admiral Spruance was in supreme command, and, besides the U.S. Fifth Fleet, he had at his disposal a British squadron commanded by Vice-Admiral Sir Bernard Rawlings.

The landings were made on the west coast of the island at Yontan and Kadena, and, as at Iwo Jima, little opposition was met with at first. But when on the 5th the XXIVth Corps, under General Hodges, turned southwards towards Shuri, it found the bulk of the Japanese garrison elaborately entrenched from shore to shore across the island. Added to this, the Japanese had opened a series of violent air attacks on the American troops and shipping. Two days later a Japanese fleet was observed steaming south of Kyushu towards the East China Sea. It had no aircraft-carriers with it, and it was at once attacked and the battleship *Yamato* sunk.

[14]*Biennial Report*, 1st July, 1943, to 30th June, 1945, p. 80.
[15]*Journal of the Royal United Service Institution*, November, 1946, p. 553.

By the date of this action, the four divisions of the XXIVth Corps had landed and the IIIrd Marine Corps, having also landed, penetrated twenty miles northwards against weak opposition. This made it clear that the Japanese intended to hold only the southern end of the island. At this time General Hodges wrote:

"It is going to be really tough. There are 65,000 to 70,000 fighting Japs holed up in the south end of the island, and I see no way to get them out except blast them out yard by yard . . .

"The Japs have tremendous amounts of artillery, and have used it far more intelligently than I have ever seen them use it to date . . .

"The terrain is decidedly rugged and cut up with many cliffs, natural and man-made, limestone and coral caves, and organized over long periods of time, and well-manned."[16]

That it was "going to be tough" proved only too true; for though the northern part of the island was rapidly overrun, the Japanese had determined to fight to the death for its southern extremity. Of the air fighting General Marshall writes:

"The ferocity of the ground fighting was matched by frequent Japanese air assaults on our shipping in the Okinawa area. By the middle of June, thirty-three U.S. ships had been sunk and forty-five damaged, principally by aerial attacks. In the Philippines campaign U.S. forces first met the full fury of the Kamikaze or suicide attacks, but at Okinawa the Japanese procedure was better organized and involved larger numbers of planes; also the Baka plane appeared, something quite new and deadly. This small, short-range, rocket-accelerated aircraft, carried more than a ton of explosives in its war-head. It was designed to be carried to the attack, slung beneath a medium bomber, then directed in a rocket-assisted dive to the target by its suicide pilot. It was, in effect, a piloted version of the German VI."[17]

This type of attack had been developed by the Japanese on account of their colossal losses in aircraft. They attempted to make good deficiency in technical superiority by an excess of valour unequalled in the history of war, and might well have succeeded had they but listened to their technicians, who urged that a more powerful war-head should be used. In the *United States Strategic Bombing Survey (Pacific War)* we read:

"From October, 1944, to the end of the Okinawa campaign, the Japanese flew 2,550 Kamikaze missions, of which 475, or 18.6 per cent were effective in securing hits or damaging near misses. Warships of all types were damaged, including twelve aircraft-carriers, fifteen battleships, and sixteen light and escort carriers. However, no ship larger than an escort carrier was

---

[16] Quoted from *General Marshall's Report*, p. 82.
[17] *Ibid.*, p. 83.

sunk.[18] Approximately forty-five vessels were sunk, the bulk of which were destroyers ... To the United States the losses actually sustained were serious, and caused great concern. Two thousand B-29 sorties were diverted from direct attacks on Japanese cities and industries to striking Kamikaze airfields in Kyushu. Had the Japanese been able to sustain an attack of greater power and concentration they might have been able to cause us to withdraw or to revise our strategic plans."[19]

While these suicide attacks were being made, the American Marines, having cleared up the northern part of the island, moved south to reinforce the XXIVth Corps, and on 13th May the 6th Marine Division broke into the outskirts of Naha. But the key to the Japanese position was an eminence called "Sugar-Loaf Hill," and it was not taken until 21st May. By the 30th, four-fifths of Naha were in American hands; the next day the whole of the town was occupied.

Fighting, however, continued, and it was not until mid-June, after the Japanese had lost 3,400 planes shot down over the Ryukyus and Kyushu and 800 destroyed on the ground, and the Americans had lost more than 1,000, that the battle began to draw towards its end, which finally came on 21st June.

How severe the fighting had been, may be judged from the casualties. In all, those of the Americans were approximately 39,000 men killed, wounded and missing, including losses of "over 10,000 naval personnel of the supporting fleet . . . 109,629 Japanese had been killed and 7,871 taken prisoner."[20]

(4) *The Strategic Bombing of Japan*, 1943-1945

When the war in the Pacific opened, neither side could, like Hitler, found its tactical operations on the first of the two strategies discussed in Chapter I—namely, annihilation. Neither had the means; Japan permanently so, and the United States temporarily so. And as regards the latter, with one fundamental difference, they were faced by a strategical situation very similar to the one Britain had been placed in by the collapse of France. Their enemy lay overseas and for the time being was out of reach. Because this meant that it would take time to close in on Japan,

---

[18]However, damage was at times considerable. Thus, on 2nd May, two suicide aircraft crashed into Admiral Mitscher's flagship, the 23,000-ton aircraft-carrier *Bunker Hill*, and reduced her to a smouldering wreck. Of her crew, 392 were killed and 264 wounded.

[19]P.10. "At the time of surrender, the Japanese had more than 9,000 planes in the home islands available for Kamikaze attack, and more than 5,000 had already been specially fitted for suicide attack to resist our planned invasion" (*Ibid.*).

[20]*General Marshall's Biennial Report*, 1st July, 1943, to 30th July, 1945, p. 83.

perforce, to start with, American strategy had to be of the exhaustive type. The difference, however, was that, whereas Germany, reinforced by the resources and manpower of the countries she had occupied as well as supported by Russia, was economically immensely strong and to all intents and purposes self-sufficient to last a long war, Japan, because the bulk of the raw materials she required to wage a war—long or short—lay, not in her own home lands, but overseas, was economically weak.

In the case of Germany, the strategic centre of gravity resided in her military strength; for until it was exhausted there was no way of reducing her economic strength other than by sea and air blockade, which, as we have seen, was a painfully slow process. But in the case of Japan, because her home lands were separated from their economic vital areas of operation by the sea, the strategical centre of gravity lay in her navy and merchant service. Were they eliminated, Japan must collapse as surely as Germany collapsed once her military strength was exhausted. Consequently, the fundamental American strategical problem was, how to eliminate them? Clearly the answer was: first, to gain command of the air and the sea, and, secondly, to centre the initiative won on the destruction of Japanese sea power.

Accepting this conclusion as logical, then, whereas the tactical problem of the American air force was to co-operate with the fleet in the destruction of the Japanese navy, its strategical problem was to concentrate on the elimination of the Japanese mercantile marine and not to dissipate its strength by striking at Japan's industries and cities unless they were directly related to her sea power. Therefore, the bulk of the U.S. Strategic Air Force should have been designed for a *guerre de course* and not, as it was, as siege artillery.

As we have seen, the tactical problem was superbly handled, and, in consequence, magnificently rewarded. But, as we shall now show, the strategical problem was not, because its centre of gravity was largely overlooked by those in control of strategic bombing. They were Douhet- or Mitchell-minded. They believed in "colossal cracks" and in the obliteration of their enemy's industries and cities, when it should have been obvious that, were the former deprived of raw materials and the inhabitants of the latter of food, Japan's factories would become inoperative and her civil population demoralized. Therefore, the blunder perpetrated in Europe was repeated, and to the vast detriment of the peace for which the war was being waged.

The *United States Strategic Bombing Survey (Pacific War)*[21] supports this contention. In it it is pointed out that Japan's economic potential was

[21]Because this report will be frequently referred to throughout this Section, to economize in space page references to it are omitted.

approximately 10 per cent of America's, and that the acreage of her arable land was no more than 3 per cent, yet it had to support a population over half as large. Also that, Japan was so "desperately vulnerable" to attack on her shipping, she could only "support a short war or a war of limited liabilities," and even had the United States been but half as strong as they were, this would have remained true.

When the war started and throughout its length, the attack on Japan's shipping was in the main handed over to America's submarines, and it was these vessels and not bombing aircraft which undertook the task of reducing Japanese mercantile marine. Admiral Spruance writes that it is difficult to over-estimate the part played by American submarines in bringing about the defeat of Japan.[22] The correctness of this remark may be judged from the following figures:

At the opening of the war Japan had 6,000,000 tons of merchant shipping of over 500 tons gross weight, and during the war an additional 4,100,000 tons were built or captured. Of the total, 8,900,000 tons were sunk or so seriously damaged as to be out of action when the war ended. Of this loss 54.7 per cent was attributed to submarines; 16.3 per cent to carrier-based aircraft; 4.3 per cent to Navy and Marine land-based aircraft; 9.3 per cent to mines, largely strewn by the Strategic Bomber Force; less than 1 per cent to surface gunfire; and 4 per cent to marine accidents.

Instead of concentrating against shipping, the Strategic Bombing Force was built to attack cities and large industrial targets. According to the *Survey*: "The total tonnage of bombs dropped by Allied planes in the Pacific War was 656,400. Of this, 160,800 tons, or 24 per cent, were dropped on the home islands of Japan. Navy aircraft accounted for 6,800 tons, Army aircraft other than B-29's for 7,000 tons, and the B-29's for 147,000 tons." Of the tonnage dropped on Japan, "104,000 tons of bombs were directed at sixty-six urban areas; 14,150 tons were directed at aircraft factories; 10,600 tons at oil refineries; 4,708 tons at arsenals; 3,500 tons at miscellaneous industrial targets; 8,115 tons at airfields and seaplane bases in support of the Okinawa operation; and 12,054 mines were sown." These figures clearly show where the bulk of the bombs fell.

Up to the spring of 1945, mainly on account of distance, strategic bombing was largely innocuous. In the autumn of 1943 it was initiated from China by B-29 attacks on industrial targets in Manchuria and Kyushu, and though damage was done, particularly to steel plants, the *Survey* considers "that the overall result achieved did not warrant the diversion of the effort entailed."

Less than a year later, Guam, Saipan and Tinian were in American hands, and the next series of blows was struck from them in November, 1944.

---

[22] *Journal of the Royal United Service Institution*, November, 1946, p. 542.

Industrial targets were again selected, but distance was still vast, and though considerable damage was done, it was in no way decisive.

Next, in the spring of 1945, it was decided to bomb the principal Japanese cities at night from an altitude averaging 7,000 feet; incendiary bombs being used instead of high explosive. The first of these attacks was on Tokyo. It took place on 9th March, when 1,667 tons of incendiaries were dropped; over fifteen square miles of the city's most densely populated area was burnt out, and 185,000 people burnt to death and injured. Other attacks followed, and on 9th June, summing up the damage done between 9th March and 31st May, the Tokyo radio reported:

"At Tokyo, 767,000 dwellings had been destroyed and 3,100,000 persons had been rendered homeless. At Nagoya there were 380,000 homeless and 96,000 buildings had been destroyed; Yokohama, 680,000 homeless and 132,000 dwellings destroyed; at Kobe, 260,000 homeless and 70,000 buildings destroyed; at Osaka, 510,000 homeless and 130,000 dwellings destroyed."[23]

"In all incendiary attacks," writes General Arnold, "over 100,000 tons of bombs were dropped in the course of more than 15,000 sorties, against sixty-six Japanese cities . . . Nearly 169 square miles were destroyed or damaged in the sixty cities for which photographic reconnaissance is available, with more than 100 square miles burned out in the five major cities attacked."[24]

The resources required to accomplish this destruction were enormous. Whereas in 1944 not more than 100 bombers had attacked Japan in a single formation, early in August, 1945, 801 Super-Fortresses attacked in a single night, and bomb loads increased from 2.6 tons in November, 1944, to 7.4 tons in July, 1945. During this last mentioned month B-29's dropped 42,000 tons on Japan, and in June, 1945, it was projected to drop 850,000 tons of incendiaries during the following nine months.

The cost of this destruction was prodigious. "The first B-29 cost $3,392,396.60,"[25] and when put into bulk production $600,000 apiece, and each machine required 57,000 man hours in its building. Two thousand, costing $1,200,000,000, were required to keep 550 in the air at one time, and the total cost of the Super-Fortress organization was $4,000,000,000.

Were the results achieved commensurate with the effort? Could not these vast sums have been more profitably spent? The answers gathered from the *Survey* are that they were not and that they could have been. These are the facts:

Though 40 per cent of the built-up area of sixty-six cities bombed was

[23]Quoted from *The Twenty-Third Quarter*, p. 302.
[24]*Third Report*, 12th November, 1945, pp. 37 and 40.
[25]*General Arnold's Second Report*, 27th February, 1945, p. 70.

destroyed, the "Plants specifically attacked with high-explosive bombs were, however, limited in number," and "The railroad system had not yet been subjected to substantial attack and remained in reasonably good operating condition at the time of surrender. Little damage was suffered which interfered with main line operations. Trains were running through Hiroshima forty-eight hours after the dropping of the atomic bomb on the city. Damage to local transport facilities, however, seriously disrupted the movement of supply within and between cities, thereby hindering production, repair work and dispersal operations." Further, that "Ninety-seven per cent of Japan's stocks of guns, shells, explosives and other military supplies were thoroughly protected in dispersal or underground storage depots, and were not vulnerable to air attack."

Though bombing and the dispersal of factories caused by it reduced production, loss of shipping was the main factor in Japan's economic decline; for it was the interdiction of coal, oil, other raw materials and food, and not the destruction of factories and urban areas which struck the deadliest blow at Japan's economy. Loss of shipping limited the import of iron ore, and want of steel limited the building of ships. Labour efficiency declined because of lack of food, and food because of lack of ships. In the *Survey* we read:

"Even though the urban area attacks and attacks on specific industrial plants contributed a substantial percentage to the overall decline in Japan's economy, in many segments of that economy their effects were duplicative. Most of the oil refineries were out of oil, the alumina plants out of bauxite, the steel mills lacking in ore and coke, and the munition plants low in steel and aluminium. Japan's economy was in large measure being destroyed twice over, once by cutting off imports, and secondly by air attack."

What this really meant was, not only the destruction of Japan's war potential, but also of her peace potential. Therefore, so far as winning the war was concerned, the latter was a pure waste of effort—it was strategically uneconomic. This shows that the centre of gravity of the problem was missed by the Combined Chiefs of Staff. Had they seen that it lay in interdicting movement and not in fire-raising, surely they would have done what the twelve civilian members of the *Survey* suggested should have been done, which is as follows:

"A successful attack on the Hakkodate rail ferry, the Kanmon tunnels and nineteen bridges and vulnerable sections of line so selected as to set up five separate zones of complete interdiction would have virtually eliminated further coal movements, would have immobilized the remainder of the rail system through lack of coal, and would have completed the strangulation of Japan's economy. This strangulation would have more effectively and efficiently destroyed the economic structure of the country than individually destroying Japan's cities and factories. It would have reduced Japan to a series of isolated communities, incapable of any sustained industrial production, incapable of moving food from the agricultural areas to the cities, and incapable of rapid large-scale movements of troops and munitions.

"The *Survey* believes that such an attack, had it been well-planned in advance, might have been initiated by carrier-based attacks on shipping and on the Hakkodate ferry in August, 1944, could have been continued by aerial mining of inland waterways beginning in December, 1944, and could have been further continued by initiating the railroad attack as early as April, 1945. The *Survey* has estimated that force requirements to effect complete interdiction of the railroad system would have been 650 B-29 visual sorties carrying 5,200 tons of high-explosive bombs."

Deduct these figures from the 15,000 sorties and 100,000 tons of incendiary bombs dropped on the sixty-six Japanese cities, and the residue is a fair measure of the waste of military means and effort, also of the strategic error of the Combined Chiefs of Staff.

Next, we will turn to the moral effect of the bombing of Japan, and the most striking thing about it is that, in face of the appalling destruction, decline in morale was exceedingly slow, and was not primarily the result of bombing.

According to Japanese estimates, 260,000 people were killed, 412,000 injured, 9,200,000 left homeless, and 2,210,000 houses demolished or burned down.[26] And be it remembered, the majority of the people killed were burnt to death. Yet in spite of this, the primary factor in the lowering of morale was shortage of food, and the secondary the defeat of the armed forces.

Prior to the attack on Pearl Harbour, states the *Survey*, "the average *per capita* caloric intake of the Japanese people was about 2,000 calories as against 3,400 in the United States," and by the summer of 1945 it was about 1,680. On so low a diet morale was bound to sink, and doubly so when coupled with one military defeat after another until bombing became the last straw. The *Survey* outlines the decline as follows:

"In June, 1944, approximately 2 per cent of the population believed

[26]*General Arnold's Third Report*, 12th November, 1945, p. 40. Apparently these figures do not include the casualties caused by the two atomic bombs. The *Survey*, which does include them, and which was published on 1st July, 1946, gives the total as 806,000, of which approximately 330,000 were fatal. "These casualties probably exceed Japan's combat casualties, which the Japanese estimate as having totalled approximately 780,000 during the entire war." The *Survey* states that 2,510,000 houses were destroyed by air attack and that 615,000 were torn down to create firebreaks.

that Japan faced the probability of defeat . . . By December, 1944, air attacks from the Marianas against the home islands had begun, defeats in the Philippines had been suffered and the food situation had deteriorated; 10 per cent of the people believed Japan could not achieve victory. By March, 1945, when the night incendiary attacks began and the food ration was reduced, this percentage had risen to 19 per cent. In June it was 46 per cent, and just prior to surrender, 68 per cent. Of those who had come to this belief over one-half attributed the principal cause to air attacks, other than the atomic bombing attacks, and one-third to military defeats."[27]

Nevertheless, the *Survey* continues: The "Emperor largely escaped the criticism which was directed at other leaders, and retained the people's faith in him. It is probable that most Japanese would have passively faced death in a continuation of the hopeless struggle, had the Emperor so ordered. When the Emperor announced the unconditional surrender the first reaction of the people was one of regret and surprise, followed shortly by relief."

Yet even without this decline in morale, the *Survey* is of opinion that the loss of shipping alone could end in nothing short of surrender. By July, 1945, steel and coal had virtually become unobtainable, whereas oil imports, which had begun to decline in August, 1943, had been eliminated by April, 1945. "It is the opinion of the *Survey* that by August, 1945, even without direct air attack on her cities and industries, the overall level of Japanese war production would have declined below the peak level of 1944 by 40 to 50 per cent solely as a result of the interdiction of overseas imports." Therefore, it would seem highly probable that had strategic bombing been centred on the destruction of Japanese merchant shipping and railways, instead of on industries and cities, by August, 1945, further resistance would have become impossible.

(5) *The Atomic Bomb and the Surrender of Japan*

Though the percentages, quoted towards the close of the above Section, show that between June, 1944, and July, 1945, among the urban population of Japan belief in victory had slumped from 98 to 42 per cent, some time before this decline set in a struggle had begun between the ruling factions which advised the Emperor on the conduct of the war. Of these factions, the two most powerful were the naval and the military, the first was inclined towards peace and the second insistent on fighting the war out irrespective of consequences.

---

[27]In accepting these estimates, it should be remembered that the Survey's work was carried out mainly in the cities which had been bombed.

In February, 1944, Rear-Admiral Takazi of the Naval General Staff, after analysing the events of the previous six months, came to the conclusion that, on account of air, fleet and shipping losses, Japan could not win the war, and, therefore, should seek a compromise peace. But it was not until the loss of Saipan in July that those who supported him were able to bring sufficient pressure to bear to force the retirement of General Tojo, premier and head of the military faction.

Tojo's successor, General Koiso, in spite of being called "The Tiger of Korea," was not sufficiently strong a man to stand up to the military faction, with the result that the situation drifted from bad to worse until 7th April, 1945, when a few days after the American landing on Okinawa, he was removed and replaced by Admiral Suzuki, whose one aim was to bring the war to an end. Next, in May, the Japanese Supreme War Direction Council considered how this could be achieved, and the first step taken was to approach Russia and ask her to intercede as mediator.

This clutching at a straw must have made clear to the Western Allies the catastrophic position Japan had reached, if only because the price Russia would demand for mediation could not possibly be less than the abandonment of all her conquests, including Manchuria and Korea. Nothing short of this would have satisfied the Russians, who had not forgotten the events of 1904-1905. This approach shows that in June the war could have been brought to an end on terms highly advantageous to Britain and the United States. By then, except for one obstacle, the military might of America had cleared the way to certain and rapid victory. But militarily the obstacle was irremovable, it was the Allied policy of unconditional surrender. By shackling both Britain and the United States, it unbarred the political road to Russia. By following it the Russians could now gain all that for forty years and more they had set their hearts upon in Eastern Asia, as unconditional surrender had already enabled them to gain more than they had ever dreamed of in Eastern Europe. Unconditional surrender spelt political victory for the U.S.S.R. Therefore, occultly, the war was being fought to stimulate and expand Communism.

Thus it came about that, caught in the toils of their self-invoked Hydra, at the crucial moment in their war in the Far East the Western Allies were compelled to surrender the political initiative to their Eastern Ally, and the war continuing, on 20th June the Emperor Hirohito once again called the six members of the Supreme War Direction Council to a conference in order to inform them that it was essential that the war should be closed on any terms short of unconditional surrender.

A month later two events simultaneously occurred: the Allied Powers met in conference at Potsdam to settle the future of Germany, and in a desert area in New Mexico, on 16th July, the first atomic bomb in history was detonated. The results of this second event were rushed to President Truman at Potsdam, and there and then he decided to drop two of these projectiles on Japan in order to shorten the war and thereby save "hundreds of thousands of lives, both American and Japanese."[28]

No sooner was the decision made than orders were sent to General Spaatz in America to drop the bombs on two of four selected cities on a day subsequent to 3rd August; whereupon "Hiroshima and Nagasaki were chosen as targets because of their concentration of activities and population."[29]

Though to save life is laudable, it in no way justifies the employment of means which run counter to every precept of humanity and the customs of war. Should it do so, then, on the pretexts of shortening a war and of saving lives, every imaginable atrocity can be justified. In fact, knowing as President Truman and Mr. Churchill did of the powers of the new weapon, its use can have implied but one thing only—namely, "Unless surrender is immediate, the slaughter of the Japanese people will be unlimited." This is corroborated by President Truman's statement of 6th August: "If they" (the Japanese), he said, "do not now accept our terms they may expect a rain of ruin from the air, the like of which has never been seen on this earth."[30] This is equivalent to a gangster saying to his victim: "Unless you do as I ask, I will shoot up your family."

If the saving of lives were the true pretext, then, instead of reverting to a type of war which would have disgraced Tamerlane, all President Truman and Mr. Churchill need have done was to remove the obstacle of unconditional surrender, when the war could have been brought to an immediate end. That this was in part realized is proved by the fact that, on 26th July, the United Kingdom, United States and China presented Japan with an ultimatum of eight terms of capitulation, of which the following were the more important.

"6. There must be eliminated for all time the authority and influence of those who have deceived and misled the people of Japan into embarking on world conquest, for we insist that a new order of peace, security and justice will be impossible until irresponsible militarism is driven from the world."

---

[28] *The Times*, 28th January, 1947. On 16th August, 1945, Mr. Churchill informed the House of Commons that "The decision to use the atomic bomb was taken by President Truman and myself at Potsdam, and we approved the military plans to unchain the dread pent-up forces." Apparently, in order to justify this decision, he informed his listeners that, had invasion been necessary, it might have cost the Americans 1,000,000, and the British 250,000 lives—that is, more than the two together lost between 1914 and 1918!

[29] *U.S. Strategic Bombing Survey Report on Atomic Bombing in Japan*, 23rd July, 1946, p. 43.

[30] *International Conciliation*, December, 1945, No. 416, p. 762.

"8. The terms of the Cairo declaration shall be carried out and Japanese sovereignty shall be limited to the islands of Honshu, Hakkaido, Kyushu, Shikoku, and such minor islands as we determine."

"10. We do not intend that the Japanese shall be enslaved as a race nor destroyed as a nation, but stern justice will be meted out to all war criminals . . ."

"13. We call upon the Government of Japan to proclaim now the unconditional surrender of all the Japanese armed forces and to provide proper and adequate assurance of their good faith in such action. The alternative for Japan is complete and utter destruction."[31]

Though, considering the amorality which characterized the war, these terms were not unreasonable, they omitted to mention a point of overriding importance—namely, the status of the Emperor. In the eyes of the people he was a divinity. Further, it was he who declared war and made peace and was in supreme command of the Japanese army, navy and air force. Was he to be held responsible for crimes they had committed? If so, was he to be listed as a "war criminal" and hung? To the masses of the Japanese this would be equivalent to acquiescing in the murder of their god. Had this point been made clear; had it been openly stated that though the Emperor's power would be curtailed in certain ways, his status as Emperor would remain inviolate, there can be no doubt whatsoever that the ultimatum would have been accepted, in which case there would be no need to use the atomic bomb.

Early on 6th August, when industrial workers had started their day's work and school children were at school, one aeroplane, a B-29, carrying a crew of eleven men approached Hiroshima, which city had been selected by General Spaatz as the first of his two targets. At 8.15 a.m. one of these men, the bomb-aimer, manipulating a lever, released the projectile attached to a parachute; whereupon the plane raced away out of the forthcoming blast.

A few moments later two balls of fire appeared over the north-west centre of the city several hundreds of feet above the ground. The tem-

---

[31] *The Times*, 27th July, 1945. This ultimatum was based on a memorandum written by Mr. Henry L. Stimson, U.S. Secretary of War to President Truman, on 2nd July, 1945, in which he suggested that the warning given to Japan should contain the following elements: "The varied and overwhelming character of the force we are about to bring to bear on the islands." . . . "The inevitability and completeness of the destruction which the full application of the force will entail." . . . "I personally think that in saying this we should add that we do not exclude a constitutional monarchy under her present dynasty, it would substantially add to the chances of acceptance." ("The Decision to Use the Atomic Bomb," Henry L. Stimson, *Harper's Magazine*, February, 1947.) This vitally important suggestion was not acted upon.

perature at their cores has been calculated at millions of degrees Centigrade and the pressure exerted at hundreds of thousands of tons per square inch. A "fire-storm" resulted in which hundreds of fires were simultaneously started, the most distant being 13,700 feet from the ground centre of the explosion. People felt the heat on their skin as far away as 24,000 feet, burns occurred at 15,000 feet, and radiation rays proved fatal within a radius of 3,000. In all, 4.4 square miles of the city were completely burnt out and 62,000 out of 90,000 houses in its urban area were destroyed. The havoc wrought has been compared to what would result by exploding a bomb twice as large as the biggest British "block-buster" over a Lilliputian town built at one inch to the foot.[32]

At the time there were probably 320,000 people in the city, and of them, according to the official casualty list, 78,150 were killed and 13,983 missing, and in all probability an equivalent number was injured. If so, the total was about 180,000.

Referring to this appalling massacre of the many by the few, on 6th August President Truman made a public statement, and among other things he said:

"Sixteen hours ago an American airplane dropped one bomb on Hiroshima, an important Japanese army base. That bomb had more power than 20,000 tons of T.N.T. It had more than two thousand times the blast power of the British 'Grand Slam' which is the largest bomb ever yet used in the history of warfare . . . It is an atomic bomb. It is a harnessing of the basic power of the universe. The force from which the sun draws its powers has been loosed against those who brought war to the Far East . . . We have spent two billion dollars on the greatest scientific gamble in history—and won."[33]

On the 8th, following in the steps of the "Fascist jackal," Mussolini, in 1940, Stalin, scenting "easy meat," declared war on Japan, and the next day the Russians crossed the Manchurian border.

The same day the second atomic bomb was dropped on Nagasaki, a city of 260,000 inhabitants, of whom probably 40,000 were killed and as many injured, and 1.8 square miles of the city destroyed. Though the bomb was more powerful[34] than the first one, the uneven terrain confined the maximum intensity of damage to the valley over which it exploded.

Thus, by means of two projectiles, a quarter of a million human beings

[32] *The Effects of the Atomic Bomb at Hiroshima and Nagasaki*, Report of the British Mission to Japan (1946), p. 5.

[33] *International Conciliation*, No. 416, pp. 760-761.

[34] The first bomb contained uranium, the second plutonium, an element created in the laboratory, and which does not exist in nature. Its atomic number is 94, and that of uranium, the last of the natural elements, is 92.

were slaughtered and maimed, and to crown the event, on this same day—9th August—President Truman broadcast to his fellow countrymen the following pious words:

"We thank God that it has come to us instead of to our enemies, and we pray that he may guide us to use it in his way and for his purpose."[35]

On the 10th a broadcast from Tokyo announced that the Japanese Government was ready to accept the terms of the Allied declaration from Potsdam on 26th July, "with the understanding that the said declaration does not compromise any demand which prejudices the prerogatives of the Emperor as a sovereign ruler."[36]

The following day the Allied reply was:

"From the moment of surrender the authority of the Emperor and the Japanese Government to rule the State shall be subject to the Supreme Commander of the Allied Powers . . ."[37]

Why was this not made clear in the declaration of 26th July? Had it been, would not the purpose of God have been more Christianly followed?

Finally, on 14th August, the Emperor accepted the provisions of the Potsdam Declaration; whereupon the "cease fire" was sounded, and on 2nd September, exactly six years since Britain and France had declared war, the Japanese envoys signed the instrument of surrender on board the U.S. battleship *Missouri* in Tokyo Bay, and the second of the World Wars ended.

Thus force triumphed over wisdom, the animal in man over the human, and for the sake of the future the brutality of the Potsdam decision to use the atomic bomb demands a moment's thought.

By the Western Allied Powers the war in the Far East, as in Europe, allegedly was fought in the names of Justice, Humanity and Christianity; yet it was won by means which mongolized war and thereby mongolized peace.

In two awful *autos da fé*, like heretics and witches in bygone ages, the inhabitants of Hiroshima and Nagasaki were charred dark brown or black, to die within a few minutes or many hours.[38]

"Where the city stood," writes Father Siemens of Hiroshima, "there is a gigantic burned-out scar . . . More and more of the injured come to us. The least injured drag the more seriously wounded. There are wounded soldiers, and mothers carrying burned children in their arms . . . Frightfully burned people beckon to us. Along the way there are many dead and

---

[35] *The Times*, 10th August, 1945

[36] *Ibid.*, 11th August, 1945.

[37] *Ibid.*, 13th August, 1945.

[38] *U.S. Strategic Bombing Survey (Atomic Bombing)*, p. 17. See also *British Mission Report*, p. 12.

dying. On the Misasi Bridge, which leads into the inner city, we are met by a long procession of soldiers who have suffered burns. They drag themselves along with the help of staves or are carried by their less severely injured comrades . . . Abandoned on the bridge, there stand with sunken heads a number of horses with large burns on their flanks."[39]

Better for the dead than the injured, for the effects of radiation were diabolical. We read: "Bloody diarrhœa followed, and the victims expired, some within two or three days after the onset and the majority within a week. Autopsies showed remarkable changes in the blood picture—almost complete absence of white blood cells, and deterioration of bone marrow. Mucuous membrances of the throat, lungs, stomach and intestines showed acute inflammation . . ." At 5,000 feet from the centre of the explosion, men were rendered sterile, and "Of women in various stages of pregnancy who were within 3,000 feet of ground zero, all known cases have had miscarriages. Even up to 6,500 feet they have had miscarriages or premature infants who died shortly after birth. In the group between 6,500 feet and 10,000 feet, about one-third have given birth to apparently normal children. Two months after the explosion, the city's total incidence of miscarriages, abortions and premature births was 27 per cent, as compared with a normal rate of 6 per cent."[40]

The influence of the bomb on morale was equally extraordinary, for it was to a large degree the inverse of what was expected. Thus we read that "The effect of the bomb on attitudes toward the war in Japan as a whole was, however, much less marked than in the target cities . . . Only in the nearest group of cities, within forty miles of Hiroshima or Nagasaki, was there a substantial effect on morale . . . Even in the target cities, it must be emphasized, the atomic bombs did not uniformly destroy the Japanese fighting spirit. Hiroshima and Nagasaki, when compared with other Japanese cities, were not more defeatist than the average . . . In Japan as a whole, for example, military losses and failures, such as those of Saipan, the Philippines, and Okinawa, were twice as important as this atomic bomb in inducing certainty of defeat. Other raids over Japan as a whole were more than three times as important in this respect. Consumer deprivations, such as food shortages and the attendant malnutrition, were also more important in bringing people to the point where they felt they could not go on with the war."[41]

From these observations it is clear that the decision to use the atomic

[39]"Eyewitness Account," Father John A. Siemens, *U.S. Manhattan Engineer District Report on Atomic Bombings of Japan*, 26th July, 1946, pp. 20-21.
[40]*U.S. Strategic Bombing Survey (Atomic Bombing)*, pp. 20-21. See also *British Mission Report*, pp. 14-17.
[41]*Ibid.*, pp. 26-27.

bomb was not only a moral but also a psychological blunder. "Even before one of our B-29's dropped its atomic bomb on Hiroshima," writes General Arnold, "Japan's military situation was hopeless."[42] Admiral Nimitz attributes Japan's surrender directly to the loss of shipping.[43] Mr. Bernard Brodie states: "Japan was completely defeated strategically before the atomic bombs were used against her,"[44] and the twelve members of the *U.S. Strategic Bombing Survey* sum up their conclusions as follows: "Based on a detailed investigation of all the facts, and supported by the testimony of the surviving Japanese leaders involved, it is the *Survey's* opinion that certainly prior to 31st December, 1945, and in all probability prior to 1st November, 1945, Japan would have surrendered even if the atomic bomb had not been dropped, even if Russia had not entered the war, and even if no invasion had been planned or contemplated."[45]

Finally, the dropping of the two atomic bombs was a political blunder of unfathomable consequences. This was noted by the Vatican City newspaper, the *Osservatore Romano*, in which on 7th August appeared the following: "Humanity did not think like da Vinci. Humanity behaved as he feared it would. It gave precedence to hatred and invented instruments of hatred. There was ever more frightful destructive competition on land, in the water, and in the air, summoning for this purpose all the spiritual and material gifts granted by God. This war provides a catastrophic conclusion. Incredibly this destructive weapon remains as a temptation for posterity, which, we know by bitter experience, learns so little from history."[46]

[42]*General Arnold's Third Report,* 12th November, 1945, p. 33.
[43]*Report on Bombing Japan,* 7th October, 1945, pp. 1 and 2.
[44]*The Absolute Weapon: Atomic Power and World Order* (1946), p. 92.
[45]*United States Strategical Bombing Survey (Pacific War),* p. 26.
[46]Quoted from *The Times,* 8th August, 1945. The reference to Leonardo da Vinci concerns his idea for a submarine. He banished the thought of it when he realized the uses to which such an invention could be put.

CHAPTER XI

FOREGROUND OF THE WAR

(1) *Policy and War*

In 1919, after four years of catastrophic war, the victorious nations learned nothing from the conflict, and now that, because of this, the Second World War has run its course, from passing events it would appear that they are learning nothing again. Then they failed to realize that since war is the instrument of policy, policy to be creative must be founded on morality, and that unless morality keeps pace with science materiality will govern the nations and inevitably reduce them to dust.

To-day science is in the saddle, morality is in collapse, and policy is therefore at a discount. In fact, it may be said that there is no policy; in its place a universal drift towards a still more catastrophic war. Instead of a reduction in armaments we see an increase, an unceasing search for more and more powerful means of destruction—a sure symptom that no fertile seeds of peace have as yet been sown.

If this drift is to be stayed, then the recent war must be examined not merely as a clash of arms, but also as a surgical operation. What the scalpel is to the surgeon, war should be to the statesman, and whatever the causes of war may be, if the aim of the statesman is purely destructive, then clearly the activities of the soldier must become those of the slaughter-house. But if, instead, the aim is constructive and curative, then these activities become those of the surgery. Due to mischance or misunderstanding, or to lack of skill, or of judgment, or of knowledge, a surgical operation may fail—it sometimes does; but when the aim of the slaughterer becomes the aim of the surgeon, it must fail, there can be no possible alternative. Therefore, once the causes of war have been diagnosed, the first problem in eliminating the disease of war lies in the political field. This holds good not only in peace-time, but during war itself. Therefore, because war—the scalpel—is a political instrument, if policy be mad, war can be nothing else than madness lethalized. War to be a sane political instrument demands a sane political end, and to be attainable that end must be strategically possible. Thus, should the aim of Salvador be to conquer the United States, because it is strategically impossible, it spells nonsense. This was the position Britain and France placed themselves in in 1939 by guaranteeing the integrity of Poland. It was strategically impossible and, therefore politically it was nonsensical, to become absolutely so once Poland was partitioned between Germany and Russia. Sane enough to see the absurdity of their strategical position, the two Western Allies shifted their aim from the political to the emotional field. Nevertheless, when Stalin annexed over half of Poland, they did not declare war on Russia as they should have done to make sense of their emotional aim that Hitler was the "evil thing." Instead, winking at one infidel, they voided their bile on the other, and by so doing squeezed all morality out of their *jehad*.

"This time we are in for a *real* crusade." So wrote Mr. Francis Neilson in his diary on 11th October, 1939. "It is to be quite different from that of the 'holy war' which began in 1914. That was comparatively easy, for it came to an end when the Germans were beaten, and everybody knows the story of the apotheosis. This crusade to stamp out Hitlerism is one that may go rambling on until the last man who wishes to boss another is exterminated.

"When Godfrey of Bouillon, the leader of the First Crusade, set out to conquer the infidel, there were those who believed it would be no difficult task to overthrow the heathen because the crusaders had the deity on their side. Somehow things did not go right, and it was necessary to have many crusades. The result of all this was, as Ernest Barker says:

" 'The Crusades may be written down as a failure. They ended not in the occupation of the east by the Christian west, but in the conquest of the west by the Mohammedan east.'

"This is most discouraging to the modern crusader, but the particular crusade undertaken by Chamberlain and Daladier against the Teutonic Saladin may occupy more time, wreck more lives, and destroy more property, without accomplishing a thing in the end to stop the greed of dictators. It should be remembered that Saladin only popped up in the twelfth century and that there were many of his kidney before he arrived upon the scene."[1]

The worst thing about crusades is that their ideological aims justify the use of all means, however abominable and atrocious. Thus, though in 1139 the Lateran Council, under penalty of anathema, forbade the use of the cross-bow "as a weapon hateful to God and unfit for Christians," it sanctioned its use against infidels. And, in the Thirty Years' War, when the common folk were dragged into the conflict by violent propaganda, because of its religious aims they came to believe that it was a sacred duty

---

[1] *The Tragedy of Europe: A Diary of the Second World War*, Francis Neilson (1940), vol. I, pp. 120-121.

to kill their enemies in the most atrocious ways[2] for the purification or preservation of the true religion, as the case might be.

An identical outlook is observed in the Second World War—a war against heresy and between dogmas. Thus, for class ideological reasons the Russians massacred ten thousand and more Polish officers at Katyn and liquidated or enslaved hundreds of thousands of "bourgeois reptiles" in the countries they occupied; whereas for racial ideological reasons the Germans exterminated hundreds of thousands of Jews and locked up hundreds of thousands of people in concentration camps.

Characteristically, for years having thundered against Stalinism, Churchill during the war concentrated the whole of his forceful personality and tremendous energy upon defeating Stalin's most deadly enemy, and thereby, with American aid, he opened the gates of Eastern Europe to the Russian invasion.

Ever consistent in his inconsistency, on 10th November, 1942, he exclaimed: "Let me, however, make this clear, in case there should be any mistake about it in any quarter . . . I have not become the King's First Minister in order to preside over the liquidation of the British Empire."[3] Yet his hatred for Hitlerism had so blinded him politically and strategically that this is exactly what he potentially did. By destroying the balance of power in Europe, he wrecked the foundations upon which the British Empire had been built, and without which it is unlikely for long to endure.

This time, by carrying unlimited warfare to its ultimate end, he not only succeeded in annihilating Germany, but in knocking the bottom out of traditional British foreign policy and strategy, which were founded, not on some wild cat crusading idea, but on solid facts of geography. Further, from the moment he became Prime Minister he put into force the Douhet theory of strategic bombing because it fitted his policy of annihilation. It would seem, therefore, and the whole course of the war supports the assumption, that in his dual capacity of Prime Minister and Minister of Defence, he let the latter run away with the former. In fact, he subordinated the political point of view to the military, and, therefore, according to Clausewitz, acted "contrary to common sense."

This point is of sufficient importance to quote in full the paragraph in which these words occur. It reads:

"That the political point of view should end completely when war begins is only conceivable in contests which are wars of life and death, from pure hatred: as wars are in reality they are . . . only the expression or manifestation of policy itself. The subordination of the political point of view to

[2]For a pictorial example see Jacques Callot's eighteen engravings entitled "*Les Misères et les Malheurs de la Guerre*," 1632.
[3]*The Times*, 11th November, 1942.

the military would be contrary to common sense, for policy has declared the war; it is the intelligent faculty, war only the instrument, and not the reverse. The subordination of the military point of view to the political is, therefore, the only thing which is possible."[4]

The reader may, however, urge that the war *was* a life and death struggle, and that therefore Mr. Churchill *was* right. Yet, even during the critical summer of 1940, it was never a life and death struggle for Britain, and for the simple reason that so long as the command of the sea was hers, it could not become a life and death struggle. In fact, after the Battle of Britain, for a long time it became a stalemate. But it was not during this period that the theory of strategic bombing could be put to the test. As we have seen, the test did not come until the spring of 1942, and only took full form twelve months later. On 19th May, 1943, at Washington in an address to Congress Mr. Churchill said:

"Opinion, Mr. President, is divided as to whether the use of air power could by itself bring about a collapse in Germany or Italy. The experiment is well worth trying, so long as other measures are not excluded. (Cheers.) Well, there is certainly no harm in finding out. (Laughter.) . . . The condition to which the great centres of German war industry, and particularly the Ruhr, are being reduced, is one of unparalleled devastation . . . It is the settled policy of our two staffs and war-making authorities to make it impossible for Germany to carry on any form of war industry on a large or concentrated scale, either in Germany, Italy, or in the enemy-occupied countries. (Cheers.) . . . This process will continue ceaselessly with ever-increasing weight and intensity until the German and Italian peoples abandon or destroy the monstrous tyrannies which they have incubated and reared in their midst."[5]

In brief, and in the words of Ferdinand II, "better a desert than a country ruled by heretics."

In this statement, the point to note is, that whatever excuses may be urged in support of a policy of annihilation in 1940 and 1941, long before May, 1943, there was none. By this date it had become clearly apparent that the tide had turned against Germany, and realizing, as Mr. Churchill must have, that the Russian way of life was more antagonistic to the British than the German way of life, had he been a far-sighted statesman, he would have done his utmost to prevent the obliteration of Germany, because, as we have stated more than once, it could only mean the establishment of a vastly more powerful and brutal hegemony over Europe than the German. Unfortunately for his own country and the world in general, far-sightedness was not Mr. Churchill's outstanding quality. The war was his personal

[4] *On War*, Carl von Clausewitz (English edition, 1908), vol. III, pp. 124-125.
[5] *The Times*, 20th May, 1943.

concern in which his reputation as a Generalissimo was at stake. Therefore, irrespective of consequences, his policy was to force a life and death struggle on Germany, and by every means in his power annihilate her.

But this was not the task of a Prime Minister, which unquestionably is to direct war towards a profitable goal—that is, to subordinate fighting power to a sane political end. In spite of, and possibly because of his masterful leadership, this Mr. Churchill utterly failed to do. And, as disastrous, so obsessed was he by hatred of his enemy that he fell back on methods of war long discarded by civilized nations.

In the Far East, events followed a parallel course, because Mr. Roosevelt's political aim was also purely a destructive one. As Ian Morrison, writing in 1943, said: "The Allies have no programme, as have the Japanese, for the future reorganization of the Far East. The lack of any specific programmes, both in Europe and Asia, is already a grave handicap to us in the actual waging of this war. It will be an even greater handicap to us after the war. Unless a little thought is devoted to these problems, academic and unreal though they may seem at the moment, there will only be chaos after a decision has been reached on the military plane, chaos leading to a speedy recurrence of those very evils which we are seeking to banish from the world."[6]

The lesson is this: Should you, when waging war, lack a politically sane and strategically possible aim, you are likely to be thrown back on an insane moral one, such as attempting to eliminate ideas with bullets or political beliefs with bombs. Hitler's aim was sane and possible and Japan's sane and impossible, though both were monstrously unjust, but not more so than the imperialistic aims of other heads of state and of other nations in the past. Though the means adopted in gaining sane aims are sometimes atrocious, in the case of insane aims they are always so. It is for this reason that crusades and civil wars are so destructive of moral values, as well as of life and property, and the Second World War was both a crusade and a European civil war.

(2) Morality and War

The war had two outstanding characteristics: It was a war of remarkable mobility and of unrivalled inhumanity—nothing like it had been seen since the Thirty Years' War. The one was conditioned by science and industry; the other by the dissolution of religion, and the emergence of what for the want of a generic name may be called "cadocracy."

The age of the superior man had ended, and the age of the inferior man had come in its stead. The gentleman—the direct descendant of the

[6] *This War against Japan*, Ian Morrison (1943), p. 99.

idealized Christian Knight—the model of warlike excellence to which many generations had aspired[7]—had been ousted by the cad. Chivalry had given way to opportunism, and everywhere the self-interested cadocrat held sway. Therefore, at bottom, the war was as much a blind revolt against Christian culture as a crusade. A revolt which took the form of a brawl between gangs of industrialized and mechanized cadocrats in which in their strugglings and strivings for economic, territorial and financial plunder they trampled under foot the spiritual and moral values which alone could give their booty worth.

Of the first characteristic, so much has already been written that little need now be added. Mobility, as we have seen, was in the main due to the adoption of the internal combustion engine on the ground and in the air, and more especially in the latter element; for it was the aeroplane which conditioned the whole war by cubing not only the battlefield, but the entire theatre of war. Though, as has been shown, the highest profitable mobility was attained when air power was integrated with land or sea power, the ability of the aeroplane to operate on its own, placed in the hands of the morally and politically blind a weapon of almost unlimited destruction.

The theory of short-cutting the prolonged agony of 1914-1918 by strategic bombing was a persuasive one. Morally, it was based on the assumption that all men are cowards and cads, and if their homes are destroyed and their wives and children mutilated or slaughtered, they will surrender to *force majeure*. It is only necessary to read the report of the Morrow Board of 1925 to realize this. It was assembled to enquire into the validity of General Mitchell's theory that air battles would prove so decisive that the nation losing them "will be willing to capitulate without resorting to further contest on land or water," and that this object could be accomplished "in an incredibly short space of time once the control of the air had been obtained."[8] But war is not a theory, it is a reality and a political instrument, and unless policy be founded on morality, a reversion from civilization to barbarism follows.

In his criticism of General Mitchell's advocacy to use bombs and gas against the enemy's civil population, Captain W. S. Pye of the U.S. Navy, who gave evidence before the Board, said that to do so would be to "strike at the root of civilization."[9] And Mr. Spaight, writing in 1930, pointed out that the advent of bombing aircraft in no way "wiped out the old distinction between combatants and non-combatants . . ." You may not, he

[7]*History of European Morals*, William Edward Hartpole Lecky (1902), vol. II, p. 260.
[8]*Hearings of the President's Aircraft Board* (Morrow Board), 1925, vol. I, 547-548.
[9]*Ibid.*, vol. I, 1231.

then wrote, "slay or wound civilians in order to destroy the moral of the enemy nation . . . It is, in fact, upon the *lethal quality* of the object attacked that your right of using homicidal violence is based."[10] Nevertheless, in 1944, he swung round in the opposite direction. "The bomber," he wrote, "*is* the Saver of Civilization . . . civilization, I believe firmly, would have been destroyed if there had been no bombing in this war. It was the bomber aircraft which, more than any other instrument of war, prevented the forces of evil from prevailing."[11]

It may seem a little strange, nevertheless it is a fact, that this reversion to wars of primitive savagery was made by Britain and the United States, the two great democratic factions of cadocracy, and not by Germany and Russia, the two great autocratic factions of that same cult. Not because the last two were the more civilized, but, as Captain Liddell Hart pertinently remarks—the more military-minded. ". . . the Germans," he writes, "having studied war more closely than most people, had come to see the ultimate drawbacks of destroying cities and industry, and the way that this damages the post-war situation . . ."[12] Much the same may be said of the Russians; for clearly they saw no profit in destroying cities they expected to plunder. Further, Captain Liddell Hart points out that, "Continental countries, with land frontiers susceptible to invasion, naturally tend to be more conscious of the drawback of a 'devastating' mode of warfare than sea-girt countries which have had relatively little experience of its effects. That is why codes of warfare, aiming at mutual limitation, have always tended to grow upon the Continent, whereas history brings out the fact that our own practice of warfare through the centuries, fostered by our relative immunity, has been more than ordinarily ruthless, or reckless, regarding the infliction of economic damage. Military men bred in the Continental tradition tend to have a legalistic attitude towards the methods of war . . . Moderation in our practice of war has been more apt to come from the humane feeling of individuals, or the gentleman's code . . ."[13]

With the disappearance of the gentleman—the man of honour and principle—as the backbone of the ruling class in England, political power rapidly passed into the hands of demagogues who, by playing upon the

[10]*Air Power and the Cities*, J. M. Spaight (1930), pp. 207 and 215.

[11]*Bombing Vindicated*, J. M. Spaight (1944), p. 7.

[12]*The Revolution in Warfare*, Captain B. H. Liddell Hart (1946), p. 70. He also writes: "The Germans' departure from this code can hardly be dated before September, 1940, when the night bombing of London was launched, following upon six successive attacks on Berlin during the previous fortnight. The Germans were thus strictly justified in describing this as a reprisal, especially as they had' prior to our sixth attack on Berlin, announced that they would take such action if we did not stop our night bombing of Berlin" (p. 72).

[13]*Ibid.*, p. 70.

emotions and ignorance of the masses, created a permanent war psychosis. To these men, political necessity justified every means, and in war-time military necessity did likewise. Thus, in order to justify the massacre of civilian populations, Marshal of the R.A.F. Sir Arthur Harris writes:

"Whenever the fact that our aircraft occasionally killed women and children is cast in my teeth I always produce (the) example of the blockade, although there are endless others to be got from the wars of the past. I never forget, as so many do, that in all normal warfare of the past, and of the not distant past, it was the common practice to besiege cities and, if they refused to surrender when called upon with due formality to do so, every living thing in them was in the end put to the sword. Even in the more civilized times of to-day the siege of cities, accompanied by the bombardment of the city as a whole, is still a normal practice; in no circumstances were women and children allowed to pass out of the city, because their presence in it and their consumption of food would inevitably hasten the end of the siege. And as to bombardment, what city in what war has ever failed to receive the maximum bombardment from all enemy artillery within range so long as it has continued resistance?"[14]

Though this may seem plausible to the semi-educated, it is a travesty of history. It is true that during the Thirty Years' War, because Magdeburg refused to surrender to Tilly, its 30,000 inhabitants were butchered. But even in that atrocious conflict this act of barbarism sent a thrill of horror throughout Christendom. It is also true that after the storming of Badajoz in 1812 fearful excesses were committed by the troops getting out of hand. But this regrettable event was not ordered or sanctioned by Wellington, and Napier describes it as "wild and desperate wickedness."[15] During the eighteenth and nineteenth centuries many cities were besieged and stormed, yet cases of purposeful atrocities following were the exception and not the rule. Not infrequently great care was taken to inflict the minimum damage on civilian life and property, as happened at the Siege of Antwerp in 1832. Marshal Gérard was besieging the citadel held by General Chassé. In order to spare the citizens the horrors of war, Chassé agreed to direct the fire of his guns on the open plains only if Gérard would agree to approach in no other direction. This plan was decided upon, and the result was that not a single non-combatant beyond the lines was harmed in person and property. Exactly one hundred years later the crowded city of Shanghai was bombed from the air and thousands of helpless Chinese were slaughtered. Though in the one case humanity was as exaggerated as barbarity was in the other, accepting the frequency of wars, well may it be

[14]*Bomber Offensive*, Marshal of the R.A.F., Sir Arthur Harris (1947), p. 177.
[15]*History of the War in the Peninsula*, Major-General Sir W. F. P. Napier (1892), vol. IV, p. 122.

asked, was not the first method the more reasonable of the two and the more likely to prevent revenge monopolizing the eventual peace?

Similarly at sea, it was always possible to bombard coastal cities, and on occasion it was done, such as the destruction of the unfortified and undefended town of San Juan del Norte in Nicaragua by an American squadron in 1854, and of Odessa, that same year, by a combined British and French squadron. Nevertheless, these incidents caused such universal denunciation that "since 1854, there has been no instance of the deliberate, wholesale destruction of a city by an enemy naval force . . ."[16] Even as late as 1900, in the Last of the Gentlemen's Wars, when Lord Roberts cornered General Cronje and his commando at Paardeburg, seeing that there were a number of women and children in the laager, he offered Cronje the opportunity of evacuating them before the bombardment opened. Though to-day such a proposal would be scoffed at as sentimental folly; yet were not our ancestors wiser than their descendants? Believing that, until wars were eliminated, the next best thing was to restrict their ravages, they saw that the simplest way to do so was to fight like gentlemen instead of cads.

Liddell Hart is, therefore, strictly correct when he compares what British airmen were pleased to call "the higher strategy" with the methods of the Mongols of the thirteenth century. Writing on the latter, Michael Prawdin gives exact parallels to this bogus strategy in his book, *The Mongol Empire*. Thus, in the chapter entitled "A War of Annihilation" we read of the conquest of Khorassan:

"The small but well-organized minority had conquered, but the land had had its fill of death and desolation. Vast cities lay in ruins and were depopulated. Never before, neither during the struggle in Mongolia nor during the campaign in China had Jenghiz' Army wrought such havoc. Terror prevailed universally from the Sea of Aral to the Persian Desert. Only in whispers did the survivors speak of 'the Accursed'."[17]

There is, therefore, nothing new in "the higher strategy," and, like Mongol warfare, it was based on the use of the more mobile arm—the aeroplane instead of the horse-archer—and, like it, it has culminated in a *Pax Tartarica*.

Lastly, as regards blockade. It may be true, as Harris quotes, that the British blockade of 1914-1918 was responsible for 800,000 deaths, but the point he misses is, that it did not devastate German cities—the foundations of civilization and culture in the enemy's land. To-day, it is not the loss of German lives during the war which has reduced Germany to a gigantic slum, but the pulverization of her cities and the destruction of her indus-

[16] *Air Power and the Cities*, p. 92.
[17] *The Mongol Empire*, Michael Prawdin (English edition, 1940), p. 194.

tries. Harris admits that "The aiming points" of his area bombardments "were usually right in the centre of the town," and it is there where normally are to be found the libraries, museums, principal churches, art galleries and historical monuments, which once destroyed are lost for ever. The blockade of 1914-1918 did not touch these material things; it did not destroy a single dwelling.

Though the obliteration of cities by bombing was probably the most devastating blow ever struck at civilization, other happenings show even more clearly the moral decline which characterized the war. Millions were enslaved; millions were deported or driven as wanderers from their homes and countries. Thousands were sterilized and tortured, and unknown numbers, like vermin, were gassed to death. Raiding parties attempted to assassinate opposing generals and their staffs, and revolt in the German occupied countries was sedulously fostered.

Perhaps more than any other, the last of these activities barbarized the war. Once the Duke of Wellington said: "I always had a horror of revolutionizing any country for a political object. I always said—if they rise of themselves, well and good, but do not stir them up; it is a fearful responsibility."[18] But Mr. Churchill thought otherwise; for not only did he encourage every resistance movement against the Germans, but he poured down from the skies thousands of tons of weapons in order to foster guerilla warfare.

What this would lead to was certain. Germans were assassinated and reprisals followed. Brutality begat brutality, and the severity of German retaliation was not due to the Germans being an exceptionally brutal people, but to the fact that guerilla warfare is always brutal. It is only necessary to read the history of the Peninsula War in Spain to realize this.

At length, to crown this moral *débâcle* came the atomic bomb, which with a suddenness almost magical, in seconds made possible all that Douhet and Mitchell had preached for years. Without it their theory was a dream, with it it became the grimmest reality which has ever faced man. Here, at length, was a weapon of such devastating powers that by using it in quantity it was possible to annihilate an enemy by the hundred thousand a second.

Writing of Tuli, the youngest son of Jenghiz Khan, Michael Prawdin says: "He never had to leave garrisons behind in occupation, for where he passed there was nothing left but uninhabited ruins. Of towns which had contained from 70,000 to 1,000,000 inhabitants nothing remained alive, 'neither a cat nor a dog'."[19]

[18]*Notes of Conversations with the Duke of Wellington*, 1831-51, Philip Henry 5th Earl Stanhope (1889), p. 69.
[19]*The Mongol Empire*, p. 191.

What essential difference is there between this horrific picture and Hiroshima and Nagasaki?

Writing on this subject, Professor Woodward says:

"The destruction of cities, the centres of integration in civilized life, has happened before, and has resulted in anarchy and darkness. The process was mainly one of slow decay, and just because it was slow, the possibilities of recovery were never entirely removed. The danger now is that we should be plunged into anarchy at once, and that we could no more organize recovery than a finely bred dog could long fend for himself if he were turned loose in the jungle. Europe at this moment is much nearer to dis location beyond recovery than we in England can imagine, but we may still hope for betterment because the area of dislocation—the number of cities destroyed—can be regarded as small in comparison with the area which still stands. We are, however, very near to the edge of an abyss, and at least for a generation to come— a longer time than our period of respite—we cannot risk a greater strain. A war in which atomic bombs were employed to destroy within as many days the twelve most important cities in the North American Continent or the twelve most important cities now remaining in Europe, might be too much for us. Human life would not disappear, but human beings would revert, helpless, without counsel, and without the physical means of recovery, to something like the culture of the late bronze age."[20]

One fact, and perhaps the most important of all, remains to be mentioned. For fifty or a hundred years, and possibly more, the ruined cities of Germany will stand as monuments to the barbarism of their conquerors. The slaughtered will be forgotten, the horrors of the concentration camps and gas chambers will dim with the passing of years; but the ruins will remain to beckon generation after generation of Germans to revenge.

(3) *Science and War*

To complete our survey of the war as a whole, one factor remains to be considered, which, so far as the present and future of war are concerned, is the most revolutionary of all.

Hitherto fighting power has followed in the footsteps of civilization and almost invariably has been a generation or two behind civil progress. Thus, in 1914, in spite of the enormous advances made by industry during the preceding forty years, in its essentials fighting power was not very different from what it had been in 1870, and tactics remained much the same. Yet before the First World War ended, industry was playing so important a

[20]*Some Political Consequences of the Atomic Bomb*, E. L. Woodward (1945), pp. 7-8.

part in waging the war that, so far as Britain and Germany were concerned, it may without exaggeration be said that *the* decisive battle was being fought between the Midlands and the Ruhr.

But when we turn to the Second World War, in addition to industrial power we find an even more puissant factor—the mobilization of science for war and the conditioning of civilization by warlike inventions. Thus, whereas in 1929, Mr. Shotwell, looking back on the First World War, stated: "During the years 1914 to 1918 . . . war definitely passed into the industrial phase of economic history . . . ,"[21] as early as 1942 in the Second World War, Mr. M. A. Stine, of the great armament firm of Du Pont, made a very different statement. His was that "The war is compressing into the space of months scientific developments which, without the spur of necessity, might have taken half a century to realize. As a result, industry will emerge from the war with a capacity for making scores of chemical and other raw materials on a scale that, only two years ago, was beyond comprehension."[22]

What does this mean? That military organization and not civil, by its alliance with science, has taken the lead, while industry gleans its after-war benefits.

Thus science became regimented by war, to form the foundations of the war state more completely than it had ever been regimented in the peace state. This, if persisted in, as undoubtedly it will be, will place civilization on a permanent footing of what may be called "wardom"; destruction and not construction becoming the focal point of man's intelligence. Thus a return will be made to the Spartan conception of civilization.

Whether this is an overstatement or not, the future alone can decide. Nevertheless, it is obvious that no fighting force of to-day or to-morrow can maintain its lethal efficiency without the scientist. In fact, just as in the First World War the industrialist became more important than the general, so in the Second did the scientist. And following in the wake of the scientist came the technician, the soldier becoming little more than the salesman of his goods. By the end of the war techniques had become as important as tactics and laboratories as essential as training grounds, until the coming of the atomic bomb raised the scientist to a position of importance only equalled by Archimedes at the Siege of Syracuse. Of him Polybius wrote: "In certain circumstances the genius of one man is more effective than any numbers whatever."[23]

It may, however, be said that because this is so, then there is a possibility that it may lead to an amelioration, for no scientist would be so

[21] *War as an Instrument of National Policy*, J. T. Shotwell (1929), p. 34.
[22] *The Times*, 9th November, 1942.
[23] *The Histories of Polybius*, Shuckburgh's trans. (1889), vol. I, p. 530.

destructively-minded as the soldier. Frankly, we see no hope of this, because in the materialistic age in which we live, as science has gone up culture and morality have gone down, until to-day, even in peace-time, science has become the barbarian in our midst. Though this is not due to seeking and gaining knowledge, during the last hundred years the unravelling of the secrets of nature has been so rapid and the decline of the religious spirit so profound that moral values have not been able to keep pace with scientific growth. Discoveries and inventions, which in a more cultured age would have proved of the greatest benefit to man, have been peddled to barbarians, who very naturally make use of them in a barbaric way. This explains why, in so many cases during the last forty to fifty years, the stimulus behind inventions has been destructiveness. To-day the atomic bomb places in man's hands a weapon of such stupendous destructive power that, so long as he remains a barbarian, it is all but a certainty that he will use it for the purpose for which it was designed. This is proved by the present universal interest in it as a weapon.

This interest is ominous, because it shows that, in spite of the war, the political situation is even more unsettled than it was before its advent. In former wars in which the political aims were sane, once a war had ended, at least some semblance of political stability was established, the belligerents grounding their arms and returning to their peaceful avocations. To-day the opposite is to be seen; for nations are more concerned than ever in preparing for the next war. Conscription has now been adopted as a peace measure by Britain, and the immense army in Russia remains on a war-footing. More portentous than these things, in these countries, as well as others also, hundreds of scientists are busily engaged in attempting to discover more and more powerful means wherewith to destroy mankind in bulk. Though the bomb which destroyed Hiroshima possessed an explosive force equivalent to the detonation of 20,000 tons of T.N.T., scientists are now searching how to increase its destructive power. Mr. John J. McCloy, a former U.S. Assistant Secretary for War, writing on this problem states: "... there can be little doubt that within the next ten years, to be conservative, bombs of a size of the power equivalent of one hundred thousand to two hundred and fifty thousand tons of T.N.T. can be made ... And if we can move to the other end of the periodic table and utilize hydrogen in the generation of energy, we would have a bomb somewhere around one thousand times as powerful as the Nagasaki bomb. I have been told by scientists who are not mere theorists, but who actually planned and made the bomb which exploded in New Mexico that, given the same intensive effort which was employed during the war towards the production of that bomb, we were within two years time at the close of the war of producing a bomb of the hydrogen-helium type, i.e., a bomb of approximately one thousand times the power of the present bombs. The rocket and jet-propulsion and biological forces, all infinitely more effective than the general public has yet comprehended, can be added to atomic warfare, and with them it does not require much imagination to understand how the rate of extermination on this planet can be increased."[24]

And what can all this striving to destroy lead to? To a veritable religion of death, in which the scientist becomes the immolating high priest and humanity the sacrificial victim. These are a few of the things we read: ". . . it is a weapon for aggressors, and the elements of surprise and terror are intrinsic to it as are the fissionable nuclei" . . . "In a world made bomb-less by treaty, the first to violate the treaty would gain an enormous advantage" . . . "Ten well-placed bombs of the Nagasaki type would eliminate the city of New York" . . . "The V2 rocket can be fitted with an atomic warhead, and thus far no defence against this weapon has been discovered" . . . "One atomic bomb costs substantially less than two fully equipped Flying Fortresses of the B-17 type"[25] . . . "It may not be impossible to smuggle atomic bombs into a country in peace-time, and to threaten to touch them off at long range,"[26] etc., etc.

This is not war; it is the conflict of gangsters. As we know them to-day, armies, navies and air forces have no place in such a struggle. And even should the atomic bomb not be used, because it may be, fighting forces will have to be redesigned to meet this possibility. Therefore, it would seem that in any case each service will have to be redesigned and, in consequence, each will have to be duplicated—for war with atomic bombs and for war without them. This makes the problem of war still more absurd. Nevertheless, absurdity does not alter the fact that in an age which has lost all trust in spiritual and moral values, the death value will remain paramount, and when fitted within the political framework of cadocracy, this value alone makes another world conflict all but a certainty.

The great powers of the world have been reduced to two in number—the United States and the U.S.S.R.—and though the world is big enough for half a dozen great powers to keep the peace in, it is too small for two to do so, and especially when they happen to possess such divergent political and social outlooks as the above two nations. Lying between them, Western Europe must eventually be drawn into the orbit of one or the other, and as Mr. Percy E. Corbett points out: "Such a clear-cut polarization of power around the two great Continental countries, the Soviet Union and the

[24] "Security in the Atomic Age," John J. McCloy, *Infantry Journal*, January, 1947, p. 10.
[25] *The Absolute Weapon: Atomic Power and World Order*, edited by Bernard Brodie (1946), pp. 73, 15, 31 and 42.
[26] *Some Political Consequences of the Atomic Bomb*, p. 9.

United States, offers scant prospect of a peaceful world co-operating in the common purpose of increased welfare."[27]

Like so many others, his solution of the problem is reliance on the United Nations' Organization. Indeed a frail reed to lean on; for were Voltaire alive to-day he would surely apply his famous aphorism to it: "United by crime and divided by interests." In any case, an operative World Organization can only be created by political equals. These do not exist, and politically and socially Soviet Russia and the United States are oil and water, they cannot mix.

Even were this possible, unless the World Organization be built on a moral foundation, it cannot become other than a tyranny. Depending on its police power to enforce its will, at the same time it will be slave to that same power, as were the Cæsars and Sultans to their Prætorian Guards and Janissaries. Clearly, if the nations want concord, a purely political organization is no solution.

"*From whence come wars and fighting among you? Come they not hence, even of your lusts that war in your members?*"

In these words of St. James is the answer which the nations can only reject at their peril. It is in the envies, greeds and fears of men that the roots of war are to be found. And these evils can only be uprooted by the Golden Rule: "*All things whatsoever ye would that men should do to you, do you even so to them.*" A rule which, without exception, is to be found on the foundation stone of every great religion, and which, therefore, is a common link between all men.

That this rule will be accepted by the world of to-day is not only unlikely but unimaginable, for it is the rule of the superior man. Nevertheless, the Law of Retribution will continue to govern the actions of men: As men sow so shall they reap, and "He that soweth iniquity shall reap calamity."

In 1919, in their Peace Treaties, the victors of the First World War sowed the wind, and, as inevitably as night follows day, in the Second World War they reaped the whirlwind. Having learned nothing and having forgotten nothing, and filled with envies, fears and greeds, they have repeated their evil, and for a second time have imposed an iniquitous peace upon the vanquished. Therefore, they have once again sown the wind, and will yet again reap the whirlwind. Evil breeds evil, and if you be blind like Samson when you cast down the pillars of the house of your enemies, its ruins will crush you.

[27] *The Absolute Weapon*, p. 165.

FINIS

APPENDIX

The Attack by Illumination

The C.D.L. was an infantry tank fitted with a powerful projector of special design emitting a fan-shaped flickering beam of light which illuminated a wide field and dazzled the eye. The projector was so protected that it could not be put out of action by anything less than a direct hit by a shell which could penetrate five inches or more of armour.

The object of this weapon was to solve the problem of night fighting on a large and organized scale, enabling an attack to be carried out more methodically and rapidly than during daylight, and far more economically and securely; for whereas the field over which the attacker advanced was brilliantly illuminated, all the defender was able to see was a wide expanse of dazzling light which obscured everything behind it, and which was so brilliant that it rendered aimed fire impossible.

The letters C.D.L. stood for "Canal Defence Light"; a name adopted in order to conceal its true use and purpose. Like the word "tank," it was a verbal camouflage.

The history of the C.D.L. is of considerable interest: (1) Because it shows how difficult it is in peace-time to get a revolutionary new weapon adopted; (2) because it shows how conservative the military-mind is during war-time; and (3) that if in this scientific and technical age future novel weapons meet with the same fate as the C.D.L., the soldier will be as completely unprepared for the next war as he was for the last.

The idea of using light as a weapon was first suggested by the late Commander Oscar de Thoren, R.N., in 1915, and in August, 1917, tests with an ordinary searchlight fitted to a tank were carried out in England. No further action was taken until 1922, when another test was made. The War Office then dropped the subject, but gave de Thoren permission to submit his idea to the French Government. This he did, but nothing definite occurred until 1933, when a syndicate to which de Thoren gave his name was formed, and the first tests in France took place in 1934. In 1936, others with improved apparatus were held at Châlons, at which representatives of the War Office attended. These trials resulted in the War Office requesting a demonstration in England. It took place in February, 1937, on Salisbury Plain, and was so satisfactory that the War Office ordered three sets of the complete apparatus for further trials, the final one of which took place on the night of 7th-8th June, 1940.

Ten days later, the War Office decided to take over the whole project and to put in hand the construction of three hundred projector turrets, a number which later on was considerably increased. Next, it was decided to create a C.D.L. School, and the first of these establishments came into being in England on 1st December, 1940. The establishment of this school eventually rose to thirty-three officers and six hundred and nineteen other ranks. In August, 1942, a second school was established in the Middle East. Also a C.D.L. establishment was set up in the United States. Approximately 6,000 officers and men passed through the English and Middle East Schools and 8,000 through the American. In all, some 1,850 tanks were converted to C.D.L. use in England, and two C.D.L. brigades were raised in England, the 1st Tank Brigade (three battalions) and the 35th Tank Brigade (two battalions) and two Armoured Groups in America (the 9th and 10th), each comprising three battalions.

Through prior to D-Day (6th June, 1944) the 1st Tank Brigade and the 10th Armoured Group were fully mobilized and ready to proceed overseas, so little interest was taken in the new weapon that it was not until 11th August that the first of these formations was landed in France, the second following eleven days later. Even then, instead of being used in the operations following on the break-through of the U.S. Third Army at Avranches, operations in which the Germans could seldom move except under cover of night,* the six battalions were never moved forward from their disembarkation camps and were gradually disbanded.

On 20th September, the U.S. 9th Armoured Group, when on the point of leaving England for France, was broken up. On 13th October, the 1st Tank Brigade suffered a similar fate, its men being drafted to other units and its tanks stripped of their C.D.L. equipment. On 27th October, orders were given to disband the American 10th Armoured Group, but owing to strong protests made by its Command, these orders were only partially carried out. In the meantime the 35th Tank Brigade had been disbanded in England.

No sooner had these steps been taken than Lord Louis Mountbatten requested that at least a brigade of C.D.L.'s be dispatched as soon as possible to India. As there was none now available, the War Office decided to re-equip 360 C.D.L.'s for S.E.A.C. and re-train new personnel. At the time, it was also decided to re-equip a C.D.L. battalion for the invasion of Germany. The men needed for these units were taken from the personnel of the C.D.L. School and such trained men of the 35th Tank Brigade as were still available. Unfortunately, there was no time to train an entire C.D.L. battalion for Germany; but two squadrons of fourteen C.D.L.'s each were hurriedly got together and on 20th February, 1945, left for France to be attached to the Twenty-First Army Group. On 1st March, 1945, the first complement of C.D.L.'s left for India, to be followed by the balance required so soon as training of officers and men had been completed.

Seemingly, because the twenty-eight C.D.L.'s dispatched to France were insufficient for any major offensive operation, eventually they were used in a purely static role for covering the crossing of the Rhine. Subsequently American C.D.L.'s were employed in an attack on the

Dortmund-Ems Canal on the night of 1st-2nd April; also in the taking of Frankfurt and the crossing of the Elbe; but so far no official report has been published on these operations. As regards the C.D.L.'s dispatched to Lord Louis Mountbatten, these arrived too late to take part in the final operations in Burma.

This sorry story of endless delays covering twenty-five years, of acceptance, of vast preparations, costing many millions of pounds, of disbandment, of resurrection and of final misuse, so far as the British C.D.L.'s were concerned, is given here in order to show that by D-Day an alternative tactics existed and that the means to carry them out were ready at hand. A tactics which did not demand "colossal cracks," or the pulverization of towns and cities, but instead one which enabled the *blitz* attack to be carried out at night-time and in conditions far more favourable to the attacker than could possibly be found in daylight.

*The following incident supports this contention. North of the Falaise pocket were the 272nd, 346th and 711th German Infantry Divisions, which, on account of the rout to the south of them, were compelled to fall back. Of this retreat, General Diestel, commander of the 346th said to Major Shulman: "As soon as we were safely lodged behind a river, we would find that our left flank had disintegrated and that we were in danger of being encircled. We would then move back again. We were never hurried in these movements because of the systematic and thoroughly organized tactics of the Allies (Twenty-First Army Group). When we had been thrown back during the day, we always knew that there would be a pause at night when the enemy would regroup for the next day's operations. It was these hours of darkness that enabled us to retire without suffering many casualties." (*Defeat in the West*, p. 163.)

INDEX

Other DA CAPO titles of interest